Nature and the Supernatural

As Together Constituting the One System of God

By

Horace Bushnell

Published by Forgotten Books 2012

Originally Published 1872

PIBN 1000300346

NATURE AND THE SUPERNATURAL

As together constituting the One System of God

BY HORACE BUSHNELL, D.D.

AUTHOR OF "THE NEW LIFE," "CHRISTIAN NURTURE," ETC.

Anchora Spei

STRAHAN & CO., PUBLISHERS

56, LUDGATE HILL, LONDON

1872

PREFACE.

THE treatise here presented to the public was written, as re
gards the matter of it, some years ago. It has been ready for
the press more than two years, and has been kept back by the
limitations I am under, which have forbidden my assuming the
small additional care of its publication. It need hardly be said
that the subject has been carefully studied, as any subject
rightly should be, that raises for discussion the great question
of the age.

Scientifically measured, the argument of the treatise is rather
an hypothesis for the matters in question, than a positive theory
of them. And yet, like every hypothesis that gathers in,
accommodates, and assimilates all the facts of the subject, it
gives, in that one test, the most satisfactory and convincing
evidence of its practical truth. Any view which takes in easily
all the facts of a subject must be substantially true. Even
the highest and most difficult questions of science are deter ·
mined in this manner. While it is easy, therefore, to raise an
attack at this or that particular point—call it an assumption, or
a mere caprice of invention, or a paradox, or a dialectically
demonstrable error—there will yet remain, after all such parti
cular denials, the fact that here is a wide hypothesis of the
world, and the great problem of life, and sin, and supernatural
redemption, and Christ, and a Christly providence, and a

divinely certified history, and of superhuman gifts entered into the world, and finally of God as related to all, which liquidates these stupendous facts, in issue between Christians and unbelievers, and gives a rational account of them. And so the points that were assaulted, and perhaps seemed to be carried, by the skirmishes of detail, will be seen, by one who grasps the whole in which they are comprehended, to be still not carried, but to have their reason certified by the more general solution of which they are a part. One who flies at mere points of detail, regardless of the whole to which they belong, can do nothing with a subject like this. The points themselves are intelligible only in a way of comprehension, or as being seen in the whole to which they are subordinate.

It will be observed that the words of Scripture are often cited, and its doctrines referred to, in the argument. But this is never done as producing a divine authority on the subject in question. It is very obvious that an argument, which undertakes to settle the truth of Scripture history, should not draw on that history for its proofs. The citations in question are sometimes designed to correct mistakes, which are held by believers themselves, and are a great impediment to the easy solution of Scripture difficulties; sometimes they are offered as furnishing conceptions of subjects, that are difficult to be raised in any other manner; sometimes they are presented because they are clear enough, in their superiority, to stand by their own self-evidence and contribute their aid, in that manner, to the general progress of the argument.

I regret the accidental loss of a few references that could not be recovered without too much labour.

H. B.

CONTENTS.

CHAPTER I.

INTRODUCTORY—QUESTION STATED.

CHAPTER II.

DEFINITIONS—NATURE AND THE SUPERNATURAL.

CHAPTER III.

CHAPTER IV.

CHAPTER V.

THE FACT OF SIN.

CHAPTER VI.

THE CONSEQUENCES OF SIN.

CHAPTER VII.

ANTICIPATIVE CONSEQUENCES.

CHAPTER VIII.

NO REMEDY IN DEVELOPMENT OR SELF-REFORMATION.

CHAPTER IX.

THE SUPERNATURAL COMPATIBLE WITH NATURE AND SUBJECT TO FIXED LAWS.

CHAPTER X.

THE CHARACTER OF JESUS FORBIDS HIS POSSIBLE CLASSIFICATION
WITH MEN.

CHAPTER XI.

CHRIST PERFORMED MIRACLES

CHAPTER XII.

WATER-MARKS IN THE CHRISTIAN DOCTRINE.

CHAPTER XIII.

THE WORLD IS GOVERNED SUPERNATURALLY IN THE INTEREST OF
CHRISTIANITY.

CHAPTER XIV.

MIRACLES AND SPIRITUAL GIFTS ARE NOT DISCONTINUED

CONTENTS.

CHAPTER XV.

CONCLUSION STATED—USES AND RESULTS.

NATURE AND THE SUPERNATURAL.

CHAPTER I.

INTRODUCTORY.   QUESTION STATED.

In the remoter and more primitive ages of the world, some times called mythologic, it will be observed that mankind, whether by reason of some native instinct, as yet uncorrupted, or some native weakness yet uneradicated, are abundantly dis posed to believe in things supernatural.   Thus it was in the extinct religions of Egypt, Phœnicia, Greece, and Rome ; and thus also it still is in the existing mythologic religions of the East.   Under this apparently primitive habit of mind, we find men readiest, in fact, to believe in that which exceeds the terms of mere nature ; in deities and apparitions of deities, that fill the heavens and earth with their sublime turmoil ; in fates and furies ; in nymphs and graces ; in signs and oracles, and in cantations ; in "gorgons and chimeras dire."   Their gods are charioteering in the sun, presiding in the mountain tops, rising out of the foam of the sea, breathing inspirations in the gas that issues from caves and rocky fissures, loosing their rage in the storms, plotting against each other in the intrigues of courts, mixing in battles to give success to their own people or defeat the people of some rival deity.   All departments and regions of the world are full of their miraculous activity. Above ground, they are managing the thunders ; distilling in showers, or settling in dews ; ripening or blasting the harvests ; breathing health, or poisoning the air with pestilential infec tions.   In the ground they stir up volcanic fires, and wrestle in earthquakes that shake down cities.   In the deep world underground, they receive the ghosts of departed men, and preside in Tartarean majesty over the realms of the shades.

The unity of reason was nothing to these Gentiles. They had little thought of nature as an existing scheme of order and Everything was supernatural. The universe itself, in all its parts, was only a vast theatre in which the gods and demigods were acting their parts.

But there sprang up at length among the Greeks, some four or five centuries before the time of Christ, a class of speculative neologists and rationalizing critics called Sophists, who began to put these wild myths of religion to the test of argument f we may trust the description of Plato, they were generally men without much character, either as respects piety or even l morals; a conceited race of Illuminati, who more often scoffed than argued against the sacred things of their religion

. it was no difficult thing for them to shake, most effectu ally, the confidence of the people in schemes of religion so intensely mythical. And it was done the more easily that the more moderate and sober-minded of the Sophists did not pro pose to overthrow and obliterate the popular religion, but only to resolve the mythic tales and deities into certain great facts and powers of nature; and so, as they pretended, to find a more sober and rational ground of support for their religious convictions. In this manner we are informed that one of their number, Eumerus, a Cyrenian, "resolved the whole doctrine, concerning the gods into a history of nature."[1]

The religion of the Romans, at a later period, underwent a ilar process, and became an idle myth, having no earnest significance and as little practical authority in the convictions the people. And when Christ came, the Sadducees were practising on the Jewish faith in much the same way. As philosophy entered, religion was falling everywhere before its nalizing processes. It was poetry on one side and dialectics· e other; and the dialectics were, in this case, more thaz latch for the poetry,—as they ever must be, until their rea] ...ness I the cheat of their pretensions are discovered. What the Christian father, Justin Martyr, says of the Sophists of his time, was doubtless a sufficiently accurate account of the others in times previous, and may be taken as a faithful picture of the small residuum of religious conviction left by them all. hey seek, he says, " to convince us that the divinity ex- s his care to the great whole and to the several kinds, but

1 Neander, vol. i. p. 6.

not to me and to you—not to men as individuals. Hence it is useless to pray to him ; for everything occurs according to the unchangeable law of an endless cycle."[1]

Or, we may take the declaration of Pliny, from the side of the heathen philosophy itself, though many were not ready to go the same length, preferring to retain religion, which they oftener called superstition, as a good instrument for the state, and useful as a restraint upon the common people. He says :— " All religion is the offspring of necessity, weakness, and fear. What God is, if in truth he be anything distinct from the world, it is beyond the compass of man's understanding to know."[2]

Thus, between the destructive processes of reason entering on one side to demolish, and Christianity on the other to offer itself as a substitute, the old mythologic religions fell, and were com pletely swept away.

And now, at last, the further question comes, viz., whether Christianity itself is also, in its turn, to experience the same fate, and be exterminated by the same or a closely similar process ? It is now to be found that Christianity is only another form of myth, and is it so to be resolved into the mere " history of nature," as the other religions were before it ? Is it now to be discovered that the prophecy and miracle of the Old Testament, and all the formally historic matters even of the gospels and epistles of the New, are reducible to mere natural occurrences, "under the unchangeable laws of an endless cycle ?" Is this process now to end in the discovery, beyond which there can be no other, that God himself is, in truth, nothing " distinct from the world ?"

This is the new infidelity : not that rampant, crude-minded, and malignant scoffing which, in a former age, undertook to rid the world of all religion ; on the contrary, it puts on the air and speaks in the character of a genuine scholarship and philosophy. It simply undertakes, if we can trust its professions, to interpret and apply to the facts of Scripture, the true laws of historic criticism. It more generally speaks in the name of religion, and does not commonly refuse even the more distinctive name of Christianity. Coming thus in shapes of professed deference to revealed religion, many persons appear to be scarcely aware

of the questions it is raising, the modes of thought it is generat
ing, and the general progress toward mere naturalism it is
beginning to set in motion. Many, also, are the more effectually
blinded to the tendency of the times, that so many really true
opinions and so many right sentiments, honourable to God
and religion, are connected with the pernicious and false
method by which it is, in one way or another, extinguishing the
faith of religion in the world. It proposes to make a science
of religion, and what can be more plausible than to have religion
become a science ?

It finds a religious sentiment in all men, which, in one view,
is a truth. It finds a revelation of God in all things, which
also is a truth. It discovers a universal inspiration of God in
human souls ; which, if it be taken to mean that they are in
herently related to God, and that God, in the normal state,
would be an illuminating, all-moving presence in them, is like
wise a truth. It rejoices also in the discovery of great and
good men, raised up in all times to be seers and prophets of
God ; which, again, is not impossible, if we take into account
the possibility of a really supernatural training or illumination,
outside of the Jewish cultus ; as in the case of Jethro, Job, and
Cornelius, including probably Socrates and many others like him,
who were inwardly taught of God and regenerated by the private
mission of his Spirit.

But exactly this the new infidelity cannot allow. All pre
tences of a supernatural revelation, inspiration, or experience, it
rejects ; finding a religion, beside which there is no other, within
the terms of mere nature itself ; a universal, philosophic, scien
tific religion. In this it luxuriates, expressing many very good
and truly sublime sentiments ; sentiments of love, and brother
hood, and worship ; quoting Scripture, when it is convenient,
as it quotes the Orphic hymns, or the Homeric and Sybilline
verses, and testifying the profoundest admiration to Jesus Christ,
in common with Numa, Plato, Zoroaster, Confucius, Mohammed,
and others ; and perhaps allowing that he is, on the whole, the
highest and most inspired character that has ever yet appeared
in the world. All this, on the level of mere nature, without
miracle, or incarnation, or resurrection, or new creation, or
anything above nature. Such representations are only historic
myths, covering perhaps real truths, but, as regards the historic
form, incredible. Nothing supernatural is to be admitted. Re-

demption itself, considered as a plan to raise man up out of thral
dom, under the corrupted action of nature—rolling back its
currents and bursting its constraints—is a fiction. There is
no such thraldom, no such deliverance, and so far Christianity
is a mistake ; a mistake, that is, in everything that constitutes
its grandeur as a plan of salvation for the world.

We have heard abundantly of these and such like aberrations
from the Christian truth in Germany, and also in the literary
metropolis of our own country. But we have not imagined any
general tendency, it may be, in this direction, as a peculiarity of
our times. If so, we have a discovery to make ; for, though it
may not be true that any large proportion of the men of our times
have distinctly and consciously accepted this form of unbelief,
yet the number of such is rapidly increasing, and, what is worse,
the number of those who are really in it, without knowing it, is
greater and more rapidly increasing still. The current is this
way, and the multitudes or masses of the age are falling into it.
Let us take our survey of the forms of doubt or denial that are
converging on this common centre, and uniting, as a common
force, against the faith of anything supernatural, and so against
the possibility, in fact, of Christianity as a gospel of salvation to
the world.

From the first moment or birth-time of modern science, if we
could fix the moment, it has been clear that Christianity must
ultimately come into a grand issue of life and death with it, or
with the tendencies embodied in its progress. Not that Christianity has any conflict with the facts of science, or they with it.
On the contrary, since both it and nature have their common
root and harmony in God, Christianity is the natural foster-
mother of science, and science the certain handmaid of Chris
tianity. And both together, when rightly conceived, must con
stitute one complete system of knowledge. But the difficulty is
here ; that we see things only in a partial manner, and that the
two great modes of thought, or intellectual methods, that of
Christianity in the supernatural department of God's plan, and
that of science in the natural, are so different, that a collision is
inevitable and a struggle necessary to the final liquidation of the
account between them ; or, what is the same, necessary to a
proper settlement of the conditions of harmony.

Thus, from the time of Galileo's and Newton's discoveries,

down to the present moment of discovery and research in geo
logical science, we have seen the Christian teachers stickling for
the letter of the Christian documents and alarmed for their safety,
and fighting, inch by inch, and with solemn pertinacity, the
plainest, most indisputable or even demonstrable facts.   On the
other side, the side of science, multitudes, especially of the mere
dilettanti, have been boasting, almost every month, some dis
covery that was to make a fatal breach upon revealed religion.

And a much greater danger to religion is to be apprehended
from science than this—viz., the danger that comes from what
may be called a bondage under the method of science,—as if
nothing could be true, save as it is proved by the scientific
method.   Whereas, the method of all the higher truths of
religion is different, being the method of faith ; a verification by
the heart, and not by the notions of the head.

Busied in nature, and profoundly engrossed with her pheno
mena, confident of the uniformity of her laws, charmed with
the opening wonders revealed in her processes, armed with
manifold powers contributed to the advancement of commerce
and the arts by the discovery of her secrets, and pressing
onward still in the inquest, with an eagerness stimulated by
rivalry and the expectation of greater wonders yet to be
revealed—occupied in this manner, not only does the mind of
scientific men but of the age itself become fastened to, and glued
down upon, nature ; conceiving that nature, as a frame of phy
sical order, is itself the system of God ; unable to imagine any
thing higher and more general to which it is subordinate.
Imprisoned in this manner by the terms and the method of
nature, the tendency is to find the whole system of God included
under its laws ; and then it is only a part of the same assump
tion that we are incredulous in regard to any modification, or
seeming interruption of their activity, from causes included in
the supernatural agency of persons, or in those agencies of God
himself that complete the unity and true system of his reign.
And so it comes to pass that, while the physical order called
nature is perhaps only a single and very subordinate term of
that universal divine system, a mere pebble chafing in the
ocean-bed of its eternity, we refuse to believe that this pebble
can be acted on at all from without, requiring all events and
changes in it to take place under the laws of acting it has
inwardly in itself.   There is no incarnation, therefore, no

miracle, nc redemptive grace, or experience ; for God's system is nature, and it is incredible that the laws of nature should bo interrupted ; all which is certainly true, if there be no higher, more inclusive system under which it may take place system atically, as a result even of system itself.

And exactly this must be the understanding of mankind, at some future time, when the account between Christianity and nature shall have been fully liquidated. When that point is reached, it will be seen that the real system of God includes two parts, a natural and a supernatural, and it will no more be incredible that one should act upon the other, than that one planet or particle in the department of nature should act upon and modify the action of another. But we are not yet ready for a discovery so difficult to be made. Thus far the tendency is visible, on every side, to believe in nature simply, and in Chris tianity only so far as it conforms to nature and finds shelter under its laws. And the mind of the Christian world is be coming, every day, more and more saturated with this propensity to naturalism ; gravitating, as it were, by some fixed law, though imperceptibly or unconsciously, toward a virtual and real un belief in Christianity itself ; for the Christianity that is become a part only of nature, or is classified under nature, is Christianity extinct. That we may see how far the mind of an age is infected by this naturalizing tendency, let us note a few of the thousand and one forms in which it appears.

First we have the relics of the old school of denial and atheism, headed most conspicuously by Mr Hume and the French philosophers. All atheists are naturalists of necessity. And atheism there will be in the world as long as sin is in it. If the doctrine dies out as argument, it will remain as a perverse and scoffing spirit. Or it will be reproduced in the dress of a new philosophy. Dying out as a negation of Hobbes or Hume, it will reappear in the positive and stolidly physical pretender- ship of Comte. But, whatever shape or want of shape it takes, destructive or positive,—a doctrine or a scoffing, a thought of the head or a distemper of the passions,—it will of course regard a supernatural faith as the essence of all unreason.

Still it cannot be said that the negations of Mr Hume are gone by, as long as they are assumed and practically held as fundamental truths, by many professed teachers of Christianity ; for it is remarkable that our most recent and most thorough-

going school of naturalists, or naturalizing critics in the Christian
Scriptures, really place it as the beginning and first principle of
criticism that no miracle is credible or possible. This they
take by assumption, as a point to be no longer debated, after the
famous argument of Hume. The works of Strauss, Hennel,
Newman, Froude, Fox, Parker, all more or less distinguished
for their ability, as for their virtual annihilation of the gospels,
are together rested on this basis. They are not all atheists ;
perhaps none of them will admit that distinction ; some of them
even claim to be superlatively Christian. But the assault upon
Christianity, in which they agree, is the one from which the
greatest harm is now to be expected, and that, in great part, for
the reason that they do not acknowledge the true genealogy of
their doctrine, and that, hovering over the gulf that separates
atheism from Christianity, they take away faith from one, with
out exposing the baldness and forbidding sterility of the other.
They have many apologies, too, in the unhappy encumbrances
thrown upon the Christian truth by its defenders, which makes
the danger greater still.

Next we have the school or schools of Pantheists ; who identify
God and nature, regarding the world itself and its history as a
necessary development of God, or the consciousness of God. Of
course there is no power out of nature and above it to work a
miracle ; consequently, no revelation that is more than a develop
ment of nature.

Next in order comes the large and vaguely-defined body of
physicalists, who, without pretending to deny Christianity, value
themselves on finding all the laws of obligation, whether moral
or religious, in the laws of the body and the world. The phreno
logists are a leading school in this class, and may be taken as
an example of the others. Human actions are the results of
organization. Laws of duty are only laws of penalty or benefit,
inwrought in the physical order of the world ; and Combe " On
the Constitution of Man " is the real gospel, of which Chris
tianity is only a less philosophic version. Thousands of persons
who have no thought of rejecting Christianity are sliding contin
ually into this scheme, speaking and reasoning every hour about
matters of duty, in a way that supposes Christianity to be only
an interpreter of the ethics of nature, and resolving duty itself, or
even salvation, into mere prudence or skill ;—a learning to walk
among things, so as not to lose one's balance and fall or be

hurt; or, when it is lost, finding how to recover and stand up again.

Closely related to these, or else included among them, we are to reckon, with some exceptions, the very intelligent, influential body of Unitarian teachers of Christianity. Maintaining, as they have done with great earnestness, the truth of the Scrip ture miracles, they furnish a singular and striking illustration of the extent to which a people may be slid away from their specu lative tenet, by the practical drift of what may be called their working scheme. Denying human depravity, the need of a supernatural grace also vanishes, and they set forth a religion of ethics, instead of a gospel to faith. Their word is practically, not regeneration, but self-culture. There is a good seed in us, and we ought to make it grow ourselves. The gospel proposes salvation ; a better name is development. Christ is a good teacher or interpreter of nature, and only so a redeemer. God, they say, has arranged the very scheme of the world so as to punish sin and reward virtue ; therefore, any such hope of for giveness as expects to be delivered of the natural effects of sin by a supernatural and regenerative experience, is vain ; because it implies the failure of God's justice and the overturning of a natural law. Whoever is delivered of sin, must be delivered by such a life as finally brings the great law of justice on his side. To be justified freely by grace is impossible.[1]

Again, the myriad schools of Associationists take it as a fun damental assumption, whether consciously or unconsciously, that human nature belongs to the general order of nature, as it comes from God, and that nothing is wanting to the full perfection of man's happiness, but to have society organized according to nature, that is, scientifically. No new creation of the soul in good, proceeding from a point above nature, is needed or to be expected. The propensities and passions of men are all right now; " attractions are proportioned to destinies " in them, as in the planets. What is wanted, therefore, is not the super natural redemption of man, but only a scientific reorganization of society.

Next we have the magnetists or seers of electricity opening other spheres and conditions of being by electric impacts, and preparing a religion out of the revelations of natural clair voyance and scientific necromancy ; the more confident of the

1 Dewey's Sermon on Retribution.

absurdity of the Christian supernaturalism, or the plan of
redemption by Christ, that they have been so mightily illumi
nated by the magnetic revelations.   They are greatly elated
also by other and more superlative discoveries, in the planets
and third heavens and the two superior states; boasting a more
perfect and fuller opening of the other world than even Christi
anity has been able to make.

Again, it will be observed, that almost any class of men,
whose calling occupies them much with matter and its laws,
have always, and now more than ever, a tendency to merely
naturalistic views of religion.   This is true of physicians.
Continually occupied with the phenomena of the body, and its
effects on the mind, they are likely, without denying Christi
anity, to reduce it practically to a form of naturalism.   So of
the large and generally intelligent class of mechanics.   Having
it for the occupation and principal study of life to adjust appli
cations of the great laws of chemistry and dynamics, and
exercised but little in subjects and fields of thought external to
mere nature, they very many of them come to be practical un
believers in everything but nature.   They believe in cause and
effect, and are likely to be just as much more sceptical in re
gard to any higher and better faith.   Active-minded, ingenious,
and sharp, but restricted in the range of their exercise, they
surrender themselves in great numbers to a feeling of unreality
in everything but nature.

Again, the tendency of modern politics, regarded as concerned
with popular liberty, is in the same direction.   Civil govern.
ment is grounded, as the people are every day informed by
their leaders, with airs of assumed statesmanship, in a social
compact—a pure fiction assumed to account for whole worlds
of fact; for everybody knows that no such compact was ever
formed, or ever supposed to be, by any people in the world.   It
has the advantage, nevertheless, of accounting for the political
state, atheistically, under mere nature, and is therefore the
more readily accepted, though it really accounts for nothing.
For if every subject in the civil state were in it as a real con
tractor, joining and subscribing the contract himself, what is
there even then to bind him to his contract, save that, in the
last degree, he is bound by the authority of God and the
sanctions of religion.   Besides, there never can be in this view
any such thing as legislation, but only an extended process of

contracting ; for legislation is the enactment of laws, and laws
have a morally binding authority on men, not as contractors,
but as subjects. It seems to be supposed that this doctrine of
a social compact has some natural agreement with popular
institutions, where laws are enacted by a major vote ; whereas
the major supposes a minor, non-assenting vote ; and as this
minor vote has been always a fact from first to last, the com
pact theory fails after all to show how majorities get a right to
govern that is better, even theoretically, than the right of any
single autocrat. There is, in fact, no conceivable basis of civil
authority and law which does not recognize the state as being,
in this form or in that, a creation of Providence, and as Provi
dence manages the world in the interest of redemption, a fact
supernatural ; which does not recognize the state as God's
minister in the supernatural works and ends of his administra
tion—appointed by him to regulate the tempers, restrain the
passions, redress the wrongs, shield the persons, and so to con
serve the order of a fallen race, existing only for those higher
aims which he is prosecuting in their history. Still we are
contriving always how to get some ground of civil order that
separates it wholly from God. A social compact, popular
sovereignty, the will of the people, anything that has an
atheistic jingle in the sound and stops in the plane of mere
nature best satisfies us. We renounce in this manner our true
historic foster-mother religion, taking for the oracle and patron
saint of our politics Jean Jacques Rousseau. And the result
is, that the immense drill of our political life, more far-reaching
and powerful than the pulpit, or education, or any protest of
argument, operates continually and with mournful certainty
against the supernatural faith of Christianity. Hence, too, it
is that we hear so much of commerce, travel, liberty, and the
natural spread of great inventions, as causes that are starting
new ideas, and must finally emancipate and raise all the nations
of mankind ; in which it seems to be supposed that there is
even a law of self-redemption in society itself. As if these
external signs or incidents of progress were its causes also ; or
as if they were themselves uncaused by the supernatural and
quickening power of Christ. Whether Christianity can finally
survive this death-damp of naturalism in our political and social
ideas, remains to be seen.

I have only to add, partly as a result of all these causes, and

partly as a joint cause with them, that the popular literature of
the times is becoming generally saturated with naturalistic senti
ments of religion.   The literature of no other age of the world
was ever more religious in the form, only the religion of it is,
for the most part, rather a substitute for Christianity than a
tribute to its honour,—a piracy on it as regards the beautiful
and sublime precepts of ethics it teaches, but a scorner only the
more plausible of whatever is necessary to its highest authority,
as a gift from God to the world.   It praises Christ as great or
greatest among the heroes; finds a God in the all, whom it
magnifies in imposing pictures of sublimity; rejoices in the con
ceit of an essential divinity in the soul and its imaginations;
dramatizes culture, sentiment, and philanthropy; and these, in
flated with an airy scorn of all that implies redemption, it offers
to the world, and especially to the younger class of the world,
as a more captivating and plausible religion.

To pursue the enumeration further is unnecessary.   What we
mean by a discussion of the supernatural truth of Christianity is
now sufficiently plain.   We undertake the argument from a
solemn conviction of its necessity, and because we see that the
more direct arguments and appeals of religion are losing their
power over the public mind and conscience.   This is true
especially of the young, who pass into life under the combined
action of so many causes, conspiring to infuse a distrust of what
ever is supernatural in religion.   Persons farther on in life are
out of the reach of these new influences, and, unless their atten
tion is specially called to the fact, have little suspicion of what
is going on in the mind of the rising classes of the world,—
more and more saturated every day with this insidious form of
unbelief.   And yet we all, with perhaps the exception of a few
who are too far on to suffer it, are more or less infected with the
same tendency.   Like an atmosphere, it begins to envelope the
common mind of the world.   We frequently detect its influence
in the practical difficulties of the young members of the churches,
who do not even suspect the true cause themselves.   Indeed,
there is nothing more common than to hear arguments advanced
and illustrations offered by the most evangelical preachers, that
have no force or meaning save what they get from the current
naturalism of the day.   We have even heard a distinguished and
carefully orthodox preacher deliver a discourse, the very doctrine
of which was inevitable, unqualified naturalism.   Logically taken

and carried out to its proper result, Christianity could have had no ground of standing left,—so little did the preacher himself understand the true scope of his doctrine, or the mischief that was beginning to infect his conceptions of the Christian truth.

In the review we have now sketched, it may easily be seen on what one point the hostile squadrons of unbelief are marching. Never before, since the inauguration of Christianity in our world, has any so general and momentous issue been made with it as this which now engages and gathers to itself, in so many ways, the opposing forces of human thought and society. Before all these combinations the gospel must stand, if it stands ; and against all these must triumph, if it triumphs. Either it must yield, or they must finally coalesce and become its supporters.

Do we undertake then, with a presumptuous and even pre posterous confidence, to overturn all the science, argument, influence of the modern age, and so to vindicate the supernatur-alism of Christianity ? By no means. We do not conceive that any so heavy task is laid upon us. On the contrary, we regard all these adverse powers as being, in another view, just so many friendly powers, every one of which has some contribution to make for the firmer settlement and the higher completeness of the Christian faith. They are not in pure error, but there is a discoverable and valuable truth for us, maintained by every one, if only it were adequately conceived and set, as it will be, in its fit place and connexion. Mr Hume's argument, for ex ample, contains a great and sublime truth, viz., that nothing ever did or will take place out of system, or apart from law— not even miracles themselves, which must, in some higher view, be as truly under law and system as the motions even of the stars. Pantheism has a great truth, and is even wanted, as a balance of rectification to the common error that places God afar off, outside of his works or above, in some unimagined altitude. No doubt there is a truth somewhere in spiritism which will yet accrue to the benefit of Christianity, or, at least, to an important rectification of our conceptions of man. So of all the other schools and modes of naturalism that I have named. I have no jealousy of science, or any fear, whether of its facts or its arguments. For God, we may be certain, is in no real disagreement with himself. It is only a matter of course that, until the great account between Christianity and science is

ever smallest doubt can be raised, at any most trivial point,
suffices to imperil everything, and the main question is taken at
the greatest possible disadvantage. The argument so stated
must inevitably be lost, as, in fact, it always is. For it has even
to be given up, at the outset, by concessions that leave it nothing
on which to stand. For no sturdiest advocate of a verbal and
punctual inspiration can refuse to admit variations of copy, and
the probable or possible mistake of this or that manuscript, in a
transfer of names and numerals. It is equally difficult to with
hold the admission here and there of a possible interpolation, or
that words have crept into the text that were once in the margin.
Starting, then, with a definition of infallibility, fallibility is at
once and so far admitted. After all, the words, syllables, iotas
of the book are coming into question ; the infallibility is logically
at an end even by the supposition. The moment we begin to ask
what manuscript we shall follow ? what words and numerals
correct ? what interpolations extirpate ? we have possibly a
large work on hand, and where is the limit ? Shall we stop
short of giving up 1 John v. 7, or shall we go a large stride
beyond, and give up the first chapters of Matthew and Luke ?
We are also obliged to admit that the canon was not made by
men infallibly guided by the Spirit ; and then the possibility
appears to logically follow that, despite of any power they had to
the contrary, some book may have been let into the canon which,
with many good things, has some specks of error in it. Besides,
if the question is thrown back upon us, at this point, we are
obliged to admit, and do, as a familiar point of orthodoxy, that
our own polarities are disturbed, our judgment discoloured, by
sin ; so that, if the book is infallible, the sense of it as infallible
is not and can not be in us ; how, then, can we affirm it, or
maintain it, in any such manner of strictness and exact percep
tion ? We could not even sustain the infallibility of God in this
manner ; i.e., because we are able to know it, item by item, as
comprehending in ourselves a complete sense of His infallibility.
We establish God's infallibility only by a constructive use of
generals, the particulars of which are conceived by us only in
the faintest, most partial manner.

Now these difficulties, met in establishing a close and punc
tual infallibility, are rather logical than real, and originate, not
in any defect of the Scriptures, but in a statement which puts
us in a condition to make nothing of a good cause—a condi-

tion to be inevitably worsted. Indeed, there is no better proof of a divine force and authority in the Scriptures, able to affirm and always affirming itself in its own right, even to the end of the world, than that they continue to hold their ground so firmly, when the speculative issue joined in their behalf has been so badly chosen, and, if we speak of what is true logically, so uniformly lost.

I see no way to gain the verdict which, in fact, they have hitherto gained for themselves, but to change our method and begin at another point, just where they themselves begin ; to let go the minima and lay hold of the principles—those great, outstanding verities, in which they lay their foundations, and by which they assert themselves. As long as the advocates of strict, infallible inspiration are so manifestly tangled and lost in the trivialities they contend for, these portentous advances of naturalism will continue. And, as many are beginning already, with no fictitious concern, to imagine that Christianity is now being put upon its last trial—whether to stand or not they hardly dare be confident—why should they be further discou raged by adhering to a mode of trial which, in being lost, really decides nothing ? Let the Church of God, and all the friends of revelation, as a word of the Lord to faith, turn their thoughts upon an issue more intelligent and significant, and one that can be certainly sustained.

CHAPTER II.

DEFINITIONS. NATURE AND THE SUPERNATURAL.

In order to the intelligent prosecution of our subject, we need, first of all, to settle on the true import of certain words and phrases, by the undistinguishing and confused use of which, more than by any other cause, the unbelieving habit of our time has been silently and imperceptibly determined. They are such as these :—"Nature," "the system of nature," " the laws of nature," " universal nature," " the supernatural," and the like. The first and last named, "nature" and the " super natural," most need our attention ; for, if these are carefully distinguished, the others will scarcely fail to yield us their true meaning.

The Latin etymology of the word *nature* presents the true force of the term, clear of all ambiguity. The nature [*natura*] of a thing is the future participle of its being or becoming—its *about-to-be*, or its *about-to-come-to-pass ;* and the radical idea is, that there is, in the thing whose nature we speak of, or in the whole of things called nature, an about-to-be, a definite futurition, a fixed law of coming to pass, such that, giving the thing, or whole of things, all the rest will follow by an inherent neces sity. In this view nature, sometimes called "universal nature," and sometimes " the system of nature," is that created realm of being or substance which has an acting, a going on or process from within itself, under and by its own laws. Or, if we say, with some, that the laws are but another name for the immediate actuating power of God, still it makes no difference, in any other respect, with our conception of the system. It is yet *as if* the laws, the powers, the actings, were inherent in the substances, and were by them determined. It is still to our scientific separated from our religious contemplation, a chain of causes and effects, or a scheme of orderly succession, determined from within the scheme itself.

Having settled thus our conception of nature, our conception of the supernatural corresponds. That is supernatural, whatever it be, that is either not in the chain of natural cause and effect, or which acts on the chain of cause and effect, in nature, from without the chain. Thus, if any event transpires in the bosom, or upon the platform of what is called nature, which is not from nature itself, or is varied from the process nature would execute by her own laws, that is supernatural, by whatever power it is wrought. Suppose, for example (which we may, for illustration's sake, even though it cannot be), that there were another system of nature incommunicably separate from ours, some "famous continent of universe," like that on which Bunyan stumbled "as he walked through many regions and countries;" if, then, this other universe were swung up side by side with ours great disturbance would result, and the disturbance would be to us supernatural, because from without our system of nature; for, though the laws of our system are acting still in the disturbance, they are not, by the supposition, acting in their own system or conditions, but by an action that is varied by the forces and reciprocal actings of the other. So if the processes, combinations, and results of our system of nature are interrupted or varied by the action, whether of God, or angels, or men, so as to bring to pass what would not come to pass in it by its own internal action, under the laws of mere cause and effect, the variations are, in like manner, supernatural. And exactly this we expect to show: viz., that God has, in fact, erected another and higher system, that of spiritual being and government for which nature exists; a system not under the law of cause and effect, but ruled and marshalled under other kinds of laws, and able continually to act upon or vary the action of the processes of nature. If, accordingly, we speak of system, this spiritual realm or department is much more properly called a system than the natural, because it is closer to God, higher in its consequence, and contains in itself the ends or final causes for which the other exists, and to which the other is made to be subservient. There is, however, a constant action and reaction between the two, and, strictly speaking, they are both together, taken as one, the true system of God; for a system, in the most proper and philosophic sense of the word, is a complete and absolute whole, which cannot be taken as a part or fraction of anything.

We do not mean, of course, by these definitions or distinctions of the natural and supernatural, to assume the impropriety of the great multitude of expressions in which these words are more loosely employed. They may well enough be so employed, the convenience of speech requires it ; but it is only the more ne cessary on that account that we thoroughly understand ourselves when we use them in this manner.

Thus we sometimes speak of " the system of nature," using the word Nature in a loose and general way, as comprising all created existence. But if we accommodate ourselves in this manner, it behoves us to see that we do not, in using such a term, slide into a false philosophy which overturns all obliga tion by assuming the real universality of cause and effect, and the subjection of human actions to that law. It may be true that men are only things determinable under the same condi tions of causality, but it will be soon enough to assert that fact when it is ascertained by particular inquiry ; which inquiry is much more likely to result in the impression that the phrase, " system of nature," understood in this manner as implying that human actions are determined by mechanical laws, is much as if one were to speak of the " system of the school-house," as supporting the inference that the same kind of frame-work that holds the timbers together is also to mortise and pin fast the moral order of the school. In the same manner we sometimes say " universal nature," when we only catch up the term to denote the whole creation or universe, without deciding any thing in regard to the possible universality of nature properly defined. To this, again, there is no objection, if we are only careful not to slide into the opinion that natural laws and causes comprehend everything ; as multitudes do, without thought, in simply yielding to the force of such a term.

The word " *Nature* " again, is currently used in our modern literature as the name of a Universal Power ; be it an eternal fate, or an eternal system of matter reigning by its necessary laws, or an eternal God who is the All, and is, in fact, nowise different from a system of matter. Nature undergoes, in this manner, a kind of literary apotheosis, and receives the mock honours of a *dilettanti* worship. And the new-nature religion is the more valued, because both the God and the worship, being creatures of the reigning school of letters, are supposed to be of a more superlative and less common quality. But, though something is here said of religion with a religious air, the word *nature*, it will be found, is used in exact accordance still with its rigid and proper meaning, as denoting that which has its fixed laws of coming to pass within itself. The only abuse consists in the assumed universal extent of nature by which it becomes a fate, an all-devouring abyss of necessity, in which God, and man, and all free beings are virtually swallowed up. If it should happen that nature proper has no such extent, but is, instead, a comparatively limited and meagre fraction of the true universe, the new religion would appear to have but a very shallow foundation, and to be, in fact, a fraud as pitiful as it is airy and pretentious.

We also speak of a nature *in* free beings, and count upon it as a motive, cause, or ground of certainty in respect of their actions. Thus we assign the nature of God and the nature of man as reasons of choice and roots of character, representing that it is " the nature of God" to be holy, or (it may be) " the nature of man to do wrong." Nor is there any objection to this use of the word " nature," taken as popular language. There is, doubtless, in God, as a free intelligence, a constitu tion having fixed laws, answering exactly to our definition of nature. That there is a proper and true nature in man we certainly know; for all the laws of thought, memory, associa tion, feeling in the human soul are as fixed as the laws of the heavenly bodies. It is only the will that is not under the law of cause and effect, and the other functions are by their laws subordinated in a degree to the uses of the will and its direct ing sovereignty over their changes and processes. And yet the will, calling these others a nature, is in turn solicited and drawn by them, just as the expressions alluded to imply, save that they have, in fact, no causative agency on the will at all. They are the will's reasons, that in view of which it acts ; so that, with a given nature, it may be expected, with a certain qualified degree of confidence, to act thus or thus ; but they are never causes on the will, and the choices of the will are never their effects. Therefore, when we say that it is " the nature of man to do this," the language is to be understood in a secondary, tropical sense, and not as when we say that it is the nature of fire to burn or water to freeze.

As little would I be understood to insist that the term *super natural* is always to be used in the exact sense I have given it Had the word been commonly used in this close, sharply-defined meaning, much of our present unbelief, or misbelief, would have been obviated ; for these aberrations result almost universally from our use of this word in a manner so indefinite and so little intelligent.   Instead of regarding the supernatural as that which acts on the chain of cause and effect in nature from without the chain, and adhering to that sense of the term, we use it very commonly, in a kind of ghostly, marvelling sense, as if relating to some apparition, or visional wonder, or it may be to some desultory, unsystematizable action, whether of angels or of God Such uses of the word are permissible enough by dictionary laws, but they make the word an offence to all who are any way inclined to the rationalizing habit.   On the other hand there are many who claim to be acknowledged as adherents of a supernatural faith, with as little definite understanding Believing in a God superior to nature, acting from behind and *through her laws*, they suppose that they are, of course, to be classed as believers in a supernatural being and religion   But the genuine supernaturalism of Christianity signifies a great deal more than this ; viz., that God is acting from without on the lines of cause and effect in our fallen world and our dis ordered humanity, to produce what, by no mere laws of nature will ever come to pass.   Christianity, therefore, is supernatural, not because it acts through the laws of nature, limited by and doing the work of the laws ; but because it acts regeneratively and new-creatively to repair the damage which those laws, in their penal action, would otherwise perpetuate.   Its very distinction, as a redemptive agency, lies in the fact that it enters into nature, in this regenerative and rigidly supernatural way, to reverse and restore the relapsed condition of sinners.

But the real import of our distinction between nature and the supernatural, however accurately stated in words, will not fully appear till we show it in the concrete ; for it does not yet appear that there is, in fact, any such thing known as the supernatural agency defined, or that there are *in esse* any beings or classes of beings, who are distinguished by the exercise of such an agency.   That what we have defined as nature truly exists will not be doubted, but that there is any being or power in the universe, who acts, or can act upon the chain of cause and effect in nature from without the chain, many will doubt and some will strenuously deny. Indeed, the great difficulty heretofore encountered, in establishing the faith of a super natural agency, has been due to the fact that we have made a ghost of it ; discussing it as if it were a marvel of superstition, and no definite and credible reality. Whereas, it will appear, as we confront our difficulty more thoughtfully and take its full force, that the moment we begin to conceive ourselves rightly, we become ourselves supernatural. It is no longer necessary to go hunting after marvels, apparitions, suspensions of the laws of nature, to find the supernatural : it meets us in what is least transcendent and most familiar, even in ourselves. In ourselves we discover a tier of existences that are above nature, and, in all their most ordinary actions, are doing their will upon it. The very idea of our personality is that of a being not under the law of cause and effect, a being supernatural. This one point clearly apprehended, all the difficulties of our subject are at once relieved, if not absolutely and completely removed.

If any one is startled or shocked by what appears to be the extravagance of this position, let him recur to our definition ; viz., that nature is that world of substance, whose laws are laws of cause and effect, and whose events transpire, in orderly succession, under those laws ; the supernatural is that range of substance, if any such there be, that acts upon the chain of cause and effect in nature from without the chain, producing thus results that, by mere nature, could not come to pass. It is not said, be it observed, as is sometimes done, that the supernatural implies a suspension of the laws of nature, a causing them, for the time, not to be—that, perhaps, is never done—it is only said that we, as powers not in the line of cause and effect, can set the causes in nature at work, in new combinations otherwise never occurring, and produce, by our action upon nature, results which she, as nature, could never produce by her own internal acting.

Illustrations are at hand without number. Thus, nature, for example, never made a pistol, or gunpowder, or pulled a trigger ; all which being done, or procured to be done, by the criminal, in his act of murder, he is hung for what is rightly called his unnatural deed. So of things not criminal ; nature

never built a house, or modelled a ship, or fitted a coat, or
invented a steam-engine, or wrote a book, or framed a constitu
tion.   These are all events that spring out of human liberty
acting in and upon the realm of cause and effect, to produce
results and combinations, which mere cause and effect could
not ; and, at some point of the process in each, we shall be
found coming down upon nature, by an act of sovereignty just
as peremptory and mysterious as that which is discovered in a
miracle, only that a miracle is a similar coming down upon it
from another and higher being, and not from ourselves   Thus
for example, in the firing of the pistol, we find materials brought
together and compounded for making an explosive gas   an
arrangement prepared to strike a fire into the substance com
pounded, an arm pulled back to strike the fire, muscles con
tracted to pull back the arm, a nervous telegraph running down
from the brain, by which some order has been sent to contract
the muscles ; and then, having come to the end of the chain of
natural causes, the jury ask, who sent the mandate down upon
the nervous telegraph, ordering the said contraction ?   And
having found, as their true answer, that the arraigned criminal
did it, they offer this as their verdict, and on the strength of
the verdict he is hung.   He had, in other words, a power to set
in order a line of causes and effects, existing elementally in nature
and then, by a sentence of his will, to start the line, doing his
unnatural deed of murder.   If it be inquired how he was able to
command the nervous telegraph in this manner, we cannot tell,
any more than we can show the manner of a miracle.   The
same is true in regard to all our most common actions.   If one
simply lifts a weight, overcoming, thus far, the great law of
gravity, we may trace the act mechanically back in the same
way ; and if we do it, we shall come, at last, to the man acting
in his personal arbitrament, and shall find him sending down
his mandate to the arm, summoning its contractions and senten
cing the weight to rise.   In which, as we perceive, he has just
so much of power given him to vary the incidents and actions of
nature as determined by her own laws—so much, that is of
power supernatural.

And so all the combinations we make in the harnessing of
nature s powers imply, in the last degree, thoughts, mandates
it will, that are, at some point, peremptory over the motions
by which we handle, and move, and shape, and combine the

substances and causes of the world. And to what extent we may go on to alter, in this manner, the composition of the world, few persons appear to consider. For example, it is not absurd to imagine the human race, at some future time, when the population and the works of industry are vastly increased, kindling so many fires, by putting wood and coal in contact with fire, as to burn up or fatally vitiate the world's atmosphere. That the condition of nature will, in fact, be so far changed by human agency, is probably not to be feared. We only say that human agency, in its power over nature, holds, or may well enough be imagined to hold, the sovereignty of the process. Meantime, it is even probable, as a matter of fact, that infections and pestilential diseases invading, every now and then, some order of vegetable or animal life, are referable, in the last degree, to something done upon the world by man. For indeed we shall show before we have done, that the scheme of nature itself is a scheme unstrung and· mistuned, to a very great degree, by man's agency in it, so as to be rather unnature after all than nature ; and for just that reason, demanding of God, even for system's sake, in the highest range of that term, miracle and redemption.

Suffice it, for the present, simply to clear, as well as we are able, this main point, the fact of a properly supernatural power in man. Thus, some one, going back to the act by which the pistol was fired, will imagine, after all, that the murderer's act in the firing was itself caused in him by some condition back of what we call his choice, as truly as the explosion of the powder was caused by the fire. Then, why not blame the powder, we answer, as readily as the man, which most juries would have some difficulty in doing, though none at all in blaming the man ? The nature of the objection is purely imaginary, as, in fact, the common sense, if we should not rather say the common consciousness of the word decides ; for we are all conscious of acting from ourselves, uncaused in our action. The murderer knows within himself that he did the deed, and that nothing else did it through him. So his consciousness testifies, so the consciousness of every man revising his actions, and no real philosopher will ever undertake to substitute the verdict of consciousness, by another, which he has arrived at only by speculation, or a logical practice in words. The sentence of consciousness is final.

was exactly this and nothing else, that the wrong-doer followed after the weakest and worst, and did not act as a reasonable being should ; and that is what his consciousness, if he could get far back enough into the sense of the moment, would report. Nor does it vary at all the conclusion that a wrong doer chooses the weakest motive, to imagine, with many loose-minded teachers, that the right is only postponed, and the wrong chosen for the moment, with a view to secure the double benefit both of the right and the wrong ; for the real question at the time is, in every such case, whether it is wisest, best, and every way most advantageous, to make the delay and try for the double benefit ; and no man ever yet believed that it was. Never was there a case of wrong or sinful choice in which the agent believed that he was really choosing the strongest or weightiest and most valuable motive.[1]

So far, then, is man from being any proper item of nature. He is under no law of cause and effect in his choices. He stands out clear and sovereign as a being supernatural, and his definition is, that he is an original power, acting, not in the line of causality, but from himself. He is not independent of nature in the sense of being separated from it in his action, but he is in it, environed by it, acting through it, partially sovereign over it, always sovereign as regards his self-determin ation, and only not completely sovereign as regards executing all that he wills in it. In certain parts or departments of the soul itself, such as memory, appetite, passion, attention, imagin-

---

[1] A certain class of theologians may, perhaps, imagine that such a view of choice takes away the ground of the Divine foreknowledge. How can God foreknow what choices men may form, when, for aught that appears, they as often choose against the strongest motive as with it? He could not foreknow anything, we answer, under such conditions, if he were obliged to find out future things, as the astronomers make out almanacs, by computation. But he is a being, not who computes, but who, by the eternal necessity even of his nature, intuits everything. His foreknowledge does not depend on his will, or the adjustment of motives to make us will thus or thus, but he foreknows everything first conditionally, in the world of possibility, before he creates, or determines anything to be, in the world of fact. Otherwise, all his purposes would be grounded in ignorance, not in wisdom, and his knowledge would consist in following after his will, to learn what his will has blindly determined. This is not the Scripture doctrine, which grounds all the purposes of God in his wisdom ; that is, in what he perceives by his eternal intuitive foreknowledge of what is contained in all possible systems and combinations before creation—"whom he did foreknow, them he also did predestinate,"—"elect, according to the foreknowledge of God." If, then, God fore knows, or intuitively knows, all that is in the possible system and the possible man, without calculation, he can have little difficulty after that in foreknowing the actual man, who is nothing but the possible in the world of possibles, set on foot and become actual in the world of actuals. So far, therefore, as the doctrine of Edwards was con trived to support the certainty of God's foreknowledge, and lay a basis for the syste matic government of the world, and the universal sovereignty of God's purposes, it ap pears to be quite unnecessary.

ation, association, disposition, the will-power in him is held in contact, so to speak, with conditions and qualities that are dominated partly by laws of cause and effect ; for these facul ties are partly governed by their own laws, and partly sub mitted to his governing will by their own laws ; so that, when he will exercise any control over them, or turn them about to serve his purpose, he can do it, in a qualified sense and degree, by operating through their laws. As far as they are concerned, he is pure nature, and he is only a power superior to cause and effect at the particular point of volition where his liberty culminates, and where the administration he is to maintain over his whole nature centres.

It is also a part of the same general view that, as all functions of the soul but the will are a nature, and are only qualifiedly subjected to the will by their laws, the will, without ever being restricted in its self-determination, will often be restricted as regards executive force to perform what it wills. In this matter of executive force or capacity, we are under physiological and cerebral limitations ; limitations of associa tion, want, condition ; limitations of miseducated thought, per verted sensibility, prejudice, superstition, a second nature of evil habit and passion, by which, plainly enough, our capacity of doing or becoming is greatly reduced. This, in fact, is the grand, all-conditioning truth of Christianity itself; viz., that man has no ability in himself, and by merely acting in himself, to become right and perfect; and that, hence, without some extension to him from without and above, some approach and ministration that is supernatural, he can never become what his own ideals require. And therefore it is the more remarkable that so many are ready, in all ages, to take up the notion, and are even doing it now, as a fresh discovery, that these stringent limitations on our capacity take away the liberty of our will. As if the question of executive force, the ability to make or become, had anything to do with our self-determining liberty ! At the point of the will itself we may still be as free, as truly original and self-active, as if we could do or execute all that we would ; otherwise, freedom would be impossible, except on the condition of being omnipotent ; and even then, as in due time we shall see, would be environed by many insuperable necessities. As long ago as when Paul found it present with him to will, but could not find how to perform, this distinction

the fact.   There was never a man, however miseducated or
suppressed by his necessities, or corrupted by bad associations,
or misled by base examples, who had not still his moral con
victions, and did not blame himself in wrongs committed.   So
firm, and full, and indestructible is this inborn, moral autocracy
of the soul, that, as certainly in Timbuctoo as in Boston, it
takes upon itself the sentence of wrong, and no matter what
inducements there may have been, no matter how brutalized
the practices in which it had been trained, recognizes still the
sovereignty of right, and blames itself in every known deviation
from it.   His judgment of what particular things are necessary
to fulfil the great idea of right may be coarse, and, as we
    ould say, mistaken ; but he acknowledges, in the deepest
convictions of his nature, that nothing done against the eternal
necessary law of right can be justified.   The fact that his wild
nature is so nearly untamable to right, or that being or becoming
the perfect good he thinks, is so far off from his capacity, so
nearly impossible under his executive limitations, is really
nothing.   Still he must, and does, condemn the bad liberty
allowed in every conscious wrong.

    Self-determination, therefore, as respects the mere will as a
power of volition, is essentially indestructible.   And it is this
gift of power, this originative liberty, constituting, as it does
the central attribute of all personality, that gives us impressions
of what is personal in character, so different from those which
we derive from anything natural.   Hence, for example, it is
that we look on the nobler demonstrations of character in man,
with a feeling so different from any that can be connected with
mere cause and effect.   In every friend we distinguish some
thing more than a distillation of natural causes ; a free, faithful
soul, that, having a power to betray, stays fast in the integrity
 f love and sacrifice.   We rejoice in heroic souls, and in every
hero we discover a majestic spirit, how far transcending the
merely instinctive and necessary actings of animal and vegetable
life   He stands out in the flood of the world's causes, strong
in his resolve, not knowing, in a just fight, how to yield, but
protesting, with Coriolanus,—

> Let the Volsces
> Plough Rome and harrow Italy, I'll never
> Be such a gosling, as to obey instinct, but stand,
> As if a man was author of himself,
> And knew no other kin.

Hence the honour we so profusely yield to the martyrs, who are God's heroes ; able, as in freedom, to yield their flesh up in the fires of testimony, and sing themselves away in the smoke of their consuming bodies. Were they a part only of nature, and held to this by the law of cause and effect in nature, we should have as much reason to honour their Christian fortitude, as we have to honour the combustion of a fire ; even that which kindled their fagots :—as much and not more.

Such is the sense we have of all great character in men. We look upon them, not as wheels that are turned by natural causes, yielding their natural effects, as the flour is yielded by a mill, but what we call their character is the majestic proprium of their personality, that which they yield as the fruit of their glorious self-hood and immortal liberty. What, otherwise, can those triumphal arches mean, arranged for the father of his country, now on his way to be inaugurated as its First Magis trate ? what those processions of women, strewing the way with flowers ? what the thundering shouts of men, seconding their voices by the boom of cannon posted on every hill ? Why this thrill of emotion just now running electrically through so many millions of hearts towards this single man ? It is the reverence they feel, and cannot fitly express, to personal great ness and heroic merit in a great cause. Were our Washington conceived in that cause of good and great action, by which he became the deliverer of his country, to be the mere distillation of natural causes, who of us would allow himself to be thrilled with any such sentiments of reverence and personal homage ? It is no mere wheel, no link in a chain, that stirs our blood in this manner ; but it is a man, the sense we have of a man, rising out of the level of things, great above all *things*, great as being himself. Here it is, in demonstrations like these, that we meet the spontaneous verdict of mankind apart from all theories, and quibbles, and sophistries of argument, testify ing that man is a creature out of mere nature—a free cause in himself—great, therefore, in the majesty of great virtues and heroic acts.

The same is true, as we may safely assume, in regard to all the other orders and realms of spiritual existence ; to angels good and bad, seraphim, principalities, and powers in heavenly places. They are all supernatural, and it is in them, as belong. ing to this higher class of existences, that God beholds the final

between volitional self-determination and executive capacity began to be recognized, and has been recognized and stated in every subsequent age till now. No one is held, even for a moment, to a bad and wrong self-determination, simply because he has not the executive force to will himself into an angel, or because he cannot become, unhelped, and at once, all that he would. He is therefore still a fair subject of blame, partly because he has narrowed his capacities or possibilities, of doing or becoming, by his former sin, and partly because he consciously does not will the right and struggle after God now, which he is under perfect obligation to do, because the terms of duty are absolute or unconditional; and, if possible, still more perfect, because he has helps of grace and favour put in his reach to be laid hold of, which, if he accepts them, will infallibly medicate the disabilities he is under.

That mankind, as being under sin, are under limitations of executive ability, unable to do and become all that is required of them by their highest ideals of thought, is then no new doctrine. Christianity is based in the fact of such a disability, and affirms it constantly as a fact that creates no infringement of responsibility and personal liberty at all, as regards the particular sphere of the will itself. And therefore it will not be expected of any Christian that he will be greatly impressed by what are sometimes offered now as original and peremptory decisions against human liberty, grounded in the fact that man is not omnipotent—not able to do or become, what he is able to think. Thus we have the following, offered as a final disposal of the question of liberty, by a very brilliant, entertaining, and often very acute writer:—" Do you want an image of the human will, or the self-determining principle, as compared with its pre-arranged and impossible restrictions? A drop of water imprisoned in a crystal; you may see such a one in any mineralogical collection. One little particle in the crystalline prism of the solid universe . . . . The chief planes of its inclosing solid are of course organization, education, condition. Organization may reduce the will to nothing, as in some idiots; and, from this zero, the scale mounts upward, by slight gradations. Education is only second to nature. Imagine all the infants born this year in Boston and Timbuctoo to change places! Condition does less, but " give me neither poverty nor riches " was the prayer of Agur, and with good reason. If there is any improvement in modern theology, it is in getting out of the region of pure abstractions, and taking these everyday forces into account." [1]

It may have been a fault of the former times that, in judgments of human character and conduct, no sufficient allowance was made for these "everyday forces," and others which might be named; if so, let the mistake be corrected; but to imagine that the freedom or self-determining liberty of the human will is to be settled by any such external references, even starts the suspicion that the idea itself of the will has not yet arrived. So when the doctrine is located as being a something in "the region of pure abstractions," because it is not found by some scalpel inspection, or out-door hunt in the social conditions of life. What can be further off from all abstractions than the immediate, living, central, all-dominating consciousness of our own self-activity? Is consciousness an abstraction? Is anything further off from abstractions, or more impossible to be classed with them? On the contrary, the very conceit here allowed, that the great question of consciousness may be settled by external processes of deduction, and by generalizations that do not once touch the fact, is only an attempt to make an abstraction of it. And yet, after it is done and seems to be finally disposed of in that manner, after the discovery is fully made out that our self-determining will is only "a drop of water imprisoned in a crystal, one little particle in the crystal line prism of the solid universe," who is there, not excepting the just now very much humbled discoverer himself, who does not know, every day of his life, and does not show, a thousand times a day, that he has the sense in him of something different? Even if he does no more than humorously dub himself Autocrat of the Breakfast Table, it will be sufficiently plain that his autocracy is a much more considerable figure with him than a drop of water in a crystal. He most evidently imagines some presiding and determining mind at the Table, that is much more of a reality and much less of an abstraction.

And so it will be found universally that, however strongly drawn, the supposed disadvantages and hindrances to virtue may be, there is, in every mind, a large and positive consciousness of being master of its own choices and responsible for them. A translation from Boston to Timbuctoo will not anywise alter

1 *Atlantic Monthly*, Feb. 1858, p. 464.

the fact.   There was never a man, however miseducated, or
suppressed by his necessities, or corrupted by bad associations,
or misled by base examples, who had not still his moral con
victions, and did not blame himself in wrongs committed.   So
firm, and full, and indestructible is this inborn, moral autocracy
of the soul, that, as certainly in Timbuctoo as in Boston, it
takes upon itself the sentence of wrong, and no matter what
inducements there may have been, no matter how brutalized
the practices in which it had been trained, recognizes still the
sovereignty of right, and blames itself in every known deviation
from it.   His judgment of what particular things are necessary
to fulfil the great idea of right may be coarse, and, as we
should say, mistaken ; but he acknowledges, in the deepest
convictions of his nature, that nothing done against the eternal,
necessary law of right can be justified.   The fact that his wild
nature is so nearly untamable to right, or that being or becoming
the perfect good he thinks, is so far off from his capacity, so
nearly impossible under his executive limitations, is really
nothing.   Still he must, and does, condemn the bad liberty
allowed in every conscious wrong.

Self-determination, therefore, as respects the mere will as a
power of volition, is essentially indestructible.   And it is this
gift of power, this originative liberty, constituting, as it does,
the central attribute of all personality, that gives us impressions
of what is personal in character, so different from those which
we derive from anything natural.   Hence, for example, it is
that we look on the nobler demonstrations of character in man,
with a feeling so different from any that can be connected with
mere cause and effect.   In every friend we distinguish some
thing more than a distillation of natural causes ; a free, faithful
soul, that, having a power to betray, stays fast in the integrity
of love and sacrifice.   We rejoice in heroic souls, and in every
hero we discover a majestic spirit, how far transcending the
merely instinctive and necessary actings of animal and vegetable
life.   He stands out in the flood of the world's causes, strong
in his resolve, not knowing, in a just fight, how to yield, but
protesting, with Coriolanus,—

Let the Volsces
Plough Rome and harrow Italy, I'll never
Be such a gosling, as to obey instinct, but stand,
As if a man was author of himself,
And knew no other kin.

Hence the honour we so profusely yield to the martyrs, who are God's heroes ; able, as in freedom, to yield their flesh up in the fires of testimony, and sing themselves away in the smoke of their consuming bodies. Were they a part only of nature, and held to this by the law of cause and effect in nature, we should have as much reason to honour their Christian fortitude, as we have to honour the combustion of a fire ; even that which kindled their fagots :—as much and not more.

Such is the sense we have of all great character in men. We look upon them, not as wheels that are turned by natural causes, yielding their natural effects, as the flour is yielded by a mill, but what we call their character is the majestic proprium of their personality, that which they yield as the fruit of their glorious self-hood and immortal liberty. What, otherwise, can those triumphal arches mean, arranged for the father of his country, now on his way to be inaugurated as its First Magis trate ? what those processions of women, strewing the way with flowers ? what the thundering shouts of men, seconding their voices by the boom of cannon posted on every hill ? Why this thrill of emotion just now running electrically through so many millions of hearts towards this single man ? It is the reverence they feel, and cannot fitly express, to personal great ness and heroic merit in a great cause. Were our Washington conceived in that cause of good and great action, by which he became the deliverer of his country, to be the mere distillation of natural causes, who of us would allow himself to be thrilled with any such sentiments of reverence and personal homage ? It is no mere wheel, no link in a chain, that stirs our blood in this manner ; but it is a man, the sense we have of a man, rising out of the level of things, great above all *things*, great as being himself. Here it is, in demonstrations like these, that we meet the spontaneous verdict of mankind apart from all theories, and quibbles, and sophistries of argument, testify ing that man is a creature out of mere nature—a free cause in himself—great, therefore, in the majesty of great virtues and heroic acts.

The same is true, as we may safely assume, in regard to all the other orders and realms of spiritual existence ; to angels good and bad, seraphim, principalities, and powers in heavenly places. They are all supernatural, and it is in them, as belong ing to this higher class of existences, that God beholds the final

causes, the uses, and the grand systematizing ideas of his uni
versal plan. Nature, as comprehending the domain of cause
and effect, is only the platform on which He establishes his
kingdom as a kingdom of minds or persons, every one of whom
has power to act upon it, and to some extent, greater or less,
to be sovereign over it. So that, after all which has been done
by the sensuous littleness, the shallow pride, and the idolatry
of science to make a total universe, or even a God, of nature,
still it is nothing but the carpet on which we children have
our play, and which we may only use according to its design,
or may cut, and burn, and tear at will. The true system of
God centres still in us, and not in it; in our management, our
final glory and completeness of being as persons, not in the
set figures of the carpet we so eagerly admire, and call it science
to ravel.

Finding, now, in this manner, that we ourselves are super
natural creatures, and that the supernatural, instead of being
some distant, ghostly affair, is familiar to us as our own most
familiar action ; also, that nature, as a realm of cause and
effect, is made to be acted on from without by us and all moral
beings—thus to be the environment of our life, the instrument
of our activity, the medium of our right or wrong doing to
ward each other, and so the school of our trial—a further
question rises, viz., what shall we think of God's relations
to nature ? If it be nothing incredible that we should act on
the chain of cause and effect in nature, is it more incredible
that God should thus act ? Strange as it may seem, this is
the grand offence of supernaturalism, the supposing that God
can act on nature from without; on the chain of cause and
effect in nature from without the chain of connexion, by which
natural consequences are propagated—exactly that which we
ourselves are doing as the most familiar thing in our lives ! It
involves, too, as we can see at a glance, and shall hereafter
show more fully, no disruption by us of the laws of nature,
but only a new combination of its elements and forces, and
need not any more involve such a disruption by Him. Nor can
any one show that a miracle of Christ (the raising, for example,
of Lazarus), involves anything more than that nature is pre
pared to be acted on by a divine power, just as it is to be acted
on by a human, in the making of gunpowder, or the making

and charging of a firearm. For though there seems to be an immense difference in the grade of the results accomplished, it is only a difference which ought to appear, regarding the grade of the two agents by whom they are wrought. How different the power of two men, creatures though they be of the same order ; a Newton, for example, a Watt, a Fulton, and some wild Patagonian or stunted Esquimaux. So, if there be angels, seraphim, thrones, dominions, all in ascending scales of endow ment above one another, they will, of course, have powers supernatural, or capacities to act on the lines of causes in nature that correspond with their natural quantity and degree. What wonder then is it, in the case of Jesus Christ, that he reveals a power over nature appropriate to the scale of his being and the inherent supremacy of his divine person ?

And yet it will not do, our philosophers tell us, to admit any such thing as a miracle, or that anything does or can take place by a divine power which nature itself does not bring to pass ! God, in other words, cannot be supposed to act on the line of cause and effect in nature ; for nature is the universe, and the law of universal order makes a perfect system. Hence a great many of our naturalists, who admit the existence of God, and do not mean to identify his substance with nature, and call him the Creator, and honour him, at least in words, as the Governor of all things, do yet insist that it must be unphilosophical to suppose any present action of God, save what is acted in and through the pre-ordained system of nature. The author of the *Vestiges of Creation*, for example (p. 118), looks on cause and effect as being the eternal will of God, and nature as the all-comprehensive order of his Providence, be sides which, or apart from which, he does, and can be supposed to do, nothing. A great many who call themselves Christian believers, really hold the same thing, and can suffer nothing different. Nature, to such, includes man. God and nature, then, are the all of existence, and there is no acting of God upon nature ; for that would be supernaturalism. He may be the originative source of nature ; he may even be the im mediate, all-impelling will, of which cause and effect are the symptoms ; that is, he may have made and may actuate the machine, in that fated, foredoomed way which cause and effect describes, but he must not act upon the machine-system outside of the foredoomed way ; if he does, he will disturb the immut-

laws! In fact, he has no liberty of doing anything, but just to keep agoing the everlasting trundle of the machine. He cannot even act upon his works, save as giving and maintain ing the natural law of his works; which law is a limit upon Him, as truly as a bond of order upon them. He is incrusted and shut in by his own ordinances. Nature is the god above God, and he cannot cross her confines. His ends are all in nature; for, outside of nature, and beyond, there is nothing but Himself. He is only a great mechanic, who has made a great machine for the sake of the machine, having his work all done long ages ago. Moral government is out of the question —there is no government but the predestined rolling of the machine. If a man sins, the sin is only the play of cause and effect; that is, of the machine. If he repents, the same is true—sin, repentance, love, hope, joy, are all developments of cause and effect; that is, of the machine. If a soul gives itself to God in love, the love is but a grinding-out of some wheel he has set turning, or it may be turns, in the scheme of nature. If I look up to him and call him Father, he can only pity the conceit of my filial feeling, knowing that it is attribut. able to nothing but the run of mere necessary cause and effect in me, and is no more in fact from me than the rising of a mist or cloud is from some buoyant freedom in its particles. If I look up to him for help and deliverance, He can only hand me over to cause and effect, of which I am a link myself, and bid me stay in my place to be what I am made to be. He can touch me by no extension of sympathy, and I must even break through nature (as He Himself cannot) to obtain a look of recognition.

How miserable a desert is existence, both to him and to us, under such conditions—to Him, because of his character; to us, because of our wants. To be thus entombed in his works, to have no scope for his virtues, no field for his perfections, no ends to seek, no liberty to act, save in the mechanical way of mere causality—what could more effectually turn his goodness into a well-spring of baffled desires and defeated sympathies, and make His glory itself a baptism of sorrow. Meantime the supposition is, to us, a mockery, against which all our deepest wants and highest personal affinities are raised up, as it were in mutinous protest. If there is nothing but God and nature, and God him self has no relations to nature, save just to fill it and keep it on its way, then, being ourselves a part of nature, we are only a link, each one, in a chain let down into a well, where nothing else can ever touch us but the next link above! Oh, it is horrible! Our soul freezes at the thought! We want, we must have, something better—a social footing, a personal, and free, and flexible, and conscious relation with our God ; that he should cross over to us, or bring us over the dark Styx of nature unto Himself, to love Him, to obtain His recognition, to receive His manifestation, to walk in His guidance, and be raised to that higher footing of social understanding and spiritual concourse with Him, where our inborn affinities find their centre and rest. And what we earnestly want, we know that we shall assuredly find. The prophecy is in us, and whether we call ourselves prophets or not, we shall certainly go on to publish it. It is the inevitable, first fact of natural conviction with us. Do we not know, each one, that he is more than a thing or a wheel, and, being consciously a man, a spirit, a creature supernatural, will he hesitate to claim a place with such, and claim for such a place ?

CHAPTER III.

NATURE IS NOT THE SYSTEM OF GOD.—THINGS AND POWERS, HOW
RELATED.

GOD is expressed but not measured by his works; least of all,
by the substances and laws included under the general term
Nature.   And yet how liable are we, overpowered, as we often
are, and oppressed by the magnitudes of nature, to suffer the
impression that there can be nothing separate and superior be
yond nature.   The eager mind of science, for example, sallying
forth on excursions of thought into the vast abysses of worlds
discovering tracts of light that must have been shooting down
ward and away from their sources, even for millions of ages, to
have now arrived at their mark; and then discovering, also, that
by such a reach of computation it has not penetrated to the
centre, but only reached the margin or outmost shore of the vast
fire-ocean, whose particles are astronomic worlds, falls back
spent, and having as it were no spring left for another trial, or
the endeavour of a stronger flight, surrenders over-mastered and
helpless, crushed into silence.   At such an hour it is anything
but a wonder that nature is taken for the all, the veritable sys
tem of God; beyond which, or collateral with which, there is
nothing.   For so long a time is science imposed upon by
nature, not instructed by it; as if there could be nothing
greater than distance, measure, quantity, and show; nothing
higher than the formal platitude of things.   But the healthy
living mind will sooner or later recover itself.   It will spring up
out of this prostration before nature, to imagine other things
which eye hath not seen, nor ear heard, nor science computed.
It will discover fires even in itself that flame above the stars.
It will break over and through the narrow confines of stellar
organization to conceive a spiritual Kosmos or divine system,

which contains and uses and is only shadowed in the faintest manner by the prodigious trivialities of external substance. Indeed, I think all minds unsophisticated by science or not disempowered by external magnitudes, will conceive God as a being whose fundamental plan, whose purpose, end, and system are nowise measured by that which lies in dimension, even though the dimensions be measureless. They will say with Zophar still, "The measure thereof is longer than the earth, and broader than the sea." And the real, proper universe of God, that which is to God the final cause of all things, will be to them a realm so far transcending the outward immensity, both in quantity and kind, that this latter will be scarcely more than some outer gate of approach, or eyelet of observation.

What I propose, then, in the present chapter, coincidently with the strain of remark here indulged, is to undertake a negative, showing what, in fact, is decisive upon the whole question, that the surrender of so many minds to nature and her magnitudes is premature and weak ; that nature plainly is not, and cannot be, the proper and complete system of God ; or, if we speak no more of God, of the universe.

It would seem that any really thoughtful person, when about to surrender himself to nature in the manner just described, must be detained by a simple glance at the manifest yearning of the human race, in all ages and nations, for something super natural. Their affinity for objects supernatural is far more evident, as a matter of history, than for objects scientific and natural. Instead of reducing their gods and religions to the terms of nature, they have peopled nature with gods, and turned even their agriculture into a concert or concurrence with the unseen powers and their ministries. Witness, in this view, the im mense array of mythologic and formally unrational religions, extinct or still existing, that have been accepted by the popula tions of the world. Notice in particular also, that, when the keen dialectics of the polished Greeks and Romans had cut away the foundations of their religions, instead of lapsing into the cold no-religion of the Sophists, the cultivated mind of their scholars and philosophers passed straight by the boasted reason to lay hold of Christianity ; and Christianity, more rational but in no degree less supernatural than the religions overturned, was ac cepted as the common faith. And what is not less remarkable,

Christianity itself, as if not supernatural enough, was corrupted by the addition of still new wonders pertaining to the virgin, the priesthood, the sacraments, and even the bones of the saints indicated all, and some of them (such as that Mary is the Mother of God) generated even by dialectic processes. And so it ever has been. Men can as well subsist in a vacuum, or on a mere metallic earth, attended by no vegetable or animal products, as they can stay content with mere cause and effect, and the endless cycle of nature. They may drive themselves into it for the moment by their speculations; but the desert is too dry and the air too thin—they cannot stay. Accordingly, we find that just now, when the propensities to mere naturalism are so manifold and eager, they are yet instigated in their eagerness itself by an impulse that scorns all the boundaries of mere knowledge and reason; that is, by an appetite for things of faith, or a hope of yet fresher miracles and greater mysteries—gazing after the Boreal crown of Fourier, and the thawing out of the poles under the heat of so great felicity to come; or watching at the gate of some third heaven to be opened by the magnetic passes, or the solemn incantations of the magic circles; expecting an irrup tion of demons, in the name of science, more fantastic than even that which plagued the world in the days of Christ, and which so many critics, in the name also of science, were iust now labouring most intently to weed out of the gospel history True, the magnetic revelations are said to be in the way of nature; no matter for that, if only they are wonderful enough · all the better, indeed, if they give us things supernatural to enjoy and live in without the name. Only we must have mysteries, and believe, and take wings, and fly clear of the dull level of comprehensible cause and substance somehow. Such is man—such are we all.

We are like the poet Shelly, who, after he had sunk into blank atheism as regards religion, could not stay content, but began forthwith to people his brain and the world with griffins and gorgons, and animated rings, and fiery serpents, and spirits of water and wind, and became, in fact, the most mythologic of all modern poets; only that he made his mythologic machinery himself, out of the delirious shapes exhaled from the deep atheistic hunger of his soul. And the new Mormon faith, or fanaticism, that strangest phenomenon of our times— what is it, in fact, but a breaking loose by the human soul, pressed down by ignorance and unbelief together, to find some element of miracle and mystery, in which it may range and feed its insatiable appetite ; a raw and truculent imposture of supernaturalism, dug up out of the earth but yesterday, which, just because it is not under reason and is held by no stays of opinion, kindles the fires of the soul's eternity to a pitch of fierceness and a really devastating energy ? And were the existing faith of powers unseen and worlds above the world of science blotted out, leaving us shut down under atheism or mere nature, and gasping in the dull vacuum it makes, I verily believe that we should instantly begin to burst up all into Mormonism, or some other newly-invented faith no better authenticated.

Into this same gasping state, in fact, we are thrown by our new school of naturalistic literature, and we can easily dis tinguish, in the conscious discontent that nullifies both our pleasure and praise, the fact of some transcendent inborn affinity, by which we are linked to things above the range of mere nature. Who is a finer master of English than Mr Emerson ? Who offers fresher thoughts in shapes of beauty more fascinating ? Intoxicated by his brilliant creations, the reader thinks, for the time, that he is getting inspired. And yet, when he has closed the essay or the volume, he is surprised to find—who has ever failed to notice it ?—that he is disabled instead, disempowered, reduced in tone. He has no great thought or purpose in him ; and the force or capacity for it seems to be gone. Surely it is a wonderfully clear atmosphere that he is in, and yet it is somehow mephitic ! How could it be otherwise ? As it is a first principle that water will not rise above its own level, what better reason is there to expect that a creed which disowns duty and turns achievement into a conceit of destiny, will bring to man those great thoughts, and breathe upon him in those gales of impulse which are necessary to the empowered state, whether of thought or of action ? Grazing in the field of nature is not enough for a being whose deepest affinities lay hold of the supernatural and reach after God. Airy and beautiful the field may be, shown by so great a master ; full of goodly prospects and fascinating images ; but, without a living God, and objects of faith, and terms of duty, it is a pasture only—nothing more. Hence the unreadi ness, the almost aching incapacity felt to undertake anything or become anything by one who has taken lessons at this school. Nature is the all, and nature will do everything, whether we will or no. Call it duty, greatness, heroism, still it is hers, and she will have more of it when she pleases. If, then, nature does not set him on also, and do all in him, there is an end. What can he expect to do in the name of duty, faith, sacrifice, and high resolve, when nature is not in the plan ? What better, indeed, is there left him, or more efficient, than just to think beautiful thoughts if he can, and surrender himself to the luxury of watching the play of his own reflec tive egoism ? Given Brama for a god and a religion, what is left us more certainly than that we ourselves become Asiatics ? Such kind of influence would turn the race to pismires, if only we could stay content in it, as happily we cannot; for if we chance to find our pleasure in it for an hour, a doom as strong as eternity in us compels us finally to spurn it as a brilliant inanity.

But we are going further with our point than we intended. Admitting the universal tendency of the race in past ages to a faith in things supernatural, it may be imagined by some that, as we advance in culture, we must finally reach a stage where reason will enforce a different demand ; they may even return upon us the list we gave in our introductory chapter, of the parties now conspiring the overthrow of a supernatural faith, requiring us to accept them as proofs that the more advanced stage of culture is now about to be reached. In that case it is enough to answer that the naturalizing habit of our times is clearly no indication of any such new stage of advancement, but only a phase of social tendency once before displayed in the negative and destructive era of the Greek and Roman religions ; also that the grand conspiracy exhibited in our own time, sig nifies much less than it would, if after all there were any real agreement among the parties. Thus it will be found that while they seem to agree in the assumption that nature includes every thing, and also to show by their imposing air of concert that, in this way the world must needs gravitate, there is yet, if we scan them more carefully, no such agreement as indicates any solid merit in their opinion, or even such as may properly entitle them to respect.

Thus we find, first of all, a threefold distribution among them that sets them in as many schools or tiers, between which there

is almost nothing in common; one section or school maintain
ing that nature is God, another that it is originally the work
of God, and a third that there is no God. If nature itself is
God, then plainly God is not the Creator of nature by his own
sovereign act; and if there is no God, then he is neither nature
nor its Creator. Their agreement, therefore, includes nothing
but a point of denial respecting the supernatural, maintained
for wholly opposite and contradictory reasons. So as regards
religion itself; to some it is a natural effect or growth in souls,
and in that view a fact that evinces the real sublimity of
nature; while to others it is itself a matter only of contempt,
a creation of priestly artifice, or an excrescence of blind super
stition. One, again, believes in the personality, responsibility,
and immortality of souls, finding a moral government in nature,
and even what he calls a gospel; another, that man is a mere
link in the chain of causalities, like the insects, responsibility a
fiction, eternity a fond illusion; and still another that, being a
mere link in the chain of causalities, he will yet for ever be,
and be happy in the consciousness that he is. The contrarieties,
in short, are endless, and accordingly the weight of their apparent
concert, when set against the general vote and appetite of the
race for something supernatural, is wholly insignificant. If it
be a token of advancing culture, it certainly is not any token
that a wiser age of reason or scientific understanding is yet
reached; and the grand major vote of the race for a super
natural faith is nowise weakened by it. Still it is a fact, the
universal fact of history, that man is a creature of faith, and
cannot rest in mere nature and natural causality. Nothing
will content him in the faith that nature is the all or universal
system of being.

But the indications we discover within the realm of nature,
or of cause and effect, are more striking even than those which
we discover in the demonstrations of our own history. We
have spoken of a system supernatural, superior to the system
of nature, and subordinating always the latter to itself; under
standing, however, that both together in the truest and most
proper sense constitute the real universal system of God. Now,
as if to show us the possibility, and familiarize to us the fact
of a subordination thus of one system and its laws to the uses
and superior behests of another, we have in the domain of

nature herself, two grand systems of chemistry, or chemical force and action ; one of which comes down upon the other, always from without, to dominate over it, decomposing substances which the other has composed, producing substances which the other could not. We speak here, it will be understood, of what is called inorganic chemistry and vital chemistry, the chemistry of matter out of life or below it, and of that which is in it and by it. The lives that construct and organize the bodies they inhabit, are the highest forms of nature, and are set in nature as types of a yet higher order of existence ; viz., spirit or free intelligence. They are immaterial, having neither weight nor dimensions of their own ; and what is yet closer to mind, they act by no dynamic force or impulsion, but from themselves ; coming down upon matter as architects and chemists, to do their own will, as it were, upon the raw matter and the dead chemistry of the world. We say not that they have in truth a will ; they only have a certain plastic instinct by which their dominating chemistry is actuated, and their architectural forms are supplied. We have thus a world immaterial within the boundaries of cause and effect ; for the plastic instinct has causes of action in itself, and acts under a necessity as absolute as the inorganic forces. It belongs to nature and not to the supernatural, because it is really in the chain of cause and effect, and is only a *quasi* power. The manner of working in these plastic chemistries no science can discover, and their products no science can imitate. Elements that are united by the laws of matter they will somehow resolve and separate, and elements which no laws of matter have ever united, they will bring into a mystic union, congenial to their own forms and uses. Thus, in place of a few distinct substances we should have were the earth left to its pure metallic state, invaded by none of these myrmidons of life and the chemistries they bring with them, we have provided for our use immense varieties of substances which cannot even be recounted — woods, meats, bones, oils, wools, furs, grains, gums, spices, sweets, the fruits, the medicines, the grasses, the flowers, the odours — representatives all of so many lives working in the clay to produce what none but their external chemistry entering into the clay in silent sovereignty can summon it to yield. They are types in nature of the supernatural and its power to subordinate the laws of nature. They come as God's mute prophets, throwing down their rods

upon the ground as Moses did, that we may see their quicken
ing and believe. We do believe that they contain a higher
tier of chemical forces, superior to the lower tier of forces in
the dead matter, and we are nowise shocked by the miracle
when we see them quicken the dead matter into life, and work
it by their magic power into substances whose affinities were not
inherent in the matter, but in the subtle chemists of vitality by
whom they were fashioned.

Nothing is better understood, for example, than that the three
elements of the sugar principle have no discoverable affinity by
which they unite, and that no utmost art of science has ever
been able under the inorganic laws of matter to unite them.
They never do unite, save by the imposed chemistry of the
sugar-making lives. And so it is of all vegetable and animal
substances. They exist because the system of vital chemistries
is gifted with a qualified sovereignty over the system of in
organic chemistry. And it would seem as if it was the special
design of God, in this triumph of the lives over the mineral
order and its laws, to accustom us to the fact of a subordination
of causes, and make us so familiar with it as to start no
scepticism in us, when the sublimer fact of a supernatural
agency in the affairs of the world is discovered or revealed.
For, if the secret workings, the dissolvings, distillations, absorp
tions, conversions, compositions, continually going on about us
and within, could be definitely shown, there is not anything in
all the mythologies of the race, the doings of the gods, the
tricks of fairies, the spells and transformations of the wizard
powers, that can even approach the real wonders of fact here
displayed. And yet we apprehend no breach or suspension of
the laws of dead matter in the manifest subordination they
suffer ; on the contrary, we suppose that the dead matter is
thus subordinated, in a certain sense, through and by its own
laws. As little reason have we to apprehend a breach upon
the laws of nature in one of Christ's miracles. Whatever yields
to Him yields by its own laws, and not otherwise. So significant is the lesson given us by these myrmidons of life that are
filling the world with their activity, preparing it to their uses,
and transforming it — otherwise a desert — into a frame of
habitable order and beauty.

It is remarkable that even Dr Strauss takes note of this
same peculiarity observable in the works of nature. "It is true,"

he says, " that single facts and groups of facts, with their con
ditions and processes of change, are not so circumscribed as to
be unsusceptible of external influence ; for the action of one
existence or kingdom in nature trenches on that of another ·
human freedom controls natural development, and material
laws react on human freedom. Nevertheless, the totality of
finite things forms a vast circle, which, except that it owes its
existence and laws to a superior power, suffers no intrusion
rom without. This conviction is so much a habit of thought
with the modern world, that in actual life the belief in a super
natural manifestation, an immediate divine agency, is at once
attributed to ignorance or imposture."[1] But, what if it should
happen that above this "totality of things" there is a grand
totality superior to things ? Wherein is it more incredible
that this higher totality should exert a subordinating "external
influence on the whole of things, than that " one kingdom in
nature trenches on another ? " Why may not men, angels,
God subordinate and act upon the whole of what is properly
called nature ? and what are all the organific powers in nature
doing but giving us a type of the truth to make it familiar ?
And then how little avails the really low appeal from such a
testimony to the current unbeliefs and crudities of a superficial
coarse-minded, unthinking world ? It is not these which can
convict such opinions of "ignorance or imposture." Had this
writer, on the contrary, observed that the subordination of one
kingdom of nature and its laws to the action of another, covers
all the difficulties of the question of miracles, he could have
had some better title to the name of a philosopher.

Meantime, while we are familiarized in this manner with the
subordination of one system of laws and forces to another, and
prepared to admit the possibility, if we should not rather say
forewarned of the actual existence of another system above
nature subordinating that, we also meet with arguments in
corporated in the works of nature that have a sturdier signi
ficance, rising up, as it were, to confront those coarse and
truculent forms of scepticism, on which, probably, the finer tokens
just referred to would be lost. The atheist denies the existence
it any being or power above nature ; the pantheist does the
same—only adding that nature is God, and entitled in some
sense to the honour of religion. Now, to show the existence of

[1] *Life of Jesus.* vol. i. p. 71.

a God supernatural, a God so far separated from nature and superior to it as to act on the chain of natural cause and effect from without the chain, the new science of geology comes forward, lays open her stone registers, and points us to the very times and places where the creative hand of God was inserted into the world, to people it with creatures of life. Thus it is an accepted or established fact in geology, that our planet was, at some remote period, in a molten or fluid state, by reason of the intense heat of its matter. Emerging from this state by a gradual cooling process, there could of course be no seeds in it and no vestiges or germs of animal life. It is only a vast cinder, in fact, just now a little cooled on the surface, but still red hot within. And yet the registers show, beyond the possibility even of a doubt, that the cinder was in due time and somehow peopled with creatures of life. Whence came they or the germs of which they sprang? Out of the fire or out of the cinder? The fire would exterminate them all in a minute of time; and it will be difficult to imagine that the cinder, the mere metallic matter of the world, has any power to resolve itself under its material laws, into reproductive and articulated forms of life.

Again, these ancient registers of rock record the fact that, here and there, some vast fiery cataclysm broke loose, submerg ing and exterminating a great part of the living tribes of the world, after which came forth new races of occupants, more numerous, and many of them higher and more perfect in their forms of organization. Whence came these? By what power ever discovered in nature were they invented, composed, articu lated, and set breathing in the air and darting through the waters of the world?

Finally, man appears, last and most perfect of all the living forms; for, while so many successive orders and types of living creatures, vegetable and animal, show us their remains in the grand museum of the rocks, no vestige, or bone, or sign of man has ever yet been discovered there. Therefore here, again, the question returns, whence came the lordly occupant? Where was he conceived? In what alembic of nature was he dis tilled? By what conjunction of material causes was he raised up to look before and after, and be the investigator of all causes?

Having now these facts of new production before us, we are

obliged to admit some power out of nature and above it, which, by acting on the course of nature, started the new forms of organized life, or fashioned the germs out of which they sprang. To enter on a formal discussion of the theory, so ambitiously attempted by some of the naturalists, by which they are ascribed to the laws of mere nature, or to natural development, would carry me farther into the polemics of geology and zoology than the limits of my present argument will suffer. I will only notice two or three of the principal points of this development theory, in which it is opposed by insurmountable facts.[1]

First of all, it requires us to believe that the original germs of organic life may be and were developed out of matter by its inorganic forces. If so, why are no new germs developed now? and why have we no well-attested facts of the kind? Some few pretended facts we have, but they are too loosely made out to be entitled, for a moment, to our serious belief. Never yet has it been shown that any one germ of vegetable or animal life has been developed by the existing laws of nature, without some egg or germ previously supplied to start the process. Besides, it is inconceivable that there is a power in the metallic and earthy substances, or atoms, however cunningly assisted by electricity, to generate a seed or egg. If we ourselves cannot even so much as cast a bullet without a mould, how can these dead atoms and blind electric currents, without any matrix, or even governing type, weave the filaments and cast the living shape of an acorn, or any smallest seed? There can be no softer credulity than the scepticism which, to escape the need of a creative miracle, resorts to such a faith as this.

But, supposing it possible, or credible, that certain germs of life may have been generated by the inorganic forces, the development scheme has it still on hand to account for the exist ence of man. That he is thus composed in full size and maturity is impossible; he must be produced, if at all, in the state of infancy. Two suppositions, then, are possible, and only two; and we find the speculations of the school vibrating apparently between them. First, that there is a slow process of advance in order, through which the lowest forms of life

1 Whoever wishes to see this subject handled more scientifically and in a most masterly manner, may consult the "Essay on Classification," prefixed to the great work of Mr Agassiz on Natural History, where the conceit that our animal and vegetable races were started in their several eras by physical agencies, without a creative Intelligence is exploded so as to be for ever incapable of resuming even a pretence of

gradually develope those which are higher and more perfect, and finally culminate in man.   Or, secondly, that there is a power in all vital natures, by which, at distant but proper intervals, they suddenly produce some order of being higher than they, much as we often see in those examples of propagation which we denominate, most unphilosophically, *lusus naturæ*, and that so, as the last and highest *lusus*, if that were a scientific con ception, man appears; being, in fact, the crown, or complete fulfilment, of that type of perfection which pertains to all, even the lowest, forms of life.   In one view the progress is a regular gradation; in the other it is a progress by leaps or stages.

As regards the former, it is a fatal objection that no such plastic, gradual movement of progress can be traced in the records of the geologic eras.   All the orders, and genera, and species maintain their immovable distinctions; and no trace can anywhere be discovered, whether there or in the now-living races, of organic forms that are intermediate and transitional. Tokens may be traced in the rocks of a transitional develop ment in some given kind or species, as of the gradual process by which a frog is developed; but there is no trace of organized being midway between the frog and the horse, or of any insect or fish, on its way to become a frog.   Besides, it is wholly in conceivable that there should be *in rerum natura* any kind of creature that is midway, or transitional, between the oviparous and mammal orders.   Still further, if man is the terminal of a slow and plastic movement or advance, what has become of the forms next to man, just a little short of man?   They are not among the living nor among the dead.   No trace of any such forms has ever been discovered by science.   The monkey race have been set up as candidates for this honour.   But, to say nothing of the degraded consciousness that can allow any crea ture of language, duty, and reason, to speak of his near affinity with those creatures, what one of them is there that could ever raise a human infant?   And, if none, there ought to be some intermediate race, yet closer to humanity, that can do it.   Where is this intermediate race?

Just this, too, is the difficulty we encounter in the second form of the theory.   There neither is nor can be any middle position between humanity and no humanity.   If the child, for child there must be, is human, the mother and father must either be human, or else mere animals.   If they have not merely the power of using means to ends, but the necessary ideas, truth, right, cause, space, time, and also the faculty of language, that is, of receiving the inner sense of symbols, which is the infallible test of intelligence [*intus lego*], then they are human ; otherwise they are animals. No matter, then, how high they may be in their order ; their human child is a different form of being, with which, in one view, they have nothing in common. And he is, by the supposition, born a child ; the son of an animal, but yet a human child. And then the question rises, what animal is there, existing or con ceivable, what accident, or .power in nature, that can nurse or shelter from death, that feeblest and most helpless of all crea tures, a human infant ? Neither do we find, as a matter of fact, that the animal races advance in their nursing and pro tecting capacity, accordingly as they advance in the scale of organization. The nearest approach to that kind of tending and protective capacity, necessary to the raising of a human infant, anywhere discernible in the animal races, is found in the marsupial animals ; which are yet far inferior, as regards both intelligence and organization, to the races of dogs, ele phants, and monkeys. Nay, the young salmon, hatched in the motherhood of the river, being cradled in the soft waters, and having a small sack of food attached underneath, to support the first weeks of their infancy, are much better off in their nursing than these most advanced races. Any theory, in short, which throws a human child on the care of an animal parentage is too nearly absurd to require refutation.

But there is a scientific reason against this whole theory of development, which appears to be irresistible, viz., that it inverts the order of causes, and makes exactly that which dis tinguishes the fact of death, the author and cause of life. For it is precisely the wonder, as was just now shown, of the living creatures, or vital powers, that, instead of being under the laws of mineral substances, they are continually triumphing over them. Never do they fall under and submit to them, till they die, and this is death. Thus, when a little nodule of living matter, called an acorn, is placed in the ground, it takes occasion, so to speak, from its new conditions, begins to quicken, opens its ducts, starts its pumps into action, sets at work its own wondrous powers of chemistry, and labours on through whole centuries, composing and building on new lengths of wood, till it has raised into the sky, against gravity and the laws of dead chemistry, a ponderous mass of many tons weight ; there to stand, waving in triumph over the vanquished chemists of the ground, and against the raging storms of ages ; never to yield the victory till the life grows old by exhaustion. Having come now to the limit of its own vital nature, the tree dies ; whereupon the laws of inorganic matter, over which it had triumphed, fall at work upon it, in their turn, to dissolve it ; and, between them and gravity, pulling it down upon the ground, it is disintegrated and reduced to inorganic dust. Now, what the theory in question proposes is, that this same living nodule was originally developed, organized, and gifted with life by the laws of dead matter—laws that have themselves been vanquished, as regards their force, by its dominating sovereignty, and never have been able to do anything more than to dissolve it after it was dead.

We are brought, then, to the conclusion, which no ingenuity of man can escape, that the successive races of living forms discovered by geology are fresh creations, by a power out of nature and above it acting on nature ; which, it will be remem bered, is our definition of supernaturalism itself. And this plainly is no mere indication, but an absolute proof, that nature is not the complete system of God. Indeed, we may say, what might well enough be clear beforehand, that, if man is not from eternity, as geology proves beyond a question, then to imagine that mere dead earth, acted on by its chemical and electric forces, should itself originate sense, perception, thought, reason, conscience, heroism, and genius, is to assert, in the name of science, what is more extravagant than all the miracles even of the Hindoo mythology.

There is yet another view of nature, at once closer at hand and more familiar, which demands a great deal more of atten tion than it has received, from those who include all existence in the term. I speak of the conflicting and mutually destruc tive elements known to be comprised in it. In one view, it appears to be a glorious and complete system of order ; in another, a confused mixture of tumult and battle. One set of powers is continually destroying what another is, with equal persistency, creating ; and the whole creation groaneth and travaileth in pain together. If, then, system is that which stands in the unity of reason, by what right are we able to call

nature a system? That it is a system, or more properly part
of a system, I do not question; for the subjective unity of
reason is an instinct so powerful in our nature, or so nearly
sovereign over it, that we can never expel the faith of such
unity, even when it is objectively undiscoverable. What I here
insist upon is, that nature, granting the most that can be said
of it as a system, is manifestly no complete system in itself.
On the contrary, it takes on appearances, in all its manifestations, that indicate the action in it, and upon it, of powers
extraneous. It seems to be no complete thing in itself, otherwise it would flow in courses of order and harmony, without
any such turbulence of conflict and mutual destruction as we
now see. We even look upon it as a realm played upon by
forces of mischief, mixed up somehow with the disorders of
disobedient powers, or, at least, penally accommodated to their
state of sin, as it was originally subordinated to their uses.
Most certain it is, that, if cause and effect are universal, and in
that view a complete universal system, such as our pantheistic
and other naturalizing writers pretend—subject to no outside
action, subordinate to no other and higher tiers of existence—
there could be no aspects of strife and tumult in the plan; all,
in such a case, must represent the necessary harmony and order
of the system; flowing together on, down the easy track of its
silent, smooth eternity. As it is, then, we have manifestly no
sufficient right to speak of system at all, in the proper and true
meaning of the term, till we bring into the account existences
above nature, such as have it in their way to will, and war,
and bring in disorder, presupposing thus a plan that includes
possibilities of strife and conflict. And then when we speak
of system, it will be in the sense of the apostle, when, passing
above the mere platitudes of things, he rises, in the manner
already described, to the contemplation of invisible dominions
and powers, and of Christ, their everlasting head, and says in-
clusively of all created beings in heaven and in earth—" For
in him all things consist." In his word " *consist*," [standing
together], we have the essential and highest conception of
system. Here is opened a glimpse of the true system of God;
anything less, or lower, or different, is only a fiction of science,
and no truth.

But we come to a point more positive and decisive, viz.,

that we do positively know existences that cannot be included in nature, but constitute a higher range, empowered to act upon it. This higher range we are ourselves, as already shown by our definition of nature and the supernatural in the last chapter. By that definition we are now prepared to assume and formally assign the grand twofold distinction of *things* and *persons*, or *things* and *powers*. All free intelligences, it was shown, the created and the uncreated, are, as being free, essentially super natural in their action ; having all, in the matter of their will, a power transcending cause and effect in nature, by which they are able to act on the lines and vary the combinations of natural causalities. They differ, in short, from everything that classes under the term nature, in the fact that they act from them selves, uncaused in their action. They are powers, not things ; the radical idea of a power being that of an agent, or force, which acts from itself, uncaused, initiating trains of effect that flow from itself.

Of the two great classes, therefore, named in our distribution, one comprehends all beings that are able to originate new trains of effects—these are the Powers ; and the other is made up of such as can only propagate effects under certain fixed laws— these are Things. At the head of one class we conceive is God, as Lord of Hosts ; who, in virtue of his all-originating power as Creator, is called the First Cause ; having round Him innumer able orders of intelligence which, though caused to exist by Him, are as truly first causes in their action as He,—starting all their trains of consequences in the same manner. In the other class we have the immense catalogue of what are called the natural sciences,—the astronomical bodies, the immaterial forces, the fluids and solids of the world, the elements and atoms of chemistry, the dynamics of life and instinct,—in all of which, what are called causes are only propagations of effects under and by fixed laws. Hence they are second causes only ; that is, causes whose causations are determined by others back of them ; never, in any sense, originative or first causes. The complete. ness of the distribution will be yet more clear, and the immense abyss of distance between the two orders or classes more visibly impassable, if we add such points of contrast as the following :—

Powers, acting in liberty, are capable of a double action,—to do or not to do (God, for example, in creating man, man in sinning) ; things can only act in one way, viz., as their law determines.

Powers are perfectible only by exercise after they are made ; things are perfect as made.

Powers are perfected, or established in their law, only by a schooling of their consent ; things are under a law mechanical at the first, having no consent.

Powers can violate the present or nearest harmony, moving disorder in it ; things are incapable of disorder, save as they are disordered by the malign action of powers.

Powers, governed by the absolute force or fiat of omnipotence, would in that fact be uncreated and cease ; things exist and act only in and by the impulsion of that fiat.

We have thus drawn out and set before us two distinct orders and degrees of being, which, together, constitute the real universe. So perfectly diverse are they in kind, that no com- mon terms of law or principle can, for one moment, be imagined to include them both ; they can be one system only in some higher and broader sense, which subordinates one to the other, or both to the same final causes. One thing is thus made clear, viz., that nature is not, in any proper sense, the universe. We know that it is not, because we find another kind of existence in ourselves, which consciously does not fall within the terms of nature. Probably the disciples of naturalism will make answer to this course of argument, by complaining that we gain our point thus easily by means of our definition, which definition is arbitrary,—drawing a distinction between nature and the super natural, or between things and powers that is not usual. Whether it be usual or not is not the question, but whether it is grounded in reality and witnessed immediately by our own con sciousness. If it has been the prime sophism of the naturalists to assume the universality of nature, and still more, if they have carried the assumption so far as to hold, in fact and even formally, that men are only things,—under the same laws of eternal necessity with things, and equally incapable of obligation, thus a part of the system of universal nature,—we certainly have as good a right to raise definitions that meet the truth of conscious ness, as they to overlook and hide them in plain defiance of consciousness. There may be something fatal in such definitions, but there certainly is nothing arbitrary.

Receiving it now as a truth sufficiently established that nature, or the realm of things, is not the system of the universe, that there is beside a realm of powers, it is difficult to close the survey taken, without glancing for a moment at the relative weight and consequence of the two realms. When such a ques tion is raised, there are many who will have it as their feeling, whether they say it in words or not, that the world of things preponderates in magnitude ; for what are we doing, a great part of us, whether men of action or men of science, but chasing the shows of our senses, and magnifying their import by the stimulation of our egregious idolatry ? And yet it would seem that any most extempore glance at the world of powers would suffice to correct us, and set the realm of things, vast as it is, in a very humble place. First, we recognize in the grand inven tory our own human race. We call them persons, spirits, souls, minds, intelligences, free agents, and we see them moving out from nature and above it consciously superior ; streaming into it in currents of causality from themselves ; subduing it, develop ing or detecting its secret laws, harnessing its forces, and using it as the pliant instrument of their will ; first causes all, in a sense, and springs of action, side by side with the Creator, whose miniatures they are, whose footsteps they distinguish, and whose recognition they naturally aspire to. Next adjacent to these we have the intelligent powers of the astronomic worlds, and all the outlying populations of the sky ; so numerous that we shall best conceive their number, not by counting the stars and increasing the census obtained by some factor or multiplier greater than the mind can definitely grasp, but by imagining the stellar spaces of infinity itself interfused and filled with their prodigious tides of life and motion. All these like us are crea tures of admiration, science, will, and duty ; able to search out the invisible in the visible, and find the footsteps of God in his works. Then again, also, we recognize a vast and gloriously-populated realm of angels and departed spirits, who, when they are sent, minister unseen about us ; mixed, we know not how, in the surroundings of our state, with unsaintly and demoniacal powers of mischief, not sent not suffered even to come, save when they are attracted by the low affinities we offer as open gates to their coming. To which, also, we are to add those un known, dimly-imagined orders of intelligences, of which we are notified in the terms of revelation,—seraphim, living creatures, thrones, authorities, dominions, principalities, and powers.

Now all these living armies or hosts of God, and God the Lord of Hosts, capable of character, society, duty, love,—

creators all, in a sense, of things that otherwise could never be, first causes all of their own acts and doings, able to adorn what is, and contrive what is not, and carry up the worlds themselves in ascending scales of improvement,—can we look on these and imagine that nature includes the principal sum and constitutes the real system of being? Are not these other forms of being the transcendent forms; and if we will inventory the universe, are they not all, in fact, that gives it an assignable value? If God Himself be a real existence, what is He by the supposition, but the major term of all existence,—the all-containing substance, a being so great that we scarcely need refer to the free populations just named, to sink all that is below Him, and is called nature, into comparative insignificance. But, when we regard Him as the uncreated power at the head of His immense family of powers, all systematized or sought to be systematized, all perfect in good or else to be perfected under one law, viz., the eternal, necessary, immutable law of *right*,— a law which He first of all accepts Himself, in which His own character of beauty and truth and even His felicity is based, and which therefore He ordains for all, to be the condition of their character, as of His own, building nature itself to it, as a field of exercise and trial; then do we, for once, catch a true glimpse of the significance of nature. It is no more that universe the philosophers speak of; it is raised in dignity by the relation it fills, and, for a like reason, sunk in quantity to comparative nothingness. Its distances no longer occupy us; its magnitudes appal us no more; the astronomic splendours are tinsel; nothing is solid, or great, or high, but those tran scendent powers whose eternities are the main substances of the worlds. Nature, in short, is only stage, field, medium, vehicle, for the universe; that is, for God and His powers. These are the real magnitudes; because they contain at once the import and the final causes, or last ends, of all created substance. The grand, universal, invisible system of God, therefore, is a system that centralizes itself in these, subordinating all mere things, and having them for its instruments. For the serving and training of these, He loosens the bands of Orion and tempers the sweet influences of Pleiades; spreading out the heavens themselves, not for the heavens' sakes, but as a tent for these to dwell in. Is it anything new that the tent is a thing less solid and of meaner consequence than the occupant?

CHAPTER IV.

PROBLEM OF EXISTENCE, AS RELATED TO THE FACT OF EVIL.

WE have reached a summit now, where a wider prospect opens, and God's true system begins to reveal its outlines. Nature, intelligently defined, is not, as we have seen, that system, but only a subordinate and humble member of it. The principal existences are not the things or magnitudes which science has for its subjects, but those everlasting populations of powers that inhabit the realm of things and do their will upon it. The real universe invests, or takes in nature, even as the blooming and succulent peach gathers its fruity parts, its fibres, veins, and circulating juices, about the nut or stone. Scientifi. cally speaking, both parts together constitute the real unity of the peach. But, if any one should claim this distinction for the stone, because of its stability, and because it is a point of inherence and a basis of reaction for the vascular and fleshy parts, it would be a good and sufficient reply that, practically, or as regarding considerations of value, the fruity part is all ; and that, when we name the peach, we commonly do not so much as think of the stone, either as being or not being included. So it is with cause and effect, laws and instincts, all that we call nature ; it is not the system of God, and is really no co-ordinate part of his universe, considered as related to the powers that have their society in it and get their reactions from it. They are the universe, practically, themselves ; only having nature as their field and the tool-house of their instru mentations.

Regarding them now as powers, and so as the grand reality of God's universal system, let us consider more carefully what their relations are to the natural forces and the general order of the system. They cannot, by the supposition, be operated under laws of causation, or be in any sense included in the order of nature. As little admissible is it, supposing the strict originality of their actions, and regarding them as properly first causes each of his own, that they are subject to any direct control or impulsion of omnipotence. We set no limits, when we thus speak, to omnipotence; we only say that omnipotence is force, and that nothing in the nature of force is applicable to the immediate direction or determination of powers. At a remove one or more degrees distant, force may concern itself in the adjustment of means, influences, and motivities related to choice; or, by spiritual permeations, it may temper and sway that side of the soul which is under the control of laws, and so may raise motivities of thought and feeling within the soul itself; but the will, the man himself as a power, is manageable only in a moral way; that is, by authority, truth, justice, beauty, that which supposes obligation or command. And this, again, supposes a consenting obedience, and this a power of non-consent, without which the consent were insignificant. Which power of non-consent, it will be observed, is a power also of deviation or disobedience, and no one can show beforehand that, having such a power, the subject will not some time use it.

So far the possibility of evil appears to be necessarily involved in the existence of a realm of powers; whether it shall also be a fact, depends on other considerations yet to be named. One of the most valued and most triumphantly asserted arguments of our new school of Sophists is dismissed, in this manner, at the outset. God, they say, is omnipotent, and, being omnipotent, He can, of course, do all things. If, therefore, He chooses to have no sin or disobedience, there will be no sin or disobedience; and if we fall on what is sin to us, it will only be a form of good to Him, and would be also to us, if we could see far enough to comprehend the good. The argument is well enough, in case men are things only and not powers; but if God made them to be powers, they are, by the supposition, to act as being uncaused in their action, which excludes any control of them by God's omnipotent force, and then what becomes of the argument? Omnipotence may be exerted, as we just said, one degree farther off, or in that department of the soul which is under conditions of nature; but it does not follow that any changes of view, feeling, motive, wrought in this manner, will certainly suffice to keep any being in the right, when he is so far a power that he can even choose the weakest and most worthless motive—as we consciously do in every wrong act of our lives.

We dismiss, in the same short manner, the sweeping inferences a certain crude-minded class of theologians are accustomed to draw from the omnipotence of God. They take the word " omnipotence" in the same undiscerning and coarse way, as if it followed indubitably that a being omnipotent can do everything he really wishes to have done ; and then the conclusion is not far off that God, for some inscrutable reason, wants sin, wants misery—else why do they exist?—therefore that the existence of sin and misery supposes no real breach of order, and that, when they come, they fall into the regular train of God's ideal harmony, as exactly as any of the heavenly motions or chemical attractions. All such idolaters of the force-principle in God will, of course, be abundantly shocked by what appears to be a limit on the sway or sufficiency of their idol. And yet, even they will be advancing unconsciously, every day of their lives, something which implies a limitation as real as any they complain of. Thus, how often will they say, without suspecting any such implication, that God could not forgive sin without a ransom, and could not provide a ransom save by the incarnate life and death of His Son. Why not, if He is omnipotent? Cannot omnipotence do everything? This very question, indeed, of the seeming limitation of God's omnipotence, implied in the sacrifice of Christ, was the precise difficulty which Anselm, in his famous treatise, undertook to solve. He states it thus :—" To show for what necessity and cause God, who is omnipotent, should have assumed the littleness and weakness of human nature for the sake of its renewal;" [1] or, as he had just been saying,[2] how He did this to restore the world, when, for aught that appears, " He might have done it merely by His will."

The difficulty was real, no doubt, to a certain class of minds in his time ; but to another class, enthralled by no such crudities in respect to force, it never was or could be any difficulty at all. As little room for question is there in our doctrine, when we say that a realm of powers is not, by the supposition, to be governed as a realm of things, that is, by direct omnipotence ; for we mean by omnipotence, not power, in the sense of influence or moral impression, but mere executive force ; we mean

<hr />

[1] *Bibliotheca Sacra*, vol. xi. p. 737.   [2] *Ibid.* p. 736.

that God, as being omnipotent, is in force to do all that force can do—this and nothing more. But force has no relation to he doing of many things. It can overturn mountains, roll ack the sea, or open a way through it; but manifestly it has nothing to do in the direct impulsion of a soul ; for a soul is a power, capable of character and responsibility, as being clear of all causation, and acting by its own free self-impulsion. There-re to say that powers, or free agents cannot be swayed abso lutely by omnipotent force, is only to deny the applicability of such force, not to place it under limitation. It might as well be called a limitation of the force of an army, to say that it can-ot compute an eclipse or write an epic ; or that of an earth quake, to say that it cannot shake a demonstration of Euclid

ie doctrine I am stating involves, in fact, no limitation of the power of God at all. It only shows that the reason of God s empire excludes, at a certain point, the absolute dominion of force. Nor is it anything new, more than in the question of Anselm above referred to, that the force of God consents to the sovereignty of his eternal reason and the counsel of wisdom in nis purposes.

But it will be peremptorily required of us at this point to answer another question, viz., Why God should have created a realm of powers or free agents if they must needs be capable, in this manner, of wrong and misery ; without acknowledging, for one moment, that I am responsible for the answer of any such question, and denying explicitly the right of any mortal to dis allow or discredit any act of God because he cannot comprehend the reason of it, I will simply say in reply, that it is enough for me to be allowed the simple hypothesis that God preferred to have powers and not things only ; because He loves character, and apart from this, cares not for all the mere things that can be piled in the infinitude of space itself, even though they be diamonds ; because, in bestowing on a creature the perilous capacity of character, he bestows the highest possibility of wealth and glory ; a capacity to know, to love, to enjoy, to be consciously great and blessed in the participation of his own divinity and character. For if all the orbs of heaven were so many solid Koh-i-noors glittering eternally in the sun, what were they either to themselves or to Him; or if they should roll eternally undisturbed in the balance of their attractions, what were they to each other ? Is it any impeachment of God that he did not care to reign over an empire of stones ? If He has deliberately chosen a kind of empire not to be ruled by force, if He has deliberately set His children beyond that kind of control, that they may be governed by truth, reason, love, want, fear, and the like, acting through their consent ; if we find them able to act even against the will of God, as stones and vegetables cannot, what more is necessary to vindicate His goodness than to suggest that He has given them, possibly, a capacity to break allegiance, in order that there may be a meaning and a glory in allegiance, when they choose it ?

There is, then, such a thing inherent in the system of powers as a possibility of wrong ; for, given the possibility of right, we have the possibility of wrong. And it may, for aught that appears, be the very plan itself of God to establish his powers in the right, by allowing them an experiment of the wrong, in which to school their liberty ; bringing them up again out of its bitterness, by a delivering process, to shun it with an in telligent and forever fixed abhorrence afterward. And then, if this should be his plan, what an immense complication of acts, events, processes, contrarieties, and caprices, must be involved in it. Nature, considered as the mere run of cause and effect, is simple as a Jew's harp. But here we have a grand concilium or republic of wills, acting each for himself, and in that capa city to be trained, governed, turned about and about, and finally brought up into the harmony of a consenting choice and a com mon love and character. The system will be one that syste. matizes the caprices and discords of innumerable wills, and works results of order through endless complications of disorder ; having, in this fact, its real wisdom and magnificence. Thus how meagre an affair to thought were our American Republic, if it were nothing but the run of causes in the climate and soil, and the mere physiology of the men ; but when it is considered as containing so many wills, acting all from themselves, incom putable in their action because they are uncaused in it ; reducing so many mixtures of contrarieties and discords to a beautiful resultant order and social unity ; striving still on, by the force of its organic *nisus*, toward a condition of historic greatness hitherto unknown to the world—considered thus, how truly sublime and wonderful a creation does it appear to be ! And yet there are many who cannot imagine that God has any system or law, in His great republic of freedom, if there be any discord, any contrariety, any infringement of His mandates, any disturbance of nature ; or, indeed, if He does not really impel and do everything Himself by His own immediate and absolute causation. Whereas, if they could rise above the feeble conceit by which they make the force of God their idol, they would see that possibly it may be the highest point of grandeur in his sys tem ; that it systematizes powers transcending nature, and even disorders in the field of nature itself.

Or, if it be objected that the admission or fact of such dis orders annihilates the unity of God's empire, leaving it in a fragmentary, cloven state, which excludes the scientific idea of a proper universe, it is a good and sufficient answer that God's unities are all, in the last degree, unities of end, or counsel as related to end ; consisting never in a perfect concert of parts or elements, but in a comprehensive order that takes up and tempers to its own purposes many antagonisms. What, in fact, is the order of heaven, or even the atomic order of particles, but a resultant of the eternal strife by which they are insti gated ? What then, if the powers are able to break loose, and do, from obligation ; when the system or plan of God is made large enough to include such a breaking loose, and deep enough in counsel, from the beginning, to handle it in terms of sovereign order ? The higher unity is not gone because discord has come in points below, and would not be even if the discord were eternal. Still it remains, comprehends everything, moving still on its ends, as little diverted or disturbed as if the powers all came to wed themselves to it in loving obedience. There is a real universe now as before, because the universal *nisus* of the plan remains, and because the regulative order that compre hends so great irregularity retains its integrity unbroken, its equilibrium undisturbed.

If now we raise the question more distinctly, what is the great problem of existence as regards the order of powers, or the human race as being such, it is not difficult to answer, fol lowing out the view thus far presented, that it is our perfection ; the perfection, that is, of our liberty, the schooling of our choice or consent as powers, so that we may be fully established in harmony with God's will and character ; unified with Him in His will, glorified with Him in the glory of His character, and so perfected with Him in His eternal beatitude. Persons or powers are creatures, we have seen, who act, not by causality, but by consent; they must, therefore, be set in conditions that invite consent, and treated also in a manner that permits the caprices of liberty. It is also a remarkable distinction, we have noted, that they are creatures perfectible only after they are made, while mere natural quantities and objects are perfect as made. Just here, accordingly, the grand problem of their life and of the world begins. They are to be trained, formed, furnished, perfected; and to this end are to be carried through just such scenes, experiences, changes, trials, variations, opera tions, as will best serve their spiritual perfection and their final fruition of each other and of God. If there are necessary perils in such a trial of their liberty, then they are to be set upon the course of such perils. Nor will it make any difference if the perils are such as breed the greatest speculative difficulties. God does not frame His empire to suit and satisfy our specu lations, but for our practical profit; to bring us up into His own excellence, and establish us eternally in the participation of His character. On this subject there would seem to be very little room for doubt. The Scripture revelation proposes this view of life, our own observation confirms it, and, besides, there is really no other in which even our philosophy can comfortably rest.

But this training of consent, this perfecting of liberty in the issues of character, it will help us at this early point to observe, is nothing different from a preparation for society, and a drill-practice in the principles of society; that is, in truth, in purity, in justice, in patience, forgiveness, love, all the self-renouncing and beneficent virtues. Accordingly the course of training will itself be social; a trial under, in, and by society. The powers will be thrown together in terms of duty as being terms of society, and in terms of society as being terms of duty. Morality and the law of religion respect society and the condi tion of social wellbeing, which is the grand felicity of powers. Things have no society or capacity of social relations. In mere nature, considered as a scheme of cause and effect, there is noth ing social, any more than there is in the members of a steam-engine. And if we really believe that we ourselves are only wheels in the play of an all-comprehending causation, it should be the end even of the feeling of society in us. Love, benefit, sympathy, injury, hatred, thanks, blame, character, worship, faith, all that constitutes the reality of society, whether of men with God or of men with each other, belongs to the fact that we are consciously powers. Strip us of this, let all these fruits be regarded as mere dynamic results, under the head of natural philosophy, and they will change at once to be mere tricks or impostures of natural magic. Our discipline, therefore, is to be such as our supernatural and social quality requires, the dis cipline of society. Since it is for society, it must be in and by society. We accordingly shall have a training as powers among other powers, such as will qualify us for a place of eternal unity and harmony with them under God, the central and First Power, so to be sent by him in a consolidated, everlasting kingdom of righteousness, and truth, and love, and peace.

And thus it is that we find ourselves embodied in matter, to act as powers upon, for, with, and, if we will, against each other, in all the endless complications of look, word, act, art, force, and persuasion ; in the family and in the state, or two and two upon each other ; in marriage, fraternity, neighbour hood, friendship, trade, association, protection, hospitality, instruction, sympathy ; or, if we will, in frauds, enmities, oppressions, cruelties, and mutual temptations, — great men moving the age they live in by their eloquence ; or shaping the ages to come by their institutions ; or corrupting the world's moral atmosphere by their bad thoughts, their fashions and vices ; or tearing and desolating all things by irruptions of war, to win a throne of empire, or the honours of victors and heroes. By all these methods do we come into society, and begin to act, each one upon the trains of cause and effect in nature ; thus upon each other, from our own point of liberty. And, accordingly, society is, in all its vast complications, an appointment—we cannot escape it. We can only say what kind of experience it shall be as regards the fruits of character in us. Meantime God is reigning over it, socially related Him self to each member, governing and training that member through his own liberty. Life, thus ordered, is a magnificent scheme to bring out the value of law and teach the necessity of right as the only conserving principle of order and happi ness ; teaching the more powerfully that it teaches, if so it must, by disorder and sorrow. And nature, it will be observed, is the universal medium by or through which the training is accomplished. The powers act on each other, by acting on the lines of cause and effect in nature; starting thus new trains of events and consequences, by which they affect each other in ways of injury or blessing. They speak and set the air in motion, as it otherwise would not move; and so the obedient air, played on by their sovereignty, becomes the vehicle of words that communicate innumerable stings, insults, flatteries, seductions, threats; or tones of comfort, love, and blessing. So of all the other elements. solid, fluid, or aerial, they are medial as between the powers. The whole play of commerce in society is through nature, and is, in fact, a playing on the causes and objects of nature by supernatural agents. All doings and misdoings are, in this view, a kind of discourse in the terms of nature, by which these supernatural agents, viz., men, answer to each other, or to God, in society. Their blasphemies, and prayers, and songs, and threats, their looks and gestures, their dress and manners, their injuries and alms, their blows and barricades and bullets and bombs, these and such like are society, the grand conversation by which our social discipline is carried on. And it is all a supernatural transaction. As a conversation in words is not reducible to mere natural causation, no more is that conversation in bullets and bombs that we call a battle. Nature could as well talk as compound her forces in cartridges and fire them with a levelled aim. Her activity in all these exchanges, or medial transactions, that are carried on so briskly, is only the activity of the powers through her, and is, in fact, supernatural. They start all these nimble couriers and set them flying back and forth, by the right they have to come down upon nature and act themselves into it. To a certain extent they are inserted into nature and conditioned by it. They live in nature and are of it, up to the point of their will, but there they emerge into qualified sovereignty. Without this inherence in nature they would have no media of action, no common terms of order, interest, or trial, and no such basis of reaction as would make the consequences of their action ascertainable or intelligible; without this sovereignty they would not be responsible. Hence God's way has been, in all ages, and doubtless in all worlds, to set his supernatural agents in the closest connexion with nature, there to have their action and there to perceive its effects on themselves and others. Even the miracles of Jesus are set as deep in nature as possible; showing the wine of

Cana to be made out of water, and not out of nothing; the multitude of the loaves out of seven, not out of none; that so the mind, being fastened to something already existent, may see the miracle as a process ; whereas, without a something in nature to begin with, there could be no process, and therefore nothing to observe.

How far this range of society extends, whether nature is not, by some inherent necessity, a medium open to the commerce of all the powers of all worlds, involving, in that manner, a perilous exposure to demoniacal irruptions, till moral defences and safeguards are prepared against them, are questions not to be answered here ; but we shall recur to them shortly in another place.

It has been already intimated, or shown as a possible thing, that the race, regarded as an order of powers, may break loose from God's control and fall into sin.   Will they so break loose ? Regarding them simply as made and set forth on the course of training necessary to their establishment in holy virtue, will they retain their innocence ?   Have we any reason to think, and, if so, what reason to think, that they will drop their allegiance and try the experiment of evil ?

It is very certain that God desires no such result.   When it takes place, it will be against His will and against every attri bute of His infinitely beneficent and pure character.   It will only be true that He has created moral and accountable beings with this peril incident, rather than to create only nature and natural things ; having it in view, us the glorious last end of His plan, finally to clear us of sin by passing us, since we will descend to it, completely through it.   He will have given us, or, at least, the original new-created progenitors, a constituently perfect mould ; so that, taken simply as forms of being, apart from any character begun by action, they are in that exact harmony and perfection that, without or before deliberation, spontaneously runs to good ; organically ready, with all heavenly affinities in play, to break out in a perfect song. So far they are innocent and holy by creation, or by the simple fact of their constituent perfection in the image of their Maker ; only there is no sufficient strength or security in their holiness, because there is no deliberative element in it.   Deliberation, when it comes, as come it must, will be the inevitable fall of it ;

and then, when the side of counsel in them is sufficiently instructed by that fall and the bitter sorrow it yields, and the holy freedom is restored, it may be or become an eternally-enduring principle. Spontaneity in good, without counsel, is weak; counsel and deliberative choice, without spontaneity, are only a character begun; issued in spontaniety, they are the solid reality of everlasting good. Still it will not, even then, be true that God has contrived their sin, as a means of the ulterior good, though it may be true that they, by their know ledge of it as being only evil, will be intelligently fixed, for ever afterward, in their abhorrence of it. Nor, if we speak of sin as permitted in this view by God, will it be any otherwise permitted, than as not being prevented, either by the non-creation, or by the uncreating of the race.

It may appear to some that such a view of God's relations to sin excludes the fact or faith of an eternal plan, showing God to be, in fact, the victim of sin; having neither power to withstand it, nor any system of purposes able to include and manage it. On this subject of foreordination or predetermined plan, there is a great deal of very crude and confused speculation. If there be any truth which every Christian ought to assume, as evident beyond all question, it is that God has some eternal plan that includes everything, and puts everything in its place. That He 'foreordains whatsoever comes to pass," is only another version of the same truth. Nor is there any the least difficulty in distinguishing the entire consistency of this with all that we have said concerning God's relations to the existence of evil—no difficulty, in fact, which does not occur in phrasing the conduct and doings even of men.

Suppose, for example, that some person, actuated by a desire to benefit or bless society, takes it in hand to establish and endow a school of public charity. In such a case, he will go into a careful consideration of all the possible plans of organi zation, with a view to select the best. In order to make the case entirely parallel, suppose him to have a complete intuition of these plans or possibilities—A, B, and C, etc., on to the end of the alphabet; so that, giving each plan or possibility, with all its features and appointments, he can see precisely what will follow—all the good, all the mischief, that will be incurred by every child that will ever attend the school. For in each of these plans or possibles there are mischiefs incident;

and there will be children attendant, who, by reason of no fault of the school, but only by their perverse abuse of it, will there be ruined. The benefactor and founder, having thus discovered that a certain plan, D, combines the greatest amount of good results and the smallest of bad ones, the question rises, whether he shall adopt that plan ? By the supposition he must, for it is the best possible. And yet, by adopting that plan, he per ceives that he will make certain also every particular one of the mischiefs that will be suffered by the abuse of it, and so the ruin of every child that will be ruined under it. As long as the plan is only a possible, a thing of contemplation, no mis chiefs are suffered, no child is ruined ; but the moment he decides to make the plan actual, or set the school on foot, he decides, makes certain, or, in that sense, foreordinates, all the particular bad conduct and all the particular undoing there to be wrought, as intuitively seen by him beforehand. Nothing of this would come to pass if the school, D, were not founded ; and, in simply deciding on the plan, with a perfect perception of what will take place under it, he decides the bad results as well as the good, though in senses entirely different. The bad are not from him, nor from anything he has introduced, or appointed ; but wholly from the abuses of his beneficence practised by others whom he undertook to bless. The good is all from him, being that for which he established the school. Both are knowingly made certain or foreordained by his act.

In this illustration it is not difficult to distinguish the true relation of God to the existence of evil. In selecting the best possible plan among the millions of possibles open to His con templation, and deciding to set on foot or actualize that parti cular universe, He also made certain all the evils or mischiefs seen to be connected with it. But they are not from Him, because they are, in this indirect manner, made certain, or fore-ordinated by Him. It is hardly right to say that they are per mitted by Him. They come in only as necessary evils that environ the best plan possible. Such are the relations of God to the existence of evil. If it comes, it is not from Him, any more than the ruin of certain children in the school, just sup posed, are from the benevolent founder. And yet He is not disappointed, or frustrated. Still He governs with a plan, a perfect and eternal plan, which comprehends, in its exact date and place, everything which every wrong-doing and revolting spirit will do, even to the end of the world.

Thus far we have spoken of God's relations to the existence of evil, or its possible prevention. We pass over now to the side of his subjects; and there we shall find reason, as regards their self-retention, to believe that the certainty of their sin is originally involved in their spiritual training as powers. Made organically perfect, set as full in God's harmony as they can be, in the mould of their constitution, surrounded by as many things as possible to allure them to ways of obedience and keep them from the seductions of sin, we shall discover still that, given the fact of their begun existence, and their trial as per sons or powers, they are in a condition privative that involves their certain lapse into evil.

If the language I employ in speaking of this matter is pecu liar, it is because I am speaking with caution, and carefully en deavouring to find terms that will convey the right, separated from any false, impression. I speak of a " condition priva- tive," it will be observed; not of any positive ground, or cause, or necessity; for, if there were any natural necessity for sin, it would not be sin. If it were caused, as all simply natural events are caused, or, what is the same, if it were a natural effect, it would not be sin. We might as well blame the run ning of the rivers, in such a case, as the wrong-doing of men; for what we may call their wrong-doing is, after all, nothing but the run of causes hid in their person, as gravity is hid in the running waters. If we could show a positive ground for sin; that man, for example, is a being whose nature it is to choose the strongest motive, as of a scale-beam to be turned by the heaviest weight, and that the strongest motive, arranged to operate on men, is the motive to do evil, that in fact would be the denial of sin, or even of its possibility; indeed it is so urged by the disciples of naturalism on every side. So again, if we could, in a way of positive philosophy, account for the existence of evil—exactly what multitudes even of Christian believers set themselves to do, not observing that, if they could execute their endeavour, they could also make as good answer for evil on the judgment day of the world—if, I say, we could properly and positively account for evil in this manner, it would not be evil any longer. When we speak of accounting for anything, we suppose a discovery of first principles to which it may be referred; but sin can be referred to no first principles; it is simply the act of a power that spurns all inductives back of the doer's will, and asserts itself, apart from all first principles, or even against them.   Therefore, to avoid all these false im plications, and present the simple truth of fact, I speak of a " condition privative; " by which I mean a moral state that is only inchoate or incomplete, lacking something not yet reached, which is necessary to the probable rejection of evil.   Thus an infant child runs directly toward, and will, in fact, run into the fire, not because of any necessity upon him, but simply because he is in a condition privative as regards the experience needed to prevent him.   I said, also, "involves the certain lapse into evil," not "produces," "infers," "makes necessary."   There is no connexion of science or law between the subject and predi cate, such that, one being given, the other holds by natural consequence; and yet this condition privative "involves," ac cording to our way of apprehending it, a certain conviction or expectation of the event stated.   Thus we often attain to expectations concerning the conduct of men, as fixed as those which we hold concerning natural events where the connexion of cause and consequence is absolute.   We become acquainted, as we say, with a certain person; we learn how he works in his freedom, or how, as a power acting from himself, he is wont to carry himself in given conditions; and, finally, we attain to a sense of him so intimate that, given almost any particular occasion or transaction touching his interest, we have an ex pectation or confidence regarding what he will do about as fixed as we have in the connexions of natural events.   The particular thing done to him " involves," in our apprehension, as the certain fact, that he will do a particular thing consequent. And yet we have no conception that he is determined in such matters by any causation or law of necessary connexion, the certainty we feel is the certainty, not of a thing, but of a power in the sovereign determination of his liberty.   In this and no other sense do we speak of a condition privative that involves a certain lapse into evil.

Having distinguished, in this careful manner, the true import of the terms employed, it now remains to look for that condi tion privative on which so much depends.   And we shall dis cover it in three particulars.

1. In the necessary defect of knowledge and consequent weak
ness of a free person or power, considered as having just begun
to be.   We must not imagine, because he is a power able in
his action to set himself above all natural causes, and act origi-
natively as from himself, that he is therefore strong.   On the
contrary, even though he begins in the full maturity of his
person, having a constitution set in perfect harmony with the
divine order and truth, he is the weakest, most unperfect of
beings.   The stones of the world are strong in their destiny,
because it stands in God under laws of causation fixed by Him.
But free agents are weak because they are free, left to act ori-
ginatively, held fast by no superior determination, bound to no
sure destiny, save as they are trained into character in and
through their experience.

Our argument forbids that we should assume the truth of
the human genesis reported in Scripture history ; for that is
commonly denied by naturalism.   I may not even assume that
we are descended of a common stock.   But this, at least, is
certain, that we each began to be, and therefore we may the
more properly take the case of Adam for an example ; because
not being corrupted by any causes back of him, as we most
certainly are, and making a beginning in the full maturity of
his powers, he may be supposed to have had some advantages
for standing fast in the right, which we have not.

As we look upon him, raising the question whether he has
moral strength to stand, we observe, first of all, that being in
a perfect form of harmony, uncorrupted, clean, in one word, a
complete integer, he must of course be spontaneous to good,
and can never fall from it until his spontaneity is interrupted
by some reflective exercise of contrivance or deliberative judg
ment.   But this will come to pass without fail in a very short
time, because he is not only spontaneous to good, but is also a
reflective and deliberative being.   And then what shall become
of his integrity ?

Entering still further into his case, as we raise this question,
we perceive that he holds a place or point in his action between
two distinct ranges of thought and motivity ; between neces
sary ideas on one hand, and knowledges or judgments drawn
from experience on the other.   In the first place, being a man,
he has necessarily developed in his consciousness the law of
right.   He thinks the right, and, in thinking it, feels himself

eternally bound by it. We may call it an idea in him, or a
law or a category of his being. He would not be a man with
out it ; for it is only in connexion with this and other neces
sary ideas that he ranges above the animals. Animals have
no necessary ideas ; these, especially such as are moral, are the
necessary and peculiar furniture of man. What could a man
do in the matter of justice, inquiring after it, determining what
it is, if the idea of justice were not first developed as a standard
thought or idea in his mind ? Who would set himself on in
quiries after true things and judgments, if the idea of truth were
not in him as a regulative thought or category of his nature ?
Thus it is, by our idea of right, that we are set to the con
ceiving or thought of duty, as well as placed under obligations
itself ; and we could not so much as raise the question of virtue
or morality, if we were not first configured to its law, and set
in action as being consciously under it. Herein, too, we are
specially resembled to God ; for, by this same idea of right,
necessary, immutable, eternal, it is that He is placed in obliga
tion, and it is by His ready and perfect homage to this that
His glorious character is built. And this law is absolute or
unconditional to Him as to us, to us as to Him. No matter
what may befall or not befall us on the empirical side of
our life. No impediment, no threat, or fear, or force, can ex
cuse us ; least of all can any mere condition privative, such as
ignorance, inexperience, or the want of opposing motive. Simply
to have thought the right, is to be under obligation to it, with
out any motive or hope in the world of experience, and despite
of all opposing motives there. Even if the worlds fall on us,
we must do the right.

Pass over now from the absolute or ideal side of our existence,
to the contingent or empirical. Here we are dealing with effects,
consequences, facts, trying our strength in attempts, computing,
comparing, judging, learning how to handle things, and how
they will handle us. And by this kind of experience we get
all the furniture of our mind and character, save what we have
as it were concreated in us in those necessary ideas of which
we have spoken, and which are pre-supposed in all experience.
What now, reverting to the case of Adam as a just-begun exist
ence, is the amount of his experimental, empirical, or historic
knowledge ? The knowledges we here inquire after, it will be
observed, are such as are gotten historically, one by one, and

one after another, under conditions of time; by seeing, doing, suffering, comparing, distinguishing, remembering, and other like operations. A man's knowledge here is represented, of course, by what he has been through, and felt, and thought. What then can he know, at the first moment of his being, when, by the supposition, he has never had a thought or an experience; or, if we take him at a point an hour or a day later, none but that of a single hour or day? Being a perfectly disposed creature, the first man sets off, we will say, in a spontaneous obedience to the right, which is the absolute law of his nature, and is in him originally, by the necessary conditions of his nature. But there comes up shortly a question regarding some act, con fessedly not right, or some act which, being forbidden, violates his sense of right. No matter what it is, he can be as properly, and will be as effectually tested, by adhering to the sense of obligation, in withholding from an apple forbidden, as in any thing else. Here then he stands upon the verge of experimental wrong, debating the choice. What it is in its idea, or obligatory principle, he knows; but what it is in the experience of its fruits or consequences, he knows not. The discord, bitterness, remorse, and inward hell of wrong are hidden, as yet, from his view. If minatory words have been used, pronouncing death upon him in case of disobedience, some degree of apprehension may have been awakened in him anticipatively, under the natural efficacy of manner and expression, which, even prior to any culture of experience, have a certain degree of power. But how little will this amount to in a way of guard or security for his virtue; for he is a knowing creature still; wanting there fore to know, and, if it were not for this noble instinct of knowledge, would not be a man. What then is this wrong he is debating, what does it signify? He does not ask whether it will bring him evil or good; for what these are, experimentally, he does not know. Enough that here is some great secret of knowledge to be opened; how can he abstain, how refuse to break through the mask of this unknown something, and know? He is tempted thus, we perceive, not by something positive placed in his way, but by a mere condition privative, a perplex ing defect of knowledge incident to the fact of his merely begun existence.

Doubtless it will be urged that no such wrong would ever be debated, if some positive desire of the nature were not first excited, some constitutional susceptibility or want drawn out in longing for its object. Even so, precisely that we have allowed ; for what is the desire of knowledge itself but a posi tive and most powerful instinct of the soul ? Only the more clear is it that, if the desired knowledge were already in pos session, the temptation itself would be over. So if some bodily appetite were excited ; how trivial and contemptible were this, or any proposed pleasure, if only the tremendous evil and woe of the wrong were already known, as it will be after years of struggle and suffering in it. The grand peril, therefore, is still seen to be of a privative and not of a positive nature. There must be positive impulses to be governed, or else there could not be a man ; and the peril is that there is yet no experimental knowledge on hand, and can be none, sufficient to protect and guard the process.

And yet the man is guilty if he makes the fatal choice. Even if the strongest motive were that way, he is yet a being able to choose against the strongest, and he consciously knows that he ought. In any view, he is not obliged to choose the wrong, more than a child is obliged to thrust his hand into the blaze of a lamp, the experience of which is unknown. The cases are, in fact, strongly analogous, save that the wrong doer knows before hand, as the child certainly does not, that the act is wrong or criminal ; a consideration by which he consciously ought to be restrained, be the consequences what they may. And yet, who can expect that he will for ever be restrained, never breaking over this mysterious line to make the bad experiment, or try what is in this unknown something eternally before his eyes ? If we rightly remember, the false prophet somewhere represents the difficulty of a certain course of virtue, by that of crossing the fiery gulf of hell upon a hair. Possibly our first man may cross upon this hair and keep his balance till he is completely over, but who will expect him to do it ? He may look upon the tree of knowledge of good and evil (rightly is it named), and pass it by. He can do it ; there is a real possibility as there is a real obligation ; but Adam, we are told, did not, neither is there any the least probability that any other of mankind, with all his advantages, ever would.

If it should be apprehended by any that a condition privative, connected as it plainly is with such perils, quite takes away the guilt of sin, that, I answer, is by the supposition impossible. It really takes away nothing. The right and only true statement is, that the guilt of sin is not as greatly enhanced as it would be, if all the knowledge needful to the strength of virtue were supplied. We differ in this matter from those naturalistic philosophers, who reduce all human wrong to weakness, and obliterate in that manner all the distinctions of good and evil. We really excuse nothing; we only do not condemn as severely as if the eternal and absolute obligation of right, revealed in every human bosom, were more thoroughly fortified by prudential and empiric knowledge.

It may also be objected, as contrary to all experience, as well as to the nature of sin itself, that sin should impart strength or increase the capacity of virtue. What in fact does it bring, but bondage, disability, and death ? Even so—this is the knowledge of sin, and no one is the more capable of holiness on account of it. It is the very point, indeed, of this knowledge, that it knows disability, helplessness, despair. And exactly this it is that prepares the possibility of a new creation. Impotence dis covered is the capacity of redemption. And then, when a soul has been truly regenerated and set in union with God, its bad experience will be the condition of its everlasting stability and strength.

It will naturally enough be objected, again, by some who hold the principle of disinterested and absolute virtue here assumed, that no mere defect of empirical knowledge—the knowledge of prudence or self-interest—creates a condition privative as regards the security of virtue ;—what need of experience to enforce obligations that are perfect, apart from all consequences ? If one is loving God, as he ought, simply for his own excellence or beauty, and living by the inspiration of that excellence, what matter is it whether he knows the practical bitterness, the woe, the hell of sin, and understands the penal sanctions of reward and penalty set against it, or not ? Is he going to fall out of his love and his inspired liberty, because he is not sufficiently shut into it by fears and apprehended miseries ? There is an appearance of force in the objection, and yet it is only an appearance. For, in the first place, it is not assumed that Adam, or any other man, put to the trial of a right life, is weak in his spontaneous obedience, because he is not sufficiently held to it by the prudential motives of fear and known destruction ; but because his curiosity, as a knowing creature, is provoked, or will be, by not so much as knowing what the motives are, in a word, by the profound mystery that overhangs the question of wrong itself.   Indeed he does not even so much as know what it will do, whether it will raise to some unknown pitch of greatness in power and intelligence or not.   In the next place, it is not assumed that the prudential motives of reward and penalty will ever recover any fallen spirit from his defections and bring him into the inspired, free state of love.   The office of such means and motives is wholly negative ; viz., to arrest the bad soul in its evil and bring it to a stand of self-renunciation, where the higher motives of the divine excellence and love may kindle it.   In the third place, it is not assumed that, when souls are recovered from evil, and finally established in holy liberty, which is the problem of their trial, they are made safe for the coming eternity by knowing how dreadfully they will be scorched by evil in case they relapse; but their safety is that, having been dreadfully scorched already by it, they have thoroughly proved what is in it, and extirpated all the fascinations of its mystery.

2. It is another condition privative, as regards the moral per fection of powers, that they require an empirical training, or course of government, to get them established in the absolute law of duty; and that this empirical training must probably have a certain adverse effect for a time, before it can mature its better results.   The eternal idea of justice makes no one just ; that of truth makes no one true ; that of beauty makes no soul beauti ful.   So the eternal law of right makes no one righteous.   All these standard ideas require a process or drill, in the field of experience, in order to become matured into characters, or to fashion character in the moulds they supply.   And this process, or drill-practice, will require two economies or courses ; the first of which will be always a failure, taken in itself, but will fur nish, nevertheless, a necessary ground for the second, by which its effects will be converted into benefits ; and then the result a holy character—will be one of course that presupposes both.

The first named course or economy is that of law ; which is called, even in Scripture, the letter that killeth.   The law ab solute, of which we just now spoke, is a merely necessary idea ; commanding us, from eternity, as it did the great Creator him self—*do right*—making no specifications and applying no mo tives, save what are contained in its own absolute excellence and authority. But the receiving it in that manner, which is the only manner in which it can be truly received, supposes a mind and temper already configured to it, so as to be in it in mere love and the spontaneous homage that enthrones it, be cause of its excellence, and God because He represents its ex cellence. Here, therefore, is the problem how to produce this practical configuration. And it is executed thus :—God, as a power and a force extraneous, undertakes for it, first of all, to enforce it empirically, by motives extraneous ; those of reward and fear, profit and loss. He takes the law absolute down into the world of prudence, re-enacting it there and preparing to train us into it, by a drill-practice under sanctions. In one view, the sanctions added are inappropriate ; for they are opposite to all spontaneity, being appeals to interest, and so far calls that draw the soul away from the more inspiring con siderations of inherent excellence. The subject is lifted by no inspiration. He is down under the law, at the best, trying to come up to it by willing, *punctuatim et seriatim*, what parti cular things are required in the specifications made by it. If we could suppose the law thus enforced to be perfectly observed under this pressure of prudential sanctions, it would only make a dry, punctilious, and painfully apprehensive kind of virtue, without liberty or dignity. The more probable result is a habitual and wearisome selfishness ; for, as long as the mind is occupied by these empirical and extraneous sanctions, it is held to the consideration of self-interest only ; and the motives it is all the while canvassing, are such as the worst mind can feel, as well as that which is truly upright. And yet there is a benefit preparing in this first or legal economy, which is indis pensable ; viz., this, that it gives adhesiveness to the law, which otherwise, as being merely ideal, we might lightly dismiss ; that the friction it creates, like some mordant in the dyeing pro cess, sets in the law and fastens it practically, or as an experi mental reality ; that the woes of penalty wage a battle for it, in which the soul is continually worsted and so broken in ; that it developes, in short, a whole body of moral judgments and convictions, that wind the soul about as cords of detention, till finally the law to be enforced becomes an experimental verity fully established. Just here the soul begins to feel a dreadful coil of thraldom round it. To get away from the law is im possible ; for it is hedged about with fire. To keep it is impossible ; for the struggle is only a heaving under self-interested motive, to get clear of a state whose bane is selfishness. What it means, the subject cannot find. He is in a condition of bitter thraldom ; his sin appears to be sin even more than ever ; and the whole discipline he is under seems only to minister the knowledge of sin ; he groans, as it were, under a body of sin and death that he cannot heave.

And so he is made ready for the second economy, that of liberating grace and redemption. For now, in Christ, the law returns, a person, clothed in all personal beauty, and offers it self to the choice, even as a friend and deliverer ; so that being taken with love to Christ, and drawing near at His call in holy trust, the bondman is surprised to find that he is loving the law as the perfect law of liberty ; which was the point to be gained or carried. And so, what began, as a necessary idea, is wrought into a character and become eternal fact. The whole operation, it will be observed, supposes a condition privative in the subject, such that he suffers, at first, a kind of repulsion by the law, and is only won to it by embracing the goodness of it in a personal friend and deliverer.

And something like this double administration of law and liberty we distinguish, in many of the matters even of our worldly life. No exactness of drill makes an army efficient or invincible, till it is fired by some free impulse from the leader, or the cause; and yet the wearisome and tedious drill is a pre vious condition, without which this latter were impossible. No great work of genius was ever written in the way of work, or before the wings were lifted by some gale of inspiration ; which gale, again, would never have begun to blow, had not the win dows of thought and the chambers of light and beauty within been opened by years of patient toil and study. The artist plods on wearily, drudging in the details of his art, till finally the in spiration takes him, and, from that point onward, his hand is moved by his subject, with no conscious drudgery or labour. In the family, we meet a much closer and equally instructive analogy. The young child is overtaken first by the discipline of the house, in a form of law ; commanded, forbidden, sent, inter dicted, all in a way of authority, and to that authority is added something which compels respect. If he is a ductile and gentle child, he will be generally obedient ; but the examples are few in which the child will not sometimes be openly restive, or even stiffen himself in wilful disobedience. In any case, it will be law, not coinciding always with the child's wishes, or his opinions of pleasure and advantage; and there will be a sense of con straint, more or less irksome, as if the authority felt were repug nant and contrary to the desired happiness. By and by, how ever, authority changes its aspect and becomes lovely. The habit of obedience, the experience had of parental fidelity and tenderness, and the discovery made of absurdity and hidden mischief in the things interdicted, as it seemed arbitrarily, gra dually abolishes the sense of law, and substitutes a control not elt before—the control of personal love and respect. So that, finally, the man of thirty will carefully and reverently anticipate the minutest wishes of a parent, and, if that can be called obe dience, will obey him; when, as a child of three, he could barely endure his authority, and submitted to it only because it was duty enforced.

Such is the analogy of common life. Law and liberty are the two grand terms under which it is passed—law first and liberty afterward. And with all this corresponds what is said in the New Testament, of law as related to gospel. It is said in one view, of the laborious ritual of Moses; yet, by this his toric reference, it is designed to lead the mind back into a more general and deeper truth. It is called "the letter that killeth " as related to "the spirit that giveth life." It is said to have s value in the development of knowledge; for by the law is 'the knowledge of sin "—" that sin by the commandment might become exceeding sinful." It is bondage introducing and preparing liberty. "The law gendereth to bondage," but the gospel, "Jerusalem that is above, is free." " If there had been a law, that could have given life, verily righteousness should have been by the law; " but that was impossible. " It the schoolmaster to bring us to Christ," and then, having embraced him, he becomes a new inspiration in our love after which we no more need "to be under a schoolmaster " " The law made nothing perfect, but the bringing in of a better hope

There is reason to suspect that many will reject what I am here advancing. They will do it, of course, for the simple reason that they know no other kind of virtue but that which s legal, having, therefore, in their consciousness, nothing which answers to the liberty of the Spirit. To them, what I have

here said will have an appearance of cant. Exactly contrary
to which, I affirm it as the only competent philosophy, perceiv
ing, I think, as clearly as I perceive anything, that the con
junction discovered in Christianity of these two ministrations is
not any casual or accidental matter, as if men had somehow
fallen under law, and God was constrained afterward to do
something for them; on the contrary, that the whole manage
ment is from before the foundation of the world, having respect
to a grand antecedent necessity, involved in the perfecting of
virtue. God never proposed to perfect a character in men by
mere legal obedience. But He instituted law originally, no
doubt, as a first stage, preparatory to a second; both of which
were to be kept on foot together, and both of which are blended,
in one way or another, probably, in the training of all holy
minds in all worlds.

3. There appears to be yet another condition privative, as
regards our security against sin, in the social relation of powers
and their trial in and through that relation; viz., that they are
at first exposed to invasions of malign influence from each other,
which can nowise be effectually prevented, save as they are
finally fortified by the defences of character. In this view, if I
am right, a great part of the problem of existence must consist
in what may be called the fencing of powers; that is, by assort
ing and separating the good from the bad, and rendering one
class inaccessible to the arts and annoyances of the other.

The individual, as we have seen, is to be perfected for so
ciety; and for that reason he must needs have his trial in and
through society. A still wider truth appears to be that the
perfect society thus preparing is to be one and universal, com
prehending the righteous populations of all worlds and ages,
for the terms of duty and religion are in their nature universal;
and for this reason it appears also to be necessary that the trial
and training should be in some open field of activity common to
all the powers. Accordingly, as we are made with social, and,
if I may use the term, commercial natures—having inlets of
sympathy and impression, by which we may feel one another;
capacities to receive and give, to wrong, to offend, to comfort,
to strengthen, to seduce, and betray one another—so there is
an antecedent probability that the terms of social exposure will
involve some possibility of access, on the part of beings un-

seen, that are not of our race. Indeed, if it should happen
that spirits are impossible to be sorted and fenced apart by
walls of matter, or gulfs of distance, or abysses of emptiness,
something like this would seem to be necessarily involved,
till they are sorted, and the gates of commerce are shut fast
by the repulsions of contrary affinities. And, accordingly, till
this takes place, there must be exposures to good and malign
influence more numerous than we can definitely mark or distin
guish.

With this corresponds, it will be observed, all that is said in
the Scriptures of the activity of ministering angels engaged to
confirm and comfort us, the insidious arts of a bad spirit to
accomplish our fall, and the manifold enticements and malignant
possessions of evil demons generally. But I advert to these
representations, it will be observed, not in a way of assuring
their authenticity, for that is forbidden by the nature of my
argument. I only cite them as offering conceptions to our mind
or imagination that may be necessary to a full comprehension of
what is included in the subject.

Many will object, most sturdily and peremptorily, I am well
aware, to the possibility of enticements and arts, practised by
unseen agents, to draw us off from our fidelity to God, alleging
that such an exposure impeaches the fatherhood of God, and
virtually destroys our responsibility. But what if it should
happen to be involved as the necessary condition of any pro
perly social existence ? And it might as well be urged that
every temptation is an impeachment of God which comes from
sources unseen, being an approach that takes us off our guard,
and upsets the balance, possibly, of our judgments, just when
we are most implicitly confiding in them. Allowing such an
objection, therefore, responsibility would be impossible ; for who
of us was ever able to see distinctly, by what avenues all of his
temptations or enticements came ? Besides, saying nothing of
bad spirits, by how many methods—by air, look, sympathy—
do we produce immediate impressions in each other, whose
sources are never noted or suspected ; conveying sentiments,
drawing to this or that, fascinating, magnetizing, playing upon
one another, by methods as subtle and secret, as if the mischief
came from powers of darkness. And yet we never imagine
that such enticements encroach at all on the grounds of our just
responsibility, and all for the manifest reason that it never mat-

ters whence our enticements come, or by what arts the colour
of our judgments is varied and their equilibrium disturbed;
still we know, in all cases, that the wrong is wrong, and know
ing that is enough to complete our responsibility.

I am well aware of the modern tendency to resolve what is
said on this subject in the Scripture into figures of speech,
excluding all idea of a literal intermeddling of bad spirits. But
that there are bad spirits, there is no more reason to doubt,
than that there are bad men (who are in fact bad spirits), and
as little that the bad spirits are spirits of mischief, and will act
in character, according to their opportunity. As regards the
possession of foul spirits, it has been maintained by many of
the sturdiest supporters of revelation, and by reference to the
words employed in one or two cases by the evangelists them
selves, that they were only diseases regarded in that light.
Others have assumed the necessary absurdity of these possessions
without argument ; and still others have made them a subject of
much scoffing and profane ridicule. For the last half century,
and contemporaneously with our modern advances in science,
there has been a general gravitation of opinion, regarding this
and many other points, toward the doctrine of the Sadducees.
Which makes it only the more remarkable, that now, at last, a
considerable sect of our modern Sadducees themselves, who
systematically reject the faith of anything supernatural, are
contributing what aid they can to restore the precise faith of
the New Testament, respecting foul spirits. They do not call
their spiritual visitors devils, or their demonized mediums
possessed persons. But the low manners of their spirits, and
the lying oracles which it is agreed that some of them give,
and the power they display of acting on the lines of cause and
effect in nature, when thumping under tables, jolting stoves,
and floating men and women through the upper spaces of
rooms, proves them to be, if they are anything, supernatural
beings ; leaving no appreciable distinction between them and
the demoniacal irruptions of Scripture. For though there be
some talk of electricity and science, and a show of reducing
the new discovered commerce to laws of calculable recurrence,
it is much more likely to be established by their experiments
as a universal fact, that whatever being, of whatever world,
opens himself to their visitation, or invites the presence of
powers indiscriminately as respects their character, whether it

be under some thin show of scientific practice or not, will assuredly have the commerce invited ! Far enough is it from being either impossible or incredible ; and exactly this is what our new school of charlatanism suggests, that immense multi tudes of powers interfused, in their self-active liberty, through all the abysses and worlds of nature, have it as the battle-field of their good or malign activity, doing in it and upon it, as the Scriptures testify, acts supernatural that extend to us. This being true, what shall be expected, but that where there is anything congenial in temper or character to set open the soul, and nothing of antipathy to repel ; or where any one, through a licentious curiosity, a foolish conceit of science, or a bad faith in powers of necromancy, calls on spirits to come, no matter from what world — in such a case what shall follow, but that troops of malign powers rush in upon their victim, to practise their arts in him at will. I know nothing at all personally of these new mysteries ; but if a man, as Townsend, and many others testify, can magnetize his patient, even at the distance of miles, it should not seem incredible that foul spirits can magnetize also. This indeed was soon discovered in the power of spirits to come into mediums, and make them write and speak their oracles. It is also a curious coincidence that no one, as we are told, can be magnetized, or become a medium, or even be duly enlightened by a medium, who is uncongenial in his affinities, or maintains any quality of antipathy in his will, or temper, or character ; for then the commerce sought is impossible. Beside it is remarkable that the persons who dabble most freely in this kind of commerce, are seen, as a general fact, to run down in their virtue, lose their sense of principles, and become addled, by their familiarity with the powers of mischief.

In these references to bad spirits, and the matter of demon-ology in general, I do not assume to have established any very decisive conclusion ; for the Scripture representations cannot be assumed as true, and the new demons of science I know nothing about, except by report. This only is made clear, that the suggestion of a condition privative in men, as regards their defence against the irruption of other powers, is one that can not be disproved by any facts within the compass of our know ledge. And since other powers doubtless exist, both good and bad, who are being sorted and fenced apart by the contrary affinities of character, nothing can be more consonant to reason than that there must be exposures to unseen mischief in our trial, till these eternal fences are raised.

We find then—this is the result of our search—that sin can nowise be accounted for ; there are no positive grounds, or principles back of it, whence it may have come. We only discover conditions privative, that are involved, as necessary incidents in the begun existence and trial of powers. These conditions privative are in the nature of perils, and while they excuse nothing,—for the law of duty is always plain,—they are yet drawn so close to the soul and open their gulfs, on either hand so deep, that our expectation of the fall is really as pressing as if it were determined by some law that annihilates liberty. Liberty we know is not annihilated. And yet we say, looking on the state of man made perilous, in this manner, by liberty, that we cannot expect him to stand.

Some persons who are accustomed to receive the Scriptures with great reverence, and whose feeling, therefore, is the more entitled to respect, may be disturbed by the apprehension, that we violate what they take for an evidently scriptural truth concerning the good angels. These are finite beings, and had a begun existence, and yet we are taught, as it will be urged that they have never fallen ; showing a complete possibility of creating free beings, or powers that will never sin ;—at which point our doctrine is seen to come into open and direct conflict with the Scriptures.

I have no pleasure, certainly, in raising a conflict with any opinion not absolutely corrupt, when it has been so long held, and with such unquestioning deference, by multitudes of Chris tian believers. But I am obliged, by the terms of my argument, to make a revision of the evidences by which this opinion is sustained. In the ante-Copernican conceptions of the universe, such an opinion was more likely to be taken up than now ; and it seems to be a relic of false interpretation then introduced. I find no clear evidence of any such opinion in the Christian Scriptures. They do affirm the existence of good angels, who, for aught that appears, have all been passed through and brought up out of a fall, as the redeemed of mankind will be. They affirm the existence also of bad angels, who certainly have not been kept from the experiment or choice of evil. A signi-

ficant intimation is supposed to be found in the text—" To the
intent that now, unto the principalities and powers in heavenly
places, might be known by the church the manifold wisdom of
God ;" as if here, for the first time, they were to be instructed
by the fact of human redemption. But everything manifestly
turns here on the epithet " manifold " [πολυποίκιλος], which,
in fact, means only *diversified*, not something new and strange ;
yielding us a hint rather which runs exactly contrary to the
common opinion, viz., that the heavenly powers discover, only
through the Church of our world, another plan of grace and
mercy unfolded different from their own. In respect to the
" new song," so often referred to in this connexion, it is suffi
cient to say that it is joined by beings not of our race, and is
abundantly new as related to a work of redemption among men ;
different in form and manner as in sphere from any other.

But the principal or hinge text on this subject is the 6th
verse of Jude's Epistle,—" And the angels that kept not their
first estate, but left their own habitation, he hath reserved,"
etc.; leaving the implication, it is supposed, that other angels
have kept their first estate, and stood fast in obedience. But
this, it has been shown by Mr Faber, in a full and somewhat
overdone discussion,[1] is a totally mistaken conception of the
passage. The term " angels," he has shown, refers to the
" sons of God," whose apostasy is set forth in the 6th chapter
of Genesis. The term αρχή, rendered " first estate," as denot
ing a moral condition, has no such meaning in any known
example. It signifies rather a *principate* or *principality*, and
the representation is, that certain persons of the Sethite, or
church people, growing lewd and dissolute in their life, went
over to the corrupt Cainites and joined them in their vices.
This also is implied in the phrase " left their own habitation "
[οίκητήριον], their domicile, or native place and country ; lan
guage entirely malapropos when referred to celestial beings.
Besides, their crime was not angelic—the " going after strange
flesh "—and, what is yet more stringent, their crime is defined
by a comparison which shows exactly what it was—" Even as
Sodom and Gomorrah, and the cities about them, in like manner,
giving themselves over to fornication and going after strange
flesh," etc. And, finally, to render this interpretation yet
more certain, it is shown that Josephus, in speaking of the

[1] *Three Dispensations*, vol. i. pp. 344-431.

"sons of God" in Genesis, calls them *angels*, and uses the same word [αρχή] *principality*, in describing their apostasy.   On the whole, it does not appear that there is any vestige of authority in Scripture for the opinion that the good angels are beings that have never sinned.

Contrary to this, there are many passages that, without being severely pressed, might be made to indicate the fact that they are all redeemed spirits.   Thus, where the desire of "angels to look into these things" is spoken of, an indication is given, not that they are unacquainted with any such fact as redemption, but of the contrary fact, that this appetite is whetted by their experience.   Why should they be so eager to look into a matter wholly unknown ?   So when the angels break into the sky at the advent of Christ, crying "Peace on earth," they seem to know in their deepest heart's feeling already what this "peace" signifies.   It is remarkable also that the one only text of Scrip ture that could fairly be insisted on, as a direct and formal declaration of Scripture on this point, is that of the apostle, when, extolling the universal headship of Christ, he says what ap pears to be directly contrary to all these assumptions,—"By him to reconcile all things unto himself, whether they be things on earth, or things in heaven."

Falling back, then, upon our own first principles, as required by the tenor of our argument, we find that angels, like men, are, by the supposition, finite beings.   If finite, then are they beings who think in succession, one thing after another, as we do.   If so, then there was a point in the early date, or first hours of their existence, when they had thought little, and had little experience, and of course knew as little as they had thought. And so, given the fact of their finite and begun existence, it seems to follow, as a conclusion, that they were in the same weakness, or condition privative, with us.   What then, can we judge, but that probably there is some ground-principle or law, common both to them and to us, that involves them in the same fortunes with us, and requires a method of training and redemp tion analogous to that which is ordained for men ?   God, as we all agree, is a being who works by system—with a glorious variety, and yet by system—and it would be singular for His plan to break down in some little department like ours, and go straight forward to its mark in other and better contrived parts of His creation.   How much better, and more consonant also to ou: feeling, to suppose that there is some antecedent necessity inherent in the conception of finite and begun existences, that, in their training as powers, they should be passed through the double experience of evil and good, fall and redemption.

At the same time, I am not anxious to carry my argument so far; and I readily concede that it might be presumptuous to insist on such a conclusion, as being one of the known truths. I only ask that a similar concession be allowed on the other side, as regards an opinion certainly not authenticated by Scrip ture; for, when that is taken out of the way as being a scriptural objection to my argument, I have no longer any concern with it. It may not be amiss to add, further, that what I have here advanced in a somewhat positive form concerning sin, I value mostly as an hypothesis. Indeed, what we want to clear our difficulties here, is not so much a doctrine, as to find that some rational hypothesis is possible. And my object is sufficiently gained when that is admitted.

If it should be objected that my doctrine or hypothesis here is only another version of the scheme that accounts for sin as being the necessary means of the greatest good, it is enough to answer that I see no great reason to be concerned for it, even if it were. Still I do not perceive that it proposes to account for sin as being a means of anything. It makes much of the knowledge of sin, or of its bitter consequences, and especially of the want of that knowledge, save as it is gotten by the bad experience itself. But the knowledge of sin is, in fact, know ing—that is the precise point of it—that it is the means of nothing good—that it is evil in all its tendencies, relations, operations, and results, and will never bring anything good to any being. If, then, the knowing of sin to be the possible means of no good is itself a means of good, wherein does it appear that I am reproducing the doctrine that sin is the neces sary means of the greatest good? Because, it may be answered, sin, as a fact of consciousness, is by the supposition the neces sary means of the knowledge of sin. But that, I reply, is a trick of argument practised on the word *means*. Undoubtedly sin, as a fact of consciousness, is the necessary *subject* of the knowledge of sin. If it were affirmed that the knowledge of certain sunken rocks, in the track of some voyage, is necessary to a safe passage, how easy to show, by just the argument here employed, that, since the rocks are a necessary means of the knowledge of the rocks, the rocks are therefore, and by necessary consequence, the necessary means of a safe passage!

There is still another point, the existence of Satan or the devil, and the account to be made of him, which is always intruded upon discussions of this nature, and cannot well be avoided.   God, we have seen, might create a realm of things, and have it stand firm in its order ; but, if He creates a realm of powers, a prior and eternal certainty confronts Him of their outbreak in evil.   And at just this point we are able, it may be, to form some just or not impossible conception of the dia bolical personality.   According to the Manichees or disciples of Zoroaster, a doctrine virtually accepted by many philosophers, two principles have existed together from eternity, one of which is the cause of good, and the other of evil ; and by this short process they make out their account of evil.   With sufficient modifications, their account is probably true.   Thus, if their good principle, called God by us, is taken as a being, and their bad principle as only a condition privative, one as a positive and real cause, the other as a bad possibility that environs God from eternity, waiting to become a fact, and certain to become a fact, whenever the opportunity is given, it is even so.   And then it follows that, the moment God creates a realm of powers, the bad possibility as certainly becomes a bad actuality, a Satan or devil *in esse;* not a bad omnipresence over against God and His equal—that is a monstrous and horrible conception—but an outbreaking evil, or empire of evil in created spirits, accord ing to their order.   For Satan or the devil, taken in the singu lar, is not the name of any particular person, neither is it a personation merely of temptation or impersonal evil, as many insist ; for there is really no such thing as impersonal evil in the sense of moral evil; but the name is a name that generalizes bad persons or spirits, with their bad thoughts and characters, many in one.   That there is any single one of them who, by distinction or pre-eminence, is called Satan or devil, is wholly improbable.   The name is one taken up by the imagination to designate or embody, in a conception the mind can most easily wield, the all or total of bad minds and powers.   Even as Davenport, the ablest theologian of all the New England Fathers, represents, in his Catechism ; answering carefully the question—" What is the devil ? "—thus :—" The multitude of apostate angels which, by pride and blasphemy against God, and malice against man, became liars and murderers, by tempt ing him to that sin."

There is also a further reason for this general unifying of the bad powers in one, or under one conception, in the fact that evil, once beginning to exist, inevitably becomes organic, and constructs a kind of principate or kingdom opposite to God. It is with all bad spirits, doubtless, as with us. Power is taken by the strongest, and weakness falls into a subordinate place of ser vility and abjectness. Pride organizes caste, and dominates in the sphere of fashion. Corrupt opinions, false judgments, bad manners, and a general body of conventionalisms that represent the motherhood of sin, come into vogue and reign. And so, doubtless, everywhere, and in all worlds, sin has it in its nature to organize, mount into the ascendant above God and truth, and reign in a kingdom opposite to God. And, in this view, evil is fitly represented in the Scripture as organizing itself under Satan, or the devil, or the prince of this world, or the prince of the power of the air—no puling fiction of superstition, as many fancy, but, rightly conceived, a grand, massive, portentous, and even tremendous reality. For though it be true that no such bad omnipresence is intended in the term Satan as some appear to fancy, there is represented in it an organization of bad mind, thought, and power, that is none the less imperial as regards resistance.

At just this point many fall into the easy mistake of suppos ing that the bad organization finds its head in a particular per son or spirit, who has all other bad spirits submissive and loyal under his will, and is called Satan as being their king. But they press the analogy too far, overlooking the fact that evil is as truly and eternally anarchy as organization. It is much better to understand, as in reference to bad spirits, what we know holds good in respect to the organic force of evil here among men. Evil is a hell of oppositions, riots, usurpations, in itself, and bears a front of organization only as against good. It never made a chief that it would not shortly dethrone, never set up any royal Nimrod or family of Nimrods it would not some time betray or expel. That the organic force of evil, therefore, has ever settled the eternal supremacy of some one spirit called devil or Satan, is against the known nature of evil. There is no such order, allegiance, loyalty, faith, in evil as that.   The stability of Satan and his empire consists, not in the force of some personal chieftainship, but in the fixed array of all bad minds, and even of anarchy itself, against what is good.

As regards the naming process by which this devil or Satan is prepared, we may easily instruct ourselves by other analogies; such, for example, as "the man of sin" and "antichrist." These are the names, evidently, of no particular person.   "The man of sin" is, in fact, *all the men of sin*, or the spirit that works in them; for the conception is that, as Christ has brought forth a gospel, so it is inevitable that sin will foul that gospel in the handling, and be a mystery of iniquity upon it.   And this mystery of iniquity, as Paul saw, was already beginning to work, as work it must, till it is taken out of the way.   And this working is to be the revelation of evil through the gospel, and of the gospel through evil.   It includes the dogmatic usurpation, the priestly assumptions, the mock sacraments, and all the church idols, brought in as improvements—everything contributed to and interwoven with the gospel by sin as a miracle of iniquity.   When that process is carried through, the gospel will be understood; not before.   It is also noticeable that what the devil or Satan is to God as a spirit, that also Antichrist is to Christ, the incarnate God-man.   Antichrist is, in fact, the devil of Christianity, as Satan is the devil of the Creation and Providence.   As the devil, too, is singled out and made eminent by the definite article, so is Antichrist spoken of in the singular as one person.   And then again, as there are many devils spoken of, so also it is declared that "now there are many antichrists."

Satan, then, is a bad possibility, eternally existing prior to the world's creation, becoming or emerging there into a bad actuality, which it is the problem of Jehovah's government to master.   For it has been the plan of God, in the creation and training of the powers, so to bring them on as to finally vanquish the bad possibility or necessity that environed Him before the worlds were made; so to create and subjugate, or by his love regenerate the bad powers loosened by His act of creation, as to have them in eternal dominion.   And precisely here is He seen in the grandeur of His attitude.   We might yield to some opinion of His weakness, when pondering the dark fatality by which he is encompassed in the matter of evil; but when we

see His plan distinctly laid, as a fowler's when he sets his net ·
that He is disappointed by nothing, and that all His counsels
told in their appointed time and order as when a general
marches on his army in a course of victory ; that He sets good
empire against evil empire, and, without high words against His
adversary, calmly proceeds to accomplish a system of order that
comprehends the subjugation of disorder, what majesty and
grandeur invest His person ! Nothing which He could have
done by omnipotence, no silent peace of compulsion, no uncon-
senting order of things, made fast by His absolute will, could
have given any such impression of His greatness and glory as
this loosening of the possibility of evil, in the purpose finally
turn it about by His counsel and transform it by His good
ness and patience. What significance and sublimity is there
folding such a view, in the ecstatic words of Christ, when just
about to finish His work—" I beheld Satan as lightning fall
from heaven !" Nor any the less when His prophet testifies
after Him— " And the great dragon was cast out, that old
serpent called the devil and Satan, which deceiveth the whole
world. ' Now is come salvation, and strength, and the king.
dom of our Lord and of his Christ."

That salvation, strength, and kingdom, be it also observed,
are not patches of mending laid upon the rent garment of a
oken plan, but issues and culminations of the eternal plan
The cross of redemption is no afterthought, but is itself
the grand all-dominating idea around which the eternal system
of God crystallizes; Jesus Christ, the " appointed heir of all
things —" the lamb slain from the foundation of the world "
Here stands out the final end or cause of all things, here emerge
the powers made strong and glorious. Weak at first, unperfect
incomplete, they are now completed and glorified—complete in
Him who is the head of all principality and power

CHAPTER V.

THE FACT OF SIN.

WE have been discussing the question of evil as a question of possibility, probability, prospect; we now come down to the question of fact—is it, or is it not, a fact that sin exists ?

But in passing to this question, it appears to be required of us to state the object we have in it, and also to indicate, in advance, at the stage we have now reached, the course or drift of our argument. We propose, then, to show, first of all, the fact of sin. This being established, we shall next go into a computation or inspection of the effects of sin, and show that it is followed and must be by a general disturbance or collapse of nature; what we call nature being, in fact, a state of un-nature induced by the penal or retributive action of causes provoked by sin. Hence, unless disorder and frustration are to be eternal, a second higher movement is required having force to restore the lapse of nature ; which higher movement is the supernatural work of grace and redemption. In this view the unity itself of the system of God comprehends, it will be seen, two ranges of existence and operative force—nature and the supernatural ; both complimentary to each other ; while the latter, comprising the powers, and all divine agencies exerted in their restoration, and containing all the last ends and highest workings and only perfect results of God's plan, is, by the supposition, chief above the other ; having that to serve its uses, and be the organ of its exercise. The creation, therefore, is made for Christianity, and without that, as a kingdom super natural, the kingdom of nature is only an absurd and frag mentary existence, having no significance or end. The argu ment will lead me, of course, to an examination of some of the supernatural facts, or supposed facts, of Christianity.

I am well aware of the necessary obscurity of this statement, but as it is offered rather to indicate the course than to convey any sufficient impression of the argument proposed, I hope it may at least satisfy the purpose intended.

I begin then with the question, whether it is a real and pro per fact that sin exists ? In discussing this question, I abstain altogether from any close theologic definition of sin. Un doubtedly there is a something called *sin* in the Christian writ ings, which is not action or wrong-doing—something not included in the Pelagian definitions of sin, as commonly pre sented. But my argument requires me to look no farther at present than to this, which is the simplest conception of the subject, inquiring whether there is any such thing in the world as properly blamable action ? Is there a transgression of right or of law—a positive disobedience to God—anything that rationally connects with remorse, or carries the sense of guilt as a genuine reality ? Of course it is implied that the trans gressor does what no mere thing, nothing in the line of cause and effect, can do—acts against God ; or, what is nowise dif ferent, against the constituent harmony of things issued from the will of God. Hence the bad conscience, the sense of guilt or blame ; that the wrong-doer recognizes in the act something from himself that is not from any mere principle of nature, not from God, contrary to God.

It appears in one view to be quite idle to raise this question. Why should we undertake the serious discussion of a question that every man has settled ? Why argue for a fact that every man acknowledges ? It would indeed be quite nugatory if all mankind could definitely see what they acknowledge. But they do not, and, what is more, many are abundantly ingenious to escape doing it. In fact, all the naturalism of our day begins just here, in the denial or disguised disallow ance of this self-evident and everywhere visible fact, the exist ence of sin. Sometimes, where no such denial is intended or thought of, it is yet virtually made in the assumption of some theory or supposed principle of philosophy, which, legiti mately carried out, conducts and will conduct other minds also to the formal denial, both of the fact of sin and of that respon sibility which is its necessary precondition. We have thus a large class holding the condition of implicit naturalism, who asserts what amounts to a denial of responsibility, and so of the

possibility of sin, without denying formally the fact, or conceiv
ing that any truth of Christianity as a supernatural religion is
brought in question • Of these we may cite, as a prominent
instance and example, the phrenologists, who are many of them
disciples and earnest advocates of the Christian doctrine. Still
it is not difficult to see that, if human actions are nothing but
results brought to pass or determined by the ratios of so many
quantities of brain at given points under the skull, then are
they no more fit subjects of reward or blame than the motions
of the stars, determined also by their quantities of matter.
Therefore some phrenologists add the conception of a higher
nature than the pulpy quantities; a person, a free-will power
presiding over them and only using them as its incentives and
instruments, but never mechanically determined by them   This
takes phrenology out of the conditions of naturalism, and, for
just the same reason, and in the same breath, renders sin a
possibility; otherwise the science, however fondly accepted as
the ally of Christianity (a sorry kind of ally at the best), is only
a tacit and implicit form of naturalism, that virtually excludes
the faith of Christianity.

On the other hand, we have met with advocates of natural
ism, who have not been quite able to deny the existence of 'sin
or who even assert the fact in ways of doubtful significance.
Thus Mr Parker, in his *Discourses of Religion*, having it for his
main object to disprove the credibility of miracles and of every
thing supernatural in Christianity, still admits in words the
existence of sin. He even accounts it one of the merits of
Calvinistic and Lutheran orthodoxy that it "shows (we quote
his own language) the hatefulness of sin and the terrible evils it
brings upon the world;"[1] and, what is yet more decisive, he
represents it as being one of the faults of the moderate school
of Protestants, that "they reflect too little on the evil that comes
from violating the law of God."[2] And yet the whole matter of
supernaturalism, which he is discussing, hinges on precisely this
and nothing else, viz., the question whether there is any such
thing as a real "violation of the law of God," any "hatefulness
in sin, any "terrible evils brought on the world" by means of
it. For to violate the law of God is itself an act supernatural,
out of the order of nature, and against the order of nature, as
truly even as a miracle, else it is nothing. The very sin of the

[1] *Discourses of Religion*, p. 453.   [2] *Ibid.* p. 465.

sin is that it is against God, and everything that comes from God ; the acting of a soul or power against the constituent frame of nature and its internal harmony, followed, therefore, as in due time we shall show, by real disorder of nature, which noth ing but a supernatural agency of redemption can ever effectually repair. Of this, the fundamental fact on which, in reality, the whole question he is discussing turns, he takes no manner of notice. Admitting the existence of sin, his speculations still go on their way, as if it were a fact of no significance in regard to his argument. If he had sounded the question of sin more deeply, ascertaining what it is and what it involves, he might well enough have spared himself the labour of his book He either would never have written it at all, or else he would have denied the existence of sin altogether, as being only a necessary condition of the supernatural.

And we are the more confirmed in the opinion that his denial of supernaturalism begins in a state of mental ambiguity re specting sin, from the fact that exactly this ambiguity is mani fested in his work itself. Thus, when speaking of the wrongs and the oppressive inequalities discovered in the distributions of society, he refers them, if we understand him rightly, to causes in human nature, not to the will, in its abuse or breach of nature. He says, " We find the root of all in man himself In him is the same perplexing antithesis which we meet in all his works. These conflicting things existed as ideas in him before they took their present concrete shape. Discordant causes [in his nature, we understand] have produced effects not harmonious. Out of man these institutions have grown ; out of his passions or his judgment, his senses or his soul. Taken together, they are the exponent which indicates the character and degree of development the race has now attained." [1] Out of his passions or his judgment, his senses or his soul ! Whence, then, did they come ? for this appears to be a little ambiguous. And what if it should happen that they came out of neither— out of no ground or cause in nature whatever, but out of the will as a power transcending nature. If these bitter wrongs of society, such as war, slavery, and the like, which Mr Parker has so often denounced in terms so nearly violent, kindling as it were, a hell of words in which to burn them before the time ; ɘ bitter wrongs are nothing but developments of " dis-

[1] *Discourses of Religion*, p. 12.

cordant causes" in human nature, then wherein are they to be blamed? " Violations of the law of God!" Do God's own causes violate His law? Bringing "terrible evils on the world!" How upon the world, when God himself has put the evils in it, as truly as he has put the legs of a frog in the tadpole out of which it grows? "Hatefulness of sin!" Is the mere develop ment of God's own constituted works and causes hateful? Is the dog-star morally hateful because it rises in July?

But the advocates of naturalism are commonly more thorough and consistent; not consistent with each other, that is too much to be expected, but consistent with themselves, in trying each to find some way of disallowing sin, or so far explaining it away, as to reduce it within the terms of mere cause and effect in nature. Thus, for example, Fourier conceives that what we call sin, by a kind of misnomer, is predicable only of society, not of the individual man. Considered as creatures of God, all men, as truly as the first man before sin, have and continue always to have a right and perfect nature, in the same manner as the stars. He accordingly assumes it as the fundamental principle of the new science, that " man's attractions," like theirs, " are proportioned to his destinies; " so that, by means of his passions, he will even gravitate naturally toward the condition of order and wellbeing, with the same infallible certainty as they. It only happens that society is not fitly organized, and that produces all the mischief. There really is no sin, apart from the fact that men have not had the science to organize society rightly. He does not appear to notice the fact that if these human stars, called men, are all harmoniously tempered and set in a perfect balance of inward attractions, by them to be swayed under the laws of cause and effect, that fact *is* organization, the very harmony of the spheres itself. And then the assumption that society is not fitly organized, or badly disorganized, is simply absurd; not less absurd the hope that man is going to scheme it into organization himself. Doubtless society is badly enough organized, but we have no place for the fact, and can have none, till we look on men as powers, not under cause and effect; capable, in that manner, of sin, and liable to it; through the bad experiment of it, to be trained up into character, which is itself the completed organization of felicity. Under this view bad organization or disorganization is possible, because sin is possible; and will be a fact, as certainly as sin is a fact—otherwise neither possible nor a fact.

But as we are dismissing, in this manner, the inconsequent and baseless theory of Fourier, there comes up, on the other side, exactly opposite to him, the very celebrated theologian of naturalism, Dr Strauss, who inverts the main point of Fourier, charging all the misdoings and miseries of the human state, commonly called sins, on the individual, leaving society blame less and even perfect. Finding the word *sin* asserting a right ful place in human language, he is not so unphilosophical as to insist on its being cast out; on the contrary, he even speaks of "the sinfulness of human nature;" but by this he under stands only that individuals must needs suffer so much of per sonal mischief and defect, in a way of carrying on the historic development of the race. In this view he says, " Humanity [*i.e.*, taken as a whole] is the sinless existence ; for the course of its development is a blameless one ; pollution cleaves to the individuals only, and does not touch the race and its history." " Sinful human nature " turns out, in this manner, to be the " sinless existence." The individuals whom we call " sinners," and regard as under " pollution," are yet seen to be " blameless " sinners ; so ingeniously " polluted," that the pollution which infects all the individuals does not once touch the race ! If there be any miracle in supernaturalism more wonderful than this, let us be informed where it is. The truth appears to be that Dr Strauss could not formally deny the fact of sin, and yet had no place for it. He threw it, therefore, into a limbo of ambiguities, where he could recognize it a fact, and yet make nothing of it.

Still there is so much of ingenuity in this method of getting rid of sin, the absurdity of it is disguised under so fine a show of philosophy, that much weaker and less cultivated men than Dr Strauss anticipated him in it, and, without knowing, as well as he, what their wise saying meant, were as greatly pleased as he with the plausible air of it. Pope rhymes it thus, a hundred ways, that,—

> "Respecting man, whatever wrong we call
> May, must be right, as relative to all."

The popular literature of our time, represented by such writers as Carlyle and Emerson, is in a similar vein ; not always denying sin, for to lose it would be to lose the spice and spirit of half their representations of humanity; but contriving rather to exalt and glorify it, by placing both it and virtue upon the common footing of a natural use and necessity. Glorifying also themselves in the plausible audacity of their offence · for it is one of the frequent infirmities of literature that it courts effect by taking on the airs of licentiousness

But this kind of originality has now come to its limit or point of reaction ; for, when licentiousness becomes a theory regularly asserted, and formally vindicated, it is then no better than truth. The poetry is gone, and it dies of its own flatness

s we have seen a volume, recently issued from the American press the formal purpose of which is to show, even as a ristian fact the blamelessness of sin ; nay more, that the main object of Jesus Christ in his mission of love, is to disabuse the world of he imposture, deliver it of the terrible nightmare si   Not to deliver it of sin itself—that is a mistake—but to deliver it of the conviction of sin, as an illusive and baneful mistake gendered by the superstition of the world! If any thing can be taken for a certain proof that mankind are in fatuated by some strange illusion, such as sin alone may breed it would seem to be the fact itself that they are able to impose upon themselves and one another, by these feeble perversities that despite of all the best known, best attested facts of life contrive to put on still the airs of science and maintain the pre tences of reason.

Passing on from these oppositions of science, falsely so called, let us refer to some of the formal proofs that sin is an existing ict. Scripture authority is out of the question, which we do ot regret ; for the practical and palpable evidences that meet ⸺ ⸺ ⸺ e simpi e inspection of humanity itself are abundantly sufficient

The question here, it will be observed, is not whether men are total y depraved or depraved at all; nor whether they sin continually; but simply whether they do actually sin ?— whether, in fact sin exists ? Nor is it implied that all sins are equally blameable ; for, beyond a question, great numbers persons are steeped in contaminating influences from their earliest childhood, and pass into life under the heaviest loads of moral disadvantage. Regarding their acts, nothing is sin to such, but what they do as sin. The object we have in view is sufficiently answered by the adequate proof of a single sin; for the argument of naturalism goes the length of denying all sin, even the possibility of sin; so that if one man is able, as a power, to break out of nature and do a sin against it, the whole theory is dissolved. The power of liberty that can do one sin can do more; and if only one man has it, he must either be a miracle himself, or else other men can do the same.

We begin with an appeal to observation, alleging as a fact that we do, by inevitable necessity, impute blame to acts of in jury done us by others. We can as easily avoid making a shadow in the sun, as we can avoid a sentiment of blame, when we are designedly injured by a fellow man. We do it, not as a pettish child may pelt a thistle on which he has trodden, not in any dispossessed state or momentary fit of anger, but even after years of reflection have passed away; nay, after we have bathed the wrong done us, for so long a time, in the cleansing waters of forgiveness. Still we condemn the wrong, and must, as long as we exist; our forgiveness itself implies that we do; for what is there to be forgiven, if there be nothing that we condemn? Thus, if there be two partners in trade, and one of them absconds with all the profits and funds of the establish ment, leaving the other, with his family, victims to the common liabilities, and to a necessary doom, for life, of poverty; by what art can either he or they ever manage to eradicate their sense of wrong, or the blame they impute to the perfidious man whose crime has been the dispoiler of their life? They may forgive him, they may follow him with their prayers to the hour of his last breath, but they will pray as for a guilty man, whose crime is the bitterness of his life, as it has been the burden of theirs.

Suppose now they turn philosophers and make the discovery that there is no sin, that all actions take place under the neces sary law of cause and effect, and manage to smooth over with this fine apology, all the crimes they hear of in the world; still that one man that robbed them of their all—how stubborn a fact is he, how unreducible to their theory! His very name means all that sin ever means, and they can as easily tear out their own heart-strings, as they can empty that name of the blame it signifies.

Or suppose a man writes a book, the precise object of which

is to show that there is, and can be no such thing as sin, and then that his work is assaulted, as he thinks, with unfair re presentations and malicious constructions, what will you more certainly see, than that he is out immediately against his ac cusers, in the most violent denunciations of their bigotry, and the wicked untruths of their criticism ? Now, if the book was true, if there is no sin that is blameable, what have they done to be so bitterly blamed ? What they have done is simply natural, and is no more to be condemned than a frosty night. It will nowise diminish the force of our supposition to add that it might well enough be given as historic fact. In which, also, we may see how certainly every man's rational and moral instincts will triumph, after all, over his theories and formal arguments, when he undertakes to deny or disprove the fact of sin.

We go farther. So confident are we in this matter that, if there be any man living who undertakes to be consistent in the denial of sin, setting it down, however firmly, as a point of will, never to blame any injury done to others or to himself, we will engage, in case he is able to spend four waking hours without any single thought or feeling of blame as against any human creature, to admit the truth of his doctrine.

We have another proof, in the fact that we as positively and necessarily blame ourselves ; not in everything—my argument does not require me to go that length—enough that we do it on particular occasions, distinctly noted and remembered. And here we are bold to affirm that every person of a mature age, and in his right mind, remembers turns or crises in his life where he met the question of wrong face to face, and by a hard inward struggle broke through the sacred convictions of duty that rose up to fence him back. It was some new sin to which he had not become familiar, so much worse perhaps in degree as to be the entrance to him consciously of a new stage of guilt. He remembers how it shook his soul and even his body ; how he shrank in guilty anticipation from the new step of wrong ; the sublime misgiving that seized him, the awkward and but half-possessed manner in which it was taken, and then afterward, perhaps, even after years have passed away, how, in some quiet hour of the day or wakeful hour of night, as the recollection of that deed—not a public crime, but a wrong, or an act of vice— returned upon him, the blood rushed back for the moment on his fluttering heart, the pores of his skin opened, and a kind of agony of shame and self-condemnation, in one word, of remorse, seized his whole person. This is the consciousness, the guilty pang of sin ; every man knows what it is.

We have also observed this peculiarity in such experiences, that it makes no difference at all what temptations we were under ; we probably enough do not even think of them ; our soul appears to scorn apology, as if some higher nature within, speaking out of its eternity, were asserting its violated rights, chastising the insult done to its inborn affinities with immutable order and divinity, and refusing to be farther humbled by the low pleadings of excuse and disingenuous guilt. To say, at such a time, the woman tempted me, I was weak, I was beguiled, I was compelled by fear and overcome, signifies nothing. The wrong was understood, and that suffices.

Nor is it only in these times of conscious compunction that we are seen to blame ourselves as transgressors. We do it tacitly or unconsciously, in ways that are even more striking. Thus it may be seen that large assemblies of men, not the worst of their species, not the ignorant, or the broken-spirited victims of depression, not the felons or outcasts of society, but the most intelligent, most honest and honourable, and generally most ex emplary as regards their conduct, will come together once in seven days, and sit down to the exposure and charge of their sin, without even a thought of offence or insult. And what is more, that kind of preaching which probes them most faithfully, and most disturbs their consciences, will most invite their at tendance, if only there is no violence or fanaticism in the manner. Any sober and rational exposure of their sin, however piercing, they will submit to, take it as their privilege, and pay for it cheerfully, year by year ! Why now is this ? Simply because they are sinners, and know the charge to be true. Were they charged in this manner with being thieves, pickpockets, or assassins, all husbands and wives arraigned as false, all children as parricides, all citizens as perjurers and traitors, all merchants and bankers as dishonest and fraudulent dealers, they would instantly repel the charge ; their indignation could not be restrained for a moment. Nor is it anything to say that they have been educated into the faith that they are transgressors, living in the guilt of sin, and submit to the charge as to one of their superstitions. It is not as being a dogma that the charge has any reality to them ; indeed they often repel it as such and deny it. It has never any power, till it is wielded in such a manner as to stir the consciousness, and draw out thence a fresh verdict of conviction.

We do then blame ourselves. It is one of the most real and tremendous facts of our consciousness ; which, if a man will seek to explain away, by resolving it into cause and effect, it will yet remain, defying and scorning all his arguments. He knows that he himself did the sin, and no cause back of him self. It is a fact, self-pronounced in his consciousness, and of which he can no more divest himself than he can stay the con sciousness of his existence. Chloroform may rid him of it, but not argument.

Again, it is a fact constantly perceived, that where men do not occupy themselves with thoughts of blame, or conscious admissions of guilt, they are yet exercised in ways that imply it, and prove it only the more convincingly. The moment we look out upon the race, and take note of mankind, as revealed in their most superficial demonstrations, we discover that they are out of rest, plagued by the foul demon of guilt. A male factor aspect invests their conduct. Not by altars only of sacrifice, smoking under every sky ; not by pilgrimages, absti nences, vigils, flagellations of the body, self-immolations, and other voluntary tortures ; not by the giving way even of natural affection before this dreadful horror of the mind, yielding up the children of the body to pacify the sins of the soul—not by these misdirected expedients and pains of guilt alone do we dis cover its existence, but by others more silent and convincing.

Take, for a single example, the remarkable fact of a univer sal shyness of God—a fact conceded by society, and made the basis even of a common law of politeness. Why is this, why is it accepted as a universal law of politeness, never to obtrude upon others the subject of religion, or of God and the soul, without some previous intimation or discovery that the subject will not be unwelcome ? Because it is presumed not to be welcome. It is not because God and the soul are questionable realities—we love to converse of things unreal or imaginary, as well as of those which are real. It is not because, being real, they are matters about which there are many different opinions—so there are about politics, literature, philosophy science, art, and almost every other subject. It is not because, being real, God is not the loftiest, purest, and, in Himself, most ennobling, most inspiring, most radiant subject of communica tion ; His government the richest fountain of wisdom ; and the soul an interest to itself that dwarfs all others. Neither is it because a population of pure, angelic intelligences, occupying this same world of ours, and immersed in similar employments, would not meet the vision of God in all His works, and would not hasten to refresh themselves in these transcendent themes. The only and true explanation is that God and the soul are themes that move disturbance. They suggest blame, they lace rate, in this manner, the comfort of the mind. So well un derstood is it that mankind are shy of God, and that humanity is itself the sign of a bad conscience, that it is tacitly voted and becomes an accepted law of politeness, never to approach this one proscribed subject, without a previous discovery that it can be done without offence.

Nor is it any excuse or clearance of the sign, to say that manifestly such subjects ought not to be promiscuously spoken of in all places and circles. This we admit. Still the question is, why they may not ? And the only answer is that which we have given, that men are under a subtle and tacit but damning sense of blame, and cannot bear, on all occasions, or anywhere but in the public assemblies of religion, to have sub jects introduced that remind them of it, and stir again the guilt of their conscience. There would never be any such places or occasions in a population of sinless beings.

Is this tacit blame, then, that appears to haunt the world and drive it from its rest, a mere fiction ? Are we still under cause and effect, as truly as a river flowing toward the ocean, only not able ourselves to discover the fact ? Bitter hardship that we cannot be allowed the placidity of the river !

We have yet another proof, in the fact that mankind are seen to be acting universally on the assumption, that wrong is done, or is likely to be done in the world. Every man of busi ness, having only ordinary intelligence, assumes it as a point of natural discretion, that he is beset with wrong-doers, who will take every advantage and seize every opportunity, and holds it as a first maxim to trust no man till he has somehow given a title to confidence. Not that men are generally weak, and prone to what is miscalled wrong, by reason of their natural infirmity.

Contrary to this, it is the very point of his concern, that they are so capable and so ready to be wicked in the use of their capacity. The smallest part of his concern is to look out fo uch as may fai him by their lack of energy or talent, and these are a class by themselves. To guard against the others is his principal study and they are so manv. sregree ̄, an p lancibla and false and hasten to the prey by so many methods that his only safety is in the presumption that every man will take ad vantage and do him a wrong if he can.

So, in what is called family government, everything is set upon a footing that anticipates wrong. Otherwise we might exist in a family state and never hear or think of a government as pertaining to it, any more than we now do of a government in the garden, to preside over the conduct of the flowers In- , if there is no danger of wrong-doing in children, the forming of pervers t the indulgence of wicked s tl e breaking down by wills unchastened, of all sacred principles why not suffer them to unfold naturally, as the flowers do , for even inexperience and neglect will as certainly blossom into vir ue, if virtue it can be called, as they into their own odours and colours. Contrary to this, we assume the need of govern- nent, that is of authority, command, correction, that the be ginnings of evil may be checked, and principles of virtue established. Doubtless there is such a thing as unrighteous and barbarous severity practised in the name of government ; still there must be government ; for whatever parent under takes to act on the assumption that the misdoing will be only mistake or inexperience, and no intended or blamable wrong is we understand some are now doing, in order to justify their theories), will assuredly find that something comes to pass, in the history of their children, that is a great deal more like wrong than they could wish !

Why, again, do we organize the civil state, why fence about society with laws enforcing them by severe and even sanguinary punishments ? If there is no blamable wrong in the world or langer of any, why so careful to defend ourselves against what our laws, by a mistake, call wrongs or crimes ; such as frauds forgeries, robberies, violations of liberty, character, and chastity murders, assassinations ? Why these manifold acts of penal legislation against wrong-doing, if wrong, as a matter of blame t of the question, or if nothing has ever occurred in the world to suggest the fact, and discover the danger of wrong ? The answer to all this will be, that what we call wrong, in this manner, is public evil, and must be restrained, but still is not really blamable, because it takes place under laws of nature, and by natural necessity. Are we then expecting, in this manner, to punish and put a stop to the laws of nature ? and so to perform, by legislation, the miracles we deny in our argu ments ? What means this array of courts, constables, and marshals, the grated prisons, the hurdles and scaffolds, the solemn farce of trials and penal sentences ? Are they simply barriers or institutes of defence, in which we array causes against the harmful action of other causes, as the Hollanders raise dykes against the sea ? Then why do we call this "*crimi nal law ?*" and why has it never occurred to the Hollanders to conceive that their dykes are raised against the criminal mis doings of the sea ?

Besides, we are afraid even of the law ; trying, by every method possible, to invent checks and balances against usurpa tions and abuses of power ; so to make power responsible, and to hedge about even our tribunals of justice by penal enactments against bribery, connivance, and arbitrary contempt of law ; as if wanting still some defence against even our defenders, and the more terrible wrongs they are like to perpetrate, in the abuse of those powers which have been committed to their hands. And then, again, when the people, groaning for long years under the misrule of a tyrant, rise up against him, insti gated by the woes they have suffered, and pluck him down from his throne, bring him to solemn trial and sentence him to die, do they lay no blame on his head, or do they only cut off the thing, as the blameless impediment to their rights and liberties ?

We perceive, in this manner, how the whole superstructure of the civil order rests on the conviction that sin is in the world. We assume it as a fact, the terrible fact, of human existence. No one doubts it, save here and there some busy Sophist, who thinks to hold his theories against all fact and experience, and against the spontaneous, practical judgments of the race—protected, while he does it, in the very liberty of his mind, and the life of his body, by laws that, under his theories, might as well set themselves to forbid the fermentation of substances, or to arraign and punish the poisonous growth of vegetables.

We have still another class of proofs, that are more subtle and closer to what may be called the latent sense of the soul ; and for just that reason, as much more convincing, when once they are brought into the light ; we speak of certain sentiments that appear to be universal, and the natural validity of which we never suspect.

Take, for a first example, the sentiment or virtue of forgive ness. Does any one doubt the reality of forgiveness ? does any one refuse to commend forgiveness as a necessary and even noble virtue ? Forgiveness to what ? Forgiveness to cause and effect, forgiveness to the weather, forgiveness to the mildew, or the fly that brings the blasted harvest ? No ! forgiveness to wrong, blamable and guilty wrong. Forgiveness and wrong are relative terms. If there is nothing to blame there is no thing to forgive. One of two things, then, must be true ; either that there has been some blamable wrong in the world, or else that the forgiveness we think of, speak of, inculcate, and com mend, is a baseless phantom, out of all reality, as destitute of dignity and beauty as of solidity and truth. Indeed, there is no place in human language for the word, any more than for the naming of a sixth sense that does not exist.

The pleasure we take in satire may be cited as another example. This pleasure consists in cauterizing, or seeing cauterized by wit, the perverse follies, the abortive pride, or the absurd airs and manners of such as morally deserve this kind of treatment. Satire supposes a free and responsible subject, who might be seriously blamed, but can be more efficiently treated by this lighter method, which, instead of denouncing the guilt, plays off the absurdities, and mocks the sorry figure of sin. Satire supposes demerit, or a blamable defect of virtue ; and, where the mark is too high to be reached by rebuke or civil indictment, even crime may be fitly chastised by it. The point to be distinctly noted is, that there is no place for satire, and we have no sympathy with it, except where there is, or is supposed to be, some kind of moral delinquency or ill desert. No poet thinks to satirize the sea, or a snow storm, or a club foot, or a monkey, or a fool. But he takes a man, a sinning man, who has deformed himself by his excesses, perversities, or crimes, and against him invokes the terrible Nemesis of wit and satire. Regarding him simply as a thing, under the laws of cause and effect, we should have as little satisfaction or pleasure in the infliction, as if it were laid upon a falling body.

We have yet another and sublimer illustration, in the abysses of the tragic sentiment—that which imparts an interest so profound to human history, to the novel and the drama, and even to the crucifixion of Jesus himself. The staple matter of emotion, all that so profoundly moves our feeling in these records of fact and fiction, is that here we look upon the conflict of good and bad powers, the glory and suffering of one, the hellish art and malice of the other, followed or not followed by the sublime vindications of providential justice. It is the war, actual or imagined, of beauty and deformity, good and evil, in their higher examples. In this view, we have a deeper sense of awe, a vaster movement of feeling, in the contemplation of a man, a mere human creature, in a character demonized by passion, than we have in the rage of the sea, or the bursting fire-storm of a volcano ; because we regard him as a power—a bad will doing battle with God and the world. Be it a Mac beth, an Othello, a Richard, a Faust, a Napoleon, or only the Jew Fagin, we follow him to his end, quivering as under some bad spell, only then to breathe again with freedom, when the storm of his destiny is over, and the wild fiery mystery that struggled in his passion is solved. But suppose it were to come to us, in the heat of our tragic exultation, as a real conviction, that these characters are, after all, only natural effects, mere frictions of things, acting from no free power in themselves ; forthwith, at the instant, every feeling of interest vanishes, and we care no more for their petty tumults than we do for the effervescence of a salt, or the skim that mantles a pool. All tragic movement ceases when the powers make their exit ; for, if now we call them men, they yet are only things, like Lion, Wall, and Moonshine, left to fill the stage with their absurd mockeries. What means it now for the Lady Macbeth to be crying to the blood, "Out, damned spot !" if there is no longer any such thing as a damned spot of guilt in her mur derous soul ? Expunge the faith of that, and the rage of her remorse turns at once to comedy—that, and nothing more.

Now, in these and other like sentiments, constantly brought into play, spontaneous, clear of all affectation, never questioned as absurdities or fictions, we encounter some of the sublimest, most irresistible evidences that men are capable of sin, and are

in it. If it is not so, then it is very clear that all the deepest
sentiments of the human bosom are only impostures of natural
weakness, destitute of dignity as of truth.

It remains to add that the objections offered to disprove the
existence of sin, and the solutions of what is called sin, advanced
by the naturalists, are insufficient and futile, and even imply
the fact itself. Most of these have been already answered in
the course of our argument, such as that the acting of a
creature against God is inconceivable ; for such a capacity was
shown to be included in the very conception of a free agent or
power ; that if God really desires no sin, He has all force to
prevent it ; for a power, it was shown, is not immediately con
trollable by force ;—that sin supposes a breach of God's system ;
for His system is a system, we have seen, not of things, but of
powers, and maintains the organic *nisus* of its aim as perfectly
among the discords it has undertaken to reduce and assimilate,
as if no act of discord had occurred. Meantime it will be seen
that the notion of evil, most commonly advanced by the natu
ralizing sceptics, is one that really involves and admits the
guilt of sin, even though advanced to clear it of the element of
guilt. " *Misdirection* " is the word they apply—they call it
misdirection—and in this, or something answering to this, they
universally agree. Even where there is only a partially deve
loped system of naturalism, and the existence of sin is not for
mally denied, a certain affinity for this word will be discovered.
Thus Mr Parker, speaking of piracy, war, and the slave trade,
suggests that these and similar evils are wrongs that come of
the "abuse, misdirection, and disease of human nature."[1] This
word *misdirection* has the advantage that it slips all recognition
of blame or responsibility, because it brings into view no real
agency or responsible agent. And hence it becomes a favourite
word, and is formally proposed by many advocates of naturalism
as the philosophic synonym of sin.

Be it so, then ; put it down as agreed that sin is misdirec
tion, and that so far there is a real something in it. Then
comes the question, Who is it, what is it, that misdirects ? Is
the misdirection of God ? That will not be said. Mr Parker
uses also, it will be observed, the term " *disease*." Will it then
be said that piracy, war, and the slave trade, are the misdirec-

[1] *Discourses of Religion*, p. 13.

tions only of disease, as when the hand of a lunatic, misdirected by a pressure on the brain, takes the life of his friend? Was it only for such innocent misdirection as this that Mr Parker inveighed so bitterly against the great statesman of New Eng land as having bowed himself to slavery? Was it then the misdirection of cause and effect in the constituent principles of human nature? This indeed appears to be intimated in another place, when it is declared that "discordant causes have pro duced effects not harmonious."[1] Is the boasted system, then, of nature a discordant, blundering, misdirecting system? If so, it should not be wholly incredible that nature may sometime blunder into a miracle. Is it then given us, for our privilege, to look over the sad inventory of the world's history, the cor ruptions of truth and religion, the bloody persecutions, the mas sacres of the good, the revolutions against oppressions and oppressors, and the combinations of power to crush them, if suc cessful, caste, slavery and the slave trade, piracy and war, tramping in blood over desolated cities and empires—can we look on these and have it as our soft impeachment to say, that they are only the misdirections of discordant causes in human nature? That has never been the sense of mankind, and never can be. There is no account to be made of these misdirections, till we bring into view man as he is, a power capable of mis directing himself and guilty in it, because he does it, swayed by no causes in or out of himself, but by his own self-determining will.

Doubtless there is abundance of misdirection; almost every thing we know is misdirected; the world is full of it; the whole creation groaneth in the sorrows, wrongs, punishments, and pe'ns of it. And then we have it as the true account of all, that ma. is the grand misdirector. He turns God's world into a hell of misdirection, and that is his sin. Apart from this, any such thing as misdirection is inconceivable. Nature yields no such thing; and if man is a part only of nature, under her necessary laws of cause and effect, there will be as little place for misdirection in his activities, as there is in the laws of chemistry, or even of the solar system. The plea of misdirec tion, therefore, is itself a concession of the fact of sin, which fact we now assume to be sufficiently established to support and be a sure foundation for our future argument.

. [1] *Discourses of Religion.* p. 12.

CHAPTER VI.

THE CONSEQUENCES OF SIN.

IT is very evident that, if sin is a fact, it must be followed
by important consequences ; for, as it has a moral significance
considered in the aspect of blameworthiness, guilt, penal desert,
and remorse, so also it has a dynamic force, considered as acting
on the physical order and sphere of nature ; in the contact and
surrounding of which its transgressions take effect. In one view,
it is the fall of virtue ; in the other, it is the disorder and penal
dislocation both of the soul and of the world. As crime, it
demolishes the sacred and supernatural interests of character ;
as a force, operating through and among the retributive causes
arranged for the vindication of God's law, it is the disruption of
nature, a shock of disorder and pain that unsettles the apparent
harmony of things, and reduces the world to a state of imperfect
or questionable beauty.

What I now propose, then, is the investigation of sin regarded in the latter of these two aspects ; or to show what consequences it operates or provokes in the field of nature.

It is not to be supposed that sin has power to annul or dis-
continue any one of the laws of nature. The same laws are in
action after the sin, or under it, as before. And yet, these laws
continuing the same, it is conceivable that sin may effect what
is really, and to no small extent, a new resolution or combina
tion, which is, to the ideally perfect state of nature, what dis
order is to order, deformity to beauty, pain to peace. This, of
course, it will do, if at all, by a force exerted in the material
world, and through the laws of nature.

At the point of his will, man is a force, we have seen, outside
of nature ; a being supernatural, because he is able to act on

the chain of cause and effect in nature from without the chain. It follows then, of course, that by acting in this manner upon nature, he can vary the action of nature from what would be its action, were there no such thing as a force external to the scheme. Nature, indeed, is submitted to him, as we have seen, for this very purpose ; to be varied in its action by his action, to receive and return his action, so to be the field and medium of his exercise.

Thus it is a favourite doctrine of our times, that the laws of the world are retributive ; so that every sin or departure from virtue will be faithfully and relentlessly punished. The very world, we say, is a moral economy, and is so arranged under its laws, that retribution follows at the heels of all sin. And by this fact of retribution, we mean that disease, pain, sorrow, de formity, weakness, disappointment, defeat, all sorts of groanings, all sizes and shapes of misery, wait upon wrong-doers, and when challenged by their sin, come forth to handle them with their rugged and powerful discipline. We conceive that, in this way, the aspects of human society and the world are, to a consider able degree, determined. But we do not always observe that nature is, by the supposition, just so far displayed under a vari ation of disorder and disease. First appear the wrongs to be chastised, which are not included in the causations of nature, otherwise they were blameless : then the laws of nature, met by these provocations, commence a retributive action, such as nature unprovoked would never display. The sin has fallen into nature as a grain of sand into the eye ; and as the eye is the same organ that it was before, having the same laws, and is yet so far changed as to be an organ of pain rather than of sight, so it is with the laws of nature, in their penal and retri butive action now begun. Sin, therefore, is, by the supposition, such a force as may suffice, in a society and world of sin, to vary the combinations and display a new resolution of the ac tivities of nature. The laws remain, but they are met and pro voked by a new ingredient not included in nature ; and so the whole field of nature, otherwise a realm of harmony, and peace, and beauty, takes a look of discord, and with many traces of its original glory left, displays the tokens also of a prison and an hospital.

Thus far we have spoken of the power there is in sin to pro voke a different action of natural causes. It also has a direct action upon nature to produce other conjunctions of causes, and so other results. The laws all continue their action as before, but the sin committed varies the combinations subject to their action, and in that manner the order of their working. Indeed, we have seen that nature is, to a certain extent, submitted by her laws to the action of free supernatural agents; which im plies that her action can be varied by their sovereignty without displacing the laws, nay, in virtue rather of the submission they are appointed to enforce. I thrust my hand, for example, into the fire, producing thus a new conjunction of causes, viz., fire, and the tissues of the hand; and the result corresponds—a state of suffering and partial disorganization. In doing this, I have acted only through the laws of nature—the nervous cord has carried down my mandate to the muscles of the arm, the muscles have contracted obediently to the mandate, the fire has done its part, the nerves of sensation have brought back their report, all in due order, but the result is a pain or loss of the injured member, as opposite to anything mere nature would have wrought by her own combinations as if it were the fruit of a miracle. So it is with all the crimes of violence, robbery, murder, assassination. The knife in the assassin's hand is a knife, doing what a knife should, by the laws which determine its properties. The heart of the victim is a heart beating on, subject to its laws, and, when it is pierced, driving out the blood from his opened side, as certainly as it before drove the living flood through the circulations of the body. But the thrust of the knife, which is from the assassin's will, makes a conjunction which nature by her laws alone would never make, and by force of this the victim dies. In like manner, a poison administered acts by its own laws in the body of the victim, which body also acts according to its laws, and the re sult ensuing is death; which death is attributable, not to the scheme of nature, but to a false conjunction of circumstances that was brought to pass wickedly by a human will. In all these cases, the results of pain, disorder, and death, are pro perly said to be unnatural; being, in a sense, violations of nature. The scheme of nature included no such results. They are disorders and dislocations made by the misconjunction or abuse of causes in the scheme of nature. And the same will be true of all the events that follow, in the vast complications and chains of causes, to the end of the world. Whatever mischief or unnatural result is thus brought to pass by sin, will be the first link of an endless chain of results not included in the scheme of nature, and so the beginning of an ever-widening circle of disturbance.   And this is the true account of evil.

But it will occur to some, that all human activities, the good as well as the bad, are producing new conjunctions of causes that otherwise would not exist.   Mere nature will never set a wheel to the waterfall, or adjust the substances that compose a house or a steamboat.   How then does it appear that the results of sin are called dislocations or disorders, or regarded as unnatural, with any great propriety than the results of virtuous industry and all right action ?   Because, we answer, the scheme of nature is adjusted for uses, not for abuses ; for improvement, culture, comfort, and advancing productiveness ; not for destruction or corruption.   Therefore it consists with the scheme of nature that water-wheels, houses, and steamboats should be built ; for all the substances and powers of nature are given to be harnessed for service, and when they are, it is no dislocation, but only a fulfilling of the natural order.

We come, also, to the same result by another and different process ; viz., by considering what sin is in its relation to God and His works.   In its moral conception, it is an act against God, or the will and authority of God.   And, since God is everywhere consistent with Himself, setting all His creations in harmony with His principles, it is of course an act against the physical order, as truly as against the moral and spiritual. Taken as a dynamic, therefore, it wars with the scheme of nature, and fills it with the turmoil of its disorders and per versities.   Or, if we take the concrete, speaking of the sinner himself, he is a substance, in a world of substances, acting as he was not made to act.   He was not made to sin, and the world was not made to help him to sin.   The mind of God being wholly against sin, the cast of every world and substance is repugnant to sin.   The transgressor, therefore, is a free power acting against God morally, and physically against the cast of every world and substance of God—acting in or among the worlds and substances as he was not made to act.

This, too, is the sentence of consciousness.   The wrong-doer says within himself—" I was not made to act thus, no laws of cause and effect, acting through me, did the deed.   I did it myself, therefore am I guilty. Had I been made for the sin, it had been no sin, but only a fulfilment of the ends included in my substance." And how terribly is this verdict certified by the discovery that the world refuses to bless him, and that all he does upon it is a work of deformity, shame, and disorder. The very substances of the world answer, as it were, in groans, to the violations of his guilty practice.

Suppose, then, what all natural philosophers assume, that nature, considered as a realm of cause and effect, is a perfect system of order; what must take place in that system, when some one substance, no matter what, begins to act as it was not made to act? What can follow, but some general disturbance of the ideal harmony of the system itself? It will be as if some wheel or member in a watch had been touched by a magnet, and began to have an action thus not intended by the maker; every other wheel and member will be affected by the vice of the one. Or it will be as if some planet or star, taking its own way, were to set itself on acting as it was not made to act; instantly the shock of disorder is felt by every other member of the system. Or we may draw an illustration, closer to probability, from the vital forms of physiology. A vital creature is a kind of unit or little universe, fashioned by the life. Thus an egg is a complete vital system, having all its vessels, ducts, fluids, quantities, and qualities, arranged to meet the action of the embryonic germ. Suppose now, in the process of incubation, that some small speck, or point of matter, under the shell, should begin, as the germ quickens, to act as it was not made to act, or against the internal harmony of the process going on, what must be the result? Either a disease, manifestly, that stops the process, or else a deformity; a chick without a wing, or with one too many, or in some way imperfectly organized. What then must follow, when a whole order of substances called men, having an immense power over the lines of causes in the world, not only begin, but for thousands of years continue, and that on so large a scale that history itself is scarcely more than a record of the fact, to act as they were not made to act? We have only to raise this question to see that the scheme of nature is marred, corrupted, dislocated by innumerable disturbances and disorders. Her laws all continue, but her conjunctions of causes are unnatural. Im mense transformations are wrought, which represent, on a large scale, the repugnant, disorderly fact of sin. Indeed, what we call nature must be rather a condition of unnature ; apostolically represented, a whole creation groaning and travailing in pain together with man, in the disorder consequent on his sin.

The conclusion at which we thus arrive is one that will be practically verified by inspection. Let us undertake, then, a brief survey of the great departments of human existence and the world, and discover, as far as we are able, the extent of the evil consequences wrought by sin.

We begin with the soul or with souls. The soul, in its normal state, including the will or supernatural power, together with the involuntary powers subordinated to it by their laws, is an instrument tuned by the key-note of the conscience, viz., *right*, to sound harmoniously with it ; or it is a fluid, we may say, whose form, or law of crystallization is the conscience. And then it follows that, if the will breaks into revolt, the instrument is mistuned in every string, the fluid shaken becomes a shapeless, opaque mass, without unity or crystalline order. Or, if we resort to the analogies of vital phenomena, which are still closer, a revolted will is to the soul, or in it, what a foreign unreducible substance is in the vital and vascular system of the egg, or (to repeat an illustration) what a grain of sand is in the eye—the soul has become a weeping organ, not an organ simply of sight. Given the fact of sin, the fact of a fatal breach in the normal state, or constitutional order of the soul, follows of necessity. And exactly this we shall see, if we look in upon its secret chambers and watch the motions of sins in the confused ferment they raise—the perceptions discoloured, the judgments unable to hold their scales steadily because of the fierce gusts of passion, the thoughts huddling by in crowds of wild suggestions, the imagination haunted by ugly and disgustful shapes, the appetites contesting with reason, the senses victorious over faith, anger blowing the overheated fires of malice, low jealousies sulking in dark angles of the soul, and envies baser still hiding under the skim of its green-mantled pools—all the powers that should be strung in harmony loosened from each other, and brewing in hopeless and helpless confusion ; the conscience meantime thundering wrathfully above and shooting down hot bolts of judgment, and the pallid fears hurrying wildly about with their brimstone torches— these are the motions of sins, the Tartarian landscape of the soul and its disorders, when self-government is gone and the

constituent integrity is dissolved.   We cannot call it the
natural state of man, nature disowns it.   No one that looks in
upon the ferment of its morbid, contesting, rasping, restive,
uncontrollable action can imagine, for a moment, that he looks
upon the sweet, primal order of life and nature.   No name
sufficiently describes it, unless we coin a name and call it a
condition of unnature.

Not that any law of the soul's nature is discontinued, or
that any capacity which makes one a proper man is taken away
by the bad inheritance, as appears to be the view of some
theologians; every function of thought and feeling remains,
every mental law continues to run; the disorder is that of
functions abused and laws of operation provoked to a penal and
retributive action, by the misdoings of an evil will.   Though it
is become, in this manner, a weeping organ, as we just now
intimated, still it is an organ of sight; only it sees through
tears.   And the profound reality of the disorder appears in the
fact that the will by which it was wrought cannot, unassisted,
repair it.   To do this, in fact, is much the same kind of impos
sibility—the phrenologists will say precisely the same—as for
a man who has disorganized his brain by over-exertion, or by
steeping it in opium, or drenching it in alcohol, to take hold, by
his will, of the millions of ducts and fibres woven together in
the mysterious net-work of its substance, and bring them all back
into the spontaneous order of health and spiritual integrity.

No! it is one thing to break or shatter an organization, and
a very different to restore it.   Almost any one can break an
egg, but not all the chemists in the world can make one whole,
or restore even so much as the slightest fracture of the shell.
As little can a man will back, into order and tune, this fear
fully vast and delicate complication of faculties; which indeed
he cannot even conceive, except in the crudest manner, by the
study of a life.

It is important also, considering the moral reactions of the
body, and especially the great fact of a propagation of the
species, to notice the disorganizing effect of sin in the body.
Body and soul, as long as they subsist in their organized state,
are a strict unity.   The abuses of one are abuses also of the
other, the disturbances and diseases of one disturb and disease
the other.   The fortunes of the body must, in this way, follow

the fortunes of the soul, whose organ it is. Sin has all its
working too in the working of the brain. To think an evil
thought, indulge a wicked purpose or passion, will, in this view,
be much as if the sin had brought in a grain of sand and lodged
it in the tissues of the brain. What then must be the effect,
when every path in its curious net-work of intelligence is travel
led, year by year, by the insulting myriads of sinning thought,
hardened by the tramp of their feet, and dusted by their
smoky trail.

But we are speaking theoretically. If we turn to practical
evidences, or matters of fact, we shall see plainly enough that
what should follow, in the effects of sin upon the body, actually
does follow. How the vices of the appetites and passions
terminate in diseases and a final disorganization of the body, is
well understood. The false conjunction made by intemperate
drink, deluging the tissues of the body with its liquid poisons,
and reducing the body to a loathsome wreck, is not peculiar to
that vice. The condition of sin is a condition of general intem
perance. It takes away the power of self-government, loosens
the passions, and makes even the natural appetite for food an
instigator of excess. Indeed, how many of the sufferings and
infirmities even of persons called virtuous, are known by all
intelligent physicians to be only the groaning of the body under
loads habitually imposed, by the untempered and really diseased
voracity of their appetites. And if we could trace all the secret
actions of causes, how faithfully would the fevers, the rheuma
tisms, the neuralgic and hypochondriacal torments, all the grim
looking woes of dyspepsia, be seen to follow the unregulated
licence of this kind of sin. Nor is anything better understood
than that whatever vice of the mind—wounded pride, unregu
lated ambition, hatred, covetousness, fear, inordinate care—
throws the mind out of rest, throws the body out of rest also.
Thus it is that sin, in all its forms, becomes a power of bodily
disturbance, shattering the nerves, inflaming the tissues, dis
tempering the secretions, and brewing a general ferment of
disease. In one view, the body is a kind of perpetual crystalli
zation, and the crystal of true health cannot form itself under
sin, because the body has within a perpetual agitating cause
which forbids the process. If then, looking round upon the
great field of humanity, and noting the almost universal working
of disease, in so many forms and varieties that they cannot be

named or counted, we sometimes exclaim with a sigh, what an hospital the world is ! we must be dull spectators, if we stop at this, and do not also connect the remembrance that sin is in the world ; a gangrene of the mind, poisoning all the roots of health, and making visible its woes by so many woes of bodily disease and death.

The particular question, whether bodily mortality has entered the world by sin, we will not discuss. That is principally a Scripture question, and the word of Scripture is not to be assumed in my argument. There obviously might have been a mode of translation to the second life, that should have none of the painful and revolting incidents which constitute the essential reality of death. We do moreover know that a very considerable share of the diseases and deaths of our race are the natural effects of sin or wrong-doing. There is great reason also to suspect, so devastating is the power of moral evil, that the infections and deadly plagues of the world are somehow generated by this cause. They seem to have their spring in some new virus of death, and this new virus must have been somewhere and somehow distilled or generated. We cannot refer them to mineral causes, or vegetable, or animal, which are nearly invariable, and they seem, as they begin their spread at some given locality, to have a humanly personal origin. That the virus of a poisonous and deadly contagion has been generated by human vices, we know as a familiar fact of history ; which makes it the more probable that other pesti lential contagions have been generated in the deteriorated populations and sweltering vices of the East, whence our plagues are mostly derived. On this point we assert nothing as a truth positively discovered ; we only design, by these references, to suggest the possible (and to us probable) extent and power of that ferment, brewed by the instigations of sin, in the diseased populations of the world. What we suggest respecting the virus of the world's plagues may be true, or it may not ; this at least is shown beyond all question, that sin is a wide-spreading, dreadful power of bodily distemper and disorganization, which is the point of principal consequence to our argument.

Passing now to society and the disorganizing effects of sin there to appear, we see at a glance that if the soul and body

are both distempered and reduced to a state of unnature, the
great interest of society must suffer in a correspondent manner
and degree. Considered as a growth or propagation, humanity is,
in some very important sense, an organic whole. If the races
are not all descended of a single pair, but of several or even
many pairs, as is now strenuously asserted by some, both on
grounds of science and of Scripture interpretation, still it makes
no difference as regards the matter of their practical and properly religious unity. The genus humanity is still a single
genus comprehending the races, and we know from geology that
they had a begun existence. That they also sinned at the be
ginning is as clear, from the considerations already advanced,
as if they had been one. Whence it follows that descendants
of the sinning pair or pairs, born of natures thrown out of har
mony and corrupted by sin, could not, on principles of physiology
apart from Scripture teachings, be unaffected by the distempers
of their parentage. They must be constituently injured or
depravated. It is not even supposable that organic natures,
injured and disordered, as we have seen that human bodies are
by sin, should propagate their life in a progeny unmarred and
perfect. If we speak of sin as action, their children may be
innocent, and so far may reveal the loveliness of innocence;
still the crystalline order is broken; the passions, tempers,
appetites, are not in the proportions of harmony and reason;
the balance of original health is gone by anticipation; and a
distempered action is begun, whose affinities sort with evil
rather than with good. It is as if by their own sin they had
just so far distempered their organization. Thus far the fruit
of sin is in them. And this the Scriptures, in a certain popu
lar, comprehensive way, sometimes call "sin;" because it is a
condition of depravation that may well enough be taken as the
root of a guilty, sinning life. They do not undertake to settle
metaphysically the point where personal guilt commences, but
only suit their convenience in a comprehensive term that desig
nates the race as sinners; passing by those speculative ques
tions that only divert attention from the salvation provided for a
world of sinners. The doctrine of physiology, therefore, is the
doctrine of original sin, and we are held to inevitable orthodoxy
by it, even if the Scriptures are cast away.

But if the laws of propagation contain the fact, in this manner,
of an organic depravation of humanity or human society, under

sin once broken loose, many will apprehend in such a fact some
ground of impeachment against God, as if He had set us on our
trial under terms of the sorest disadvantage. If we start, they
ask, under conditions of hereditary damage, with natures depra
vated and affinities already distempered by the sin of proge itors,

uly as if we had commenced the bad life ourselve , hat s
our bad life when we begin it but the natural issue of our hope
less misbegotten constitution? It is no sufficient answer to
say hat no blame attaches to the mere depravation supposed
whether it be called sin or by any other name ; it shocks them
to hear it even suggested that a good being like God can ha
set us forth in our trial under such immense disadvantages
Probably enough they assail the doctrine of inherited depravity
in terms of fiery denunciation, whether taken as a dogma set up by
th ologians, or as being affirmed by Christian revelation itself,
not observing that it is the inevitable fact also of human history
——, ————— ——— ——— —— ——, a necessary deduction even of
physiological science.

Now, so far from admitting the supposed disadvantage incurred by this organic depravation of the race, or the mode
of existence to which it pertains as a natural incident, we are
led to an opinion exactly opposite. Indeed, there appears to be
no other way possible, in which the race could have been set
—— —— ——— ———— with as good chances of a successful and
happy issue.

Thus, taking it for granted that God is to create a moral
population or a population of free intelligences, that, having a
begun existence, are to be educated into and finally established
in good there were obviously two methods possible. They
might always be created outright in full volume, like so many
Adams, only to exist independently and apart from all repro
ductive arrangements, or they might be introduced, as we are,
in the frail and barely initiated existence of the infantile state,
each generation born of the preceding, and altogether composing
a rigidly constituent organic unity of races.

In the former case they would have the advantage of a
perfectly uncorrupted nature, and, if that be any advantage, of
ma   ty in what may be called the raw staple of their
functions But such advantages amount to scarcely more than
the opportunity of a greater and more tremendous peril · for
)eing all, by supposition, under the same conditions privative

with the first man of Scripture,[1] they would as certainly do the
same things, descending to the same bad experiment, to be in
volved in the came consequent fall and disorder. They would
only be more strictly original in their depravation, having it as
the fruit of their own guilty choices.

And then, as regards all mitigating and restoring influences,
the comparative disadvantage would be immense. Self-centred
now, every man in his sin, and having no ligatures of race and
family and family affection to bind them together, the selfish
ness of their fall would be unqualified, softened by no mitiga
tions. Spiritual love they cannot understand, because they
never have felt the natural love of sex, family, and kindred, by
which under conditions of propagation, a kind of inevitable
first-stage virtue is instituted ; such as mitigates the severities
of sin, softens the sentiments to a social, tender play, and offers
to the mind a type, everywhere present, of the beauty and true
joy of a disinterested spiritual benevolence. They compose
instead a burly prison-gang of probationers, linked together by
no ties of consanguinity, reflecting no traces of family likeness,
bent to each other's and God's love by no dear memories.
Society there is none. Law is impossible. Society and law
suppose conditions of organic unity already prepared. Every
man for himself, is the grand maxim of life ; for all are atoms
together in the medley of the common selfishness ; only the
old atoms have an immense advantage over the young ones
fresh arrived ; for these new-comers of probation come, of
course, to the prey, having no guardians or protectors, and no
tender sentiments of care and kindred prepared to shelter them
and smooth their way. Besides, the world into which they
come must have been already fouled and disordered by the sin
of the prior populations, and must therefore be a frame of being
wholly inappropriate to their new-created innocence ; or else
if not thus disordered, must have been a casement of iron, too
rigid and impassive to receive any injury from sin, and therefore
incapable of any retributive discipline returned upon it. There
is, in short, no condition of trial which, after all, is seen to be
so utterly forbidding and hopeless as just this state of Adamic
innocence, independence, and maturity of faculty, which many
are so ready to require of God, as the only method of promise
and fair advantage in the beginning of a responsible life.

[1] Chapter iv. p. 71.

How different the condition realized where men are propa·
gated as a race or races! Then are they linked together by a
necessary, constituent, anticipative love. Moved by this love,
the progenitors are immediately set to a work of care and hope
beautifully opposite to the proper selfishness of their
The delicate and tender being received to their embrace
circulates their blood, will bear their name, and is looked upon
even by their selfishness, as a multiplied and dearer self They
are even made to feel, in a lower and more rudimental way
what joy there is in a disinterested love ; and they pour out
their fondness in ways that even try their invention, instigated
by the compulsory bliss of sacrifice. They want the best things
too for their child, even his virtue ; and probably enough his
religious virtue ; for they dread the bitter woes of wrong-doing
his is true, at least, of all but such as have fallen below
ature in their vices, and ceased to hear her voice. They even
undertake to be a providence, and do for their child all which
the love of God, even till now rejected, has been seeking to do
for themselves, commanding him away from wrong, and warn
ing him faithfully of its dangers. Besides, it is a great point
in the scheme of propagated life, that the child learns how to
be grown, so to speak, into, and exist in, another will ; which is
an immense advantage to the religious nurture, even where the
parental character is not good. He is not like a population of
untutored, unregulated Adams, who have just come to the finding
of a man s will in them, and do not know how to use it, least of
all how to sink it obediently in the sovereign will and authority
of God. The child's will grew in authority, and he comes out
gently in the reverence of a subordinated habit, to choose the
way of obedience, having his religious conscience configured and
trained by a kind of family conscience previously developed
There is almost no family, therefore,—none except the very
worst and most depraved,—in which the rule of the house is not
a great spiritual benefit, and a means even of religious virtue
How much more, where the odour of a heavenly piety fills the
house and sanctifies the atmosphere of life itself ? Instead of
being set forth as an overgrown man, issued from the Creator's
hand to make the tremendous choice, undirected by experience
he is gently inducted, as it were, by choices of parents before
his own, into the habit and accepted practice of all holy obedi
ence ; growing up in the nurture of their grace, as truly as of

their natural affection. Furthermore, as corruption or deprava.
tion is propagated under well-known laws of physiology, what
are we to think but that a regenerate life may be also propa
gated, and that so the Scripture truth of a sanctification from
the womb may some time cease to be a thing remarkable and
become a commonly expected fact ? And then, if a point
should finally be reached, under the sublime *palingennesia* of
redemption, when Christian faith, together with its fruits of
nurture and sanctified propagation, should be nearly or quite
universal, and the world, which is now in its infancy, should
roll on millions of ages after, training its immense populations
for the skies, how magnificently preponderant the advantages of
the plan of propagation, which at first we thought could be
only a plan to set us out in the wrong, and sacrifice our virtue
by anticipation !

This comparison, which might otherwise seem to be a digres
sion, will effectually remove those false impressions so generally
prevalent concerning God's equity in the fact of natural corrup
tion ; and if this be done, a chief impediment to all right
conceptions of the human state. as affected by sin, will be re
moved. In this manner, wholly apart from the Scriptures,
instructed only by the laws of physiology, we discover the
certain truth of an organic fall or social lapse in the race ; we
find humanity broken, disordered, plunged into unnature by
sin ; but dark and fearful as the state may be, there is nothing
in it unhopeful, nothing to accuse. We are only where we
should be, each by his own act, if we were created indepen.
dently, with immense advantages added to mitigate the hope.
lessness of our disorder.

It is very true that, under these physiological terms of pro
pagation, society falls or goes down as a unit, and evil becomes
in a sense organic in the earth. The bad inheritance passes,
and fears, frauds, crimes against property, character, and life,
abuses of power, oppressions of the weak, persecutions of the
good, piracies, wars of revolt, and wars of conquest, are the
staple of the world's bitter history. All that Mr Fourier has
said of society, in its practical operation, is true ; it is a pitiless
and dreadful power, as fallen society should be. And yet it is
a condition of existence far less dreadful than it would be, if the
organic force of natural affinities and affections were not opera
tive still, in the desolations of evil, to produce institutions,

construct nations,[1] and establish a condition of qualified unity and protection. Otherwise, or existing only as separate units, in no terms of consanguinity, we should probably fall into a state of utter non-organization, or, what is the same, of univer sal prey. The grand woe of society, therefore, is not, as this new prophet of science teaches, the bad organization of society ; but that good organization, originally beautiful and beneficent, can only mitigate, but cannot shut away, the evils by which it is infested. The line of propagation is, in one view, the line of transmission by which evil passes ; but it is, at the same time, a sure spring of solidarity and organific power, by which all the principal checks and mitigations of evil, save those which are brought in with the grace of supernatural redemption, are supplied. Otherwise the state of evil, untransmitted and purely original in all, would make a hell of anarchy, unendur able and final.

Nothing, in this view, could be more superficial than Mr Fourier's conception of the woes of society. Ignoring at the outset the existence of sin, and assuming that every man comes from the hand of his Maker in a state that represents the Maker's integrity, even as the stars do, he lays it down as a fundamental maxim of science, that all the passions and appe tites of the race are, like gravity itself, instincts that reach after order—in his own rather pretentious and extra scientific language, that " attractions are proportioned to destinies." The attrac tions of the worlds of matter adjust their positions ; so the perfect order of the heavens. So the attractions of men, to wit, their lusts, appetites, passions, will adjust the perfect order of society. Why, then, do they not ? Because of social mal-organization. And, with so many impulses or passions gravitating all toward order, whence came the mal-organization ?—why are not the heavens, too, mal-organized, and with as good right ? But I refer to these insane theories of social science, not for any purpose of argument against them, but simply to get light and shade for my subject. The woe of society is deeper and more difficult ; not to be mended by artificial reconstructions apart from all ties of consanguinity, not by contracts of good will and mutual service, not by bonds of interest and licenses of passion. It lies, first of all, in the fall of man himself, which includes the

1 The word itself represents upon its face the common life of a common root or parentage.

fall of passion ; a fall which is mitigated even compulsorily by the organific power of consanguinity, but can, by no human wisdom, or skill, or combination, be restored. Organization will do what it can, it will be more or less bad as it is more or less perverted by injustice, or misdirected and baffled by the instigations of selfishness and the bad affinities and demonized passions of sin.

It now remains to carry our inquest one step farther. If sin has power, taken as a dynamic, to affect the soul, the body, and society, in the manner already indicated, reducing all these departments of nature to a state unnatural, it should not be incredible that it may also have power to produce a like disorder in the material or physical world. The immense power of the human will over the physical substances of the world and the conjunctions of its causes, is seldom adequately conceived. Almost everything, up to the moon, is capable of being somehow varied or affected by it. Being a force supernatural, it is con tinually playing itself into the chemistries and external com binations of matter, converting shapes, reducing or increasing quantities, transferring positions, framing and dismembering conjunctions, turning poisons into medicines, and reducing fruits to poisons, till at length scarcely anything is left in its properly natural state. Some of these changes, which it is the toil of human life to produce, are beneficent ; and a multitude of others represent, alas ! too faithfully, the prime distinction of sin ; the acting of a power against God, or as it was not made to act. Could we only bring together into a complete inventory all the new structures, compositions, inventions, shapes, qualities, already produced by man, which are, in fact, the furniture only of his sin—means of self-indulgence, instruments of violence, shows of pride, instigations of appetite, incitements and institutes of corrupt pleasure—all the leprosies and leper-houses of vice, the prisons of oppression, the hospitals and battle-fields of war, we should see a face put on the world which God never gave it, and which only represents the bad conversion it has suffered, under the immense and ever-industrious perversities of sin.

But we must carry our search to a point that is deeper and more significant. In what is called nature, we find a large admixture of signs or objects, which certainly do not belong to an ideal state of beauty, and do not, therefore, represent the mind of God, whence they are supposed to come. The fact is patent everywhere, and yet the superficial and hasty multitudes appear to take it for granted, that all the creations of God are beautiful of course. They either assume it as a necessary point of reverence or deduce it as a point of reason, that whatever comes from God represents the thought of God ; being cast in the mould of His thought, which is divine beauty itself. Not only do the poets and poetasters in prose go the round of nature, sentimentalizing among her dews and flowers, and pav ing their worship at her shrine, as if the world were a gospel even of beauty; but our philosophers often teach it as a first principle, and our natural theologians assume it also in their arguments that the forms of things must represent the perfect forms of the Divine thought, by which they were fashioned It would seem that such a conceit might be dissipated by a single glance of revision ; for God is the infinite beauty, and who can imagine, looking on this or that half dry and prosy scene of nature, that it represents the infinite beauty ? The fact of creation argues no such thing. For what if it should happen to have been a part of God's design in the work to represent, not Himself only as the Pure and Perfect One the immutable throne of law and universal order, but quite as truly and in immediate proximity, to represent man to himself · that he may see both what he is for, and what he is, and strugole up out of one into the other. Then, or in that view, it would be the perfection of the world, taken in its moral adaptations that it is not perfect, and does not answer to the beauty of the creative mind, save under the large qualification specified.

And exactly this appears to be the true conception of the physical world. What does it mean, for example, that the vital organizations are continually seen to be attempting pro ducts which they cannot finish ? Thus a fruit tree covers. itself with an immense profusion of blossoms, that drop and do not set in fruit. And then, of those fruits which are set an immense number fall, strewing the ground with deaths— tokens all of an abortive attempt in nature, if we call it nature to execute more than she can finish. And this we see in all the growths of the world—they lay out more than they can perform. Is this the ideal perfection of nature, or is there some touch of unnature and disorder in it ? Is God the Creator, represented in this ? Does He put Himself before us in this manner, as a being who attempts more fruits than He can produce ? or is there a hint in it, for man, of what may come to pass in himself? an image under which he may con ceive himself and fitly represent himself in language ? a token, also, and proof of that most real abortion, to which he may bring even his immortal nature, despite of all the saving mercies of God ?

Swedenborg and his followers have a way of representing, I believe, that God creates the world through man, by which they understand that what we call the creation is a purely gerundive matter—God's perpetual act—and that he holds the work *to man*, at every stage, so as to represent him always at his present point, and act upon him fitly to his present taste. Not far off is Jonathan Edwards' conception of God's upholding of the universe—it is, in fact, a perpetual reproduction ; the creation, so called, being to His person what the image in a mirror is to the person before it, from whom it proceeds and by whom it is sustained. Indeed this latter conception runs into the other, and becomes identical with it, as soon as we take in the fact that God is always being and becoming to man, both in counsel and feeling, what is most exactly fit to man's character and want ; for, in that view God's image, otherwise called His creation, will be all the while receiving a colour from man, and will so far be configured to him. Accordingly, we look, in either view, to see the Kosmos or outward frame of things held to man, linked to his fortunes to rise and fall with him, and so, under certain limitations, to give him back his doings and represent him to himself—representing God, in fact, the more adequately that it does.

The doctrine of types in the physical world, to represent con ditions of character and changes of fortune in the spiritual, is only another conception of the same general truth. And this doctrine of types we know to be true in part ; for language itself is possible only in virtue of the fact that physical types are pro vided, as bases of words, having each a natural fitness to repre sent some spiritual truth of human life ; which is, in fact, the principal use and significance of language. Whence also it follows that if human life is disordered, perverted, reduced to a condition of unnature by sin, there must also be provided, as the necessary condition of language, types that represent so great a change ; which is equivalent to saying that the fortunes

of the outer world must, to some very great extent, follow the
fortunes of the occupant and groan with him in his disorders.

Or we are brought to a conclusion essentially the same, by
considering the complete and perfect unity of natural causes;
how they form a dynamic whole, resting in an exact balance of
mutual relationship, so that if any world or particle starts from
its orbit or position, every other world and particle feels the
change.   What then must follow when the given force or sub
stance man begins, and for long ages continues, to act as he
was not made to act; out of character, against God, refusing
place, and breaking out on every side from the general scheme
of unity and harmony, in which the creation was to be com
prehended?   What can his human disorder be, but a propa
gating cause of disorder? what his deformity within, but a
soul of deformity without, in the surroundings of the field he
occupies?

And this again is but another version of the fact that the
final causes of things are moral; the arrangement being that
natural causes shall react upon all wrong-doing, in retributive
diseases, discords, and pains, to correct and chasten the wrong;
which, indeed, is the same thing as to say that the world was
made to share the fortunes of man, and fall with him in his
fall.

Whichever of these views we take, for at bottom they all
coalesce in the same conclusion, we see at a glance, that given
the fact of sin, what we call nature can be no mere embodi
ment of God's beauty and the eternal order of His mind, but
must be, to some wide extent, a realm of deformity and abor
tion; groaning with the discords of sin, and keeping company
with it in the guilty pains of its apostasy.   Even as the apostle
says—meaning doubtless all which his words most naturally
signify—" For the whole creation groaneth and travaileth in
pain together."

We need not therefore scruple to allow and also to maintain
the judgment, that many things we meet are not beautiful;
we should rather look for many that are not.   Thus we have
growths in the briars and thorns that do not represent the
beauty and benignity of God; but under His appointment take
on their spiny ferocity from man, whose surroundings they are,
and whose fortunes they are made to participate.   The same
may be said of loathsome and disgusting animals.   Or we may

take the pismire race for an example—a race of military vermin, who fight pitched battles, and sometimes make slaves of their captives ; representing nothing surely in God, save his purpose to reflect, in keenest mockery, the warlike chivalry and glory of man.   It was our fortune once to see a battle of these insect heroes.   On a square rod of ground it raged for two whole days, a braver field than Marathon or Waterloo, covered with the dead and dying, and with fierce enemies rolled in the dust, still fight ing on in a deadly grapple of halves, after the slender connexion of their middle part had been completely severed in the en counter.   That these creatures image God in their fight cannot be supposed, save as God may reveal, by a figure so powerful, the sense He has of what we call our glory, the bloody glory of our sin.

Under the same principle that the world is linked to man and required to represent him to himself, we are probably to account for the many and wide-spread tokens of deformity round us in the visible objects of nature.   Whoever may once set his thought to this kind of inquiry, will be amazed by the constant recurrence of deformities or things which lack the beauties of form.   After all the fine sentimentalities, lavished by rote and without discriminating thought on the works and processes of nature, he will be surprised to find that the world is not as truly a realm of beauty, as of beauty flecked by injury.   The growths are carbuncled and diseased, and the children have it for a play to fetch a perfect leaf.   Fogs and storms blur the glory of the sky, and foul days, rightly so called, interspace the bright and fair.   The earth itself displays vast deserts swept by the horrid simoom ; muddy rivers, with their fenny shores, tenanted by hideous alligators ; swamps and morasses, spreading out in provinces of quagmire, and reeking in the steam of death.   In the kingdom of life, disgusting and loathsome objects appear, too numerous to be recounted ; such as worms and the myriads of base vermin, deformed animals, dwarfs, idiots, leprosies, and the rot of cities swept by the plague ; history itself depicting the mushrooms sprouting in the bodies of the unburied dead, and the jackals howling in the chambers at their dreadful repast.   Even more significant still is the fact, because it is a fact that concerns the honour even of our personal organism, that no living man or woman is ever found to be a faultless model of beauty and proportion.   When

I

the sculptor will fashion a perfect form, he is obliged to glean for it, picking out the several parts of beauty from a hundred mal-proportioned, blemished bodies in actual life. And what is yet more striking, full three-fourths of the living races of men are so ugly, or so far divested of beauty in their mould, that no sculptor would ever think of drawing on them for a single feature !

This word *deformity*, which is properly a word of sight, may be used too in its largest and most inclusive import, to cover all the ground of the senses, together with a whole family of words in *de* or *dis*, that indicate a relation of disjunction—the dis-gusts of the taste and the smell ; the dis-easement or pain of the sensibility ; the dis-cords and the unmelodious notes that storm the offended ear of music ; the manifold braying, cawing, screeching, yelling sounds, such as would be low in a farce, but are issued still from as many badly-voiced pipes in the great organ of nature. And then, besides, we have dis-tempers, dis proportions, dis-tortions, dis-orders, de-rangements, answering all, shall we say, to the dis-location of our inward harmony, and revealing in that manner the desolating effects of our sin.

If it should be urged that all these deformities and discords are necessary contrasts, to enliven the beauty and heighten the music of nature, it is enough to answer that pain is as necessary to joy, eternal pain to eternal joy ; or better still, because the analogy is closer and more exact, that moral deformity is just as necessary in God to the sufficient impression of His moral beauty. Though, if we take them altogether in their moral import and uses—the abortions, the deformed growths and landscapes, and the strange jargon of sounds—regarding them as prepared by the Almighty Father, fitly to insphere a crea ture supernatural whom He is correcting in his sins and training unto Himself, then do they rise into real dignity and reveal a truly divine magnificence. This, we say, is indeed the tre mendous beauty of God ; and the strange, wild jargon of the world, shattered thus by sin, becomes to us a mysterious, transcendent hymn. Still it is deformity, jargon, death, and the only winning side of it is, that it answers to the woe, and meets the want of our sin.

CHAPTER VII.

ANTICIPATIVE CONSEQUENCES.

In the account offered of the consequences of sin, we have spoken of these consequences as effects transpiring under laws, and so as matters *post* in respect to the fact of sin. The result stated coincides, in all but the positive or inflictive form, with the original curse denounced on man's apostasy, as represented in the Adamic history or sin-myth, as some would call it, of the ancient Scriptures. That primal curse, it is conceived, penetrates the very ground as a doom of sterility, covers it with thorns and thistles and all manner of weeds to be subdued by labour, makes it weariness to live, brings in death with its armies of pains and terrors to hunt us out of life, and so unparadises the world. Call it then a myth, disallow the notion of a positive infliction as being unphilosophical; still the matter of the change, or general world-lapse asserted in it, is one of the grandest, most massive, best-attested truths included in human knowledge. It is just that which ought to be true under the conditions, and which we have found, by inspection also, to be true as a matter of fact.

Still there is a difficulty, or a great and hitherto insufficiently explored question, that remains. It is the question of date or time; for when we speak, as in the previous chapter, of the consequences of sin, we seem to imply that, upon or after the fact of sin, the physical order of the world, affected by the shock, underwent a great change that amounted to a fall; becoming, from that point onward, a realm of deformity and discord, as before it was not, and displaying, in all its sceneries and combinations, the tokens of a broken constitution. All which, it will readily occur to any one, cannot in that form

be true.   For the sturdy facts of science rise up to confront us
in such representations, testifying that death, and prey, and
deformed objects, and hideous monsters, were in the world long
before the arrival of man.   Nay, the rocks open their tombs and
show us that older curses than the curse, older consequences
ante-dating sin, had already set their marks on the world, and
had even made it, more than once, an Aceldama of the living
races.

"I need scarce say," remarks Hugh Miller, "that the palæ
ontologist finds no trace in nature of that golden age of the
world, of which the poets delighted to sing, when all creatures
lived together in unbroken peace, and war and bloodshed were
unknown.   Ever since animal life began upon our planet, there
have existed, in all the departments of being, carnivorous classes,
who could not live but by the death of their neighbours, and who
were armed in consequence for their destruction, like the
butcher with his knife, and the angler with his hook and
spear."[1]   This being true, the paradisiac history, as commonly
understood, is still farther off from a possible verification, un
less we suppose the curse to be there reported as a fact subse
quent, though latently incorporate before, because it is there
discovered, and plainly could not be conceived, at that time, as
the facts of future science may require.

For the true solution of this apparent collision between
geologic revelations and the paradisiac history lies in the fact,
which many have not considered, that there are two modes of
consequence, or two kinds of consequences; those which come
as effects under physical causes, and have their time as events
subsequent; and those which come anticipatively, or before the
facts whose consequences they are, because of intellectual
conditions, or because intelligence, affected by such facts, appre
hended before the time, could not act as being ignorant of them.
These two modes of consequence, and particularly the latter,
now demand our attention.

As regards the former—the consequences of suffering and
dislocation that follow sin, as effects in time subsequent—there
is happily not much requiring to be said; for the truth on that
subject is familiar, and is in fact overmuch insisted on by the
modern teachers.   Only it happens that, while they so frequently

[1] *Testimony of the Rocks,* p. 99.

make a gospel of the mere retributive principle thus arrayed against evil, they do also contrive to narrow the bad consequences of sin to a range so restricted, and to results of mischief so nearly trivial, that really nothing is involved in disobedience, except in cases of extreme viciousness and moral abandonment. They do not conceive such a thing as the real dissolution of the primal order and harmony even of the soul, and the ceasing to be any longer a complete integer, when it drops its moral in tegrity. What I have so abundantly shown in the previous chapter, they do not allow themselves to see, that any beginning or outbreak of sin carries with it the inevitable fact of a shock to the general state of order ; starting trains of penal and re tributive consequences, which have no assignable limit, and which none but a supernatural and divine agency can reverse. Anything entering into God's world, or falling out in it, that is against His will, breaks of course the crystalline order, and how far the fracture will go no one can tell.

When, therefore, we meet any given token of lapse or dis order, it may not be clear to us on mere inspection how it came in, whether among the subsequent or the anticipative consequences of sin.   Thorns and thistles—did they take on their spiny and savage armour before the sin of man, or after ? Possibly after.   No man can tell beforehand how far such a beginning of disobedience and apostasy from God might pene trate the fabric, and poison the substance, and so determine the form of growths in the world ; for, in a scheme of perfect reason, any violation of wrong travels fast and far, and no one can guess how far.   But if the geologist, opening the hidden registers of the world, finds the portrait, or even the indis putable analogon of a thistle in the stone, that is the end of the inquiry.

The substance then of what I would desire to say on this particular point is, that without some conviction of evil and pain following after sin, as its necessary effect, there could be no such thing as a practically real moral government in the world.   That such evil and pain do follow, with inevitable certainty, even as all effects follow after their causes, we perceive and almost uni versally admit; for they are distinguishable in all the four great departments of being—the body, the soul, society, and the world. And since it is theoretically true that, in any perfect system of being, the disturbance of a particle disturbs the whole, we are to

admit, without difficulty, and as it were by intellectual require
ment, that evils most remote, deepest, widest, and most com
prehensive, may be effects or inevitable sequents of human
transgression.   On this point our faith should properly be
shocked by nothing ; for it is a fact visible beforehand, all time
apart, that sin must be a grand, all-penetrating sacrament of woe
to the world that contains it.   And we shall most naturally take
all the evils we meet to be the dynamical effects of sin, till we
find them penetrating also the pre-Adamite conditions of being,
and setting their type in the registers of the geologic ages.

We come now to the matter of the anticipative consequences,
where it will be required of us to speak more carefully and to
dwell longer.

And here the first thing to be noted, as respects the conse
quences of sin in our particular world, is, that the subsequent
effects of the sin of other beings might very well bring in dis
orders here that anticipate the arrival of man.   There had
been other moral beings in existence doubtless before the creation of man.   So, in fact, the Scriptures themselves testify.
They also testify that some such were evil, and, as we are left
to judge, fixed in a reprobate character by long courses of evil.
As they are shown to have had access to our world, after we
came in as a race to possess it, so doubtless they had been
visitors and travellers in it, if we may so speak, during all the
long geologic eras that preceded our coming—hovering, it may
be, in the smoke and steam, or watching for congenial sounds
and sights among the crashing masses and grinding layers, even
before the huge monsters began to wallow in the ooze of the
waters, or the giant birds to stalk along the hardening shores.
What they did, in this or that geologic layer of the world, we of
course know not.   As little do we know in what numbers they
appeared, or by what deeds of violence and wrong they disfigured
the existing order.   We do not even know that the successive
extinctions of so many animal races, and the deformities found
in so many of the now existing races, were not somehow referrible to the audacity of their wrongs and the bitter woe of
their iniquities.   As already intimated,[1] the fencing of spirits
may be an essentially moral affair—such that having, by their
very nature, the freedom originally of the physical universe, the

<hr />

1 Chapter iv. pp. 80-84.

universe might well be visited by all such myrmidons of evil, and being so visited, might show, as a necessary consequence, the tokens of their evil contact or inhabitation. Indeed it might well enough show such tokens of their sin in worlds they had never visited ; for the universe, as we have seen, is a whole, and a shock to any part of that whole must have its effects of some kind in every other. How far the solidarity of the universe and its fortunes extends, or how many things it embraces, we certainly do not know, and are therefore not qualified to assume that " the whole creation" does not neces sarily feel the touch of every bad mind and act, and suffer some consequent disorder in every part. Finding then tokens of deformity and prey, and objects of disgust appearing in the world, long ages before it was inhabited by man, we are not hastily to infer that these are not actual consequences of sin. They may be such, in the strictest terms of retributive causality, though not as related to the sins of man. Preceding that, by long ages of time, they may yet be subsequent and penal effects, as related to older, vaster, outlying populations of sinners that had visited, or sent the shock of their sin into the world, before the human race appeared.

It is not proposed, however, to account for all the previously existing marks of evil in the world in this manner. It is most agreeable not to do it. For we shall easily convince ourselves that vast realms of consequences, and these as real as any, pre cede, and, in rational order, ought to precede their grounds or occasions. Indeed, it is the peculiar distinction of consequences mediated by intelligence that they generally go before, and pre pare the coming of events to which they relate. Whoever plants a state erects a prison, or makes the prison to be a necessary part of his plan ; which prison, though it be erected before any case of felony occurs, is just as truly a consequence of the felonies to be as if it were erected afterward, or were a natural result of such felonies. All the machinery of disci pline in a school or an army is prepared by intelligence, per ceiving beforehand the certain want of discipline hereafter to appear, and is just as truly a consequence of the want as if it were created by the want itself, without any mediation of in telligence.

So also any commander, who is managing a campaign and has gotten hold of the intended plan of his enemy, will be

utterly unable to project a plan for himself, or even to order
the manœuvres of a day, so as not to show a looking at the
secret he has gained, and also to prepare innumerable things
that are, in some sense, consequences of it. What then shall
we look for, since God's whole plan of government is, in some
highest view, a campaign against sin, and is from the beginning
projected as such, but that all the turnings of His councils and
shapings of his creations should have some discoverable refer
ence to it? And how, in that case, could they be more truly
and rigidly consequences of it? Indeed, all consequences *post*,
are, in fact, anticipative first, and are as really existent, in
the laws ordained by intelligence to bring them to pass, as they
are in their actual occurrence in time afterward. It is by no
fiction therefore, and as little by any fetch of ingenuity, that
we speak of anticipative consequences; for they are the unfail
ing distinction of every plan ordered by intelligence; every
system or scheme comprehended in the moulds of reason will
disclose, in the remotest and most subtle beginnings, marks
that relate to events future, and even to issues most remote.

This, too, so far from being any subject of wonder, is even
a kind of necessary incident of intelligence. For everything
that comes into the view of intelligence must also pass into the
plans of intelligence. How can any intelligent being frame a
plan so as to make no account of what is really in his know
ledge? Or how could the all-knowing God arrange a scheme
of providential order, just as if He did not know the coming fact
of sin, eternally present to His knowledge? Mind works under
conditions of unity, and, above all, Perfect Mind. What God
has eternally in view, therefore, as the certain fact of sin, that
fact about which all highest counsel in His government must
revolve, and upon the due management of which all most event
ful and beneficent issues in His kingdom depend, must pervade
His most ancient beginnings, and crop out in all the layers and
eras of His process, from the first chapter of creative movement,
onward. As certainly as sin is to be encountered in His plan,
its marks and consequences will be appearing anticipatively, and
all the grand arrangements and cycles of time will be somehow
preluding its approach, and the dire encounter to be maintained
with it. To create and govern a world, through long eras of
time, and great physical revulsions, yet never discover to our
view any token that He apprehends the grand cataclysm of sin

hat is approaching, till after the fact is come, He must be much
ess than a wise, all-perceiving Mind. Much room would be left
or the doubt, whether He is any mind at all; for it is the way
)f mind to weave all counsel and order into a web of visible unity.

It accords also with this general view of the subject, as related
.o mind, that our most qualified teachers in science discover so
nany tokens of premeditation, or anticipative thought, in the
arlier types and creations of the world. " Premeditation prior
.o creation "[1]—this is the grand, intellectual fact which Mr
Agassiz verifies with a confidence so calmly scientific, in his late
ntroduction to the study of Natural History. All sciences, he
shows, are in things, because the Creator's premeditative thought
.s there; every first thing accordingly shows some premeditative
:oken of every last. " Enough has been already said," he re-
narks, " to show that the leading thought which runs through
:he successions of all organized beings in past ages is manifested
igain in new combinations, in the phases of the development of
iving representatives of these different types. It exhibits every-
vhere the working of the same creative Mind, through all time,
ind upon the whole surface of the globe."[2] He passes directly
)n, accordingly, in his next section, to speak of the " Prophetic
Types among Animals," discovering, in the earlier types of
inimated being, what reads "like a prophecy" of all the types
:o come after. " There are entire families," he says, " among
:he representatives of older periods, of nearly every class of
inimals, which, in the state of their perfect development, exem
plify such prophetic relations, and afford, within the limits of the
inimal kingdom, at least, the most unexpected evidence that the
plan of the whole creation had been maturely considered long
before it was executed."[3] All this, it will be observed, by the
mere dry light of reason and of positive science, apart from any
consideration of a service to be rendered to revealed religion.

Professor Dana, in like manner, though with a somewhat
lifferent purpose, observes, in " the survey of geological facts,
a remarkable oneness of system, binding together, in a single
plan or scheme, the successive events or creations, from the earliest
coral or shell-fish to man."[4] The whole geologic series or pro
gress constitutes, in this manner, he maintains, " one grand history
with the creation of man, the last act in the drama of creation."

[1] *Essay on Classification*, p. 9.   [2] *Ibid*. p. 116.   [3] *Ibid*. p. 117.
[4] *New Englander*, vol. xvi. p. 96.

The point of conviction reached by these great masters of science, and stated thus in terms of the truest intellectual in sight, is still not the end of all reason as pertaining to the sub ject in question. If we speak of "prophetic types" fulfilled or perfected by future creations, there will, in the same manner, be types also that have their fulfilment, after all creations are ended, in the spiritual state of men, and the remotest issues and last ends of human existence. And as all that God or dains or previously creates, will have some respect to these last ends, and the conditions of trial and bad experience through which they are to be reached, it is even probable that, if we had a perfect insight of any humblest thing, be it only a mol lusc or an insect, we should find some subtle type or reference in it to the grandest and most radical facts of the spiritual history of the universe. For the premeditation of God and the intellectual unity of His thought comprehend more than any mere matter of species or frame of geological order; viz., that for which all species and all facts of science and all objects of scientific study exist.

So, also, if we speak with Professor Dana of a "remarkable oneness of system," geology is, in real fact, no system of God, except as we say it by accommodation, which doubtless he would also admit; for there is but one system, and can be only one, as there is but one systematizing mind and one last end, about which the inferior combinations, sometimes called systems, revolve. When, therefore, it is remarked that God's one system visibly comprehends all the creation, from coral and shell-fish up to man, why not also, we ask, to something farther?—to what man will do, and what will be done upon him and for him, and finally to all that he will become, when God's last end, that in which all system centres, and for which it works, is finally consummated? And what can we look for in this view but that God's premeditations about sin, the images it raises, the coun sel it requires, the deaths and abortions it works, and the new creations it necessitates, will be coming into view, in all the immense, ante-dated eras and mighty revolutions of the geologic process. By the mere unity of God's intellectual system they ought to appear, and, when they do, they will as truly be con sequences of sin as if they were mere physical effects, subsequent in time to the facts.

There is also another account to be made of these anticipative

consequences of sin, viz., that they are necessary for great and
important uses, in the economy of life, as a spiritual concern.
Were there no tokens of death, deformity, prey, and abortion,
in the geologic eras, previous to man's arrival, and were it left
us to believe that just then and there discord broke loose, and
the whole frame of paradisiac order was shaken to the fall, we
might imagine that God was overtaken by some shock for which
He was not prepared, and that the world fell out of His hands
by some oversight, which probably enough He can never effectu
ally repair.   But with so many tokens of anticipative recogni
tion found labouring, and heard groaning, through so many eras
of deaths and hard convulsions, prior to the sin they represent,
we see, every one of us, in our state of wrong-doing and denial
of God, that He understands His work from the beginning, is
taken by no surprise, meets no shock for which he is unpre
pared, and holds every part of His kingdom, even from the
foundation of the world, in fit connexion with the tragic history
of sin and salvation afterward to be transacted in it.   In part
we see the world reduced to unnature, infected with disease,
shaken by discord, marred by deformity, subsequently to the
fact of sin, just as it must be by the retributive action of causes,
or by the false conjunctions produced by the wrongs and abuses
of sin.   For the rest, it was anticipatively disordered for the
sake of order, or in terms of necessary unity and counsel, as
pertaining to the Governing Mind ; displaying thus, in clearer
and diviner evidence, the eternal insight and all-comprehending
intelligence of His appointments.   For, in being set with types
all through and from times most ancient, of suffering and de
formity, prefiguring, in that manner, the being whose sublime
struggles are to have it for their field, and showing him, when
he arrives, how Eternal Forethought has been always shaping
it to the mould of his fortunes—thus and thus only could he be
fitly assured, in the wild chaos of sin, of any such Counsel or
Power as can bring him safely through.

How magnificent also is the whole course of geology, or the
geologic eras and changes, taken as related to the future great
catastrophe of man, and the new-creating, supernatural grace of
his redemption !   It is as if, standing on some high summit, we
could see the great primordial world rolling down through gulfs
and fiery cataclysms, where all the living races die ; thence to
emerge, again and again, when the Almighty fiat calls it forth,

a new creation covered with fresh populations; passing thus through a kind of geologic eternity in so many chapters of deaths, and of darting, frisking, singing life; inaugurating so many successive geologic mornings over the smoothed graves of the previous extinct races; and preluding in this manner the strange world-history of sin and redemption, wherein all the grandest issues of existence lie.   This whole tossing, rending, recomposing process, that we call geology, symbolizes evidently as in highest reason it should, the grand spiritual catastrophe and Christian new-creation of man; which, both together comprehend the problem of mind, and so the final causes or last ends of all God's works.   What we see is the beginning conversing with the end, and Eternal Forethought reaching across the tottering mountains and boiling seas to unite begin ning and end together.   So that we may hear the grinding layers of the rocks singing harshly—

> Of man's first disobedience and the fruit
> Of that forbidden tree;

and all the long eras of desolation, and refitted bloom and beauty, represented in the registers of the world, are but the epic in stone of man's great history before the time.

And of this we are the more impressed, in the fact so power fully shown by Mr Agassiz, that the successive new populations of the geologic eras are, beyond a question, fresh creations of God summoned into being by His act, and fashioned in the moulds of His thought, impossible to be created or fashioned by any existing laws and forces in nature.   He does not say dis tinctly that they are supernatural creations, he might not so understand the word as to be clear of all disrespect in regard to it, but the fresh act of creation which he affirms and even scientifically proves, exactly answers to our definition of the supernatural, as being the action of some agent on the condi tions of nature from without those conditions, and so as to pro duce results which the laws of cause and effect in nature could not produce.   What a consideration, then, is it that the great question of the supernatural, which is now put in issue, and upon which depends even the faith of Christianity, as a grand supernatural movement of God on the world, is settled, over and over again, and the verdict as many times recorded in the rocks of the world!

In these great anticipative facts of the world, it is very

nearly impossible to resist the conviction of the eternal and
original subserviency even of its solid material structure to re
ligion, and especially to Christianity.   And exactly this ought
to be true, if the Christ and his religion be such, and so related
to the creation as we suppose him to be.   All God's most
ancient works are of course to be found thus in the interest of
Christianity, answering to it from their distant past, types of
its coming in the distant future, one with it in design, as being
issues of the same Eternal Mind.

It is difficult also to resist the conviction of a use more
specific and pointed than those to which we have referred.
Thus, in respect to misshapen monsters and deformed growths,
it is a remarkable fact that, as the layers of geology rise, and
creatures are produced that stand higher in the scale of organic
perfection, the number of deformities and retrograde shapes is
multiplied.   This fact has been strikingly exhibited by Hugh
Miller, in refutation of the development theory.   It permits
another use, taken as a moral type, of human history.   Thus
the serpent race makes no appearance, he observes, till we
ascend to the tertiary formation, and there it wriggles out into
being, contemporaneously with the more stately and perfect
order of mammalia.   When the mammoth stalks abroad as
the gigantic lord of the new creation, the serpent creeps out
with him, on his belly, with his bag of poison hid under the
roots of his feeble teeth, spinning out three or four hundred
lengths of vertebræ, and having his four rudimental legs
blanketed under his skin ; a mean, abortive creature, whom the
angry motherhood of nature would not go on to finish, but shook
from her lap before the legs were done, muttering, ominously,
" Cursed art thou for man's sake above all cattle ; upon thy
belly shalt thou go, and dust shalt thou eat all the days of thy
life,"—powerful type of man, the poison of his sin, the degrada
tion of his beauty under it, the possible abortion of his noble
capacities and divine instincts !

It is also shown by Miller, in the same manner, that the fishes
lost ground, or grew deformed in organization, as the human era
drew nigh.[1]   Regarding man as the highest form of organization,
having a head, neck, two hands, and two feet—the latter an
swered by the four legs of the beasts, the two wings and legs of
the birds, and the four fins of the fishes—every creature

[1] *Footprints of the Creator*, pp. 183-191.

will be most perfect in form when his parts are adjusted most nearly according to the human analogies ; and it is found that all the first fishes were actually in this type of agreement.   In the second formation, the forward fins are found to have slid up, not seldom, and struck themselves close upon the head, leaving no neck ; much as if a man were to appear with his arms fastened to his head close behind his ears.   In a later formation, both fins, representing hands and feet, have mounted into the same position ; and, as if this were uncomfortable, some races have dropped a pair altogether.   Then, next, in the chalk formation, where the nearest vicinage to man is attained, appears the remarkable order that includes the plaice, turbot, halibut, and flounder ; the two latter of which are familiar in our American waters.   They have the four fins stuck close upon the head.   They are capsized so as to swim on the flat side. The mouth is twisted so as to accommodate their false position. The two sides of the jaw do not match, one being much larger and having three or four times as many teeth as the other. The backbone is lateral, occupying one side of the body.   One eye is fixed in the middle of the forehead, and the other, which is much smaller, is thrust out upon one of the side promontories of the face.

What now does this strange process of deformity, chronicled in the rocks of the world, signify ?   What but that God is preparing the field for its occupant ; setting it with types of obliquity that shall match, and faithfully figure to man the obliquity and deformity of his sin !   Now, then, he at last appears, the lord of the creation, a being supernatural, clothed in God's image, a power to be trained up to greatness and glory—only he will find his way to the magnificent destiny of character appointed him, by struggling on, through falls, dis orders, and perishing abortions, and deformities of misdoing, that implicate the whole creation, causing it to groan and travail with him in his trial.

It will signify much to such a being, and especially in the advanced ages of time, when he seems to be conquering the world by his sciences, to find that, as the creation of God was rising in order, and the higher forms of life were appearing, in a series to be consummated or crowned by the appearing of man, tokens also of retrogradation, abortion, defect, deformity, were also beginning to appear ; as if to foretoken the moral history he will begin, and the humiliations through which he will require to be led. Coming in originally as lord and occupant to have dominion, and taking possession of it finally in the higher dominion of science, a most strange, powerfully humbling lesson meets him, exactly suited to his want, and one that ought to moderate all undue conceit of science in him, and temper him to that teachable state of inquiry that allows the nobler and diviner truths of Christianity to visit his heart. What does it mean—let any student of nature answer—what does it mean that a Perfect Mind, whose very thoughts are beauty, generates in the same era and side by side with man, such outrageous deformities, as we see, for example, in the halibut species ? Here is a deep lesson, worthy of much study. There is plainly no account to be made of such appearances, or facts, till we bring in the sovereignty of moral ideas, and assume the necessity of moral types and lessons.

On the whole, as the result of this inquiry into the anticipative consequences of sin, we must naturally take up the con viction, that the world, or what we call the creation, is not so much a completed fact as a *conatus*, struggling up concomitantly with the powers that are doing battle in it for a character; falling with them in their fall, rising with them or to rise, to a condition, finally, of complete order and beauty. There is much to be said for such an expectation, and it appears to be just what is held up, in the promise of a new heavens and earth, wherein dwelleth righteousness.

The pantheistic form of naturalism, it is well known, makes a very different account of the abortions and deformities of the world, and also of its future possibilities. It assumes, for a fact, that nature is an incomplete or partially developed form of being, going on toward perfection, under laws of develop ment contained in itself; therefore necessarily plunging into mischances, and producing uncomely or unperfect fruits. Ac cordingly God, who is in fact the all of nature, is a tardy but sublime Naturus, who is some time about to be, if He can attain to a more complete consciousness in His children, and be cleared of the blundering process of development by which necessity is at work to shape him into order. Meantime, we ourselves are blundering on with Him, they suppose, undergoing a like de velopment. What we called sin, before we became philosophers, we now call development, and excuse ourselves from all blame in it, because we are only parts of nature, subject to her laws; parts, that is, of God, and subject to the eternal fate that rules

That a soul, pressed down by the great questions of exist ence should some time reel into this gulf, is scarcely a subject of wonder; but no healthy, manly soul, none but one that is hag-ridden by the dark and spectral difficulties of the world will long stay in it. There is in the scheme, at first view, a certain imposing air of rational magnificence — it includes so ___ ___ _ s 'en G 1 and His n. story s coolly, and clears the question of evil by a solution so easy

But after all it is not cleared. We have called our con sciousness a fool it is true. in reporting such a thing as sin, and have taken the police of our souls into custody to escape the conviction of it, and still the sin is here—in us and around us We cannot act our part. for any two hours of our life without assuming its reality. What then becomes of our grea philosophy, when amusing itself thus in its lofty airs of reason,

is yet confronted every moment by the plain, simple denial and even scorn of our consciousness!

With this too comes the argument of our woe. The air of such a creed is too thin to support our life. There is no object meeting us to fill our want, there is no meaning or heart, in the mute, dead All; nothing in existence to give it significance, or inspire any great act or sentiment. We live in a disabled, stunted subjectivity. The inspiration of faith is replaced by the impotence of conceit. The world is a blunder, consciousness is a lie, the dark things of sin are developments and the All is a Universal Mockery. And then what remains but to go back and set up again the great first truth, which no mortal can spare for a day, that *whatever is wanted, is*—there fore God, the Living God shall be our faith; for Him we want as the complemental good, without which existence is but a name for starvation?

How many things too are there in the world, after all that can nowise be accounted for by this pantheistic theory? If the disorders and deformities of nature are God in partial develop ment, how is it conceivable that any being, in a state so raw uld ever have organized such complicated structures—human bodies for example—where the design is so evident, the parts so many and delicate, the offices so manifold, the unity so perfect? It is inconceivable that any power—call it God. or nature. or by whatever name — capable of constructing an organization so wonderful, should still be struggling up into order, through such grotesque and misbegotten shapes as are here accounted for, by the necessary imperfection of its or His development; composing first the glorious order of the astro nomic mechanism, then faltering afterward in the absurd com position of a flounder; able to fashion a creature of reason, but not to stand the criticism of reason; able to start new races of living creatures in the successive eras of geology, but having yet no will to start anything, apart from the control of fate. And what can such a doctrine make of Jesus Christ. what place does it provide in the world for such a being? If nature can develope nothing perfect; if, by reason of inherent defect, it must needs develope itself in blunders of abortion, deformity, and pain; will it still suffice to form the mind, fashion the beauty, finish the character of a Jesus?

But I am assuming here a superiority and perfection of order in the character of Jesus that may not be admitted by the pantheist, and as the question is hereafter to be discussed, and will be made a point of consequence in the argument, I desist for the present; only requiring it of such as look for a God in development, to answer how their blind force, called nature. staggering on through the disorders. abortions, and deformities of so many ages, and even falling into retrogradations as remarkable as its improvements, can be imagined to have pro duced such a soul and character as that of Jesus; a being, whether perfect or not, so high, so peculiar, original, pure, wise, great in goodness?

In this and the preceding chapter, we have now traced the consequences of sin : there the consequences that must needs follow it, as effects their causes, showing what results of mis chief and disorder it reveals in the soul, the body, society. and the world ; here accounting for a large display of correspondent facts in the geologic history precedent, or before the arrival of man, showing that they still are as truly consequences of the fact of sin as the others, being only just those marks that God's intelligence, planning the world and shaping it, even from eternity, to the uses and issues of a trial comprehending sin, must needs display. Sin, it will be seen, is, in this view, a

very great world-transforming, world-uncreating fact, and no
such mere casualty, or matter by the way, as the superficial
naturalism, or half-naturalistic Christianity of our time, sup
poses.   It is that central fact, about which the whole creation
of God and the ordering of His providential and moral govern .
ment revolves.   The impression of many appears to be, that
sin is this or that particular act of wrong which men sometimes
do, but which most men do not, unless at distant intervals ; and
who can imagine that anything very serious depends on these
rather exceptional misdeeds, when, on the whole, the account is
balanced by so many shows of virtue ?   The triviality and
shallowness of such conceptions are hardly to be spoken of with
patience.   It is not seen that when a man even begins to sin he
must needs cast away the principle, first, of all holy obedience,
and go down thus into a general lapse of condition, to be a soul
broken loose from principle and separated from the inspirations
of God.   Only a very little philosophy too, conceiving the fact
that sin is the acting of a substance, man, as he was not made
to act, must suffice to the discovery that, in a system or scheme
of perfect order, it will start a ferment of discord among causes
that will propagate itself in every direction, carrying wide-spread
desolation into the remotest circles.   The whole solidarity of
being in the creation, physical and spiritual, is necessarily
penetrated by it and configured to it.   Character, causes, things
prior and *post*, all that God embraces in the final causes of
existence, somehow feel it, and the whole creation groans and
travails for the pain of it.   The true Kosmos, in the highest and
most perfectly ideal sense of that term, does not exist.   Nature
is become unnature, and stopping at the point reached, which of
course we do not, we must even say that the creation of God is
a failure.

But there is an objection to be anticipated here which re
quires our attention before we dismiss this part of our subject.
It is that no proper Kosmos, no crystalline order of nature, ac
cording to the view stated in this chapter, has ever yet existed.
For, if we speak of the state of unnature as a consequence of
sin, that state of unnature has existed, in part, or as far as it
should, anticipatively, through all the precedent eras and geo
logic processes of the world.   The true ideal system of nature,
therefore, has never existed, and there was never any such con
dition or chime of order to fall from, or to shatter by sin, as

we are trying all the while to suppose. All which is certainly
true, if we must go entirely back of God's purposes and beyond
them to find it ; for what we have been tracing as the anticipative consequences of sin is nothing but the working of His
ancient counsel concerning it. But the real truth is that nature,
original and true nature, has existed and does now exist ; for, if
we call our present state, as we truly should, a condition of unnature, we mean by it nothing more than that the causes
included in pure nature are working now more or less retributively, painfully, diseasedly, and so as to create a state of
dislocation in the outward harmonies ; a state of incapacity and
bondage in the spiritual aspirations of the soul. Nature is unnature when her causes are acting retributively,—they are not,
in such cases, discontinued, or thrown out of their law ; but
they act, in their law and under it, as perfectly and systemati
cally as ever. The unnaturalness of our present state under sin
consists, not in the fact that nature is gone by, or is broken up,
but only in the fact that her causes are all at work on the con
trary ingredient, sin. It is as if a good and healthy stomach
were at work upon a stone to digest it—still it is acting by its
own laws and powers, as truly as if the stone were meat, though
its acting is only a throe of distress. Were everything, indeed,
now rolling on in sweetest bonds of harmony, according to the
pure ideal of what we call nature, nothing of bad consequence
or penal and retributive action anywhere appearing in it, no disorder of sin visible anywhere as a fact of anticipation, still
nature would not be more truly extant than now ; for the dis
order and unnature we speak of are really order and nature
chastising the false fact, sin ; which process of chastisement and
groaning we call unnature, only because it does not answer,
thus far, to the ideal working of the scheme, disturbed by no
such enemy of God and all good as it has here met. Nor does
it make any the least difference, except with some speculative
wordsman, grubbing under space and time, whether death and
prey and other like consequences of sin began to work, before
the arrival here of man, or only after. If God's Whole Plan re
spects the fact of sin before the fact, the scheme of nature was
none the less real or perfect, because of the unnature working
anticipatively in it, any more than it follows that the unnature
subsequent has discontinued nature, whose retaliatory action it
really is, and nothing more.

Unnature then—this is our conclusion—a far-reaching, all-comprehensive state of unnature, is the consequence of sin.   It mars the body, the soul, society, the world, all time before and after.   What an argument then have we, and especially from the ante-dated tokens of evil, for the belief that God's original p an comprehends a rising side, an economy supernatural, that shall complement the disorder and fall of nature, having power roll back its currents of penal misery, and bring out souls into the established liberty and beauty of holiness.   How mani-:est is it in the world's birth that God, from the first, designs for a second birth ; some grand *palingennesia* that shall raise e tall of nature and make existence fruitful.   It has been a great fault, as was just now intimated, that we have made so e of sin.   It is either nothing, or else it is a great deal more than it is conceived to be by the multitude who admit its existence.   The mental and moral philosophers make nothing of it, going on to construct their sciences, so called, precisely as the soul had received no shock of detriment ; and even the most orthodox theologians do scarcely more than score it with guilty conviction, regarding it seldom as a dynamic force, and then with a comprehension too restricted to allow any true im pression of its import.   Hence, in great part, the general in credulity in regard to the supernatural facts of Christianity There can be nothing supernatural, we think, because it would violate the integrity of nature.   The integrity of nature ! What but a world of unnature has it become already ?   And what has sent these hard pangs into it and through it but a supernatural force, even the human will ? for this, we have seen, is a power supernatural as truly as God, though not equal in degree ; able to act on the lines of causes and vary their conjunctions from without, even as He is represented in the Christian truth to do.   Hence the disorder and disease ; hence the groaning and travailing in pain together of the whole crea tion—it is all the supernatural work, the bad miracle of sin No other name will fitly name it.   Indeed, if there should be somewhere in the universe a race of beings that have never sinned, and they should have it set before them in all its conse quences to the physical order of things, they would look upon it, we suspect, as a miraculous agency, exerted in God's universe opposite to Himself.   And they would begin, we fear, to say with Mr Hume, unless they were better philosophers than he that such a miracle is wholly incredible; that the confidence they have in the beneficent, harmonious action of nature, is too strong to be broken by any possible testimony to such doings. Therefore this tremendous, all-revolutionizing miracle must be a fiction.

Of course it is not a miracle. It is only a fact supernatural —a grand assault of man's supernatural agency upon the world. We shall speak more definitely of miracles hereafter. For the present, we only say that the supernatural agency of God in the world's redemption is now shown to be most clearly wanted; and we do not perceive wherein it is more incredible that God should act, in His way, upon the lines of natural causes, than that we should do it in ours. Of course He will act with a higher sovereignty worthy of Himself. His divine supernatural power will be divine, our human will be human. If we have broken or clouded the crystal and cannot restore its transparency, He can. If we bring deformity, He will bring beauty. If we die, He will bid us live. Will He do this? That is now the question that remains.

CHAPTER VIII.

NO REMEDY IN DEVELOPMENT OR SELF-REFORMATION

WE are now at the point of catastrophe in God's plan, whe
it is next in order to look about for some remedial agency
dispensation that shall restore the lapse and bring out those r
sults of order and happiness that were proposed by God, as v
must believe, in His act of creation. Are we then shut up t
nature and the hope that she will surmount her own catas
trophe, or may we believe that her inherent weakness will b
complemented by a supernatural and divine movement tha
shall organize a new economy of life ?

The former is the ground taken by all the naturalizing classe
of our time. Nothing can take place, they say, which is no
operated under and by the laws of nature. To believe that any
thing can take place which is from without, or from above the
laws of nature, is unphilosophical and sa urs o cre uity
That there is such a thing as misdirection they will admit, and
some will admit a. so th ac o s n, an- -- —·· be a e d b
t l that, in consequence either of misdirection or of sin

wai

emedy. Our present object is to look into their principa
emedies, or grounds of e cted restoration, and try wha
e is in them , of presented under two
listinct forms, both of which may be taken as rival gospels
opposite to Christianity.

By e class who formally reject or ignore Christianity
develo ment is regarded as the universal panacea—all the
appare vils of the world are to be cured by development.

The class who professedly teach and believe the Christian

gospel, reducing it still to a mere scheme of ethics or natural virtue, rely more on the individual will to be exerted in self-government, self-culture, and the doing of justice, mercy, and other good works.

Of these rival gospels, both from within the terms of nature, I will now speak in their order.

I. Of development, or, as it is often phrased, the natural progress of the race.

The world is just now taken, as never before, with ideas of progress. The human race, it is conceived, exists under laws of progress. The philosophers, or would-be philosophers, have even undertaken to reduce the laws of progress to a scientific statement. They conceive that all the advanced races of man kind began at the level of the savage state, and have been set forward to their present pitch of culture, civilization, wealth, and liberty, by laws of development in mere nature. The mul titude go after them, embracing the welcome idea of progress only the more enthusiastically, that they are so much taken with the new word *development*, conceiving that there is great science in it, or, at least, some unknown kind of power. If there are any evils, or bitter woes in society, development is going to cure them; for the laws of development are at work to produce progress, and they will as certainly do it as the laws of matter will determine its motions. All crime and sin are going finally to be cured in this manner, and character is going finally to blossom, on the broken stock of nature, even as flowers are developed out of stocks not broken, and roots not poisoned by disease. Finding thus a gospel of progress in the world itself and the mere laws of existence, what need of any such antiquated mythology as the Christian gospel brings us? Or, if the argument is not openly stated in this manner, still it is virtually adopted; for how many that suppose Christianity to be true, still have it only as a thing by the way, a straw floating down this flood and passing on with us, to see the brave work human progress is doing. If it is not called a myth or wild tradition, still the really trusted gospel is phreno logy, chemistry, and the other new sciences, with their grand economic creations, such as telegraphs, railroads, steamboats, and the like—(not omitting the new and better bible discovered in the oracles of necromancy)—and these are going at last to raise the world, no thanks to Christianity, into a state of uni-

versal brotherhood and felicity! The lowest charlatans,
some of the most cultivated savans, hold much the same lan
guage, and trust in the same gospel of development

Now that there is or should be such a thing as development
we certainly admit. All the human faculties are capable o
development by exercise or training, and every human being
will, of necessity, be developed to a certain degree, both in
mind and body, by the growth of years and the necessary
struggles of life. But that human society was ever carried
forward by a single shade, in the matter of religious virtue,
under mere laws of natural development, we utterly deny. It
is even a fair subject of doubt whether any nation or race of
men was ever advanced in civilization by inherent laws of progress. Certain it is that no individual was ever cleared of sin
by development, or restored even proximately to the state of
primal order and uprightness; equally so that the vast, far-
spreading, organic woes of the world are for ever immedicable
by any such remedy.

In one view, it may be rightly said that the whole object of
God, in our training, is to develope in us a character of eternal
uprightness; developing also, in that manner, as a necessary
consequence, grand possibilities of social order and wellbeing;
though, when we thus speak, we include the fact of sin and the
engagement with it of a supernatural grace, to lift up the otherwise remediless fall of nature. But this, if we must have the
word, is Christian development; a development accomplished
by carrying us across and up out of the gulf of unnature, where
the hope of all progress and character was ended. We are
developed, in this sense, by and through an experience of that
state of wrong, whose woe it is that it is the fall of nature, and,
in that sense, the end of all development. But this, it will be
seen, is not the popular doctrine of progress, which assumes the
fact of a progress in right li

Consider, first, the savage state, whence it is continually as
sumed that history and civilization spring. The doctrine is, that
all the advanced nations of mankind began as savages, and that
all the peoples of the world now existing are on their way up out
of the savage state into civilization and a state of social virtue.
Contrary to this, no savage race of the world has ever been
raised into civilization, least of all into a state of virtue by
mere natural development. All which is evident by just that
which distinguishes the savage state; for it is the principal and,
in fact, only comprehensive distinction of the savage races, that
they are such as have fallen below progress, living on from age
to age without progress, and sometimes quite dying out; for
the simple reason, that there is no sufficient capacity of progress
left to perpetuate their life in proximity with more advanced
races. They are beings or races physiologically run down or
become effete under sin; fallen at last below progress, below
society, become a herd no longer capable of public organization,
and a true, social life. It signifies nothing for such races to
ask more time; time can do nothing for them better than ex
termination. It is well if even a gospel and a faith above
nature can now get such hold of them as to raise them. They
are, in fact, just as far off from the original unpractised unde
veloped state of nature, as the most advanced races; and, as
David said over the child—" I shall go to him, but he shall not
return to me," so it is possible for the living and advanced
races to go downward, but never for these dead ones, unassisted,
to rise. We have proofs enough that peoples advanced in cul.
ture may become savages, but no solitary example of a race of
savages that have risen to a civilized state by mere development.
And the real fact is, that we may much better assert a law of
natural deterioration than a law of natural progress; for, apart
from some influence or aid of a supernatural kind, the deterio
ration of society, under the penal mischiefs of sin, would be
universal. By the supposition it should be so; for, as all so
ciety is under sin, it is of course suffering the retributive action
of penal causes; and as all discord propagates only greater dis
cord and cannot propagate harmony, it follows that the run of
society under sin must be downward, from bad to worse, unless
interrupted by some remedial agency from without.

It is somewhat difficult to test our particular opinion on this
subject by actual examples; for we cannot commonly trace

the unhistoric and subtle methods, in which any race of men may have been impregnated with new possibilities; somctimes by other religions, with which they are made conversant by commerce and travel; sometimes by sporadic and supernatural revelations; traces of which are decernible, not only in the extra-Jewish examples of Jcthro, Job, and Cornelius, but in the literature of all the cultivated races, and sometimes, here and there, in the demonstrations even of the wild races. That the old Pelasgic race was raised, by a mere natural progress, to the high pitch of culture displayed by the Greek civilization, we have no reason whatever to believe. Their literature, from Hesiod downward, is sprinkled with too many traces of senti ment derived from the Jewish and Egyptian religions, to suffer the opinion that they are a nation thus advanced, by the simple motherhood of nature. The Roman civilization was, in fact, a propagation of the Greek, with the advantage of a right infusion from her serious and venerable fathers, who, like Numa, com muned with invisible powers in retired groves and silent grottoes. The Teutonic race, often named as an example of natural development, is known to have been set forward by the civilizations it conquered and its early conversion to the Chris tian faith. Meantime how many great and powerful races have become extinct. We look for the Ninevites with as little hope as for Ninus himself. The Assyrians, Babylonians, and Medes are also vanished. The Egyptians, Phœnicians, Etruscans, Romans, once the great powers of history and civilization, are extinct. The Aztec race, run down to such a state of incapacity as not even to understand their own monuments, or know by whom they were built, we rightly call savages, and look upon as having just now come to their vanishing point.

What now does it mean that so many races, empires, lan guages of the world, have become extinct? Is this a token of infallible development? Do we see in this the proof that all the evil and sin of the world are going, at last, to be surmounted and cleared by the inevitable law of progress? What would our new prophets of development say, if they were told, when exult ing so confidently in the glorious future of their own and all other nations, that a day will certainly be reached, when the Anglo-American race is become an extinct race, Washington a contested locality, and the Constitution of the United States a hopeless search of the world's antiquarians? Distant as such an expectation may be from our thoughts, and contrary as it may be to the illimitable progress of which we hear so often, it is only that which has happened a hundred times already, and may as well happen again.

We have spoken of the evident falsity of the supposition, that all the advancement of the world begins at an originally savage state; that being, in fact, no first, but an old and decayed state rather, where long ages of deterioration under sin have finally extirpated the original possibilities of advance ment. The first stage of human society was simply a stage of crudity, or crude capacity, and was not more remote from the state of high civilization than it was from the low, decrepid, animalized condition which we now designate by the term *savage*. All races begin together at the state of simple being, or crude capacity, and only make the fatal leap of sin together. After that they separate, some ascending, led up by their holy seers and lawgivers, and others, not having or not giving heed to such, going down the scale of penal deteriorations to become savages. A full half the globe is peopled thus by tribes which are either reduced to the savage condition, or else are far on their way toward it; humbled in capacity, physically deterio rated, and that to such a degree, that the springs of recuperative force appear to be quite gone. Considering now the certain fact, that all these had their beginning in a simply crude state, having the same high possibilities and affinities, which the races had that are now most advanced, what are we to think of mere de velopment? This advantage or condition of crude possibility they had, many thousands of years ago, and the result is what we see. Having run down thus miserably under the boasted gospel of natural progress, what hope is there in this gospel for the final restoration of all things?

It is fatally opposed too by the geologic analogies. Here it stands, the settled verdict of science itself, that the successive eras of vegetable and animal life have not been introduced, by any law of progress, or by any mere development of nature and her forces. The attempts that have been made to show this are even pitiable failures. They ask us, in fact, to believe greater miracles in the name of development than any we encounter in the gospel history. Thus, we have displayed in the new crea tions of the rocks themselves, a standing type of that moral new creation, by which the distempered and fallen races of the world

are to be raised up. Lest we should think any such divine in
tervention incredible, and try to find some better hope for man
in the gospel of development, we are here familiarized with the
fact, that no such law of development has been able to carry on
the geologic progress of the planet, and that God has been wont,
in all its ancient depopulations, to insert new germs of life
creatively, and people it with living creatures fresh from His
hand.

Again, it is a consideration scarcely less impressive, that God
has managed to insert into the physiological history of animals
and vegetables an always-present, living type of the process
itself, by which, as transcending all mere development, His
supernatural remedy operates ; so that we may see it, as it
were, with our eyes, and become familiar with it. I refer to
that wondrous, inexplicable function of healing, discovered in
the restoration or repair of animals and vegetables, that are
wounded or sick. When a tree, for example, is hacked or
bruised, a strange nursing process forthwith begins, by which
the wound is healed. A new bark is formed on the edges of
the wound, by what method no art of man can trace, the dead
matter is thrown off, and a growth inward narrows the breach,
till finally the two margins meet and the tissues interweave,
and not even a scar is left. So in all the flesh wounds of
animals, and the fractures even of bones. So too in regard to
all diseases not terminating mortally ; they pass a crisis, where
the healing function, whatever it be, triumphs over the poison
of the disease, and a recovery follows, in which the whole flesh
and fibre appear even to be produced anew.

Here, then, is a healing power whose working we can no
way trace, and one that, if we look at the causes of disintegra
tion present, appears even to accomplish what is impossible.
Regarding the body as a machine—and taken as a merely
material organization, what is it more ?—it is plainly impossible
for it to heal, in this manner, and repair itself. The disordered
watch can never run itself into good repair. In machines, dis
order can only propagate and aggravate disorder till they become
a wreck. The physicians and physiologists call the strange
healing function the *vis medicatrix ;* as if it were some gentle,
feminine nurse hidden from the sight, whose office it is to expel
the poisons, knit the fractures, and heal the wounds of bodies.
And as names often settle the profoundest questions, so it ap-

pears to be commonly taken for granted here, that the healing accomplished is wrought by a nursing function thus named, as one of the inherent properties of vital substances. It may be so or it may not; for the whole question is one that is involved in the profoundest mystery. The healing property may be one of the incidents of life itself, or it may be a distinct power whose office it is to be the guard and medicating nurse of life, or it may be the working of a grand supernatural economy set in closest vicinage to nature, to be the physical, visible, always present token of a like supernatural economy in the matters of character and the soul. But whatever view we take of this healing power in physiology, or whatever account we make of it, these two points are clear.

First, that the healing accomplished is no fact of develop ment. There is no difficulty in seeing how existing tissues and organs may create extensions within their own vascular sphere; and this is development. But where a new skin or bark is to be created, or a new interlocking made of parts that are sun dered, the ducts and vesicles that might act in development, being parted and open at their ends, want mending themselves. Thus, when the parts of a fractured bone are knit together, and we see them reaching after each other, as it were across a chasm, where there are no vessels to bridge it or carry across the lines of connexion, development might well enough make the parts longer, but how could it make them unite across the fracture by which they are separated ? The development of a tree, wounded by some violence, would only enlarge the wound, just in proportion to the enlargement of the surface which the bark should cover. A fevered body does not cure itself by development. As little can we imagine that the restored health and volume of the body is created by the development of the fever. No shade of countenance, therefore, is given to the hope that human development, under the retributive woes of sin, will be any sufficient cure of its disorders, or will set the fallen subjects of it forward in a course of social progress.

This also, secondly, is equally clear, that, as the mysterious healing of bodies yields the development theory no token of favour, it is only a more impressive type, on that account, of some grand restorative economy, by which the condition of un-nature in souls and the world is to be supernaturally regencrated—just such a type as, regarding the relations of matter to mind, and of things natural to things spiritual, we might expect to find incorporated in some large and systematic way, in the visible objects and processes of the world.   And how much does the healing of bodies signify, when associated thus with the grand elemental disorder and breakage of sin !   What is it, in fact, but a kind of glorious, everywhere visible sacrament, that tokens life, and hope, and healing invisible, for all the retributive woes and bleeding lacerations of our guilty fallen state, as a race apostate from God.

Hence too, probably, the fact that transactions of healing are so closely connected, the world over, with sentiments of religion.   Perhaps the fact is due, in part to some latent association that connects diseases with sin, and, to much the same extent, connects the hope of healing with some possibility of a divine medication.   However this may be, the mystery of healing, as we are constituted, stands in close affinity with God and the faith of His supernatural operation.   Thus it was that the priests both of the Egyptians and the Greeks were their physicians, and that their precepts and prescripts of healing were kept in their temples.   Æsculapius, too, the god of medicine, had his own altars and priests.   At a later period, the Essenes and the Christian monks, accounted by some to be their successors, had their pious explorations of diseases and the sacred powers of remedies ;   reducing medicine itself to a function of religion.   Later still, Paracelsus himself began the restoration of medicine, as a kind of chemical theosophy.   And as Christianity itself classes healings among the spiritual gifts, and calls the elders of the Church to pray for the sick ;   so we find that some of our Indian tribes have traditions of one whom, as related to the Great Spirit, they call the Uncle, and who came into the world by a mysterious advent, long ages ago, and instituted the " Grand Medicine," which is, in fact, their religion.

It is difficult to resist the impression, in such demonstrations as these, of some very profound connexion between the healing of bodies and the faith of a supernatural grace of healing for the disorders of souls.   Else why this persistent tendency in men's opinions of healing, to associate the fevered body and the leprous mind, and seek the medication of both in the common rites of religion ?

But there is a shorter argument with the scheme that pro poses to find a remedy for all the ills of character and society, in what it calls a more complete development. It is this : That no one ever dares practically to act on the faith of such a doctrine, whether in the state or the family. The civil law is, in fact, and to a very great extent, a restraint on develop ment, and has its merit in the fact that it is. It forbids men to unfold themselves freely, in their base passions and criminal instigations, and deters them from it. Were it not for the state protecting itself by such means against development, society would be quite dissolved. What we discover in families is even more remarkable. There are multitudes of parents that believe, as they suppose, with all their hearts, in the good day coming through the progress of human development. And as part of the same general faith, their views of education make it to consist simply in educing or developing just what is in the child's nature. But they do not act on that principle in the house, and dare not; though probably enough they are never aware of the fact. They maintain a family regimen that con sists, to a great degree, not in development but in repression. To let the child have his way and act himself out freely, with out restraint, is no part of their plan. Probably it never occurs to them as a rational possibility. Just contrary to this, they lay their foundations in a restriction of natural development ; hoping in that manner to extirpate unruly and base instigations, and form a habit in the child of doing better things than he would most naturally do. And it is remarkable that, in the fulfilling of their office, which is so far an office of repression, they are acting as a force supernatural. According to our definition, it will be remembered that human wills are strictly supernatural in their action, and the child, we here discover, spends all the first years of his life under the regulative and repressive action of such wills. He is in them, in fact, more truly than he is in nature, and the house is a little creation made for him by their keeping. He is handled in infancy as they direct, fed as they direct when he begins to ask for food, clothed as they direct, commanded, limited, forbidden, repressed, and so is finally grown up to an age of self-regulation. The process may be called his development, but the most remark able thing in it is that it is a restraint of development. Why this restraint ? If development is going to be the gospel of the world's redemption, what makes it wise, in the common sense of the wor d, to res rain that gospel ? Are the ills of society and the world going to be cured too soon ? If development can do is promised, why not give it a hearty godspeed everywhere, and let every human creature, old and young, act out at is , in the speediest, most unrestricted manner ssible ? A glance in this direction is sufficient to show us that all we hear of inevitable progress, and the necessary laws of development, is hollow and deceitful. It is not development but new creation that can bring us the remedies we look for Nature has powers and capabilities that want development. Reduced to real unnature (which is her present state), she also has disordered passions, base instigations, greedy appetites, ferocious animosities, propensities to cunning and falsehood, which want no development, and which, if they are developed unrestrained, annihilate all chance of progress, and even forbid e :e society. Mere development therefore promises nothin

We come now—

II. To the other rival gospel, that which proposes to dispense wi h all supernatural aids, and to restore the disorders and the fallen character of sin by a self-cultivated or self-originated

Expectation is here rested on the human will, which, in our view, may be done, it will be said, with greater reason, since we make it even by definition, a supernatural power. But there are different orders or degrees, it must be observed, of supernatural power ; the human, the angelic, the divine ; which are all alike in the fact that the will acts from itself, uncaused in ts action, but very unlike as regards potency, or the extent of their efficacy What we are endeavouring in our argument to how is, the fact of a divine supernatural agency concerned in he upraising or redemption of man. But if man can raise imse own will, that is, by his humanly supernatural force, then plainly there is no need of a divine intervention from without and above nature to regenerate his fallen state. Still it will not be denied by the class of teachers most forward in maintaining this form of naturalism, that all religious virtue is dependent, in a certain sense, on the concourse and spiritual helping of God. Only that concourse and helping, it will be said, belongs to the scheme of nature, and never undertakes to help us out of the retributive woes and disorders of nature ; for nature is the system of God, including all He does or can rationally be expected to do. To imagine that such a mode of piety or religious virtue should be maintained by the human will, would be less extravagant if there were no sin, no conse quent woes and disorders ; though even then it would be the faith of a God imprisoned or entombed in the inexorable laws of nature ; with whom the soul could aspire to no real con verse, and could have no social sympathy, more than with a wall. Before this unbending prisoner of fate, this nature-God, this dead wall, he might go on to dress up a character and fashion a merely ethical virtue ; cultivating truth, honesty, justice, temperance, kindness, piling up acts of merit, and doing legal works of charity ; but to call this character religious, how ever plausible the show it makes, is only an abuse of the term. Religious character is not legal. It is an inspiration—the Life of God in the Soul of man ; and no such life can ever quicken a soul except in the faith of a Living God, which here is manifestly wanting. Not even the pure angels could subsist in such a style of virtue ; for it is the strength and beatitude of their holiness, that it is no will-work in them, but an eternal, immediate inspiration of God. Consciously it is not theirs, but the inbreathing life of their father.

But this ethical gospel, this religion acted as in pantomime, becomes even more insipid and absurd, when the fact of sin, with all its consequences of distemper and disorder, is admitted. Now the problem is to find by what power the original har mony of nature can be reconstructed, and its currents of penal disaster turned back. Can the human will do this ? That it can act upon the courses of nature we know,—sin itself indeed is the staring and incontrovertible proof that it can. But it does not follow, as we have said already, that the power which has broken an egg, or shivered a crystal, can mend it. That is a thing more difficult, and demands a higher power.

Consider simply the change that is needed to restore the lapsed integrity of a soul. Its original spontaneity to good is gone, its silver cord of harmony is broken, the sweet order of life is turned into a tumult of inward bitterness, its very laws are become its tormentors. All its curious, multiform, scarcely conceivable functions, submitted by its laws to the will, are now contesting always with each other, and are wholly intractable to its sovereignty. And still it is expected of the will, that it is going to gather them all up into the primal order, and recon struct their shattered unity ! Why, it were easier, a thousand-fold, for man's will to gather all the birds of the sky into martial order, and march them as a squadron through the tempests of the air ! Manifestly none but God can restore the lapsed order of the soul. He alone can reconstruct the crystal-line unity. Which, if He does, it will imply an acting on those lines of causes in its nature, by whose penal efficacy it is dis tempered ; and that is, by the supposition, a supernatural operation.

Besides, the work is really not done, till the subject is re stored to a virtue whose essence is liberty. And how is man by his mere will, to start the flow of liberty ? He may do this and do that, and keep doing this and that, carefully, punctili ously, suffering no slackness. But it will be work, work only and the play of liberty will never come. He can never reach the true liberty till an inspiration takes him, and the new birth of God's Spirit makes him a son. The light he manufactures will be darkness, or at best a pale phosphorescence, till Christ is revealed within. His self-culture may fashion a picture with many marks of grace, but the quickening of God alone can make it live. If he relish his work in a degree, it will be the relish of conceit, not the living fountain of a heavenly joy, bursting up from unseen depths within. He will advance fit-fully, eccentrically, and without balance, making a grimace here while he fashions a beauty there ; for there is no balance of order and proportion till his faith is rested in God, and his life flows out from the divine plenitude and perfection. Meantime his ideals will grow faster than his attainments, and if he is not wholly drunk up in conceit, he will be only the more afflicted and baffled the greater his pertinacity. Oh, if there be any kind life most sad, and deepest in the scale of pity, it is the dry, cold impotence of one who is honestly set to the work of his own self-redemption !

Do we then affirm, it will be asked, the absolute inability of a man to do and become what is right before God ? That is the Christian doctrine, and there is none that is more obviously true Wherein, then, it may also be asked, is there any ground of blame for continuance in sin ? Because, we answer, there is a Living God engaged to help us, and inviting always our acceptance of His help. Nor is this any mere gracious ability, such as constitutes the joy of some and the offence of others. No created being of any world, not even the new-formed man before his fall, nor the glorified saint, nor the spotless angel, had ever any possibility of holiness, except in the embrace of God. This is the normal condition of all souls, that they be filled with God, acted by God, holding their will in His, irradiated always by His all-supporting life. Just this it is that constitutes the radical idea of religion, and differs it from a mere ethical virtue. God is the prime necessity of all religious virtue, and is only more emphatically so to beings under sin. The necessity is con stituent, not penal; it becomes penal only when communications originally given to the fallen, but now cast away by their sin, require to be restored.

There is really no difficulty in this question of disability under sin, save that which is created by the fogs of unintelli gent speculation. It is taken extensively, as if it were a ques· tion regarding man's inherent, independent ability, when in fact he has no such ability to anything. Can he obey God or not ? is he able to do God's will or not ? is the question raised; and it is understood and discussed as being a question that turns on the absolute quantities of the man, and not in any respect on relative aids and conditions without; much as if the question were whether he has weight, apart from all relative weights or attractions? or whether he can stand alone apart from anything to stand upon ? or whether he has power to live a year, apart from all food and light and shelter and air ? The true question of ability is different. It is this : Whether the subject is able to rise into a holy life, taken as insphered in God, and all the attractive, transforming, and supporting influences of the grace of God ? Apart from this, he certainly is not able. By mere working on himself and manipulating, as it were, his body of sin and death, he can do just nothing in the way of self-perfection ; and, if he could even do everything as regards self-transformation, there would be no religious character in the result, any more than if his works were done before the moon. Religious character is God in the soul, and without that all pretences of religious virtue are, in fact, atheistic. Such is the disability of a fallen man, taken as acting on himself; and the condition of an angel, acting in that manner, is no better; for he could not begin to act thus, without being himself fallen, at

the instant.   But if the question be what a man has power to
do taken in the surroundings of Divine truth and mercy, which
in fact include the co-operating grace of the Divine Spirit, the
true answer is that he can do all things.   He has at every
moment a complete power as respects doing what God requires of
him at that moment, and is responsible according to his power
And yet, when we say a complete power, we mean, not so much
that he is going even then to do something himself, as that he
is going to have something done within by the quickening and
transforming power of his divine Lord, in whom he trusts   His
power is to set himself before power, open his nature to the
rule of power and so to live.   Even as we may say that a tree
has power to live and grow, not by acting on itself and willing
to grow, but as it is ministered unto by its natural surround
ings the soil, the sun, the dew, the air.   It has only to offer
itself openly and receptively to these, and by their force to
grow.

Where then, it may be asked, is the significance of free will
which we have even shown to be a power supernatural?   If the
isordered soul cannot restore itself, or by diligent self-culture
regain the loss it has made by sin, wherein lies the advantage
such a power, and where the responsibility to a life of holy
Our answer is, that by the freedom of the will we
understand simply its freedom as a volitional function · but
mere volitions, taken by themselves, involve no capacity to re
generate or constitute a character.   Holy virtue is not an act
or compilation of acts taken merely as volitions, but it is a new
tate or *status* rather, a right disposedness, whence new action
may flow.   And no mere volitional exercise can change the state
or disposedness of the soul, without concurrent help and grace
We can will anything, but the execution may not follow   To
will may be present, but how to perform it may be difficult to
nnd,—difficult, that is, when simply acting in and upon our-
se ves ; never difficult, never possible to fail in doing. when
acting before and toward a Divine Helper, trustfully appealed
to.   And this is the power of the will, as regards our moral
recovery   It may so offer itself and the subordinate capacities
to God, that God shall have the whole man open to His do
minion and be able to ingenerate in him a new divine state or
principle of action ; while, taken as a governing, cultivating
and perfecting power in itself, it has no such capacity whatso-

ever. And this is the only rational and true verdict. Say what we may of the will as a strictly self-determining power, raise what distinctions we may as regards the kinds of ability, such as natural and moral, antecedent and subsequent, we have no ability at all, of any kind, to regenerate our own state, or restore our own disorders. Salvation is by faith, or there is none.

There is then, we conclude, no hope of a restoration of society, or of a religious upraising of man, except in a super natural and Divine operation. Progress under sin, by laws of natural development, is a fiction—there is no hope of progress, apart from the regenerative and quickening power of a grace that transcends mere natural conditions and causes. As little room is there to expect that men will be able to heal their own spiritual maladies and cultivate themselves into heaven's order, by a merely ethical regimen maintained in the plane of nature. The only remedy for the human state, under sin, is that which comes into nature as the revelation of a divine force.

Suppose now there might be found some great and profound thinker, who has never come under the impress of Christianity, or even heard of such a thing as a plan of supernatural redemp tion; a man of the highest culture, least under the power of superstition; a free-thinker as regards the religion of his country and times; and suppose that he, by the mere force of his own thought, struggling with the great problem of humanity, society, and progress, should be found to rest his hope deliber ately on some supernatural remedy, as the only sufficient remedy for the world; giving forth a testimony that has been audited and accepted by the greatest and best minds of all subsequent ages; revealing, as it were, a Christianity before the time, as far as the want of it and the fact of some such operative power are concerned; how unlikely will it be that some new science of development, or some more rational gospel of self-culture, has just now discovered the essential weakness or childishness of a supernatural faith? Precisely such a witness we have in the great Plato, seconded by the coincident testimony of many others, only less conspicuous than he.

Beginning at the base note of human depravity, he says, "1 have heard from the wise men that we are now dead, and that the body is our sepulchre."[1]   Again he says, "The prime evil is inborn in souls;" "it is implanted in men to sin."[2]   Again, "The nature of mankind is greatly degenerated and depraved all manner of disorders infest human nature, and men being impotent, are torn in pieces by their lusts, as by so many wild horses.   He also speaks of an "evil nature," "an evil in nature," "a disease in nature," "a destruction of harmony in the soul," and much more to the same effect.   Then again, tracing the origin of this diseased state, he says, "That in times past, the divine nature flourished in men ; but, at length being mixed with mortal custom, it fell into ruin ; hence an inundation of evils in the race."[4]   Again, "The cause of corruption is from our parents, so that we never relinquish their evil way, or escape the blemish of their evil habit."[5]

Inquiring now for the remedy which is able to restore and re-establish the virtue lost, he discusses at large the question whether virtue can be taught, and deliberately concludes that it can be produced by no mere teaching.   He says, "If, in this whole disputation, we have rightly conceived the case, virtue is acquired, neither by nature's force, nor by any institutes of discipline or teaching, but it comes to those that have it by a certain divine appointment [or inspiration], over and above the mind's own force or exertion."[6]   He also adds that, if we could be dressed up into a show of virtue by teaching, it would be the same as "to be adorned with a shadow, whereas virtue s a thing real and solid,"—rooted, that is, in the heart's in most life.   The same conviction is expressed in a different form when he says, "That after the golden age, the universe, by reason of that confusion that came upon it, would have been quite dissolved, had not God again taken it upon him to sit at the helm and govern the world, and restore its disordered and almost disjointed parts to their primeval order."[7]   And accor dantly with such a conviction, he recommends a faith in divine help and supernatural guidance, and says, "He who prayeth to God, and trusteth in His good favour, shall do well."[8]   Again "God is the beginning and end of all being, and whoever follows His guidance shall be happy."[9]   And that he means by this, to commend a faith in supernatural aid, is evident when he says, in his Timæus, " That beatitude, or spiritual liberty, is only to have the demon," that is, the good spirit, " dwelling in us," alluding probably to the remarkable declara tion of his teacher Socrates, " that a certain demon, or good spirit, had followed him even from his childhood, with his good suggestion or influence, signifying what he should do."[1] He brings in Socrates also maintaining this remarkable dialogue with his pupil Alcibiades : " Dost thou know by what means thou mayest avoid the inordinate motions of thy mind ? " He answers, " Yes." *Soc.* " How ?" *Al.* " If thou *wilt*, Socrates." *Soc.* " Thou speakest not rightly." *Al.* " How then must I speak ?" *Soc.* " Say, if God will,"[2] etc.

Here, then, we have a man rising up out of heathenism, one of the greatest of mankind, testifying his conviction of the disability and ruin of human nature, and his confidence in some supernatural aid, as the only hope of the world—all this instructed by his own consciousness, and by so many years of philosophic study, in the great problem of humanity and human progress. For no teacher, even of our modern time, is more intent on the possibility of some better ideal state of the world and society than he. In this problem, indeed, it may even be said that he wore out his life.

Seneca speaks quite despairingly of our possible recovery by any means. He says, " Our corrupt nature has drunk in such deep draughts of iniquity, which are so far incorporated in its very bowels, that you cannot remove it, save by tearing them out." And yet he conceives, in the faintest manner, some possibility of supernatural aid. " No man is able to clear him self, let some one give him a hand, let some one lead him out "—as if asking for some Christ unknown, to come and bring the soul forth from its thraldom.

He also says, as if he were writing out another seventh chap ter of the Romans, " What is it, Lucilius, that, when we set ourselves in one way, draws us another, and when we desire to avoid any course, drives us into it ? What is it that so wrestles with our mind, allowing us never to settle any good resolution once for all ?"[4]

And Ovid also joins in the same confession—" If I could, I would be more sane. But some unknown force drags me against my will. Desire draws me one way, conviction another.

1 *Theages*, 128.   2 *Alcib.* 135.   3 *Ep.* 52.   4 *Ep.* 52.

I see the better and approve, the worse I follow."[1]   " O wretched man that I am, who shall deliver ?" is the sigh that interprets and fitly concludes their confession.

Passages in great number could be cited from other ancient writers, in which they express the same conviction, that man can never be raised out of his sin by any mere natural force. But these are points of opinion. We prefer to add, as being more significant, some illustrations also of the practical longing they had for the appearance of some divine helper, and the manifestation of God in some gracious revelation of His presence. In illustrations of this kind, we shall see exactly what would be our own condition, if these supernatural manifestations, denied by so many in our times, were taken away, and we were really set back, as we require ourselves to be, in the proper darkness of nature. It was a continual source of misery to the most enlightened of the pagan scholars, and philosophers, that whatever they seemed to discover, or to establish by the light of natural reason, was yet never discovered, never established, but was still overhung by a cloud of uncertainty. Thus we hear Xenophanes closing off his work on nature, in these words —"No man has discovered any certainty, nor will discover it, concerning the gods, and what I say of the universe. For if he uttered what is even most perfect, still he does not know it, but conjecture hangs over all."

Oppressed by this feeling of uncertainty, they were only goaded the more painfully in their search after the real meaning of life, and waited, with a longing only the more hungry, for some revelation of divine things, if haply it might some time be given. Thus Plato, speaking in his Phædo of the soul and its destiny, says—"It appears to me that to know them clearly in the present life is either impossible or very difficult; on the other hand, not to test what has been said of them in every possible way, not to investigate the whole matter, and exhaust upon it every effort, is the part of a very weak man. For we ought, in respect to these things, either to learn from others how they stand, or to discover them for ourselves; or, if both these are impossible, then, taking the best of human reasonings, that which appears the best supported, and embarking on that, as one who risks himself on a raft, so to sail through life—unless one could be carried more safely, or with

1 *Metam.* vii 19

less risk, on a secret conveyance or some Divine Logos."
What a condition of hunger for knowledge!—a great and
mighty soul, prying at the gates of life, to force them open,
catching the faintest gleams of truth or opinion, and committing
his all tenderly to them as to a slender raft upon the sea, only
venting, with a sigh, the mysterious hint of a Divine Logos,
who will possibly come to him within, and be a surer light, a
safer guide.   And this dim hint of a better revelation is ven
tured more boldly in his Alcibiades, when he says—" We must
wait patiently until some one, either a god or some inspired
man, teach us our moral and religious duties, and, as Pallas in
Homer did to Diomede, remove the darkness from our eyes."
How little incredible was it to him, the highest philosophic in
tellect the world has ever seen, that some incarnate messenger
of God, or teacher supernaturally sent, may some time come to
enlighten the world !   What in fact does he tell us, but that
he is waiting for Jesus the Christ !
    At a later period, or about the time of Christ, when the
faith of the ancient religion or mythology had become more
nearly extinct, the struggle of souls, shut up to the mere dark
ness of nature and reason, became more sad and painful.
Strabo, for example, falling back on the religion of Moses, re
ceived from him a faith in one Supreme Essence, who he
thought should be worshipped without images in sacred groves ;
and there, he said, " the devout should lay themselves down to
sleep, and expect signs from God in dreams." [1]   Not daring to
look for any waking experience of God supernaturally revealed
in the soul, he must still indulge the hope that the Eternal
will, at least, come to it in the land of sleep and dreams.
Poor Pliny, confessing too the wretched hunger of his soul, saw
no relief to it better than suicide.   "It is difficult," he writes,
" to say whether it might not be better for men to be wholly
without religion, than to have one of this kind [viz., that of
his country], which is a reproach to its object.   The vanity of
man and his insatiable longing after existence, have led him
also to dream of a life after death.   A being full of contra
dictions, he is the most wretched of creatures, since the other
creatures have no wants transcending the bounds of their
nature.   Man is full of desires and wants that reach to infinity,
and can never be satisfied.   Among these so great evils, the

[1] Lib xvi. chap. 2.

best thing God has bestowed on man is the power to take his
~~~ ~~~. Scarcely less sad is the desperation of the pagan
Cecilius, represented in the dialogue of Minutius Felix, as
maintaining that, without any reasonable evidence for the old
religion, they must yet cling to it as a tradition; for he felt
that they must have some semblance of a religion, some opinion
of a supernatural care and a converse of Deity with men.
How much better is it," he said, "to receive just what our
fathers have told us, to worship the gods they taught us to
reverence even before we could have any true knowledge of
them, to allow ourselves no right of private judgment; but to
elieve our ancestors, who, in the infancy of mankind, near the
rtn of the world, were even considered worthy of having the
gods for their friends " What a strait is this for an intelligen
being to be in—holding fast, by his will, upon the belief of a
supernatural approach of the gods, in times gone by, without
any present evidence!

It is a very fine thing for many, saturated as they are with
Christian truth, and all but oppressed with the evidences of a
new creating grace and gospel, to invent speculative difficulties,
and finally take it up as wisdom or the better reason, to believe
n nothing but mere nature and her laws. But the recoil of
tne soul from such negations will come after, and it will be
terrible quite beyond their conception. We see this in the
facts just stated, and yet more affectingly in the history of
Clement the Roman, and of his conversion. He tells how he
was harassed from his childhood, by questions which paganism
could not help him to answer; such as relate to his being and
immortality, the origin of the world and its continuance, when
began, when it will end, and whither his present life is to
carry him. "Incessantly haunted," he says, "by such thoughts
as these which came I knew not whence, I was sorely troubled
~~ ~~~~ l grew pale and emaciated. . . . I resorted to
the schools of the philosophers, hoping to find some certain
foundation. I saw nothing but the piling up and tearing down
of theories. Thus was I driven to and fro, by the different
representations, and forced to conclude that things appear, not
as they are in themselves, but as they happen to be presented on
this or that side. I was made dizzier than ever, and, from the
ottom of my heart, sighed for deliverance." [2] Then he tells

how he resolved to visit Egypt, the land of mysteries and appa
ritions, there to hunt up some magician who could summon a
spirit for him from the other world ; for he thought, if he could
see a spirit, that would settle the question of immortality, and
give him a fixed point of truth. But in this unhappy state, in
quiring, distressed, agitated, he fell in with a Christian gospel,
heard it preached, there discovered what his soul had been
aching so long and bitterly to find, and there he found rest.

These illustrations from history show us most effectually how
little of true science there is, after all, in those who boast the
laws of progress, or a gospel of self-cultivation, as more rational
and hopeful than a gospel of faith. After all, they may see that,
when left to the proper darkness of nature, it is no such rational
and luminous state as they thought, but a night of gloom, a
longing vacancy, a hunger insupportable. Nature has no
promise for society, least of all any remedy for sin.

CHAPTER IX.

THE SUPERNATURAL COMPATIBLE WITH NATURE AND SUBJECT TO FIXED LAWS.

, as we have shown, there is no hope for man, or huma
ciety, under sin, save in the supernatural interposition of God
e are led to inquire, in the next place, what rational objectio
ere may be to such an interposition? And we find tw
jections alleged. *First*, That any such interference of super
tural agency is incompatible with the order of nature
condly, That the supernatural agency supposed is itself dis
nsed without law, and contrary, in that view, to reason. O
ese I will speak in their order. And—

I. I undertake to show that the supernatural divine agency,
[uired to provide an efficacious remedy for sin, is wholly com-
ible with nature; involving no breach of her laws, or dis-
bance of their systematic action.

I have already shown that nature is not, in any proper and
nplete sense, the system of God, but is in fact a subordinate
mber only, of a higher and virtually supernatural system, to
se uses it is subject. It is, in fact, a Thing; while the
l kingdom of God is a kingdom of Powers, Himself the
al Power. Both He and they are continually using the
ng, and pouring their activity into it, as the medial point
heir relationship; and this in a way we now propose to
v that is nowise incompatible with its laws; for the very
cient reason that, by these laws, it is originally submitted
heir activity. Not even what we call the dist

will be seen that not even miracles, wrought by a supernatural divine agency, necessarily imply any removal or suspension of such laws ; for nature is subjected by her laws, both to God's activity and to ours, *to be* thus acted on and varied in her operation by the new combinations or conjunctions of causes they are able to produce. Accordingly every result produced in this manner, whether by God or by men, represents nature supernaturally acted on, not nature overturned ; that is, it is natural in one view, in another supernatural ; natural as com ing to pass under and by the laws of nature ; supernatural as coming to pass by new conjunctions of causes, which are made by the action of wills upon nature.

What an immense action upon nature are we ourselves seen to have, as a race, when we consider the multifarious wheels and engines we have put at work, the heavy burdens we carry round the globe in our ships, the structures we raise, the culti vation we practise ! We make the world, in fact, another world. All of which is referrible to a force supernatural in the last degree. Nature, unapplied or uncombined by our wills, could do no such thing. Wills only have this power, and wills are supernatural. If now we have a power so immense over the world, as we see in all our works and wonders of contrivance, is it credible that God can have no way of access to nature, no power at all over nature ? Is He the only will excluded from a sovereignty over it ?

To illustrate this point yet farther, we will suppose a com pany of youth or children engaged in playing at ball. The ball is an inert spherical substance that will lie on the ground for ever, unless it is raised by some cause out of itself, and will never act save as it is acted on. It has a certain tenacity of parts and an elastic body, but no power in itself to move. Nevertheless we see it flying through the air in lively play, smitten, caught, thrown—the central object and instrument of what is called a game ; that is of a social strife between the players. It is, for the time, a medium of commerce in the lively battle of its motions between so many contesting agents. But the motions it has in the air, we observe, represent so many arms throwing it by its weight or driving it by its elasticity. So far its play is natural only. Then, if we inquire what moves the arms, we discover that it is done by the sudden con traction of muscles, acting under purely mechanical principles,

and this is natural. If now we push our inquiry still farther,
asking why the muscles contracted thus and thus, we discover
that this also happened by reason of mandates sent down to
them on the nervous cord, which, again, was equally natural.
But if we go still farther and ask what originated or caused the
wills to originate the mandates, the true answer is, that it was
the wills themselves acting by no causation, able to act or
not ; so that, if some one or more of the players is a truant
from school, or from home, transgressing, in the play, a direct
order of restriction, he will know that he is doing wrong, and
blame himself for the wrong he does, simply because it is an
immediate, irresistible conviction of his mind that he is im
pelled to his disobedience by no cause whatever. Doubtless
he has ends, reasons, motives, but these are no causes of his
act ; for he knows that he could and ought to have resisted
them all. Here then we finally arrive at a power supernatural,
moving all the hands and bats of the players. The ball is at
one end of so many chains of causes, and the free wills of the
players at the other. The ball would never have stirred but
for the arms, nor these but for the contractions of the muscles,
nor these contracted but for the mandates sent down to them,
which mandates, in the last degree, are the peremptory acts of
so many free wills or powers that act supernaturally from no
causation. Just here, then, rises the question, if the play is
thus carried on by causes which, in the last degree, are super
natural, is there any overturning or disorder of nature implied
in it ? Manifestly not ; and for the simple reason that the
bats, and arms, and hands, and muscles, are by their very laws
subordinated, as chains of causes, to the supernatural power that
wields them. The play is natural, therefore, as being through
and by those subordinated agents ; and supernatural, as being
from that power. We have no thought of a miracle in the case,
or of any implied overturning of nature which is shocking to
our faith. On the contrary, the event is so common, so remote
from anything extraordinary, that we are very likely to look
upon it as a transaction wholly in the world of natural cause
and effect.

We come now to the application. Nature is to God and his
spiritual and free creatures what the ball is to the players.
In one view, we may regard the Almighty Ruler of the world
us the sensorium and active brain of the world ; having an

immediate power of action through every member and every line of causes in it ; able, in that manner, to maintain a con stant living agency in its events, without really infringing its order, or obstructing and suspending its laws in any instance. Nature is pliant thus to Him, as the body of the players to them ; and as the natural order of their body is not violated by the mandates they put upon it, so there is full opportunity for God to do his wonders of power and redemption in the earth, without violating any condition of natural order and system whatever. His access to all the lines of causes in nature may be as truly normal as that which the soul has, at that secret point of the brain where it delivers its mandates to the body.

We are speaking here, it will be observed, not of God's possible activity, as being the activity of nature. That is a different conception. What we now say is, that, supposing all the forces and laws of nature to continue for ever, there is also room for the perpetual acting of God upon the lines of causes in nature, doing His will supernaturally in it, or upon it, just as we do, and yet in perfect compatibility with the laws and the settled order of nature. He may as well act Himself into the world as we, and nature will as little be overturned by His action as by ours. Nor will it create any difficulty that He acts like Himself, and in ways proportionate to His infinite majesty.

That nature is in fact submitted to His action, as to ours, in the manner supposed, is evident from the report of science it self. For when the geologists show that new races of animal and vegetable life have taken a beginning, at successive points in the history of the creation, that whole realms of living creatures disappear again and again, to be succeeded by others fresh from the hand of God, what does it signify but that the atoms and elemental forces of nature are so related to God that they do, by their own laws, submit themselves to His will, flowing into new combinations, and composing thus new germs of life ? These successive repopulations of the rocks were not produced by so many overturnings of nature—that is too ex travagant for belief, and stands in no harmony with what we know of God. On the contrary, every element of force and every atom of matter concerned in these new births of life was acting, we are to believe, in its moment of new combination, precisely as, according to its inherent properties and laws, it ever had done and ever will do.   It was only instigated by a divine force not in its natural laws ; and in the quickening of that yielding itself up, by these laws, to organize and live. Nor was the visitation of Mary, glorious and sacred as the mystery was, a transaction at all different in principle, or one that involved, in fact, any violation of nature not involved in the other just named.   So also when we discover the world, or human race, groaning under the penal disorders and bondage of sin, the deliverance of those disorders by a supernatural power involves no overturning of the causes at work, or the laws by which they work, but only that these causes are, by their laws, submitted to the will and supernatural action of God, so that He can arrange new conjunctions, and accomplish, in that man ner, results of deliverance.   Indeed, a physician does precisely the same thing in principle, when, appealing as he thinks to the laws of substances, he brings them into combinations that are from himself, and places them in connexions to exert a healing force.

It will further assist our conceptions and modify our impres sions of this subject, if we inquire briefly into the office and probable use of what is called nature.   That nature is not appointed as any final end of God, we have before shown.   It is only ordained, as we then intimated, to be played upon by the powers ; that is, by God Himself and all free agents under Him.   Instead of being the veritable system or universe of God, as in our sensuality or scientific conceit we make it, we may call it more truly the ball or medial substance occupied by so many players ; that is, by the spiritual universe under God as the Lord of Hosts.   There could be no commerce of so many players in the game referred to, without some medium or medial instrument ; and the instrument needed to be a constant, invariable substance, as regards shape, weight, size, elasticity, inertia, and all the natural properties pertaining to it.   If the ball changed weight, colour, density, shape every moment, no skill could be acquired or evinced in the use of it ; there would be no real test in the game, and no social commerce of play in the parties using it.   Therefore it needed to be, so far, a con stant quantity.   So, demonstrably, there needs to be, between us and God, and between us and one another, some constant quantity, so that we can act upon each other, trace the effects of our practice and that of others, learn the mind of God, the misery and baseness of wrong, the worth of principles, and the blessedness of virtue, from what we experience ; attaining thus to such a degree of wisdom, that we can set our life on a footing of success and divine approbation. What we call nature is this constant quantity interposed between us and God, and between us and each other—the great ball, in using which, our life battle is played. Or, considering the grand immensity of planetary worlds, careering through the fields of light, all these, we may say, rolling eternally onward in their rounds of order, bearing their wondrous furniture with them, such as science discovers, and weaving their interminable lines of causes, are the ball of exercise, in which, and by which, God is training and teaching the spiritual hosts of His empire. They are set in a system of immutable order and constancy for this reason ; but with the design, beforehand, that all the free beings or powers shall play their activity on them and into them, and that He, too, by the free insertion of His, may turn them about by His counsel, and so make Himself and His counsel open to the commerce of His children.

So far, therefore, from discovering anything undignified or superstitious in the admission of a supernatural agency and government of God in the world, it is, in fact, the only worthy and exalted conception. It no more humbles the world or de ranges the scientific order of it to let God act upon it, than to let man do the same ; as we certainly know that he does, without any thought of overturning its laws. On the other hand, to imagine, in the way of dignifying the world, that God must let it alone and simply see it go, is only to confess that it was made for no such glorious intent as we have supposed.

To serve this intent, two things manifestly are wanted, and one as truly as the other ; viz., nature and the supernatural, an invariable, scientific order, and a pliant submission of that order to the sovereignty and uses of wills, human and divine, without any infringement of its constancy. For if nature were to be violated and tossed about by capricious overturnings of her laws, there would be an end of all confidence and exact intelli gence. And if it could not be used, or set in new conjunctions, by God and his children, it would be a wall, a catacomb, and nothing more. And yet this latter is the world of scientific naturalism—a world that might well enough answer for the

housing of manakins, but not for the exercise of living men.
It would seem to be enough to for ever dissipate any such un
believing tendencies, simply to have caught, for once, the differ
ence between the constancy of causes separated from uses, and
the constancy of causes limbered and subjected to the uses of
eternal freedom and intelligence. That is the world of causation, this of religion ; that a dumb-bell exercise for arms that
are dumb-bells themselves, this a living order, set in the contact
and consecrated to the uses of spirit ; that a world as being a
world, this is a grand gymnasium of powers whom God is train
ing for society and commerce with Himself.

Furthermore, it is plain that, if there is no supernatural
agency of God permissible or credible in the world, then there
is practically no government over it. It makes no difference,
touching the point here in question, whether we regard nature
as being literally a machine, wound up to run by its own causes
apart from God, or whether we regard the causes and laws as
being themselves the immediate action of God, always present
to them and in them.   For if He is present thus, only as the
soul of its causes or the will operating in its laws, then that
presence, if restricted, as naturalism requires, to the mere run
of nature, and allowed no liberty of help in the disorders of
evil, is scarcely better than the presence of Ixion at his wheel.
If we speak of God, the Almighty, He is a being mortgaged for
eternity to the round of nature ; a grim idol for science to
worship, but no Father to weakness or Redeemer to faith.

Or if we imagine that God has so planned the world of nature
that, running on by its own inherent laws and causes, it will
always, by a pre-established harmony, bring just the events to
pass that are wanted ; soothe the sorrows, comfort the re
pentances, hear the prayers, redress the wrongs, chastise the
crimes of his subjects ; still it is with our faith practically as
if it were living in a mill, and not as if it were concerned, hour
by hour, with the living God. God is really not accessible.
We have access only to the mill we are in, with joy to feel it
running !   There is no such reciprocity between us and God as
to answer the wants of our hearts, or the necessities of our moral
training.

Besides, if it be maintained that nature is the proper uni
verse of God, and that no conception is admissible of powers
outside of nature acting upon it to vary the action it would

otherwise have by itself, then follows the very shocking conse quence that, since the creation, God has had and can hereafter have no work of liberty to do. Nature is His monument, and not His garment. Not only are miracles out of the question, but counsel and action also. He is under a scientific embargo, neither hearing nor helping His children, nor indeed giving any signs of recognition. And the reason is worse, if possible, and more chilling than the fact, viz., that if He should stir, He would move something that science requires to be let alone! A great many Christians are confused and chilled by a difficulty resembled to this feeling, when they go to God in worship or prayer, that nothing can reasonably be expected of Him, because reason allows Him to do nothing. It is as if He were one of those spent meteors to which the Indians offer sacrifice—a hard, cold rock of iron, which they worship for the noise it made a long time ago, when it fell from the sky, and not because it is likely ever to make even a noise again.

Just here, the view we are advancing is seen to have an im. mense practical as well as speculative consequence. It finds how to conceive God in a state of as great activity now as He was when He made the world—always active from eternity to eternity. Every work of His hand is pliant still to His counsel. He is doing something, able to do all we want. In all events and changes He has a present concern. He turns about not the clouds only, but all the wheels of nature, by His ever-living power and government. He is an Agent, as much more real than Nature, as He is wider in his reach and more sovereign. He can produce variant results through invariable causes, and so can make the world of things keep company with the vari ant demands of want, weakness, wickedness, and merit ; of love, truth, justice, and holy supplication, in His children. It is no longer as if, at some given point in the solitude of His eternity, He waked up and created the worlds, since which time He has neither done nor can ever be expected to do anything more, because it is the right now of the laws of nature to do every thing uninterrupted. Contrary to this, He is the Living God, and can as readily meet us and bend Himself and His works to our condition or request, as a man, without any infringement of his body can bend it to his uses. Nature is seen to be subjected to His constant agency by its laws themselves, which laws He has never to suspend, but only to employ, having the great

realm of nature flexible as a hand to His will for ever.   Now H
is no more fenced away from us by nature, no more closeted be
hind it, to sleep away his deaf and idle eternity; but He is wit
us and about us, filling all things with His potent energy an
fatherly counsel.   He maintains a relationship as real an
practical with us as we have with each other.

II. I undertake, in opposition to the objection which sup
poses that the supernatural agency of God is itself subject to n
law or system, to show that it is regulated and dispensed b
immutable and fixed laws.   As intelligent creatures, we cai
have no comfort under a condition ruled by no law or system
and conformed to no principles of intelligence.   We instinctively
demand that everything in God's plan shall stand in the stric
unity of reason, even as the old astronomers strive to comprehend the heavenly bodies and their motions, in the figures oi
geometry and the fixed proportions of arithmetic.   This high
instinct of our nature, God, we may be sure, will never violate.

1. Since God has inserted in our nature this instinctive
opinion of law, as necessary to the honour of His government,
and the comfort of our reason under it, we have, in the fact, a
very certain proof that His government will be such as to meet
our respect, and satisfy the yearnings of our intelligence.

2. The fa   na ure is a realm, organized under fixed
laws is itself ⏐ ⏐ ╀ ╴ ╛ ──── satisfactory evidence that such
is the manner of God also in things supernatural.   Who that
simply looks on the heavenly worlds, for example, can suffer a
doubt afterward, that God will do everything in terms of law
and strict systematic unity.

3. Since God is the sovereign intelligence, the Perfect Reason,
He will Himself have an affinity for law and systematic unity,
as much stronger than we, as He is higher in order than we,
and broader in the comprehension of His understanding.   Hence
it is impossible to believe that in anything, even the smallest,
He will deviate from rules of universal application—least of all
in the highest order of His works, even such as He displays in
the grace of our redemption.

4. The moral and religious need we have of such a faith
makes it indispensable.   To let go of such a faith, or lose it, is
to plunge at once into superstition.   If any Christian, the most
devout, believes in a miracle, or a providence that is done outside of all system and law, he is so far on the way to polytheism.

The unity of God always perishes when the unity of order and law is lost. And we may as well believe in one God acting on or against another, as in the same God acting outside of all fixed laws and terms of immutable order. Indeed, I suppose it was in just this way that polytheism began. The transition is easy and natural, from a superstitious belief in one God who acts without system, to a belief in many who will much more naturally do the same.

But the main difficulty here is not to establish a reasonable conviction that the supernatural works of God must be dis pensed by fixed laws; it is to find how this may be, or be intelligently conceived. And here lies the main stress of our present inquiry.

To open the way, then, to a just and clear conception of the great fact stated, it will be necessary to enter into some im portant distinctions concerning law, or what is properly meant by the word *law*.

The word is used with many varieties of meaning, but always, and in all its varieties, having one element that is constant, viz., the opinion had of its uniformity; as that, in exactly the same circumstances, it will always and for ever do, bring to pass, direct, or command precisely the same thing. Without this no law is ever regarded as a law.

Observing this fundamental fact, we notice the distinction next of natural and moral law. Natural law is the law by which any kind of being or thing is made to act invariably, thus or thus, in virtue of terms inherent in itself; as when any body of matter gravitates by reason of its matter, and according to the quantity of its matter.

Moral law pertains never to a thing, or to any substance in the chain of cause and effect, but only to a free intelligence, or self-active power. Its rule is authority, not force. It com mands, but does not actuate or determine. It speaks to assent or choice, inviting action, but operating nothing apart from choice. It imposes obligation, leaving the subject to obey or not, clear of any enforcement, save that of conviction before hand, and penalty afterward.

It will be seen at once that God's supernatural works in Christ and the Spirit are not reducible under either of these two kinds of law, the natural or the moral. To a certain ex tent, God's nature will be a law to His action, even as ours is a necessary law to us. Thus, if we are intelligent, our intelli gent nature will manifest effects of intelligence. If we form necessary ideas of figure, space, time, truth, right, justice, there will be something in our action, that reveals these ideas. In ike manner, if we are free agents, it is made impossible for us by a fixed law of nature, to act as mere things, under the law of cause and effect. So, if God is infinite in His nature then it is a fixed law of His nature that he shall indicate infinity in His action, and if He has geometric ideas, that His works shall, by a necessary consequence, have some fixed relation to the laws of geometry; such as we discover in the spheres, and orbits, and projectile curves, and in the subtle triangulations of light. Thus it is rightly affirmed by the great Hooker, that " the being of God is a kind of law to His working."[1] And so far does he carry this opinion as to hint the probable neces sity that God, being both one and three, an essential unity and a threefold personality, there will, of course, be something in His works correspondent with His nature.

So again, if we speak of the law moral, that is a law as com pletely sovereign over God as it is over us. It is the eternal necessary law of right or of love; a law that He acknowledges with a ready and full assent for ever; that which determines the immutable order, and purity, and glory of His character. And then, of course, the law accepted in His own character will be a law published to his subjects to be the rule of theirs. Moral law then, by the free consent of God, shapes the divine character, and so the character and ends of his govern. ment.

But though natural law and moral law have much to do, as here discovered, in determining and moulding all the conduct of God, we do not immediately conceive what is meant by the fact, that the supernatural works of God are dispensed by fixed laws, till we bring into view a third kind of law, viz., the law of one's end, or the law which one's reason imposes in the way of attaining his end. Moral law, we have said, shapes the char acter of God, and that determines His end. Since he is a morally perfect being in His character, moral perfection or holi ness will be the last end of His being, that for which He creates and rules; for, if He were to value holiness only as the means of some other end, such as happiness, then He would even disrespect holiness, rating it only as a convenience; which is not the character of a holy being, but only an imposture in the name of such a character. Regarding holiness, then, as God's last end, His world-plan will be gathered round the end proposed, to fulfil it, and all His counsels will crystallize into order and system, subject to that end. For this nature will exist, in all her vast machinery of causes and laws; to this all the miracles and supernatural works of redemption will bring their contributions. Having this for His end, and the supernatural as means to His end, the divine reason will of course order all under fixed laws of reason, which laws will be so exact and universal as to make a perfect system.

How this may result we can see from a simple reference to ourselves. Thus, if a man undertakes to be honest, having that for an end, then it will be seen that his end so far becomes a law to all his actions; that is, a law self-imposed, one which his reason prescribes, and which, in accepting his end, he freely accepts. So if a man's end is to be rich, we shall see that his end is a law to his whole life-plan, or at least so far a law that it fails only where his reason or judgment falls short of a perfect perception. Or we may take a case more exact and palpable, the case of a player at the game of chess. The end he proposes is to win the game, and that end, subordinating his reason or skill, will become a law to every move he makes on the diagram, except where his skill is at fault, or his understanding short of comprehension. If now we suppose him to be gifted with a perfect skill or an all-perceiving reason, it will result that every move made will be determined with such exactness and uniformity, that, if he were to play the game over a million of times, he would never in a single case move differently in exactly the same circumstances.

Here, then, is what we mean by affirming that all God's supernatural acts, providences, and works, supernatural though they be, will yet be dispensed in all cases by immutable, universal, and fixed laws. It will be so because His end never varies, and His reason is perfect. Therefore His world-plan, though comprehending the supernatural, will be an exact and perfect system of order, centered in the eternal unity of reason about His last end. There will be nothing desultory in it, nothing irregular, nothing so particular as to happen apart from rule and universal counsel. The order of the heavens, and the

angles of the light will not be more perfect, because the reason
f the supernatural is equally precise and clear.   The same
work will always be done in the same circumstances, withou a
semblance of variation.   Even as the dial, under the laws of
nature will make the same shadow, at the same hour, for an
eternal succession of days, so the good gift and perfect from
above will come down from the Father of lights, punctual and
true in its order, as from one whose counsel is perfect, and with
whom is no variableness, neither shadow of turning   Order
everlasting order, reigns where least we look for it, and where
the unthinking and crude mind of superstition would deem it
even a merit that God had broken loose from His eternity of
law to bless the world at will.

But how is it conceivable, some one may ask, that such
works as are comprehended in the range of human redemption
should take place systematically under fixed laws ?   To this we
answer that it is not necessary to such a conviction that we
should be able to conceive *how* these operate, or what they are
All we need is to find the possible and probable fact ; which
having found we can as little doubt or dismiss the conviction
of some presiding law as we can the faith of universal laws in
nature, where we do not know the laws or cannot discover the
secret of their action.   For example, we know in general what
is the law of miracles, viz., that they are wrought as attesta
tions of a Divine mission in those by whom they are wrought ;
but their particular occasions, times, and properties, why
wrought by this and not by another, why at one time, or in one
age, and not in succeeding ages, we may not be able to discover
The aw is beyond our investigation, but that there is a law
and that exactly the same miracles will be wrought, if wrought
at all in exactly the same conditions or spiritual connexions
even to eternity, we have no more room to doubt than we have
to question God's intelligence.   For if God's end is the same
He can never deviate or omit to do exactly the same things in
exactly the same circumstances, without some defect of intelli
gence.   Either now or before He must confess to a mistake   If
He is perfect in wisdom now, He was not then ; if then He is
not now.   But when we say " exactly the same circumstances,"
it is important for us to notice the extent of the qualification ;
or this will bring into view a great principle of distinction
between the natural and the supernatural, apart from which the

extraordinary and apparently desultory manifestations of the latter cannot be understood. Nature is a machine, compounded of wheels and moved by steady powers. Hence it goes in rounds or cycles, returning again and again into itself, produc ing thus seasons, months, and years; repeating its dews, and showers, and storms, and varied temperatures; in the same circumstances or times, doing much the same things. But it is not so in the affairs of a mind, a society, or an age. There the motion is never in circles, but onward, eternally onward. Nothing is ever repeated. No mind or spirit can reproduce a yesterday. No age, the age or even year that is past. The combinations of circumstances may have a certain analogy, but they are never the same, or even nearly so. If they are near enough to require a repetition by the Saviour of His miracle of the loaves, they will yet be so far different as to require a dif ference in the miracle. And where the outward conditions appear to be exactly the same, the inward states and spiritual connexions may be so various as to take away all resemblance; requiring Paul to raise a Publius out of his fever at Malta, and leave a Trophimus sick at Miletum. We have no argument against uniformity and law in such diversities, for in reality there is no recurrence of circumstances and conditions such as at first view might be supposed. So if miracles appear in one age and not in another, it is because the world is moving on in a right line, reproducing no conditions and circumstances of the past, but, by conditions always new, is demanding a treatment correspondently new. Hence, while the course of nature is a round of repetitions, the course of the supernatural repeats nothing, and for that reason takes an aspect of variety that appears even to exclude the fact of law. But it is so only in appearance. God's perfect wisdom still requires the same things to be done in the same circumstances, and, when not the same, as nearly the same as the circumstances are nearly resembled. Everything transpires in the uniformity of law.

Thus we may assert as confidently, as if it occurred a hun dred times a day, that a supernatural event, never known to occur but once, takes place under an immutable and really universal law; such, for example, as the great, world-astound ing miracle of the incarnation. In exactly the same conditions, if they were to occur a million of times in the universe (which may or may not be a violent supposition), precisely the same miracle also would recur, and that with as great certainty as the natural law of gravity will cause a stone to fall, when for the millionth time its support is taken away. Living here upon this ant-hill, which we call the world, and seeing only the yard of space and the day of time our field occupies, we are likely to judge that an event which never occurred but once since the world began must be an event apart from all order and system ; even as a savage, but a little more childish than we, might imagine that some new deity is breaking into the world when he sees the air-stone fall, because he never saw the like before. Indeed, we have only to look into the appearings of the Jehovah angel, previous to the incarnate appearing of the Word, noting all the approaches and gradual preparations of the event, to see how certainly God has a way and a law for it, and will not bring it to pass till the law decrees it and the fulness of time is come. Could we look into the history, too, of the innumerable other worlds God has comprehended in His reign, what a lesson might we thence derive from events counterpart to this of the incarnation, varied only to meet the varied conditions of their want, character, and destiny. Though we may not be able, creatures of a day, to unfold the law of this grand miracle, and reduce it to a formula of science, how little reason have we in our inability to question the fact of such a law ?

Besides, it is a fact that the laws of a great many of God's supernatural works are made known or discovered to us. Thus God dispenses the Holy Spirit by fixed laws. Prayer, also, is heard by laws as definite as the laws of equilibrium in forces. And what is called the doctrine of the Spirit and the doctrine of prayer, as given in the Scriptures, is, in fact, nothing more nor less than the unfolding to us, if we could so regard it, of the laws of the Spirit and the laws of prayer, as pertaining to the supernatural kingdom of God. Indeed, there is wanting now for the more intelligent guidance of Christian disciples to con solidate their faith and save them from the extravagancies of fanaticism, a practical treatise on the laws of prayer, of spiritual gifts, and of the dispensation of the Holy Spirit generally, These two great powers, the hearing of prayer and the dispens ing of the Spirit, are like the waterfalls and winds of nature, to which we set our wheels and lift our sails, and so by their known laws take advantage of their efficacy. A crystal or

gem that is being distilled and shaped in the secret depths of
the world, is not shaped by laws as well understood as the law
of the Spirit of life when it moulds the secret order and beauty
of a soul.

Our conclusion therefore is, that all God's works, even such
as are most distinctly supernatural, are determined by fixed
laws. This is true of all supernatural events, with the single
exception of the bad and wicked actions of men. And these
are out of all terms of law, not because they are supernatural,
but only because they are bad. Indeed, it is a somewhat
singular and even curious fact, that while so great jealousy is
felt in our time of miracles and all immediate spiritual opera
tions of God, as being so many violations of order and fixed
law in the universe, the only known events in the world, of
which that is really true, are the bad actions of bad men, or of
bad spirits generally. These are not subject to any fixed laws;
they consent to no law. They are determined neither by the
laws of causality, nor by the laws of a good end ; which are laws
of reason, truth, and beneficence. They have no agreement
with the world, or with God, or even with the constituent wellbeing of the doers themselves. All that can be apprehended of
miracles is true of them, and even more. Their damning
miracle is everywhere, and the confusion they make is real.
If those persons who are so ready to apprehend some destruc
tion, or implied destruction of law in the faith of miracles, would
turn their thoughts upon these real disorders, and conceive
them as the only known facts in our world that have no subjec
tion to law, they would have a good point of beginning for the
cure of their scepticism generally.

It cannot be necessary to pursue this topic farther. But it
may be well to notice, before we drop the subject, one or two
false impressions very commonly entertained by the natural
philosophers and poets of nature, whose scepticism is oftener
grounded in such impressions than in formal arguments. They
are greatly impressed by the immutable reign of order and law
in nature, deeming it the highest point of sublimity, in all the
known manifestations of God. Not seldom, indeed, is this
point magnified by them, in terms of admiration, that reflect a
certain contempt on the Christian ideas of God ; as if it were
possible only to an over-easy credulity, to imagine that God will

descend from His high position of law to do such things as the preaching and praying disciples of Christianity expect of Him. Gazing into the sky, and beholding the eternal, changeless roll of the worlds, every orb in the track, where the astrologers of Babylon and Egypt saw it long ages ago, never to vary or falter in the longer ages to come—image, how sublime, they exclaim, of the divine greatness! Greater and sublimer still, that the same undeviating rule of law is equally conspicuous in the smallest things; that in every salt and pebble there is a little astronomy of atoms whose laws are as old as the stars, and whose constancy is a reflection of theirs! No, the wonder of God's way is not here, but it is that He can make constancy flexible to so many myriads of uses, and the uses themselves— all but the abuses—a system of order and law as complete and perfect as that of the stars. Constancy, as a mere post or position, has no dignity. The true dignity and miracle of order is constancy made flexible to use and expression. Sir Charles Bell had no such thought as that he could magnify the beauty of God's way in the hand, by simply showing the curious articu lations by which it is mechanically strengthened in its gripe; the chief wonder, the real miracle of beauty in the instrument, as he well understood, lies in its flexibility, its ready submission to so many and such endlessly varied uses. Let us not be taken by the mere stability of nature, because it compliments our vanity by the easy understanding it permits. Magnitudes, weights, distances, regularities, are not the highest symbols of God's creative dignity. The glory, the true sublimity of God's architectural wisdom is that, while His work stands fast in immutable order, it bends so gracefully to the humblest things, without damage or fracture, pliant to all free action, both His and ours; receiving the common play of our liberty, and becom ing always a fluent medium of reciprocal action between us; to Him a hand showing His handiwork, or even a tongue which day unto day uttereth speech, and night unto night showeth forth knowledge of Him; to us the ground of our works, the instrument of our choices, and yet, in the order, all, of a perfect counsel and of laws as immutable as His throne. In this rests the doctrine of faith, the doctrine that justifies prayer, enables the disciple to believe that God can notice him, and move among causes to help him; raising him thus into a state of ennobled consciousness, how superior to the low mechanical

scepticism which thinks itself dignified in the discovery that
God, incrusted in the stiffness of his scientific order, has no
longer any power to bend Himself to man.

The other point alluded to has reference to the comparative
estimate of nature and the supernatural. Unexercised in the
great world of Christian thought, uninitiated by years of holy
experience in its deep mysteries, the natural philosopher and
poet very commonly look upon the supernatural, or, what is the
same, Christianity, as comprised of a few stray facts or ghostly
wonders, much less credible than they might be, and turn away
with a kind of pity from a field so narrow, to what they call a
broader and more satisfactory teaching—that of the great school
of nature. Here is variety, they say, beauty, magnificence,
greatness, and a sound, consistent order, worthy of God. This,
they imagine, is the true revelation.

How little do such minds conceive what the world of super
natural fact comprises. Go to nature for the great and quick
ening thoughts, the wonders and broad truths! Call nature
the grand revelation! Is it more to go to nature and know it,
than to know God? Are there deeper depths in nature, higher
sublimities, thoughts more captivating and glorious? In the
mineral and vegetable shapes are there finer themes than in the
life of Jesus? In the storms and gorgeous pilings of the
clouds, are there manifestations of greatness and beauty more
impressive than in the tragic sceneries of the cross? Nature
is the realm of things, the supernatural is the realm of powers.
There the spinning worlds return into their circles and keep
returning. Here the grand life-empire of mind, society, truth,
liberty, and holy government, spreads itself in the view, unfold
ing always in changes, vast, various, and divinely beneficent.
There we have a Georgic, or a hymn of the seasons; here an
epic that sings a lost Paradise. There God made the wheels of
His chariot and set them rolling. Here He rides forth in it,
leading His host after Him; vast in counsel, wonderful in
working; preparing and marshalling all for a victory in good
and blessing; fashioning in beauty, composing in spiritual
order, and so gathering in the immense populations of the
worlds to be one realm—angels, archangels, seraphim, thrones,
dominions, principalities, powers, and saints of mankind—all to
find, in His works of guidance and new-creating grace, a volume
of wisdom. which it will be the riches of their eternity to study.

Thus we conceive, alas! too feebly, the true scale of dignity in God's two realms. In one the order is superficial and palpable. In the other it is deep as eternity, mysterious and vast as the counsel that comprehends eternity, in its development. Still it is counsel, it is order, it is truth and reason. Even as the Revelation of John contrives, in so many ways, to intimate, by the using of exact numbers for those which are not; in the seven angels, and seven trumpets, and seven vials; in the four beasts, and four and twenty elders; in the hundred forty and four thousand of them that are sealed; in the city, the new Jerusalem, that is four-square, having its height, length, and breadth equal; with twelve gates, tended by twelve angels, resting on twelve foundations, that are twelve manner of precious stones—by such images, and under such exact notations of arithmetic, does this man of vision put us on conceiving, as we best can, the glorious and exact society God is reconstructing out of the fallen powers. We shall see it to be all in law; settled in such terms of order, that all counsel, act, and joy, both His and ours, will be in terms of everlasting truth and reason, a realm as much more wonderful than nature, as liberties of mind are more difficult to master than material quantities.

CHAPTER X.

THE CHARACTER OF JESUS FORBIDS HIS POSSIBLE CLASSIFICATION WITH MEN.

THE need of a supernatural, divine ministration, to restore the disorders of sin, is now shown; also that such a ministration is compatible with the order of nature, and, being in that view a rational possibility, that it may well be assumed as a probable expectation. In this manner we are brought directly up to con front the main question—Is the exigency met by the fact? is the supernatural divine ministration actually set up, and shown to be by adequate evidence?

Here we raise a question, for the first time, that puts the Christian Scriptures in issue; for it is the grand peculiarity of these sacred writings, that they deal in supernatural events and transactions, and show the fact of a celestial institution finally erected on earth, in the person of Jesus Christ, which is called the kingdom of God or of heaven, and is in fact a perpetual, supernatural dispensatory of healing and salvation for the race. Christianity is, in this view, no mere scheme of doctrine, or of ethical practice, but is instead a kind of miracle, a power out of nature and above, descending into it; a historically super natural movement on the world, that is visibly entered into it, and organized to be an institution in the person of Jesus Christ. He, therefore, is the central figure and power, and with Him the entire fabric either stands or falls.

To this central figure, then, we now turn ourselves; and, as no proof beside the light is necessary to show that the sun shines, so we shall find that Jesus proves Himself by His own self-evidence. ' The simple inspection of His life and character will suffice to show that He cannot be classified with mankind (man though He be), any more than what we call His miracles can be classified with mere natural events.   The simple demon strations of His life and spirit are the sufficient attestation of His own profession, when He says—"I am from above"— "I came down from heaven."

Let us not be misunderstood.   We do not assume the truth of the narrative by which the manner and facts of the life of Jesus are reported to us; for this, by the supposition, is the matter in question.   We only assume the representations them. selves, as being just what they are, and discover their necessary truth in the transcendent, wondrously self-evident picture of divine excellence and beauty presented in them.   We take up the account of Christ in the New Testament, just as we would any other ancient writing, or as if it were a manuscript just brought to light in some ancient library.   We open the book, and discover in it four distinct biographies of a certain remark able character, called Jesus Christ.   He is miraculously born of Mary, a virgin of Galilee, and declares Himself, without scruple, that He came out from God.   Finding the supposed history made up, in great part, of His mighty acts, and not being disposed to believe in miracles and marvels, we should soon dismiss the book as a tissue of absurdities too extravagant for belief, were we not struck with the sense of something very peculiar in the character of this remarkable person.   Having our attention arrested thus by the impression made on our re spect, we are put on inquiry, and the more we study it the more wonderful as a character it appears.   And before we have done, it becomes, in fact, the chief wonder of the story; lifting all the other wonders into order and intelligent proportion round it, and making one compact and glorious wonder of the whole picture—a picture shining in its own clear sunlight upon us, as the truest of all truths—Jesus, the Divine Word, coming out from God, to be incarnate with us, and be the vehicle of God and salvation to the race.

On the single question, therefore, of the more than human character of Jesus, we propose in perfect confidence, to rest a principal argument for Christianity as a supernatural institu tion; for, if there be in Jesus a character which is not human, then has something broken into the world that is not of it, and the spell of unbelief is broken.

Not that Christianity might not be a supernatural institution,

if Jesus were only a man ; for many prophets and holy men, as
we believe, have brought forth to the world communications
that are not from themselves, but were received by inspira
tions from God.   There are several grades, too, of the super
natural, as already intimated ;   the supernatural human,
the supernatural prophetic, the supernatural demonic and
angelic, the supernatural divine.   Christ, we shall see, is the
supernatural manifested in the highest grade or order, viz., the
divine.

We observe, then, as a first peculiarity at the root of His
character, that He begins life with a perfect youth.   His child
hood is an unspotted, and withal a kind of celestial flower.
The notion of a superhuman or celestial childhood, the most
difficult of all things to be conceived, is yet successfully drawn
by a few simple touches.   He is announced beforehand as
" that Holy Thing ;" a beautiful and powerful stroke to raise
our expectation to the level of a nature so mysterious.   In His
childhood, everybody loves Him.   Using words of external de
scription, He is shown growing up in favour with God and man,
a child so lovely and beautiful that heaven and earth appear to
smile upon Him together.   So, when it is added that the child
grew and waxed strong in spirit, filled with wisdom, and, more
than all, that the grace or beautifying power of God was upon
Him, we look, as on the unfolding of a sacred flower, and seem
to scent a fragrance wafted on us from other worlds.   Then, at
the age of twelve, He is found among the great learned men of
the day, the doctors of the temple, hearing what they say, and
asking them questions.   And this without any word that indi.
cates forwardness or pertness in the child's manner, such as
some Christian Rabbi or silly and credulous devotee would cer
tainly have added.   The doctors are not offended, as by a child
too forward or wanting in modesty, they are only amazed that
such a degree of understanding can dwell in one so young and
simple.   His mother finds Him there among them, and begins
to expostulate with Him.   His reply is very strange ; it must,
she is sure, have some deep meaning that corresponds with His
mysterious birth, and the sense He has ever given her of a some
thing strangely peculiar in His ways ; and she goes home keep
ing His saying in her heart, and guessing vainly what His
thought may be.   Mysterious, holy secret, which this mother

hides in her bosom, that her holy thing, her child whom she
has watched during the twelve years of His celestial childhood,
now begins to speak of being "about His Father's business,"
in words of dark enigma, which she cannot fathom.

Now we do not say, observe, that there is one word of truth
in these touches of narration. We only say that, whether they
be fact or fiction, here is given the sketch of a perfect and
sacred childhood—not of a simple, lovely, ingenuous, and pro
perly human childhood, such as the poets love to sketch, but
of a sacred and celestial childhood. In this respect the early
character of Jesus is a picture that stands by itself. In no
other case that we remember, has it ever entered the mind of
a biographer, in drawing a character, to represent it as begin
ning with a spotless childhood. The childhood of the great
human characters, if given at all, is commonly represented, ac
cording to the uniform truth, as being more or less contrary to
the manner of their maturo age ; and never as being strictly
one with it, except in those cases of inferior eminence where
the kind of distinction attained to is that of some mere prodigy,
and not a character of greatness in action, or of moral excel
lence. In all the higher ranges of character, the excellence
portrayed is never the simple unfolding of a harmonious and
perfect beauty contained in the germ of childhood, but it is a
character formed by a process of rectification, in which many
follies are mended and distempers removed ; in which confidence
is checked by defeat, passion moderated by reason, smartness
sobered by experience. Commonly a certain pleasure is taken
in showing how the many wayward sallies of the boy are, at
length, reduced by discipline to the character of wisdom, justice,
and public heroism so much admired.

Besides, if any writer, of almost any age, will undertake to
describe, not merely a spotless, but a superhuman or celestial
childhood, not having the reality before him, he must be some
what more than human himself, if he does not pile together
a mass of clumsy exaggerations, and draw and overdraw, till
neither heaven nor earth can find any verisimilitude in the
picture.

Neither let us omit to notice what ideas the Rabbis and
learned doctors of this age were able, in fact, to furnish, when
setting forth a remarkable childhood. Thus Josephus, drawing
on the teachings of the Rabbis, tells how the infant Moses, when

the King of Egypt took him out of his daughter's arms, and playfully put the diadem on his head, threw it pettishly down and stamped on it. And when Moses was three years old, he tells us that the child had grown so tall, and exhibited such a wonderful beauty of countenance, that people were obliged, as it were, to stop and look at him as he was carried along the road, and were held fast by the wonder, gazing till he was out of sight. See, too, what work is made of the childhood of Jesus himself, in the Apocryphal gospels. These are written by men of so nearly the same era, that we may discover, in their embellish ments, what kind of a childhood it was in the mere invention of the time to make out. While the gospels explicitly say that Jesus wrought no miracles till His public ministry began, and that He made His beginning in the miracle of Cana, these are ambitious to make Him a great prodigy in His childhood. They tell how, on one occasion, He pursued, in His anger, the other children, who refused to play with Him, and turned them into kids ; how, on another, when a child accidentally ran against Him, He was angry, and killed him by His mere word ; how, on another, Jesus had a dispute with His teacher over the alphabet, and when the teacher struck Him, how he crushed him, withered his arm, and threw him down dead. Finally, Joseph tells Mary that they must keep Him within doors; for everybody perishes against whom He is excited. His mother sends Him to the well for water, and having broken His pitcher, He brings the water in His cloak. He goes into a dyer's shop, when the dyer is out, and throws all the cloths He finds into a vat of one colour, but, when they are taken out, behold, they are all dyed of the precise colour that was ordered. He commands a palm-tree to stoop down and let Him pluck the fruit, and it obeys. When He is carried down into Egypt, and all the idols fall down wherever He passes, and the lions and leopards gather round Him in a harmless company. This the Gospel of the Infancy gives us a picture of the wonderful childhood of Jesus. How unlike that holy flower of paradise, in the true gospels, which a few simple touches make to bloom in beautiful self-evidence before us !

Passing now to the character of Jesus in His maturity, we discover at once that there is an element in it which distin guishes it from all human characters, viz., innocence. By this we mean, not that He is actually sinless ; that will be denied, and therefore must not here be assumed.   We mean that, viewed externally, He is a perfectly harmless being, actuated by no destructive passions, gentle to inferiors, doing ill or injury to none.   The figure of a lamb, which never was, or could be, applied to any of the great human characters, without an im plication of weakness fatal to all respect, is yet, with no such effect, applied to Him.   We associate weakness with innocence, and the association is so powerful, that no human writer would undertake to sketch a great character on the basis of innocence, or would even think it possible.   We predicate innocence of infancy, but to be a perfectly harmless, guileless man, never doing ill even for a moment, we consider to be the same as to be a man destitute of spirit and manly force.   But Christ ac complished the impossible.   Appearing in all the grandeur and majesty of a superhuman manhood, He is able still to unite the impression of innocence, with no apparent diminution of His sublimity.   It is, in fact, the distinctive glory of His character, that it seems to be the natural unfolding of a divine innocence, a pure celestial childhood, amplified by growth.   We feel the power of this strange combination, but we have so great diffi culty in conceiving it, or holding our minds to the conception, that we sometimes subside or descend to the human level, and empty the character of Jesus of the strange element unawares. We read, for example, His terrible denunciations against the Pharisees, and are shocked by the violent, fierce sound they have on our mortal lips ; not perceiving that the offence is in us, and not in Him.   We should suffer no such revulsion, did we only conceive them bursting out, as words of indignant grief, from the surcharged bosom of innocence ; for there is nothing so bitter as the offence that innocence feels, when stung by hypo crisy and a sense of cruelty to the poor.   So, when He drives the money-changers from the temple, we are likely to leave out the only element that saves Him from a look of violence and passion.   Whereas it is the very point of the story, not that He, as by mere force, can drive so many men, but that so many are seen retiring before the moral power of one—a mysterious being, in whose face and form the indignant flush of innocence reveals a tremendous feeling they can nowise comprehend, much less are able to resist.

Accustomed to no such demonstrations of vigour and decision

in the innocent human characters, and having it as our way to
set them down, without further consideration, as
"Incapable and shallow innocents,"
we turn the indignant fire of Jesus into a fire of malignity;
whereas it should rather be conceived that Jesus here reveals
His divinity, by what so powerfully distinguishes God Himself,
when He clothes His goodness in the tempests and thunders of
nature. Decisive, great, and strong, Christ is yet all this,
even the more sublimely, that He is invested withal in the
lovely but humanly feeble garb of innocence. And that this
is the true conception is clear, in the fact that no one ever
thinks of Him as weak, and no one fails to be somehow im
pressed with a sense of innocence by His life; when His enemies
are called to show what evil or harm He hath done, they can
specify nothing, save that He has offended their bigotry. Even
Pilate, when he gives Him up, confesses that he finds nothing
in Him to blame, and, shuddering with apprehensions he cannot
subdue, washes his hands to be clear of the innocent blood!
Thus He dies, a being holy, harmless, undefiled. And when
He hangs a bruised flower drooping on His cross, and the sun
above is dark, and the earth beneath shudders with pain, what
have we in this funeral grief of the worlds, but a fit honour
paid to the sad majesty of His divine innocence?

We pass now to His religious character, which, we shall dis
cover, has the remarkable distinction that it proceeds from a
point exactly opposite to that which is the root or radical
element in the religious character of men. Human piety begins
with repentance. It is the effort of a being, implicated in
wrong and writhing under the stings of guilt, to come unto
God. The most righteous, or even self-righteous, men blend
expressions of sorrow and vows of new obedience with their
exercises. But Christ, in the character given Him, never
acknowledges sin. It is the grand peculiarity of His piety, that
He never regrets anything He has done or been; expresses
nowhere a single feeling of compunction, or the least sense of
unworthiness. On the contrary, He boldly challenges His
accusers, in the question—Which of you convinceth me of sin?
and even declares, at the close of His life, in a solemn appeal
to God, that He has given to men, unsullied, the glory divine
that was deposited in Him.

Now the question is not whether Christ was, in fact, the faultless being assumed in His religious character. All we have to notice here is that He makes the assumption, makes it not only in words, but in the very tenor of His exercises them selves, and that by this fact His piety is radically distinguished from all human piety. And no mere human creature, it is certain, could hold such a religious attitude, without shortly displaying faults that would cover him with derision, or excesses and delinquencies that would even disgust his friends. Piety without one dash of repentance, one ingenuous confession of wrong, one tear, one look of contrition, one request to heaven for pardon—let any one of mankind try this kind of piety, and see how long it will be ere his righteousness will prove itself to be the most impudent conceit! how long before his passions, sobered by no contrition, his pride kept down by no repentance, will tempt him into absurdities that will turn his pretences to mockery! No sooner does any one of us begin to be self-righteous, than he begins to fall into outward sins that shame his conceit. But, in the case of Jesus, no such disaster follows. Beginning with an impenitent or unrepentant piety, He holds it to the end, and brings no visible stain upon it.

Now, one of two things must be true. He was either sinless, or He was not. If sinless, what greater, more palpable excep tion to the law of human development, than that a perfect and stainless being has for once lived in the flesh! If not, which is the supposition required of those who deny everything above the range of human development, then we have a man taking up a religion without repentance, a religion not human, but celestial, a style of piety never taught him in his childhood, and never conceived or attempted among men—more than this, a style of piety, withal, wholly unsuited to his real character as a sinner, holding it as a figment of insufferable presumption to the end of life, and that in a way of such unfaltering grace and beauty, as to command the universal homage of the human race! Could there be a wider deviation from all we know of mere human development.

He was also able perfectly to unite elements of character, that others find the greatest difficulty in uniting, however unevenly and partially. He is never said to have smiled, and yet He never produces the impression of austerity, moroseness, sadness, or even of being unhappy. On the contrary, He is described as one that appears to be commonly filled with a sacred joy; "rejoicing in spirit," and leaving to His disciples, in the hour of His departure, the bequest of His joy—"that they might have my joy fulfilled in themselves." We could not long endure a human being whose face was never moved by laughter, or relaxed by a gladdening smile. What sym pathy could we have with one who appears, in this manner, to have no human heart? We could not even trust him. And yet we have sympathy with Christ; for there is somewhere in Him an ocean of deep joy, and we see that He is, in fact, only burdened with His sympathy for us to such a degree, that His mighty life is overcast and oppressed by the charge He has undertaken. His lot is the lot of privation, He has no power· ful friends, He has not even where to lay His head. No human being could appear in such a guise, without occupying us much with the sense of His affliction. We should be descending to him, as it were, in pity. But we never pity Christ, never think of Him as struggling with the disadvantages of a lower level, to rise above it. In fact, He does not allow us, after all, to think much of His privations. We think of Him more as a being of mighty resources, proving Himself, only the more sublimely, that He is in the guise of destitution. He is the most unworldly of beings, having no desire at all for what the earth can give, impossible to be caught with any longing for its benefits, impassable even to its charms, and yet there is no ascetic sourness or repugnance, no misanthropic distaste in His manner; as if He were bracing Himself against the world to keep it off. The more closely He is drawn to other worlds, the more fresh and susceptible is He to the humanities of this. The little child is an image of gladness, which His heart leaps forth to embrace. The wedding and the feast and the funeral have all their cord of sympathy in His bosom. At the wedding He is clothed in congratulation, at the feast in doctrine, at the funeral in tears; but no miser was ever drawn to his money with a stronger desire than He to worlds above the world. Men undertake to be spiritual, and they become ascetic; or, endeavouring to hold a liberal view of the comforts and pleasures of society, they are soon buried in the world, and slaves to its fashions; or, holding a scrupulous watch to keep out every particular sin, they become legal, and fall out of liberty; or, charmed with the noble and heavenly liberty, they run to negligence and irresponsible living; so the earnest become violent, the fervent fanatical and censorious, the gentle waver, the firm turn bigots, the liberal grow lax, the benevolent ostentatious.   Poor human infirmity can hold nothing steady. Where the pivot of righteousness is broken, the scales must needs slide off their balance.   Indeed, it is one of the most difficult things which a cultivated Christian can attempt, only to sketch a theoretic view of character, in its true justness and proportion, so that a little more study, or a little more self-experience, will not require him to modify it.   And yet the character of Christ is never modified, even by a shade of rectification.   It is one and the same throughout.   He makes no improvements, prunes no extravagances, returns from no eccentricities.   The balance of His character is never disturbed or readjusted, and the astounding assumption on which it is based is never shaken, even by a suspicion that He falters in it.

There is yet another point related to this, in which the attitude of Jesus is even more distinct from any that was ever taken by man, and is yet triumphantly sustained.   I speak of the astonishing pretensions asserted concerning His person. Similar pretensions have sometimes been assumed by maniacs, or insane persons, but never, so far as I know, by persons in the proper exercise of their reason.   Certain it is that no mere man could take the same attitude of supremacy toward the race, and inherent affinity or oneness with God, without fatally shocking the confidence of the world by his effrontery. Imagine a human creature saying to the world—"I came forth from the Father"—"Ye are from beneath, I am from above;" facing all the intelligence and even the philosophy of the world, and saying, in bold assurance—"Behold, a greater than Solomon is here"—"I am the light of the world"—"the way, the truth, and the life;" publishing to all peoples and religions—"No man cometh to the Father, but by me;" promising openly in His death—"I will draw all men unto me;" addressing the Infinite Majesty, and testifying—"I have glorified thee on the earth;" calling to the human race— "Come unto me," "follow me;" laying His hand upon all the dearest and most intimate affections of life, and demanding a precedent love—"He that loveth father or mother more than me, is not worthy of me." Was there ever displayed an example of effrontery and spiritual conceit so preposterous? Was there ever a man that dared put himself on the world in such pretensions?—as if all light was in him, as if to follow him and be worthy of him was to be the conclusive or chief excellence of mankind! What but mockery and disgust does he challenge as the certain reward of his audacity! But no one is offended with Jesus on this account; and what is a sure test of His success, it is remarkable that, of all the readers of the gospel, it probably never even occurs to one in a hundred thousand to blame His conceit, or the egregious vanity of His pretensions.

Nor is there anything disputable in these pretensions, least of all, any trace of myth or fabulous tradition. They enter into the very web of His ministry, so that if they are extracted and nothing left transcending mere humanity, nothing at all is left. Indeed, there is a tacit assumption, continually maintained, that far exceeds the range of these formal pretensions. He says—"I and the Father that sent me." What figure would a man present in such language—I and the Father? He goes even beyond this, and apparently without any thought of excess or presumption, classing Himself with the Infinite Majesty in a common plural, He says—"*We* will come unto him, and make *our* abode with him." Imagine any, the greatest and holiest of mankind, any prophet, or apostle, saying *we*, of himself and the great Jehovah! What a conception did He give us concerning Himself, when He assumed the necessity of such information as this—"My Father is greater than I;" and above all, when He calls Himself, as He often does, in a tone of condescension—"the Son of Man." See Him also on the top of Olivet, looking down on the guilty city and weeping words of compassion like these—imagine some man weeping over London or New York, in the like— 'How often would I have gathered thy children together, as a hen doth gather her chickens under her wings, and ye would not!' See Him also in the supper, instituting a rite of remembrance for Himself, a scorned, outcast man, and saying This is my body"—"This do in remembrance of me."

I have dwelt thus on the transcendent pretensions of Jesus, because there is an argument here for His superhumanity, which cannot be resisted. For eighteen hundred years these prodigious assumptions have been published and preached to a world that is quick to lay hold of conceit, and bring down the lofty airs of pretenders, and yet, during all this time, whole nations of people, composing as well the learned and powerful as the ignorant and humble, have paid their homage to the name of Jesus, detecting never any disagreement between His merits and His preten sions, offended never by any thought of His extravagance. In which we have absolute proof that he practically maintains His amazing assumptions! Indeed it will even be found that, in the common apprehension of the race, He maintains the merit of a most peculiar modesty, producing no conviction more distinctly than that of His intense lowliness and humility. His worth is seen to be so great, His authority so high, His spirit so celestial, that instead of being offended by His pretensions, we take the impression of one in whom it is even a condescension to breathe our air. I say not that His friends and followers take this im pression, it is received as naturally and irresistibly by unbe lievers. I do not recollect any sceptic or infidel who has even thought to accuse Him as a conceited person, or to assault Him in this, the weakest and absurdest, if not the strongest and holiest, point of His character.

Come now, all ye that tell us in your wisdom of the mere natural humanity of Jesus, and help us to find how it is, that He is only a natural development of the human; select your best and wisest character; take the range, if you will, of all the great philosophers and saints, and choose out one that is most competent; or if, perchance, some one of you may imagine that he is himself about upon a level with Jesus (as we hear that some of you do), let him come forward in this trial and say— "Follow me"—"Be worthy of me"—"I am the light of the world"—"Ye are from beneath, I am from above"—"Behold a greater than Solomon is here;" take on all these transcendent assumptions, and see how soon your glory will be sifted out of you by the detective gaze, and darkened by the contempt of mankind! Why not; is not the challenge fair? Do you not tell us that you can say as divine things as he? Is it not in you too, of course, to do what is human? are you not in the front rank of human developments? do you not rejoice in the power to rectify many mistakes and errors in the words of Jesus? Give us then this one experiment, and see if it does not prove to

you a truth that is of some consequence; viz., that you are a
man, and that Jesus Christ is—more.

But there is also a passive side to the character of Jesus,
which is equally peculiar, and which also demands our atten
tion.   I recollect no really great character in history, excepting
such as may have been formed under Christianity, that can
properly be said to have united the passive virtues, or to have
considered them any essential part of a finished character.
Socrates comes the nearest to such an impression, and there
fore most resembles Christ in the submissiveness of his death.
It does not appear, however, that his mind had taken this turn
previously to his trial, and the submission he makes to the
public sentence is, in fact, a refusal only to escape from the
prison surreptitiously; which he does, partly because he thinks
it the duty of every good citizen not to break the laws, and
partly, if we judge from his manner, because he is detained by
a subtle pride, as if it were something unworthy of a grave
philosopher to be stealing away, as a fugitive, from the laws
and tribunals of his country.   The Stoics, indeed, have it for
one of their great principles, that the true wisdom of life con
sists in a passive power, viz., in being able to bear suffering
rightly.   But they mean by this the bearing of suffering so
as not to feel it; a steeling of the mind against sensibility,
and the raising of the will into such power as to drive back the
pangs of life, or shake them off.   But this, in fact, contains
no allowance of passive virtue at all; on the contrary, it is an
attempt so to exalt the active powers, as to even exclude every
sort of passion or passivity.   And Stoicism corresponds, in this
respect, with the general sentiment of the world's great char
acters.   They are such as like to see things in the heroic vein,
to see spirit and courage breasting themselves against wrong,
and, where the evil cannot be escaped by resistance, dying in a
manner of defiance.   Indeed, it has been the impression of the
world generally, that patience, gentleness, readiness to suffer
wrong without resistance, is but another name for weakness.
But Christ, in opposition to all such impressions, manages to
connect these non-resisting and gentle passivities with a cha
racter of the severest grandeur and majesty; and, what is more,
convinces us that no truly great character can exist without
them.

Observe Him, first, in what may be called the common trials of existence. For if you will put a character to the severest of all tests, see whether it can bear, without faltering, the little, common ills and hindrances of life. Many a man will go to his martyrdom with a spirit of firmness and heroic composure, whom a little weariness or nervous exhaustion, some silly prejudice, or capricious opposition would, for the moment, throw into a fit of vexation or ill-nature. Great occasions rally great principles, and brace the mind to a lofty bearing, a bearing that is even above itself. But trials that make no occasion at all, leave it to show the goodness and beauty it has in its own disposition. And here precisely is the superhuman glory of Christ as a character, that He is just as perfect, exhibits just as great a spirit in little trials as in great ones. In all the history of His life, we are not able to detect the faintest indica tion that He slips or falters. And this is the more remarkable, that He is prosecuting so great a work with so great enthusiasm ; counting it His meat and drink, and pouring into it all the energies of His life. For when men have great works on hand, their very enthusiasm runs to impatience. When thwarted or unreasonably hindered, their soul strikes fire against the obstacles they meet, they worry themselves at every hindrance, every disappointment, and break out in stormy and fanatical violence. But Jesus, for some reason, is just as even, just as serene, in all His petty vexations and hindrances, as if He had nothing on hand to do. A kind of sacred patience invests Him everywhere. Having no element of crude will mixed with His work, He is able, in all trial and opposition, to hold a condition of serenity above the clouds, and let them sail under Him, without ever obscuring the sun. He is poor, and hungry, and weary, and despised, insulted by His enemies, deserted by His friends, but never disheartened, never fretted or ruffled. You see, meantime, that He is no Stoic ; He visibly feels every such ill as His delicate and sensitive nature must, but He has some sacred and sovereign good present to mingle with His pains, which, as it were naturally and without any self-watching, allays them. He does not seem to rule His temper, but rather to have none ; for temper, in the sense of passion, is a fury that follows the will, as the lightnings follow the disturbing forces of the winds among the clouds ; and accordingly where there is no self-will to roll up the clouds and hurl them through the sky, the lightnings hold their equilibrium, and are as though they were not. _

As regards what is called pre-eminently His passion, the scene of martyrdom that closes His life, it is easy to distinguish a character in it which separates it from all mere human martyrdoms. Thus, it will be observed, that His agony, the scene in which His suffering is bitterest and most evident, is, on human principles, wholly misplaced. It comes before the time, when as yet there is no arrest, and no human prospect that there will be any. He is at large to go where He pleases, and in perfect outward safety. His disciples have just been gathered round Him in a scene of more than family tenderness and affection. Indeed it is but a very few hours since that He was coming into the city, at the head of a vast procession, followed by loud acclamations, and attended by such honours as may fitly celebrate the inaugural of a king. Yet here, with no bad sign apparent, we see Him plunged into a scene of deepest distress, and racked, in his feeling, with a more than mortal agony. Coming out of this, assured and comforted, He is shortly arrested, brought to trial, and crucified; where, if there be anything questionable in His manner, it is in the fact that He is even more composed than some would have Him to be, not even stooping to defend Himself or vindicate His inno cence. And when He dies, it is not as when the martyrs die. They die for what they have said, and remaining silent will not recant. He dies for what He has not said, and still is silent.

By the misplacing of His agony thus, and the strange silence He observes when the real hour of agony is come, we are put entirely at fault on natural principles. But it was not for Him to wait, as being only a man, till He is arrested and the hand of death is before Him, then to be nerved by the occasion to a show of victory. He that was before Abraham, must also be before His occasions. In a time of safety, in a cool hour of retirement, unaccountably to His friends, He falls into a dread ful contest and struggle of mind; coming out of it, finally, to go through His most horrible tragedy of crucifixion, with the serenity of a spectator?

Why now this so great intensity of sorrow? why this agony? Was there not something unmanly in it, something unworthy of a really great soul? Take Him to be only a man, and there probably was ; nay, if He were a woman, the same might be said. But this one thing is clear, that no one of mankind, whether man or woman, ever had the sensibility to suffer so intensely ; even showing the body, for the mere struggle and pain of the mind, exuding and dripping with blood. Evidently there is something mysterious here ; which mystery is vehicle to our feeling, and rightfully may be, of something divine. What, we begin to ask, should be the power of a superhuman sensibility ? and how far should the human vehicle shake under such a power ? How too should an innocent and pure spirit be exercised, when about to suffer in His own person, the greatest wrong ever committed ?

Besides, there is a vicarious spirit in love ; all love inserts itself vicariously into the sufferings and woes, and, in a certain sense, the sins of others, taking them on itself as a burden. How then, if perchance Jesus should be divine, an embodiment of God's love in the world—how should He feel, and by what signs of feeling manifest His sensibility, when a fallen race are just about to do the damning sin that crowns their guilty history ; to crucify the only perfect being that ever came into the world ; to crucify even Him, the messenger and representa tive to them of the love of God, the deliverer who has taken their case and cause upon Him ! Whosoever duly ponders these questions, will find that he is led away, more and more, from any supposition of the mere mortality of Jesus. What he looks upon, he will more and more distinctly see to be the pathology of a superhuman anguish. It stands, he will per ceive, in no mortal key. It will be to him the anguish visibly, not of any pusillanimous feeling, but of holy character itself ; nay, of a mysteriously transcendent, or somehow divine, character.

But why did he not defend His cause and justify His inno cence in the trial ? Partly because He had the wisdom to see that there really was and could be no trial, and that one who undertakes to plead with a mob only mocks his own virtue, throwing words into the air that is already filled with the clamours of prejudice. To plead innocence in such a case, is only to make a protestation, such as indicates fear, and is really unworthy of a great and composed spirit. A man would have done it, but Jesus did not. Besides, there was a plea of innocence in the manner of Jesus, and the few very significant words that He dropped, that had an effect on the mind of Pilate, more searching and powerful than any formal protesta tions.   And the more we study the conduct of Jesus during the whole scene, the more shall we be satisfied that He said enough ; the more admire the mysterious composure, the wis dom, the self-possession, and the superhuman patience of the sufferer.   It was visibly the death scene of a transcendent love. He dies not as a man, but rather as some one might who is mysteriously more and higher.   So thought aloud the hard-faced soldier—" Truly this was the Son of God."   As if he had said—" I have seen men die—this is not a man.   They call him Son of God—He cannot be less."   Can He be less to us ?

    But Christ shows Himself to be a superhuman character, not in the personal traits only, exhibited in His life, but even more sublimely in the undertakings, works, and teachings by which He proved His Messiahship.
    Consider then the reach of His undertaking ; which if He was only a man, shows Him to have been the most extravagant and even wildest of all human enthusiasts.   Contrary to every religious prejudice of His nation and even of His time, contrary to the comparatively narrow and exclusive religion of Moses itself, and to all His training under it, He undertakes to organize a kingdom of God or kingdom of heaven on earth. His purpose includes a new moral creation of the race—not of the Jews only and of men, proselyted to their covenant, but of the whole human race.   He declared thus, at an early date in His ministry, that many shall come from the east and the west and sit down with Abraham, and Isaac, and Jacob in the king dom of God ; that the field is the world ; and that God so loves the world as to give for it His only begotten Son.   He also declared that His gospel shall be published to all nations, and gave His apostles their commission, to go into all the world and publish His gospel to every creature.
    Here, then, we have the grand idea of His mission—it is to new-create the human race and restore it to God, in the unity of a spiritual kingdom.   And upon this single fact, Reinhard erects a complete argument for His extra-human character ; going into a formal review of all the great founders of states and most celebrated lawgivers, the great heroes and defenders

of nations, all the wise kings and statesmen, all the philosophers, all the prophet-founders of religions, and discovering as a fact that no such thought as this, or nearly proximate to this, had ever before been taken up by any living character in history; showing also how it had happened to every other great character, however liberalized by culture, to be limited in some way to the interest of His own people or empire, and set in opposition or antagonism, more or less decidedly, to the rest of the world. But to Jesus alone, the simple Galilean carpenter, it happens otherwise; that, having never seen a map of the world in his whole life, or heard the name of half the great nations on it, He undertakes, coming out of His shop, a scheme as much vaster and more difficult than that of Alexander, as it proposes more, and what is more divinely benevolent! This thought of a universal kingdom, cemented in God —why, the immense Roman empire of His day, constructed by so many ages of war and conquest, is a bauble in comparison, both as regards the extent and the cost! And yet the rustic tradesman of Galilee propounds even this for His errand, and that in a way of assurance as simple and quiet, as if the immense reach of His plan were, in fact, a matter to Him of no consideration.

Nor is this all; there is included in His plan, what, to any mere man, would be yet more remote from the possible confidence of His frailty; it is a plan as universal in time, as it is in the scope of its objects. It does not expect to be realized in a lifetime, or even in many centuries to come. He calls it, understandingly, his grain of mustard seed; which, however, is to grow, He declares, and overshadow the whole earth. But the courage of Jesus, counting a thousand years to be only a single day, is equal to the run of His work. He sees a rock of stability, where men see only frailty and weakness. Peter himself, the impulsive and always unreliable Peter, turns into rock and becomes a great foundation, as he looks upon Him. "On this rock," He says, "I will build my church, and the gates of hell shall not prevail against it. His expectation, too, reaches boldly out beyond His own death; that, in fact, is to be the seed of his great empire—" Except a corn of wheat fall into the ground and die, it abideth," He says, " alone." And if we will see with what confidence and courage He adheres to His plan when the time of His death approaches—how far He is from giving it up as lost, or as an exploded vision of His youthful enthusiasm—we have only to observe His last inter view with the two sisters of Bethany, in whose hospitality He was so often comforted. When the box of precious ointment is broken upon His head, which Judas reproves as a useless expense, He discovers a sad propriety, or even prophecy, in what the woman has done, as connected with His death, now at hand. But it does not touch His courage, we perceive, or the confidence of His plan, or even cast a shade on His prospect. " Let her alone. She hath done what she could. She is come aforehand to anoint my body to the burying. Verily I say unto you, wheresoever this gospel shall be preached throughout the whole world, this also that this woman hath done shall be told for a memorial of her." Such was the sublime confidence He had in a plan that was to run through all future ages, and would scarcely begin to show its fruits during His own life time.

In this great idea, then, which no man ever before conceived, the raising of the whole human race to God, a plan sustained with such evenness of courage, and a confidence of the world's future so far transcending any human example—is this a human development ? Regard the benevolence of it, the universality of it, the religious grandeur of it, as a work readjusting the relations of God and His government with men—the cost, the length of time it will cover, and the far off date of its com pletion—is it in this scale that a Nazarene carpenter, a poor uneducated villager, lays out His plans and graduates the confi dence of His undertakings ? There have been great enthusiasts in the world, and they have shown their infirmity by lunatic airs, appropriate to their extravagance. But it is not human, we may safely affirm, to lay out projects transcending all human ability, like this of Jesus, and which cannot be completed in many thousands of years, doing it in all the airs of sobriety, entering on the performance without parade, and yielding life to it firmly as the inaugural of its triumph. No human creature sits quietly down to a perpetual project, one that proposes to be executed only at the end or final harvest of the world. That is not human but divine.

Passing now to what is more interior in His ministry taken as a revelation of His character, we are struck with another dis tinction, viz., that He takes rank with the poor, and grounds all the immense expectations of His cause on a beginning made with the lowly and dejected classes of the world. He was born to the lot of the poor. His manners, tastes, and intellectual attainments, however, visibly outgrew His condition, and that in such a degree that, if He had been a mere human character, He must have suffered some painful distaste for the kind of society in which He lived. The great, as we perceive, flocked to hear Him, and sometimes came even by night to receive His instructions. He saw the highest circles of society and influence open to Him, if He only desired to enter them. And, if he was a properly human character, what virtuous but rising young man would have a thought of impropriety, in accepting the elevation within his reach, considering it as the proper reward of his industry, and the merit of his character—not to speak of the contempt for his humble origin, and his humble associates, which every upstart person of only ordinary virtue is so commonly seen to manifest. Still He adheres to the poor, and makes them the object of His ministry. And what is more peculiar, He visibly has a kind of interest in their society, which is wanting in that of the higher classes; perceiving, apparently, that they have a certain aptitude for receiving right impressions which the others have not. They are not the wise and prudent, filled with the conceit of learning and station, but they are the ingenuous babes of poverty, open to conviction, prepared, by their humble lot, to receive thoughts and doctrines in advance of their age. Therefore He loves the poor, and, without descending to their low manners, He delights to be identified with them. He is more assiduous in their service than other men have been in serving the great. He goes about on foot, teaching them and healing their sick; occupying His great and elevated mind, for whole years, with details of labour and care, which the nurse of no hospital had ever laid upon him—insanities, blind eyes, fevers, fluxes, leprosies, and sores. His patients are all below His level, and unable to repay Him, even by a breath of congenial sympathy; and nothing supports Him but the consciousness of good which attends His labours.

Meantime, consider what contempt for the poor had hitherto prevailed, among all the great statesmen and philanthropists of the world. The poor were not society, or any part of society. They were only the conveniences and drudges of society; appendages of luxury and state, tools of ambition, material to be used in the wars. No man who had taken up the idea of some great change or reform in society, no philosopher who had con ceived the notion of building up an ideal state or republic, ever thought of beginning with the poor. Influence was seen to re side in the higher classes, and the only hope of reaching the world, by any scheme of social regeneration, was to begin with them, and through them operate its results. But Christ, if we call Him a philosopher, and, if He is only a man, we can call Him by no higher name, was the poor man's philosopher ; the first and only one that had ever appeared. Seeing the higher circles open to Him, and tempted to imagine that if He could once get footing for His doctrine among the influential and the great, He should thus secure His triumph more easily. He had yet no such thought. He laid his foundations, as it were, below all influence, and, as men would judge, threw Him self away. And precisely here did He display a wisdom and a character totally in advance of His age. Eighteen centuries have passed away, and we now seem just beginning to under stand the transcendent depth of this feature in His mission and His character. We appear to be just waking up to it as a dis- covery, that the blessing and upraising of the masses are the fundamental interest of society—a discovery, however, which is only a proof that the life of Jesus has, at length, begun to penetrate society and public history. It is precisely this which is working so many and great changes in our times, giving liberty and right to the enslaved many, seeking their education, encouraging their efforts by new and better hopes, producing an aversion to war, which has been the fatal source of their misery and depression, and opening, as we hope, a new era of comfort, light, and virtue in the world. It is as if some higher and better thought had visited our race —which higher thought is in the life of Jesus. . The schools of all the philoso- phers are gone, hundreds of years ago, and all their visions have died away into thin air ; but the poor man's philosopher still lives, bringing up His poor to liberty, light, and character, and drawing the nations on to a brighter and better day.

At the same time, the more than human character of Jesus is displayed also in the fact that, identifying Himself thus with the poor, He is yet able to do it without eliciting any feelings of

partisanship in them.   To one who will be at the pains to reflect
a little, nothing will seem more difficult than this ; to become
the patron of a class, a down-trodden and despised class, with
out rallying in them a feeling of intense malignity.   And that
for the reason, partly, that no patron, however just or magna
nimous, is ever quite able to suppress the feelings of a partisan
in himself.   A little ambition, pricked on by a little abuse, a
faint desire of popularity playing over the face of his benevolence,
and tempting him to loosen a little of ill-nature, as tinder to the
passions of his sect—something of this kind is sure to kindle
some fire of malignity in his clients.

Besides, men love to be partisans.   Even Paul and Apollos
and Peter had their sects or schools glorying in one against
another.   With all their efforts, they could not suppress a
weakness so contemptible.   But no such feeling could ever get
footing under Christ.   If His disciples had forbidden one to
heal in the name of Jesus, because he followed not with them,
He gently rebuked them, and made them feel that He had
larger views than to suffer any such folly.   As the friend of
the poor and oppressed class, He set Himself openly against
their enemies, and chastised them as oppressors, with the most
terrible rebukes.   He exposed the absurdity of their doctrine,
and silenced them in argument; He launched His thunder
bolts against their base hypocrisies ; but it does not appear
that the populace ever testified their pleasure, even by a cheer,
or gave vent to any angry emotion under cover of His leader
ship.   For there was something still, in the manner and air of
Jesus, which made them feel it to be inappropriate, and even
made it impossible.   It was as if some being were here, taking
their part, whom it were even an irreverence to applaud, much
more to second by any partisan clamour.   They would as soon
have thought of cheering the angel in the sun, or of rallying
under him as the head of their faction.   On one occasion, when
He had fed the multitudes by a miracle, He saw that their
national superstitions were excited, and that, regarding Him as
the Messiah predicted in the Scriptures, they were about to
take Him by force and make Him their king ; but this was a
national feeling, not the feeling of a class.   Its root was super.
stition, not hatred.   His triumphal entry into Jerusalem,
attended by the acclamations of the multitude, if this be not
one of the fables or myths which our modern criticism rejects,

is yet no demonstration of popular faction or party animosity. Robbing it of its mystical and miraculous character, as the in augural of the Messiah, it has no real signification.   In a few hours, after all, these hosannahs are hushed.   Jesus is alone and forsaken, and the very multitudes He might seem to have enlisted, are crying " Crucify him !."   On the whole, it can not be said that Jesus was ever popular.   He was followed at times by great multitudes of people, whose love of the marvellous worked on their superstitions, to draw them after Him.   They came also to be cured of their diseases.   They knew Him as their friend.   But there was yet something in Him that forbade their low and malignant feelings gathering into a conflagration round Him.   He presents indeed, an in stance that stands alone in history, as God at the summit of the worlds, where a person has identified himself with a class, without creating a faction, and without becoming a popular character.

Consider Him next as a teacher ; His method and manner, and the other characteristics of His excellence, apart from His doctrine.   That will be distinctly considered in an another place.

First of all, we notice the perfect originality and indepen dence of His teaching.   We have a great many men who are original, in the sense of being originators, within a certain boundary of educated thought.   But the originality of Christ is uneducated.   That he draws nothing from the stores of learning, can be seen at a glance.   The impression we have in reading His instructions, justifies to the letter the language of His contemporaries, when they say, " This man hath never learned."   There is nothing in any of His allusions or forms of speech that indicates learning.   Indeed, there is nothing in Him that belongs to His age or country—no one opinion, or taste, or prejudice.   The attempts that have been made, in a way of establishing His mere natural manhood, to show that He borrowed His sentiments from the Persians and the eastern forms of religion, or that He had been intimate with the Essenes and borrowed from them, or that He must have been acquainted with the schools and religions of Egypt, deriving His doctrine from them—all attempts of the kind have so pal pably failed, as not even to require a deliberate answer.   If He is simply a man, as we hear, then He is most certainly a new and singular kind of man, never before heard of, one who visibly is quite as great a miracle in the world as if He were not a man. We can see for ourselves, in the simple directness and freedom of His teachings, that whatever He advances is from Himself. Shakspere, for instance, whom we name as being probably the most creative and original spirit the world has ever produced, one of the class, too, that are called self-made men, is yet tinged, in all his works, with human learning. His glory is, indeed, that so much of what is great in history and historic character, lives and appears in his dramatic creations. He is the high-priest, we sometimes hear, of human nature. But Christ, understanding human nature so as to ad. dress it more skilfully than he, never draws from it historic treasures. He is the high-priest, rather, of the divine nature, speaking as one that has come out from God, and has nothing to borrow from the world. It is not to be detected by any sign, that the human sphere in which He moved imparted any thing to him. His teachings are just as full of divine nature, as Shakspere's of human.

Neither does He teach by the human methods. He does not speculate about God as a school professor, drawing out conclu sions by a practice on words, and deeming that the way of proof; He does not build up a frame of evidence from below by some constructive process, such as the philosophers delight in ; but He simply speaks of God and spiritual things as one who has come out from Him, to tell us what He knows. And His simple telling brings us the reality ; proves it to us in its own sublime self-evidence ; awakens even the consciousness of it in our own bosom ; so that formal arguments or dialectic proofs offend us by their coldness, and seem, in fact, to be only opaque substances set between us and the light. Indeed, He makes even the world luminous by His words—fills it with an imme diate and new sense of God, which nothing has ever been able to expel. The incense of the upper world is brought out in His garments, and flows abroad, as a perfume, on the poisoned air.

At the same time, He never reveals the infirmity so commonly shown by human teachers, when they veer a little from their point, or turn their doctrine off by shades of variation, to catch the assent of multitudes. He never conforms to an expecta tion, even of His friends. When they look to find a great pro phet in Him, He offers nothing in the modes of the prophets.

When they ask for places of distinction in His kingdom, He rebukes their folly, and tells them he has nothing to give, but a share in His reproaches and His poverty. When they look to see Him take the sword as the Great Messiah of their nation, calling the people to His standard, He tells them He is no war rior and no king, but only a messenger of love to lost men; one that has come to minister and die, but not to set up or restore the kingdom. Every expectation that rises up to greet Him is repulsed; and yet, so great is the power of His manner, that multitudes are held fast, and cannot yield their confidence. Enveloped as He is in the darkest mystery, they trust Him·still; going after Him, hanging on His words, as if detained by some charmed influence, which they cannot shake off or resist. Never was there a teacher that so uniformly baffled every ex pectation of His followers, never one that was followed so persistently.

Again, the singular balance of character displayed in the teachings of Jesus, indicates an exception from the standing infirmity of human nature. Human opinions are formed under a law that seems to be universal. First, two opposite extremes are thrown up, in two opposite leaders or parties; then a third party enters, trying to find what truth they both are endeavour ing to vindicate, and settle thus a view of the subject that includes the truth and clears the one-sided extremes, which op posing words or figures, not yet measured in their force, had produced. It results, in this manner, that no man, even the broadest in his apprehensions, is ever at the point of equilibrium as regards all subjects. Even the ripest of us are continually falling into some extreme, and losing our balance, afterward to be corrected by some other who discovers our error, or that of our school.

But Christ was of no school or party, and never went to any extreme—words could never turn Him to a one-sided view of anything. This is the remarkable fact that distinguishes Him from any other known teacher of the world. Having nothing to work out in a word-process, but everything clear in the simple intuition of His superhuman intelligence, He never pushes Himself to any human eccentricity. It does not even appear that He is trying, as we do, to balance opposites and clear extravagances, but He does it, as one who cannot imagine a one-sided view of anything. He is never a radical, never a con-

servative.   He will not allow His disciples to deny Him before
kings and governors, He will not let them renounce their allegi
ance to Cæsar.   He exposes the oppressions of the Pharisees in
Moses' seat, but, encouraging no factious resistance, says—"Do
as they command you."   His position as a reformer was uni
versal—according to His principles almost nothing, whether in
church or state, or in social life, was right; and yet He is thrown
into no antagonism against the world.   How a man will do,
when he engages only in some one reform, acting from his own
human force ; the fuming, storming frenzy, the holy rage and
tragic smoke of his violence, how he kindles against opposition,
grows bitter and restive because of delay, and finally comes to
maturity in the character thoroughly detestable—all this we
know.   But Christ, with all the world upon His hands, and a
reform to be carried in almost everything, is yet as quiet and
cordial, and as little in the attitude of bitterness or impatience,
as if all hearts were with Him, or the work already done ; so
perfect is the balance of His feeling, so intuitively moderated is
it by a wisdom not human.

We cannot stay to sketch a full outline of this particular and
sublime excellence, as it was displayed in His life.   It will be
seen as clearly in a single comparison or contrast, as in many,
or in a more extended inquiry.   Take, then, for an example,
what may be observed in His open repugnance to all superstition,
combined with His equal repugnance to what is commonly
praised as a mode of liberality.   He lived in a superstitious age,
and among a superstitious people.   He was a person of low
education, and nothing, as we know, clings to the uneducated
mind with the tenacity of a superstition.   Lord Bacon, for example, a man certainly of the very highest intellectual training,
was yet infested by superstitions, too childish to be named with
respect, and which clung to him, despite of all his philosophy,
even to his death.   But Christ, with no learned culture at all,
comes forth out of Galilee, as perfectly clean of all the super
stitions of His time as if He had been a disciple from His child
hood of Hume or Strauss.   " You children of superstition think,"
He says, " that those Galileans, whose blood Pilate mingled
with their sacrifices, and those eighteen upon whom the tower
in Siloam fell, must have been monsters to suffer such things.
I tell you, nay ; but except ye repent, ye shall all likewise
perish."   To another company He says—" You imagine, in your

Pharisaic and legal morality, that the Sabbath of Moses stands in the letter ; but I tell you that the Sabbath is made for man, and not man for the Sabbath ; little honour, therefore, do you pay to God when you teach that it is not lawful to do good on this day. Your washings are a great point, you tithe herbs and seeds with a sanctimonious fidelity, would it not be as well for you teachers of the law, to have some respect to the weightier matters of justice, faith, and benevolence ? " Thus, while So-crates, one of the greatest and purest of human souls, a man who has attained to many worthy conceptions of God hidden from his idolatrous countrymen, is constrained to sacrifice a cock to Æsculapius, the uneducated Jesus lives and dies superior to every superstition of His time ; believing nothing because it is believed, respecting nothing because it is sanctified by custom and by human observance. Even in the closing scene of His life, we see His learned and priestly associates refusing to go into the judgment-hall of ~~Caiaphas~~ lest they should be ceremonially defiled and disqualified for the feast ; though detained by no scruple at all as regards the instigation of a murder ! While he on the other hand, pitying their delusions, prays for them from His cross—"Father, forgive them, for they know not what they do."

And yet Christ is no liberal, never takes the ground or boasts the distinction of a liberal among His countrymen, because it is not a part of His infirmity, in discovering an error here to fly to an excess there. His ground is charity, not liberality ; and the two are as wide apart in their practical implications, as ad hering to all truth and being loose in all. Charity holds fast the minutest atoms of truth, as being precious and divine, of fended by even so much as a thought of laxity. Liberality loosens the terms of truth ; permitting easily and with careless magnanimity variations from it ; consenting, as it were, in its own sovereignty, to overlook or allow them ; and subsiding thus, ere long, into a licentious indifference to all truth, and a general defect of responsibility in regard to it. Charity extends allowance to men ; liberality to falsities themselves. Charity takes the truth to be sacred and immoveable ; liberality allows it to be marred and maimed at pleasure. How different the manner of Jesus in this respect from that unreverent, feeble laxity, that lets the errors be as good as the truths, and takes it for a sign of intellectual eminence, that one can be floated comfortably in the abysses of liberalism. "Judge not," He says, in holy charity, "that ye be not judged;" and again, in holy exactness, "Whosoever shall break, or teach to break, one of these least commandments, shall be least in the kingdom of God;" in the same way, "He that is not with us is against us;" and again, "He that is not against us is for us;" in the same way also, "Ye tithe mint, anise, and cummin;" and again, "These things ought ye to have done, and not to leave the other undone;" once more, too, in the same way, "He that is without sin, let him cast the first stone;" and again, "Go and sin no more." So magnificent and sublime, so plainly divine, is the balance of Jesus. Nothing throws Him off the centre on which truth rests; no prejudice, no opposition, no attempt to right a mistake, or rectify a delusion, or reform a practice. If this be human, I do not know for one what it is to be human.

Again, it is a remarkable and even superhuman distinction of Jesus, that, while He is advancing doctrines so far transcend ing all deductions of philosophy, and opening mysteries that defy all human powers of explication, He is yet able to set His teachings in a form of simplicity, that accommodates all classes of minds. And this, for the reason that He speaks directly to men's convictions themselves, without and apart from any learned and curious elaboration, such as the uncultivated can not follow. No one of the great writers of antiquity had even propounded, as yet, a doctrine of virtue which the multitude could understand. It was taught as being τὸ καλὸν (the good), or τὸ πρέπον (the becoming), or something of that nature, as distant from all their apprehensions, and as destitute of motive power, as if it were a doctrine of mineralogy. Considered as a gift to the world at large, it was the gift of a stone, not of bread. But Jesus tells them directly, in a manner level to their understanding, what they want, what they must do and be, to inherit eternal life, and their inmost convictions answer to His words. Besides, his doctrine is not so much a doctrine as a biography, a personal power, a truth all motivity, a love walking the earth in the proximity of a mortal fellowship. He only speaks what goes forth as a feeling and a power in His life, breathing into all hearts. To be capable of His doctrine, only requires that the hearer be a human creature wanting to know the truth.

Call Him then, who will, a man, a human teacher; what

human teacher ever came down thus upon the soul of the race, as a beam of light from the skies—pure light, shining directly into the visual orb of the mind, a light for all that live, a full transparent day, in which truth bathes the spirit as an element? Others talk and speculate about truth, and those who can may follow; but Jesus is the truth, and lives it, and, if He is a mere human teacher, He is the first who was ever able to find a form for truth at all adequate to the world's uses. And yet the truths He teaches out-reach all the doctrines of all the phi losophers of the world. He excels them, a hundred-fold more, in the scope and grandeur of His doctrine, than He does in His simplicity itself.

Is this human, or is it plainly divine? If you will see what is human, or what the wisdom of humanity would ordain, it is this—exactly what the subtle and accomplished Celsus, the great adversary of Christianity in its original promulgation, alleges for one of his principal arguments against it. "Woollen manufacturers," he says, "shoemakers, and curriers, the most uneducated and boorish of men are zealous advocates of this religion; men who cannot open their mouths before the learned, and who only try to gain over the women and children in fami lies."[1] And again, what is only the same objection under a different form, assuming that religion, like a philosophy, must be for the learned, he says, "He must be void of understanding who can believe that Greeks and barbarians, in Asia, Europe, and Lybia—all nations to the ends of the earth—can unite in one and the same religious doctrine."[2] So also Plato says, "It is not easy to find the Father and Creator of all existence, and when He is found, it is impossible to make Him known to all."[3] "But exactly this," says Justin Martyr, "is what our Christ has effected by His power." And Tertullian also, glory ing in the simplicity of the Gospel, as already proved to be a truly divine excellence, says, "Every Christian artisan has found God, and points Him out to thee, and, in fact, shows thee everything which is sought for in God, although Plato main tains that the Creator of the world is not easily found, and that when He is found, He cannot be made known to all." Here then, we have Christ against Celsus, and Christ against Plato. These agree in assuming that we have a God whom only

---

1 Neander's *Memorials of Christian Life*, p. 19. 2 *Ibid.* p. 33. 8 Timæus.
4 Neander's *Memorials of Christian Life*, p. 19.

the great can mount high enough in argument to know. Christ
reveals a God whom the humblest artisan can teach, and all
mankind embrace, with a faith that unifies them all.

Again, the morality of Jesus has a practical superiority to
that of all human teachers, in the fact that it is not an artistic
or theoretically elaborated scheme, but one that is propounded
in precepts that carry their own evidence, and are, in fact, great
spiritual laws ordained by God, in the throne of religion.   He
did not draw long arguments to settle what the *summum bonum*
is, and then produce a scheme of ethics to correspond.   He
did not go into the vexed question, what is the foundation of
virtue ? and hang a system upon His answer.   Nothing falls
into an artistic shape, as when Plato or Socrates asks what kind
of action is beautiful action ? reducing the principles of morality
to a form as difficult for the uncultivated as the art of sculpture
itself.   Yet Christ excels them all in the beauty of His precepts,
without once appearing to consider their beauty.   He simply
comes forth telling us, from God, what to do, without deducing
anything in a critical way ; and yet, while nothing has ever yet
been settled by the critics and theorizing philosophers, that
could stand fast and compel the assent of the race even for a
year, the morality of Christ is about as firmly seated in the con
victions of men, as the law of gravity in their bodies.

He comes into the world full of all moral beauty, as God of
physical ; and as God was not obliged to set Himself to a course
of æsthetic study, when He created the forms and landscapes of
the world, so Christ comes to His rules by no critical practice
in words.   He opens His lips, and the creative glory of His
mind pours itself forth in living precepts—Do to others as ye
would that others should do to you—Blessed are the peace
makers—Smitten upon one cheek, turn the other—Resist not
evil Forgive your enemies—Do good to them that hate you
Lend not, hoping to receive—Receive the truth as little
children.   Omitting all the deep spiritual doctrines He taught,
and taking all the human teachers on their own ground, the
ground of perceptive morality, they are seen at once to be
meagre and cold ; little artistic inventions, gleams of high con
ceptions caught by study, having about the same relation to the
Christian morality that a statue has to the flexibility, the self-
active force, and flushing warmth of man, as he goes forth in
the image of his Creator, to be the reflection of His beauty and

the living instrument of His will. Indeed, it is the very dis
tinction of Jesus that He teaches, not a verbal, but an original,
vital, and divine morality. He does not dress up a moral
picture, and ask you to observe its beauty, He only tells you
how to live ; and the most beautiful characters the world has
ever seen have been those who received and lived His precepts
without once conceiving their beauty.

Once more it is a high distinction of Christ's character, as
seen in His teachings, that He is never anxious for the success
of His doctrine. Fully conscious of the fact that the world is
against Him, scoffed at, despised, hated, alone too in His cause,
and without partisans that have any public influence, no man
has ever been able to detect in Him the least anxiety for the
final success of His doctrine. He is never jealous of contradic
tion. When His friends display their dulness and incapacity,
or even when they forsake Him, He is never ruffled or disturbed.
He rests on His words, with a composure as majestic as if He
were sitting on the circle of the heavens. Now the consciousness of truth, we are not about to deny, has an effect of this
nature in every truly great mind. But when has it had an
effect so complete ? What human teacher, what great philoso
pher has not shown some traces of anxiety for his school, that
indicated his weakness ; some pride in his friends, some dislike
of his enemies, some traces of wounded ambition, when disputed
or denied ? But here is a lone man, a humble, uneducated
man, never schooled into the elegant fiction of an assumed com
posure, or practised in the conventional dignities of manners,
and yet, finding all the world against Him, the world does not
rest on its axle more firmly than He upon His doctrine.
Questioned by Pilate what He means by truth, it is enough to
answer—" He that is of the truth heareth my voice." If this
be human, no other man of the race, we are sure, has ever
dignified humanity by a like example.

Such is Christ as a teacher. When has the world seen a'
phenomenon like this ; a lonely uninstructed youth, coming
forth amid the moral darkness of Galilee, even more distinct
from His age, and from everything around Him, than a Plato
would be rising up alone in some wild tribe in Oregon, assum
ing thus a position at the head of the world, and maintaining it,
for eighteen centuries, by the pure self-evidence of His life and
doctrine ! Does He this by the force of mere human talent or

genius ? If so, it is time that we begin to look to genius for miracles ; for there is really no greater miracle.

There is yet one other and more inclusive distinction of the character of Jesus, which must not be omitted, and which sets Him off more widely from all the mere men of the race, just because it raises a contrast which is at once total and experi mental. Human characters are always reduced in their emin ence, and the impressions of awe they have raised, by a closer and more complete acquaintance. Weakness and blemish are discovered by familiarity ; admiration lets in qualifiers ; on approach, the halo dims a little. But it was not so with Christ. With His disciples, in closest terms of intercourse, for three whole years ; their brother, friend, teacher, monitor, guest, fellow-traveller ; seen by them under all the conditions of public ministry and private society, where the ambition of show, or the pride of power, or the ill-nature provoked by annoy ance, or the vanity drawn out by confidence, would most cer tainly be reducing Him to the criticism even of persons most unsophisticated, He is yet visibly raising their sense of His degree and quality ; becoming a greater wonder and holier mys tery, and gathering to His person feelings of reverence and awe, at once more general and more sacred. Familiarity operates a kind of apotheosis, and the man becomes divinity, in simply being known. At first, He is the son of Mary and the Nazarene carpenter. Next, He is heard speaking with authority, as con trasted even with the scribes. Next, He is conceived by some to be certainly Elias, or some one of the prophets, returned in power to the world. Peter takes Him up, at that point, as being certainly the Christ, the great, mysterious Messiah ; only not so great that he is not able to reprove Him, when He begins to talk of being killed by His enemies ; protesting—" Be it far from thee, Lord." But the next we see of the once bold apostle, he is beckoning to another, at the table, to whisper the Lord and ask who it is that is going to betray Him ; unable himself to so much as invade the sacred ear of his Master with the audible and open question. Then, shortly after, when he comes out of the hall of Caiaphas, flushed and flurried with his threefold lie, and his base hypocrisy of cursing, what do we see but that, simply catching the Great Master's eye, his heart breaks down, riven with insupportable anguish, and is utterly

dissolved in childish tears ?   And so it will be discovered in all
the disciples, that Christ is more separated from them, and
holds them in deeper awe, the closer He comes to them and the
more perfectly they know Him.   The same too is true of His
enemies.   At first, they look on Him only as some new fanatic,
that has come to turn the heads of the people.   Next, they
want to know whence He drew His opinions, and His singular
accomplishments in the matter of public address ; not being, as
all that knew Him testify, an educated man.   Next, they send
out a company to arrest Him, and, when they hear Him speak,
they are so deeply impressed that they dare not do it, but go
back, under a kind of invincible awe, testifying—" Never man
spake like this man."   Afterward, to break some fancied spell
there may be in Him, they hire one of His own friends to
betray Him ; and even then, when they are come directly
before Him and hear Him speak, they are in such tremor of
apprehension, lest He should suddenly annihilate them, that
they reel incontinently backward and are pitched on the ground.
Pilate trembles visibly before Him, and the more because of
His silence and His wonderful submission.   And then, when
the fatal deed is done, what do we see but that the multitude,
awed by some dread mystery in the person of the crucified,
return home smiting on their breasts for anguish, in the sense
of what their infatuated and guilty rage has done.

   The most conspicuous matter, therefore, in the history of
Jesus is, that what holds true in all our experience of men is
inverted in Him.   He grows sacred, peculiar, wonderful, divine,
as acquaintance reveals Him.   At first He is only a man, as
the senses report him to be ; knowledge, observation, familiarity,
raise Him into the God-man.   He grows pure and perfect, more
than mortal in wisdom, a being enveloped in sacred mystery, a
friend to be loved in awe—dies into awe, and a sorrow that con
tains the element of worship !   And exactly this appears in the
history, without any token of art, or even apparent consciousness
that it does appear—appears because it is true.   Probably no
one of the evangelists ever so much as noticed this remarkable
inversion of what holds good respecting men in the life and
character of Jesus.   Is this character human, or is it plainly
divine ?

   We have now sketched some of the principal distinctions of

the superhuman character of Jesus. We have seen Him unfold
ing as a flower, from the germ of a perfect youth ; growing up
to enter into great scenes, and have His part in great trials ;
harmonious in all with Himself and truth, a miracle of celestial
beauty. He is a Lamb in innocence, a God in dignity ; reveal
ing an impenitent but faultless piety, such as no mortal ever
attempted, such as, to the highest of mortals, is inherently im
possible. He advances the most extravagant pretensions, with
out any show of conceit, or even seeming fault of modesty. He
suffers without affectation of composure, and without restraint of
pride, suffers as no mortal sensibility can, and where, to mortal
view, there was no reason for pain at all ; giving us not only an
example of gentleness and patience in all the small trials of life,
but revealing the depths even of the passive virtues of God, in
His agony and the patience of His suffering love. He undertakes
also a plan, universal in extent, perpetual in time, viz., to unite
all nations in a kingdom of righteousness under God ; laying
His foundations in the hearts of the poor, as no great teacher
had ever done before, and yet without creating ever a faction,
or stirring one partisan feeling in His followers. In His teach.
ings He is perfectly original, distinct from His age and from all
ages ; never warped by the expectation of His friends ; always
in a balance of truth, swayed by no excesses, running to no
oppositions or extremes ; clear of all superstition, and equally
clear of all liberalism ; presenting the highest doctrines in the
lowest and simplest forms ; establishing a pure. universal
morality, never before established ; and, with all His intense
devotion to the truth, never anxious, perceptibly, for the success
of His doctrine. Finally, to sum up all in one, He grows more
great, and wise, and sacred, the more He is known—needs, in
fact, to be known, to have His perfection seen. And this, we
say, is Jesus the Christ ; manifestly not human, not of our world
—some being who has burst into it, and is not of it. Call Him
for the present that " Holy Thing," and say, " By this we be
lieve that thou camest from God."

Not to say that we are dissatisfied with this sketch, would be
almost an irreverence of itself, to the subject of it. Who can
satisfy himself with anything that he can say of Jesus Christ ?
We have seen how many pictures of the sacred person of Jesus
by the first masters, but not one among them all that did not
rebuke the weakness which could dare attempt an impossible

subject. So of the character of Jesus. It is necessary for the holy interest of truth, that we should explore it, as we are best able; but what are human thoughts and human conceptions on a subject that dwarfs all thought, and immediately outgrows whatever is conceived? And yet, for the reason that we have failed, we seem also to have succeeded. For the more impos sible it is found to be to grasp the character and set it forth, the more clearly is it seen to be above our range—a miracle and a mystery.

Two questions now remain, which our argument requires to be answered. And the first is this—Did any such character, as this we have been tracing, actually exist? Admitting that the character, whether it be fact or fiction, is such as we have seen it to be, two suppositions are open, either that such a character actually lived, and was possible to be described, be cause it furnished the matter of the picture itself; or else, that Jesus, being a merely human character as He lived, was adorned or set off in this manner, by the exaggerations of fancy and fable and wild tradition afterward. In the former alternative, we have the insuperable difficulty of believing that any so per fect and glorious character was ever attained to by a mortal. If Christ was a merely natural man, then was He under all the conditions privative as regards the security of His virtue that we have discovered in man. He was a new created being, as such to be perfected in a character of steadfast holiness, only by the experiment of evil and redemption from it. We can be lieve any miracle, therefore, more easily than that Christ was a man, and yet a perfect character such as here is given. In the latter alternative, we have four different writers, widely distin guished in their style and mental habit—inferior persons, all, as regards their accomplishments, and none of them remarkable for gifts of genius—contributing their parts, and coalescing thus in the representation of a character perfectly harmonious with itself and with all—a character whose ideal no poet had been able to create, no philosopher, by the profoundest effort of thought, to conceive and set forth to the world. What is more, these four writers are, by the supposition, children all of credu lity, retailing the absurd gossip, and the fabulous stories of an age of marvels, and yet, by some accident, they are found to have conceived and sketched the only perfect character known to mankind. To believe this requires a more credulous age than these writers ever saw. We fall back, then, upon our con clusion, and there we rest. Such was the real historic charac ter of Jesus. Thus He lived, and the character is possible to be conceived, because it was actualized in a living example. The only solution is that which is given by Jesus Himself, when He says—" I came forth from the Father, and am come into the world."

The second question is this—Whether this character is to be conceived as an actually existing, sinless character, in the world ? That it is I maintain, because the character can no otherwise be accounted for in its known excellences. How was it that a simple-minded peasant of Galilee was able to put Himself in advance, in this manner, of all human teaching and excellence ; unfolding a character so peculiar in its combinations, and so plainly impossible to any mere man of the race ? Because His soul was filled with internal beauty and purity, having no spot or stain, distorted by no obliquity of view or feeling, lapsing therefore into no eccentricity or deformity. We can make out no account of Him so easy to believe, as that He was sinless ; indeed, we can make no other account of Him at all. He re alized what are, humanly speaking, impossibilities ; for His soul was warped and weakened by no human infirmities, doing all in a way of ease and naturalness, just because it is easy for clear waters to flow from a pure spring. To believe that Jesus got up these high conceptions artistically, and then acted them, in spite of the conscious disturbance of His internal harmony, and the conscious clouding of His internal purity by sin, would involve a degree of credulity, and a want of perception, as re gards the laws of the soul and their necessary action under sin, so lamentable as to be a proper subject of pity. We could sooner believe all the fables of the Talmud.

Besides, if Jesus was a sinner, He was conscious of sin as all sinners are, and therefore was a hypocrite in the whole fabric of His character ; realizing so much of divine beauty in it, maintaining the show of such unfaltering harmony and celestial grace, and doing all this with a mind confused and fouled by the affectations acted for true virtues ! Such an example of successful hypocrisy would be itself the greatest miracle ever heard of in the world.

Furthermore, if Jesus was a sinner, then He was, of course,

a fallen being ; down under the bondage, distorted by the perversity of sin and its desolating effects, as men are. The root therefore of all His beauty is guilt. Evil has broken loose in Him, He is held fast under evil. Bad thoughts are streaming through His soul in bad successions ; His tempers have lost their tune ; His affections have been touched by leprosy ; remorse scowls upon His heart ; His views have lost their balance and contracted obliquity ; in a word, He is fallen. Is it then such a being, one who has been touched, in this manner, by the demonic spell of evil—is it He that is unfold ing such a character ?

What then do our critics in the school of naturalism say of this character of Christ ? Of course they are obliged to say many handsome and almost saintly things of it. Mr Parker says of him, that " He unites in Himself the sublimest precepts and divinest practices, thus more than realizing the dream of prophets and sages ; rises free from all prejudice of His age, nation, or sect ; gives free range to the spirit of God in His breast ; sets aside the law, sacred and true—honoured as it was, its forms, its sacrifice, its temple, its priests ; puts away the doctors of the law, subtle, irrefragable, and pours out a doctrine beautiful as the light, sublime as heaven, and true as God." [1] Again—as if to challenge for His doctrine the distinc tion of a really superhuman excellence—" Try Him as we try other teachers. They deliver their word, find a few waiting for the consolation who accept the new tidings, follow the new method, and soon go beyond their teacher, though less mighty minds than he. Though humble men, we see what Socrates and Luther never saw. But eighteen centuries have past since the Sun of humanity rose so high in Jesus ; what man, what sect has mastered His thought, comprehend His method, and so fully applied it to life ! " [2]

Mr Hennel, who writes in a colder mood, but has, on the whole, produced the ablest of all the arguments yet offered on this side, speaks more cautiously. He says, " Whilst no human char acter, in the history of the world, can be brought to mind which, in proportion as it could be closely examined, did not present some defects, disqualifying it for being the emblem of moral perfection, we can rest, with least check or sense of incongruity, on the imperfectly known character of Jesus of Nazareth." [3]

[1] *Discourses of Religion*, p. 294. ' [2] *Ibid.* p. 303. [3] *Inquiry*, p. 451.

But the intimation here is that the character is not perfect; it is only one in which the sense of perfection suffers "least check." And where is the fault charged? Why, it is discovered that Jesus cursed a fig-tree, in which He is seen to be both angry and unreasonable. He denounced the Pharisees in terms of bitter animosity. He also drove the money-changers out of the temple with a scourge of rods, in which He is even betrayed into an act of physical violence. These and such like specks of fault are discovered, as they think, in the life of Jesus. So graceless in our conceit, have we of this age grown, that we can think it a point of scholarly dignity and reason to spot the only perfect beauty that has ever graced our world, with such discovered blemishes as these! As if sin could ever need to be made out against a real sinner, in this small way of special pleading; or as if it were ever the way of sin to err in single particles or homœopathic quantities of wrong! A more just sensibility would denounce this malignant style of criticism as a heartless and really low-minded pleasure in letting down the honours of goodness.

In justice to Mr Parker, it must be admitted that he does not actually charge these points of history as faults or blemishes in the character of Jesus. And yet, in justice also, it must be added that he does compose a section under the heading— "*The Negative Side, or the Limitations of Jesus*,"—where these, with other like matters, are thrown in by insinuation, as possible charges sometimes advanced by others. For himself, he alleges nothing positive, but that Jesus was under the popular delusion of His time, in respect to devils or demoniacal possessions, and that He was mistaken in some of His references to the Old Testament. What now is to be thought of such material, brought forward under such a heading, to flaw such a character! Is it sure that Christ was mistaken in His belief of the foul spirits? Is it certain that a sufficient mode of interpretation will not clear His references of mistake? And so, when it is suggested, at second hand, that His invective is too fierce against the Pharisees, is there no escape, but to acknowledge that, "considering His youth, it was a venial error?" Or, if there be no charge but this, "at all affecting the moral and religious character of Jesus," should not a just reverence to one whose life is so nearly faultless, constrain us to look for some more favourable construction that takes the

solitary blemish away ?   Is it true that invective is a necessary
token of ill-nature ?   Are there no occasions where even holi
ness will be most forward in it ?   And when a single man
stands out alone, facing a whole living order and caste, that
rule the time—oppressors of the poor, hypocrites and pretend
ers in religion, corrupters of all truth and faith, under the
names of learning and religion—is the malediction, the woe,
that He hurls against them, to be taken as a fault of violence
and unregulated passion ; or, considering what amount of force
and public influence He dares to confront and set in deadly
enmity against His person, is He rather to be accepted as
God's champion, in the honours of a great and genuinely heroic
spirit ?

Considering how fond the world is of invective, how ready to
admire the rhetoric of sharp words, how many speakers study
to excel in the fine art of excoriation, how many reformers are
applauded in vehement attacks on character, and win a great
repute of fearlessness, just because of their severity, when, in
fact, there is nothing to fear—when possibly the subject is a
dead man, not yet buried—it is really a most striking tribute
to the more than human character of Jesus, that we are found
to be so apprehensive respecting Him in particular, lest His
plain, unstudied, unrhetorical severities on this or that occa
sion, may imply some possible defect or " venal error " in Him.
Why this special sensibility to fault in Him? save that, by His
beautiful and perfect life, He has raised our conceptions so high
as to make, what we might applaud in a man a possible blemish
in His divine excellence.

The glorious old reformer and blind poet of Puritanism—
vindicator of a free commonwealth and a free, unprelatical re
ligion—holds, in our view, a far worthier and manlier conception
of what Christ does, in this example, and of what is due to all
the usurpations of titled conceit and oppression in the world.
With truly refreshing vehemence he writes—" For in times of
opposition, when against new heresies arising, or old corrup
tions to be reformed, this cool, impassionate mildness of positive
wisdom is not enough to damp and astonish the proud resistance
of carnal and false doctors, then (that I may have leave to soar
awhile, as the poets use) Zeal, whose substance is ethereal, arm-
ing in complete diamond, ascends his fiery chariot, drawn by
two blazing meteors figured like beasts, but of a higher breed

than any the zodiac yields, resembling those four which Ezekiel and St John saw, the one visaged like a lion, to express power, high authority, and indignation, the other of man, to cast derision and scorn upon perverse and fraudulent seducers —with them the invincible warrior, Zeal, shaking loosely the slack reins, drives over the heads of scarlet prelates and such as are insolent to maintain traditions, bruising their stiff necks under his flaming wheels.   Thus did the true prophets of old combat with the false; thus Christ, Himself the fountain of meekness, found acrimony enough to be still galling and vexing the prelatical Pharisees.   But ye will say, these had immediate warrant from God to be thus bitter ; and I say, so much the plainer is it found that there may be a sanctified bitterness against the enemies of the truth." [1]

And what other conception had Christ Himself of the mean ing and import of His conduct in the matter in question ?   He felt a zeal within Him, answering to Milton's picture, which could not, must not, be repressed.   He knew it would be blamed, or set in charge against Him, by false critics and un charitable doubters ; and He said, " The zeal of thy house hath eaten me up."   And still it was, when rightly viewed, only a necessary outburst of that indignant fire, which is kindled in the sweet bosom of innocence, by the insolence of hypocrisy and oppression.

I conclude, then, (1.) that Christ actually lived and bore the real character ascribed to Him in the history.   And (2.) that He was a sinless character.   How far off is He now from any possible classification in the genus humanity !   Having reached this point, we are ready to pass, in the next chapter, to the Christian miracles, and show that Christ, being Himself the greatest of all miracles, in his own person, did, in perfect con sistency, and without creating any greater difficulty, work miracles.

But before we drop a theme like this, let us note more dis tinctly the significance of this glorious advent, and have our congratulations in it.   This one perfect character has come into our world, and lived in it; filling all the moulds of action, all the terms of duty and love, with His own divine manners, works, and charities.   All the conditions of our life are raised

[1] *Apology for Smectymnus*, sect. i.

thus by the meaning He has shown to be in them, and the
grace He has put upon them. The world itself is changed, and
is no more the same that it was; it has never been the same
since Jesus left it. The air is charged with heavenly odours,
and a kind of celestial consciousness, a sense of other worlds, is
wafted on us in its breath. Let the dark ages come, let society
roll backward and churches perish in whole regions of the earth,
let infidelity deny, and, what is worse, let spurious piety dis
honour the truth; still there is a something here that was not,
and something that has immortality in it. Still our confidence
remains unshaken, that Christ and His all-quickening life are
in the world, as fixed elements, and will be to the end of time;
for Christianity is not so much the advent of a better doctrine
as of a perfect character; and how can a perfect character, once
entered into life and history, be separated and finally expelled?
It were easier to untwist all the beams of light in the sky, sepa
rating and expunging one of the colours, than to get the cha
racter of Jesus, which is the real gospel, out of the world. Look
ye hither, meantime, all ye blinded and fallen of mankind, a
better nature is among you, a pure heart, out of some pure
world, is come into your prison, and walks it with you. Do you
require of us to show who He is, and definitely to expound His
person? We may not be able. Enough to know that He is
not of us—some strange being out of nature and above it,
whose name is Wonderful. Enough that sin has never touched
His hallowed nature, and that He is a friend. In Him dawns
a hope—purity has not come into our world, except to purify.
Behold the Lamb of God that taketh away the sins of the world!
Light breaks in, peace settles on the air, lo! the prison walls
are giving way—rise, let us go.

CHAPTER XI.

CHRIST PERFORMED MIRACLES.

It used to be the practice of theologians to cite the miracles of Christ as proofs of His doctrine, and even of the gospel history ; not observing that the conditions of the question are entirely changed since the days of the first witnesses.   To the contem. poraries and attendants on the ministry of Jesus, He might well enough be approved of God, by miracles and signs; for, being themselves eye-witnesses, they could easily be sure of the facts. But to those who saw them not, to us who have heard of them only by the report of history, they can never be cited as proofs, because the main thing to be settled with us is the verity of the facts themselves.   The gospel history, instead of being attested to us by the miracles, has them rather as a heavy burden rest ing on its own credibility.   Doubtless it is true that, if such a being as Christ were to come into the world, on such an errand as the gospel reports, we should look to see him verify his mis sion by miracles, and without the miracles we should suspect the authenticity of his pretensions.   As far, therefore, as the miracles sort with the person of Christ and his mission, as set forth in His gospels, there is a harmony of parts in the history, that is one of the evidences of its truth.   It is even a necessary evidence, yet scarcely a sufficient evidence by itself.   We still require to be certified that the miracles reported are facts.   This done, Christianity, as a supernatural revelation of God, is estab lished.   Until then, the miracles are, it must be admitted, a subtraction from its rational evidence ; even though the subject-matter of the history be incomplete, and so far wanting in rational evidence, without them.

The ground taken against the Christian miracles by Spinoza,

in which he is followed by Mr Parker, is this : that they dis
honour God, as involving the opinion that His great revelation
in nature is insufficient, and needs afterward to be amended,
and that, in doing it by miracles, He is conceived to overturn
His own laws, and break up the order of His work.

Hume was an atheist, and, of course, had nothing to say of
God, or the confusion of His plan. Assuming that we know
nothing save by experience, he argued that we know by experi
ence the fallibility of all testimony, and the uniformity of the
laws of nature.   Hence that no amount of testimony can justify
our belief in a miracle ; for we have, and must have, a stronger
faith in the uniformity of the laws of nature, than we can have
in any testimony.   ·

Assisted in this sceptical tendency by modern science, which
has set the laws of nature, for the time, in such prominence, as
to operate a real suppression of thought in the spiritual direc
tion, Dr Strauss assumes the incredibility of miracles, without
much care for the argument, and bases on that assumption his
deliberate and powerful assault upon the gospel history.

Against these and similar modes of denial, which distinguish
the naturalistic tendencies of our time, we now undertake,
assisted by the material already prepared in the preceding chap
ters, to establish the fact of the Christian miracles.   Our argument will not prove every one of them, or, in fact, any particular
one ; for the question will still be open, for such as choose to
engage in it, whether this, or that, or some of them, are not to
be discredited for particular reasons, which display the mistake
or credulity of the narrators.   We shall only show that Christ
wrought miracles, which is the great point in issue.

Let us endeavour, then, first of all, as a matter on which
everything depends, to settle what is to bo understood by a
miracle, or what a miracle is.

We have raised a clear distinction already between nature
and the supernatural ; viz., that nature is the chain of cause
and effect—that coming to pass which is determined by the
laws of cause and effect in things.   The supernatural is that
which acts *on* the chain of cause and effect, from without the
chain ; not being caused in its action, but acting from itself,
under no conditions of previous causality.   The distinction of
nature and the supernatural is the distinction, in fact, between

propagations of causality and original causality, between *things* and *powers*.   In this view, man, as a power, together with all created spirits, good and bad, is a supernatural being co-ordinate with God, in so far as he acts freely and morally.   If he moves but a limb in his freedom, he acts on the lines of cause and effect in nature ; and if, in moving that limb, he has committed a murder, we blame him for it, and bring him to a felon's punishment ; simply because he was not caused to do the deed, by any efficient cause back of him, but did it of himself ; or, as the common law has it, "by malice aforethought."

But we do not call these free moral actions of man miracles because they are common, and because there is no attribute of wonder connected with them.   What then is a miracle ?   It is a supernatural act, an act, that is, which operates on the chain of cause and effect in nature from without the chain, producing in the sphere of the senses, some event that moves our wonder, and evinces the presence of a more than human power.   Observe three points.   (1.) It is by some action *upon*, not *in*, the line of cause and effect ; (2.) it is in the sphere of the senses, for, though the regeneration of a soul may require as great power as the raising of Lazarus, it is yet no proper miracle, because it is no sign to the senses ; (3.) it must be understood to evince a superhuman power, otherwise feats of jugglery and magic would be miracles.   We commonly suppose, in miracles, a deific power, though sometimes we refer them to a subordinate, angelic, or demoniacal power ; as when we speak of signs and lying wonders, that are wrought by no divine agency.   The word *miracle*, which is a Latin diminutive, properly denotes some limited or isolated fact that we wonder at.   It takes the diminutive form probably because it relates to something parcelled off from the whole of nature, which, in that view, is small or partial.   The Scripture uses several terms or names to denote such events, calling them "signs," "wonders," "powers ;" and once, παράδοξα, translated "strange things."

To make our definition yet more exact, or to clear it yet farther of ambiguity, let us add the following negatives :—

1. A miracle is not, as our definition itself implies, any wonderful event, developed under the laws of nature, or of natural causation.   Some religious teachers have taken this ground, suggesting that nature was originally planned or performed, so as to bring out these particular surprises at the

points where they occur. Doubtless God's original scheme, taken as a whole, was so planned or performed; but that scheme included more than mere nature, viz., all supernatural agencies and events, and even His own works or actions in the higher, vaster field of the supernatural. But it is a very differ ent thing to imagine that nature is everything, and that the surprises are all developments of nature.

2. A miracle is no event that transpires singly, or apart from system; for the real system of God is not nature, as we have seen, but that vaster whole of government and order, including spirits, of which nature is only a very subordinate and compara tively insignificant member. In this higher view, a miracle is in such a sense part of the integral system of God, that it would be no perfect system without the miracle. Hence all that is said against miracles, as a disruption of order in God's kingdom—therefore incredible and dishonourable to God—is without foundation.

3. A miracle is no contradiction of our experience. It is only an event that exceeds the reach of our experience. We have a certain experience of what is called nature and the order of nature. But what will be the effect, in the field of nature, when the supernatural order meets it, or streams into it, we cannot tell; our experience here is limited to the results or effects that may be wrought by our own supernatural agency. What the supernatural divine, or angelic or demonic agency may be able to do in it, we know not. Therefore, all that is alleged by Mr Hume falls to the ground. It may be more difficult to believe, or more difficult to prove such facts, wrought by such agencies; but not because they are contrary, in any proper sense to our experience. They are only more strange to our experience.

4. A miracle is no suspension or violation of the laws of nature. Here is the point where the advocates of miracles have so fatally weakened their cause by too large a statement. The laws of nature are subordinated to miracles, but they are not suspended or discontinued by them. If I raise my arm, I subordinate the law of gravity and produce a result against the force of gravity, but the law or the force is not discontinued. On the contrary, it is acting still, at every moment, as uniformly as if it held the arm to its place. All the vital agencies main tain a chemistry of their own, that subordinates the laws of in-

organic chemistry. Nothing is more familiar to us, than the fact of a subordination of natural laws. It is the great game of life, also, to conquer nature and make it what, of itself, by its own laws of cause and effect, it is not. We raised the supposition, on a former occasion, of another physical universe, separated from the existing universe, and placed beyond a gulf, across which no one effect ever travels. If now that other universe were swung up side by side with this, it would instantly change all the action of this—not by suspending its laws, but by an action that subordinates and varies its action. So the realm of spirits is a realm that is permitted, or empowered to come down upon this other, which is called nature, and play its activity upon it, according to the plan God has before adjusted; but this activity suspends no law, breaks no bond of system. Nature stands fast, with all her terms of cause and effect, as before, a constant quantity, interposed by God to be a medium between supernatural beings in their relative actions. They are to have their exercise in it, and upon it, and so, by their activity, they are to make a moral acquaintance with each other; men with men, all created spirits with all, God with creatures, creatures with God; acquaintance also with the need of laws by the wrongs they suffer, and with their own bad mind by seeing what wrongs they do; so by their whole experience to be trained, corrected, assimilated in love, and finished in holy virtue. There is no more a suspension of the laws of nature when God acts than when we do; for nature is, by her very laws, subjected to His and our uses, to be swayed, and modified, and made a sign-language, so to speak, of mutual acquaintance between us.

By these four negatives, distinctly premised, we seem to have cleared the faith of miracles of all needless incumbrances, and, in that way, to have cut off the principal objections urged against their credibility. Before proceeding, however, to inquire after the more positive proofs of the Christian miracles, it may be well to glance at the positions taken by some of the principal advocates of naturalism, and especially to the admissions they are sometimes constrained to make.

Thus it is conceded by Mr Hennel, that "it seems beyond the power of intellect to decide *a priori*, whether a miraculous revelation, or instruction through nature alone, be more suitable

to the character of God."[1]   There is then n
in the supposition, that God, as the spring
and order in His works, should yet perform
ever doubts we suffer of their reality must be groun
of historic evidence.   This is a large concession.

Coincidently with this, Mr Parker admits, that " there is
antecedent objection " to miracles, if only they are wrought " in
conformity with some law out of our reach."[2]   And exactly this
is true of all supernatural divine agency, as we have abundantly
shown—only the laws of God's supernatural agency are laws of
reason, or such as respect His last end, and the best way of
compassing that end ; which laws are yet so stable and so
exactly universal, that He will always do exactly the same
things, in exactly the same circumstances or conditions.

The admissions of Dr Strauss are even more remarkable.
We have already referred to his admission that one " kingdom
in nature many intrench on another," and that " human free
dom " may, in this way, modify " natural development."[3]
Ask the question accordingly, wherein is it less credible that
the freedom of God may do as much ? and we have, as the
necessary answer, what contains the whole doctrine of miracles.
Doubtless it will be added that man belongs to " the totality of
things," and that God does not; that man is in "the vast circle"
of nature and natural laws, and that God is not.   But the
answer, we reply, is grounded in an assumption, as regards man,
that is justified by no evidence, and is contradicted even by the
evidence of consciousness.   Man, as a being of free will, is no
part of nature at all, no arc in the circle of nature.   He belongs,
we have abundantly shown, to a higher kingdom and order ;
having it for his prime distinction that he acts supernaturally,
acts upon the circle of nature from without, and never as being
determined by the causalities of nature.   All the free intelligences of the universe are acting on the circle of nature in this
manner, and why then may not God Himself ?

But we have another concession that is even more to our
purpose.   Adverting to the fact that the ancient peoples,
especially of the East, begin at God, and see all changes take
their spring in His immediate agency, while the moderns
begin at things, and see all changes come to pass, under

1 *Inquiry*, p. 96.   2 *Discourses of Religion*, pp. 269, 270.
3 *Life of Jesus*, vol. i. p. 72.

... laws, he distinctly rejects the latter, as being, by itself ... complete and sufficient view of the subject. ' It must be confessed," he says, " on nearer investigation, that this modern explanation, although it does not exactly deny the existence of God, yet puts aside the idea of Him, as the ancient view did the idea of the world. For this is, as it has often been well remarked, no longer a God and Creator, but a mere finite artist, who acts immediately upon his work only during its first production, and then leaves it to itself; who becomes excluded with his full energy from one particular sphere of existence."[1]

There is then, he admits, no validity in the modern opinion which assumes that all things take place by force of second causes, and without an immediate divine agency. Indeed he explicitly acknowledges, on the next page, that "our idea of God requires an immediate, and our idea of the world a mediate divine operation." He only manages to quite take away the value of the admission, by raising the question, how to combine or settle the relative adjustment of the mediate and immediate operation, and by so conducting the process as to come out in the conclusion, that "God acts upon the world as a whole immediately; but on each part, only by means of His action on every other part," that is to say, "by the laws of nature." And so miracles are excluded.

But there is a mistake here, first in his premises, and next in his conclusion. It is not true that our " idea of the world" requires us to hold the faith of a merely " mediate " action of God upon it. Exactly contrary to this, the idea of the world, taken as disordered by sin, demands His immediate action. It is not only necessary in order to realize the idea of God, or make room for His practical existence, that we conceive Him to have some kind of immediate action, but the world, under its disorders, asks for it, and waits for the restoring grace of it. It is very true that if the world, as an organized frame of scientific order, under second causes, were in no way disturbed by our immediate action upon it, there would seem to be no demand or even place for an immediate operation of God. Why should the watchmaker turn the hands of his watch directly by the key, when he has made them to go mediately by the spring? But this is not any true statement of the question; the world is in no such state of primal and ideal order. Making due account of sin, as our philosophers, alas! never do, we have a condition that, for order's sake, asks an intervention of God's supernatural and powerful hand. The world, in fact, was made, including man, as a thing necessarily unperfect; made to want, thus, interventions and immediate operations, to carry it on and bring it out, in the final realiza tion of its perfected ends. Even as a watch, being no infallible machine, is submitted to external action by means of the regulator; and as, without a regulator prepared for the imme diate touch of some hand, it would be no manageable or service able thing, so it is the particular merit of nature, that it is originally ordered to receive the touch of free-will forces from without; first of such as are human, and then, as the only sufficient power of conservation, of such as are divine.

The error referred to, in the conclusion at which Dr Strauss arrives in his analysis, is too obvious to require a particular refutation. Enough that any one but a mere words-man will find some difficulty in conceiving how God should act "imme diately on the whole" of the world, without acting immediately on some one or all of the parts. Acting in or upon some one wheel of a watch, the whole action of the watch will be affected; so when every wheel is acted on; but what is that immediate action upon the whole of a watch that does not immediately act on any one of the parts? Besides, the argument by which all particular action is excluded, would require that God should never have begun to act immediately anywhere. Creation is thus philosophically impossible. God, therefore, has had no thing to do, but to be chained to the wheel from eternity, acting immediately on some eternal whole that is self-existent as He; allowed to begin nothing, vary no part or particle, held by a doom to His eternal totality. Is it this which "the idea of God" requires, this by which our idea of God is fulfilled?

On this particular question, however, of an immediate and a mediate divine agency, we are not disposed to spend a great deal of time. We strongly suspect there is a sophism in the question, much as if the inquiry were whether God, who is above time, acts in this tense or the other? All that we can say with confidence on this subject appears to be that, so far as we can see, it is necessary for *us*, under conditions of time, to hold the two conceptions of a nature set on foot in some past time, and a divine force acting supernaturally upon it now; and that God so distributes His action or plan, as to give us what will thus accommodate our finite conditions. Nature, practically viewed, and wholly apart from speculation, is a kind of third quantity between us and God, to be reciprocally acted on; so that we can see what we are doing toward Him, and what He is doing toward us. It is words to the great life-talk of duty, a medium of action and reaction that interprets to us the divine relationship in which we stand. Laying hold of nature by her laws and causes, to build, produce, possess, and also to frame a scientific knowledge, we get a footing and a basis of reaction for our freedom. If we descend into sin, we set the causes of nature in courses of retributive action, and this reveals what is in our sin. Then, as God will redeem us, we are able to see a force entered into nature which is not nature's force. One may be as truly a divine force as the other, but they are yet so ordered as to be relative forces to our apprehension, acting one upon or into the other. In all Christian experience, and in times of prayer, we get a divine help entered into our state which we apprehend distinctly, and with a conscious intelligence, as we could not if all divine agency were homogeneous. But while we need so manifestly to think God's agency in this manner, under a twofold distribution, it is by no means certain that He, from His height of eternity, classifies His action under our finite categories of tense and re lative causality. It is very certain, as we have already shown, that nature is not to Him the universal system. All His doings, whether past or present, mediate or immediate, rest in laws of reason determined by His end; and it is in these, not in the physical laws magnified by science, that He beholds the real system of His universe. In this view, nature may be to Him a kind of continuous creation, coalescing, as it flows from His will, in a common stream with His supernatural action, and crystallizing with it in the unity of His end. Enough that to us a conception of His work is given which better meets our finite conditions. Enough that we may call it natural and supernatural, cause and effect and miracle, mediate and imme diate; and that so, without any real error, we may have our human want accommodated. The twofold distinction is per mitted as a practically valid form of thought, without which we could have no sense of relationship with God under the experience of life ; and without which nothing done by Him, as prior to our sin, in the way of judicial arrangement, or posterior in the way of recovery, could ever be intelligible.

Having noted some of the admissions of the naturalizing teachers, we will now proceed to adduce some proofs of the Christian miracles, or rather to gather up the proofs already supplied by the course of our argument itself.

1. We have seen that man himself acts supernaturally in all his free accountable actions. That is, he acts upon the chain of cause and effect in nature, uncaused himself, in his action. This is no miracle, but it involves all the speculative difficulties encountered in miracles. These are nothing but acts, every way similar to ours, of God or superhuman agents on the lines of causes in nature, only different in effect or degree as they are different beings from us. We have only to suppose that nature is, by her very laws, submitted to them as to us, and that is the end of all difficulty. We may wonder at their manifestations and not at our own ; but our wonder alters nothing, creates no derangement of nature, any more than if we were so familiar with such doings as to experience no wonder at all. If the sun darkens, or the earth shudders with Christ in His death, that sympathy of nature is just as appropriate for Him as it is for us, that our skin should blush or our eye distil its tears when our guilt is upon us, or our repentances dissolve us. It is not cause and effect that blushes or that weeps, but it is that cause and effect are touched by sentiments which connect with our freedom. Nature blushes and weeps, because she was origin ally submitted so far to our freedom, or made to be touched by our actions ; but she could not even to eternity raise a blush or a tear of contrition if we did not command her.

2. Consider how near the fact of sin, which is the act of a supernatural human agency, approaches to the rank of a miracle. Sin, as we have shown in a previous chapter, is the acting of a free being as he was not made to act ; for if it were the acting of a being under laws of cause and effect established by God, then it would be no sin. God made sin possible, just as He made all lying wonders possible, but He never made it a fact, never set anything in His plan to harmonize with it. Therefore it enters the world as a forbidden fact against everything that God has ordained. And then what follows ? A general dis-

ruption of everything that belongs to the original paradisiac
order of the creation.   The soul itself begins at the first mo
ment to feel the terrible action of it, and becomes a crazed and
disordered power.   The crystal form of the spirit is broken,
and it is become an opaque element, a living mal-formation.
The conscience is battered and trampled in its throne. · The
successions of the thoughts have become disorderly and wild,
the tempers are out of tune, the passions kindle into guilty
fires, and burn with a consuming heat, the imagination is a
hell of painful, ugly phantoms, the body a diseased thing,
scarred by deformity.   Society is out of joint, and even the
physical world itself, as we have shown, is marred in every part
by abortions, deformities visible, and discords audible, so as no
more to represent the perfect beauty of its author.   What devil
now of confusion has thrown a magnificent creature, and a
realm of glorious natural order, into so great confusion ?
Where are those sovereign laws of beauty and order which they
tell us nothing can disturb ?   We care not to call sin a miracle.
We only say that no one miracle, nor all miracles, ever heard
of or reported, can be imagined to have wrought a thousandth
part of the disturbance actually wrought by sin, the sin of man
kind.   Whoever then has yielded to the really shallow dogma
of rationalism, which teaches that cause and effect in nature must
have their way, fulfilling causes of ideal harmony, and forever
excluding the possibility of a miracle, need not go far to find a
corrective.   Let it be distinctly noted then—

3. That what we call nature, and what the mere naturalists
are so bold to assume cannot be mended or altered by any
interference of miracle, does, in fact, no longer exist.   Sin has
so far unmade the world that the divine order is broken.   The
laws are all in action as at the first, never discontinued or
annihilated, but the false fact or lying wonder of sin, has made
false conjunctions of causes, and set the currents of causality in
a kind of malign activity, which displaces for ever the proper
order of nature.   It is with nature as with a watch in which
some wheel has been made eccentric in its motions by abuse.
The whole machine is in disorder, though no one part is want
ing.   It is no longer a watch or time-keeper, but a jumble of
useless and absurd motions.   So nature, under sin, is no longer
nature, but a condition of unnature.   Yet this it is that our
scientific naturalism assumes to be the perfect order ; which

not even God may touch by a miracle, without a breach of its integrity! It is nature, they say, and God who is the God of nature, will not, cannot touch it, without either consenting to its original imperfection, or producing a general wreck of its perfection. Why, the perfection of it is gone long ages ago! From the moment, when a substance or power located in it, viz., man, began to act as he was not made to act, that is to sin, it has been a disordered fabric of necessity. No longer does it represent only the beautiful mind of its Author, but quite as often the shame, and discord, and deformity consequent upon sin. And no man, we are sure, who regards it for a mo ment, will have any the least apprehension that a miracle wrought in it by its Author can be anything but a hopeful sign for its systematic integrity. That He would never work a miracle in nature proper, as it came from His hands, we are quite willing to admit; but since nature is gone, fallen with man in the bad experiment of evil, and since it was originally designed to be acted on, both by man and by Himself, in a process of training that carries him through a fall, and brings him out in redemption, we see nothing to discourage the faith of miracles, but much to prove the contrary. This brings us to speak—

4. Of the fact that, without a putting forth of the divine power, in some action sovereign as miracle, there can be no reconstruction of the proper order of nature, no recovery of the broken state of man. The laws of nature, without him and within, are now running perversely as laws of sin and death. The crystalline order of souls and of the world is broken, and it is plain, at a glance, that no being but God, the Almighty, can avail to restore the disturbance. The laws have no power of self-rectification, any more than the laws of a disordered machine have power to cure the disorder by running. As certainly, therefore, as sinners are to be restored, as certainly, that is, as that all God's ends in the world and human exist ence are not to fail, there will be, must be, miracles or puttings forth, at least, of a divinely supernatural power. Every thing in the whole creation is groaning and travailing in the expectation of so great a redemption. The very plan was originally, as we have shown, to bring out the grand results of spiritual order and character intended, by means of a double administration; that is by the creation and the new-creation, the creation disordered by

sin, the new-creation raised up and glorified by grace and its miracles. Go back then a moment—

5. To things precedent and see what considerations and facts may be gathered there. First, we discover what the natural ists and men chiefly occupied with matters of science so gene rally overlook, the fact that nature never was, and never was designed to be, the whole empire of God; that the final. ends of God are not contained in nature at all; and that it was appointed by Him to be only a means to His ends, a mere field for the training of His children. In this view spiritual crea tures, creatures supernatural, compose the real body and sub stance of His empire, and to these nature was to be subjected, by these to be played upon in the great life-battle of their trial—disordered by them and restored by Himself. Accord ingly, it is not implied that the divine system is, in any degree, marred or broken by His miracles. On the contrary, every thing done by Him will be done as fulfilling that system. There is no change, no reconsideration, no breach of unity, but a doing of precisely that which was set down to be done at the first. He proceeds, in fact, by laws predetermined, in His miracles them selves ; of course by a perfect and orderly system.

Observe, again, the fact that God has either never done or can do anything, or else that He may as well be supposed to do a miracle now. To create anything that was not, to set any plan on foot that was not on foot, was itself a miracle that involved all the difficulties of a miracle subsequent. To create a scheme called nature and retire to see it run, is itself a miracle, and we may just as well suppose that He continues to work as that He so began. He has either never done anything, or else He may do something now. There is no way to escape the faith of miracles and hold the faith of a personal God and Creator. It is only pantheism, or what is not far different, atheism, that can rationally and consistently maintain the im possibility of miracles. Any religion too absolute to allow the faith of miracles, is a religion whose God never did anything, and is therefore no God.

Again, it is discovered and proved, by science itself, that God has performed, at least, one miracle, or class of miracles, in the world, previous to the date of human existence. We speak of the great geological discovery that new races of animals and plants have, at different times, been created, and finally man himself. The mere metallic earth, which, at one time, was the all of nature, did not make or sprout up into any form of life. That would be a greater miracle, done by nature, than the raising of Lazarus—as great as if the earth had raised him, yea, as great as if the earth had invented and shaped him, and breathed intelligence into him. Here then is proved to us, out of the infallible registers of the rocks, that God had sometime wrought a miracle upon nature. And, as we said just now, one miracle proved, decides the question ; for there may as well be a thousand as one. We pass now—

6. To the subject of our last chapter, where we meet a proof that concludes all argument. We there showed, by a full and critical examination of the character of Jesus, that He is plainly not a human character, and cannot be rightly classed in the genus humanity ; also, that the character is not an invention, but that such a person must have lived, else He could not be described ; also, that being such, in external description, He must have been, what He Himself claimed to be, a sinless being. Here, then, is a being who has broken into the world, and is not of it ; one who has come out from God, and is even an expression to us of the complete beauty of God—such as He should be, if He actually was, what He is affirmed to be, the Eternal Word of the Father incarnate. Did He work miracles ? this is now the question that waits for our decision—did He work miracles ? By the supposition, He is superhuman. By the supposition, too, He is in the world as a miracle. Agreeing that the laws of nature will not be suspended, any more than they are by our own supernatural action, will they yet be so subordinated to His power as to permit the performance of signs and wonders, in which we may recognize a superhuman force ? Since He is shown to be a superhuman being, manifestly nature will have a relation to Him, under and by her own laws, such as accords with His superhuman quality, and it will be very singular if He does not do superhuman things ; nay, it is even philosophically incredible that He should not. An organ is a certain instrument, curiously framed or adjusted in its parts, and prepared to yield itself to any force which touches the keys. An animal runs back and forth across the key-board, and produces a jarring, disagreeable jumble of sounds. Thereupon he begins to reason, and convinces himself that it is the nature of the instrument to make such sounds, and no other. But a skilful

player comes to the instrument, as a higher presence, endowed with a super-animal sense and skill. He strikes the keys, and all-melodious and heavenly sounds roll out upon the enchanted air. Will the animal now go on to reason that this is impossible, incredible, because it violates the nature of the instrument, and is contrary to his own experience? Perhaps he may, and men may sometimes not be wiser than he. But the player himself, and all that can think it possible for him to do what the animal cannot, will have no doubt that the music is made by the same laws that made the jargon. Just so Christ, to whose will or touch our mundane system is pliant as to ours, may be able to execute results through its very laws, subordinated to Him, which to us are impossible. Nay, it would be itself a contradiction of all order and fit relation, if He could not. To suppose that a being out of humanity will be shut up within all the limitations of humanity, is incredible and contrary to reason. The very laws of nature themselves, having Him present to them, as a new agent and higher first term, would require the development of new consequences and incidents in the nature of wonders. Being a miracle Himself, it would be the greatest of all miracles if He did not work miracles.

Let it be further noted, as a consideration important to the argument, that Christ is here on an errand high enough to justify His appearing, and also of a nature to exclude any suspicion that He is going to overthrow the order of God's works. He declares that He has come out from God to be a restorer of sin, a regenerator of all things, a new moral creator of the world; thus to do a work that is, at once, the hope of all order, and the greatest of all miracles. Were He simply juggling with our curiosity, in the performance of idle and useless wonders, doing it for money, or to show what is of no consequence; as that He is a priest, or has the power of second sight, or that the sun shines, or that he is right in asserting some insignificant opinion, it is allowed that we should have no right to believe in Him. But he tells us, on the contrary, that He is come out from God, to set up the kingdom of God, and fulfil the highest ends of the divine goodness in the creation of the world itself; and the dignity of His work, certified by the dignity also of His character, sets all things in proportion, and commends Him to our confidence in all the wonders he performs.

But our human supernatural action, it will be suggested, is

through the body, while the raising of Lazarus dispenses with all natural media and instruments. And yet, as our body is a part of nature, it will be seen that we act upon the body as being itself nature, without media between it and our will, in the same manner. The relationship existing between different orders of being and nature, may also vary according to their degree. On this subject we know nothing. We cannot even say that, to such a being as Christ incarnate in it. the whole realm of physical existence was not present as a sensorium, quickened by His life. Mere ignorance is not competent here to hold an objection. If we cannot see how Christ could work His miracles, or send His will into things around him, there is nothing singular in the fact. There are many things that we cannot understand.

Nor shall we apprehend in His miracles any disruption of law; for we shall see that He is executing that true system, above nature and more comprehensive, which is itself the basis of all stability, and contains the real import of all things. Dwelling from eternity in this higher system Himself, and having it centred in His person, wheeling and subordinating thus all physical instruments, as doubtless He may, to serve those better ends in which all order lies, it will not be in us, when He comes forth from the Father, on the Father's errand, to forbid that He shall work in the prerogatives of the Father. Visibly not one of us, but a visitant who has come out from a realm of spiritual majesty, back of the sensuous orb on which our moth-eyes dwell as in congenial dimness and obscurity of light, what shall we think when we see diseases fly before Him, and blindness letting fall the scales of obscured vision, and death retreating from its prey, but that the seeming disruption of our retributive state under sin, is made to let in mercy and order from above. For, if man has buried himself in sense, and married all sense to sin, which sin is itself the soul of all disorder, can it be to us a frightful thing that He lays His hand upon the perverted causalities, and says, "Thou art made whole?" If the bad empire, the bitter unnature, of our sin, is somewhere touched by His healing power, must we apprehend some fatal shock of disorder? If, by His miraculous force, some crevice is made in the senses to let in the light of heaven's peace and order, must we tremble lest the scientific laws are shaken, and the scientific causes violated? Better is it to say—" This beginning of miracles did

Jesus make in Galilee, and manifested forth his glory, and wo believe in him." Glory breaks in through His incarnate person, to chase away the darkness. In Him peace and order descend to rebuild the realm below they have maintained above. Sin, the damned miracle and misery of the groaning creation, yields to the stronger miracle of Jesus and His works, and the great good minds of this and the upper worlds behold integrity and rest returning, and the peace of universal empire secure. Out of the disorder that was, rises order; out of chaos, beauty. Amen! Alleluia! for the Lord God omnipotent reigneth!

Once more, it is a powerful evidence for the historic verity of the Christian miracles, that their deniers can make no account of them, as reported in the Christian narratives, which is rational or even credible. Dr Strauss maintains that they are myths or legendary tales, that grew up out of the story-telling and marvelling habit of the disciples of Christ, within the first thirty years after their Master's death, at which time many of the eye-witnesses of the miracles were still living. That such a conversion of history into fable should have taken place in the traditions of a much longer period of time, is not impossible. But he is compelled to shorten his time in this manner, as it would seem, because there is no allusion made in the Gospels to the fall of Jerusalem as an accomplished fact. For, had they been written after the overthrow by Titus, it is inconceivable that his name should not have been mentioned in those chapters of the Gospels that foretell the overthrow, and also that the shocking scenes of the siege should not have been even too distinctly described. On the supposition, too, that the first age of discipleship was fertile enough in the mythical tendency to have generated so many miraculous stories within the short period of thirty years, this grand catastrophe of the nation must have been set off with a profuse garnish of fictions, and Christ Himself, coming in the clouds of heaven to be the avenger of the Cross, must have had such prominence in the transaction as to quite leave the Roman commander in the shade. Hence the necessity that so short a time should be fixed. And thus we are required to believe that all these myths were developed and recorded in the lifetime of the eye-witnesses of Christ's ministry, and some of them recorded by eye-witnesses themselves. The faith of miracles, we think, would be somewhat easier than this. And still the difficulty is further increased by the fact that the

THE MIRACLES IS TENABLE.

Epistles, the genuineness of which is indisputable, present exactly the same Christ, and refer to the same miracles, in a manner clear of all pretence of myth or extravagance.

But the mythologic hypothesis of this critic breaks down more fatally, if possible, in the necessary implication, that four common men are able to preserve such a character as that of Christ, while loading down the history thus with so many mythical wonders that are the garb of their very grotesque and childish credulity. By what accident, we are compelled to ask, was an age of myths and fables able to develope and set forth the only conception of a perfect character ever known in our world? Were these four mythologic dreamers, believing their own dreams and all others beside, the men to produce the perfect character of Jesus, and a system of teachings that transcend all other teachings ever given to the race? If there be a greater miracle or a tax on human credulity more severe, we know not where it is. Nothing is so difficult, all human literature testifies, as to draw a character, and keep it in its living proportions. How much more to draw a perfect character, and not discolour it fatally by marks from the imperfection of the biographer. How is it, then, that four humble men, in an age of marvels and Rabbinical exaggerations, have done it—done what none, not even the wisest and greatest of mankind, have ever been able to do?

So far even Mr Parker concedes the right of my argument. "Measure," he says, "the religious doctrine of Jesus by that of the time and place He lived in, or that of any time and any place. Yes, by the doctrine of eternal truth. Consider what a work His words and deeds have wrought in the world. Remember that the greatest minds have seen no farther, and added nothing to the doctrine of religion; that the richest hearts have felt no deeper, and added nothing to the sentiment of religion; have set no loftier aim, no truer method than His, of perfect love to God and man. Measure Him by the shadow He has cast into the world—no, by the light He has shed upon it. Shall we be told such a man never lived—the whole story is a lie? Suppose that Plato and Newton never lived. But who did their wonders, and thought their thought? It takes a Newton to forge a Newton. What man could have fabricated a Jesus? None but a Jesus." [1]

1 *Life of Jesus*, p. 363.

Exactly so. And yet, in the middle of the very paragraph from which these words are gleaned, Mr Parker says, " We can learn few facts about Jesus;" also, that in certain things—to wit, His miracles, we suppose—" Hercules was His equal, and Vishnu His superior." Few facts about Jesus! all the miracles recited of Him as destitute of credibility as the stories of Her cules and Vishnu! And yet these evangelists, retailing so many absurd fictions and so much childish gossip, have been able to give us a doctrine upon which the world has never advanced, a character so deep that the richest hearts have felt nothing deeper, and added nothing to the sentiment of it. They have done, that is, the difficult thing, and broken down under the easy! preserved, in the life and discourses of Jesus, what exceeds all human philosophy, all mortal beauty, and yet have not been able to recite the simplest facts! Is it so that any intelligent critic will reason? Suppose, if it please, that they are not infallible in their narrative, for we have not proved them to be. Still, as we would trust a carrier who has brought us a case of the rarest diamonds, set in the frailest and most delicate tissues, proving at once his capacity and his honest fidelity to his trust, so much more will we trust these simple men who have given us the perfect life of Jesus, discoloured by no stain from their own fond prejudices and weaker in firmities. Nor, if this carrier may have once stumbled at our door, when bringing us some bundle of meaner consequence, do we set him down, after bringing us the casket safely, as one who is unreliable in these common errands. No more can we set down our evangelists, as unreliable in matters of fact, after they have brought us the glorious, self-evidencing character of Jesus, even though, to suppose the worst, they should be suspected, once or twice, of mistake in the external facts of His ministry. But there are objections to be considered.

First objection. That if the miracles of Christ are to be believed, why not those also of Hercules and Vishnu, and the ecclesiastical miracles of the Papal Church? Undoubtedly they must be, if they are wrought by such a character as Jesus, engaged in such a work. But it is rather too much to insist that, because we take good money, we ought therefore in con sistency to take counterfeit money. If it be said that the Popish miracles are as well attested as those of Jesus, we have made nothing at all, let it be observed, of the mere testimony of witnesses. We have proved the witnesses by that which stands in glorious self-evidence before us, and not the miracles by the mere testimony of the witnesses. We will believe the miracles also of Hercules, when Hercules is seen, by the holy beauty of his perfect character, to have certainly come out from God. So, too, we might well enough agree to believe the miracles of the apocryphal gospels, that, for example, of the Infancy of Jesus, could the writer only manage to give us the character of that infancy, without reducing it to a disgusting picture of pettishness and passion. Until then we must dis cover, in what is called his gospel, how certain it is that the pen which gives us only myths and marvels, for the facts of a perfect history, will give us, for a perfect character, what is wilder still and more absurd.

Second objection. That, according to our definition, there may be false miracles. That is certainly the doctrine of Scrip ture. Neither is there anything essentially incredible in it. They are wrought, of course, by no concurrence of divine power, but only by such power as belongs to the grade of the spirit by whom they are wrought—by "him whose coming is with signs and lying wonders," "by the spirits of devils, working miracles." According to our definition, any invisible spirit, who can do what is superhuman, can do a miracle. That there are invisible spirits, we have no doubt, and what kind of access they may have to nature, in what manner qualified or restrained, we do not know. But it will never be difficult to distinguish their prodigies and freaks of mischief from any divine operation. Their character will be evident in their works, and no one that loves the divine truth will ever be taken by their impostures. We express no opinion of the utterances and other demonstra tions which many are accepting in our times, as the effusions of spirits—they are beyond our range of acquaintance. We say that if these things are really done or communicated by spirits, then they are miracles, bad miracles, of course ; and thus we have it established as a curious phenomenon, that the men who are boasting their rejection of all divine miracles, are themselves deepest in the faith of those which are wrought by demons. Nor is it impossible that God has suffered this late irruption of lying spirits, to be at once the punishment and the rectification of that shallow unbelief which distinguishes our age—thus to shame the absurd folly of what is here called science, and bring

us back to a true faith in the spiritual realities and powers of a
supernatural kingdom.

Third objection.   That if miracles are credible in any particular time or age, that, for example, of the New Testament, they
must be now and always credible.   To this we answer that they
are now and always credible.   But it does not follow that they
are now and always a fact.   That must depend upon historic
evidence.   The Scriptures nowhere teach, what is often assumed, the final discontinuance of miracles, and it is much to
be regretted that such an assumption is so commonly made ; for
when it is taken for an authorized doctrine, that God will no
more allow any real miracle to be wrought since the apostolic
times, it renders even the New Testament miracles just so much
more difficult to be believed.   There is no certain proof that
miracles have been wrought in every age of the Christian
Church.   There is certainly a supernatural and divine causality
streaming into the lives and blending with the faith of all good
men, and there is no reason to doubt that it may sometimes
issue in premonitions, results of guidance and healing, endow-
ments of force, answers to prayer that closely approach, in many
cases, if they do not exactly meet, our definition of miracles.

We answer again, that if miracles have been discontinued,
even for a thousand years, they may yet be revived in such
varieties of form, as a different age may require.   They will be
revived without fail, whenever the ancient reason may return,
or any new contingency may occur demanding their instrumentality.

And yet, again, we answer that there may have been good
and sufficient reasons why the more palpable miracles of the
apostolic age could not be continued, or must needs be inter-
spaced by agencies of a more silent character.   It may have
been that they would by and by corrupt the impressions and
ideas even of religion, setting men to look after signs and prodigies with their eyes, inducing a contempt of everything else,
and so, instead of attesting God to men, making them unspiritual
and even incapable of faith.   Traces of this mischief begin to
appear even in the times of the apostles themselves.   Therefore, when the fire is kindled, the smoke, it may be, ceases ; or
rather it becomes transparent, so that we do not so readily see
it, though it is there.   Christianity, it is very obvious, inaugu-
rates the faith of a supernatural agency in the world.   It is

either supernatural or it is a nullity. Hence, to inaugurate such a faith, it must needs make its entry into the world, through the fact of a divine incarnation and other miracles. In these we have the pole of thought, opposite to nature, set before us in distinct exhibition. And then the problem is, having the two poles of nature and the supernatural presented, that we be trained to apprehend them conjunctively, or as working together in silent terms of order. For, if the miracles continue in their palpable and staring forms of wonder, and take their footing as a permanent institution, they will breed a sensuous, desultory state of mind, opposite to all sobriety, and all genuine intelli gence. The invalid will now pray to be healed by pure miracle, and will never learn or be taught how to pray, in a manner that contemplates a unifying of the supernatural force with nature and the system of natural causes. At a certain point the miracles were needed as the polar signs of a new force, but, for the reasons suggested, it appears to be necessary, also, that they should not be continuous; otherwise the supernatural will never be thought into any terms of order, as a force conjoined with nature in our common experience, but will only instigate a wild, eccentric temper, closely akin to unreason and to all practi cal delusion. And yet there may be times, even to the end of the world, when some outburst of the miraculous force of God will be needed to break up a lethargy of unbelief and sensuous dulness, equally unreasoning and desultory.

Fourth objection. That whatever may be true of miracles in other respects, they are only demonstrations of force; there fore, having in themselves no moral quality, there is no rational or valuable, or even proper place for them in a gospel, con sidered as a new-creating grace for the world. To this we answer that it is a thing of no secondary importance for a sinner, down under sin, and held fast in its bitter terms of bondage, to see that God has entered into his case with a force that is adequate. These mighty works of Jesus, which have been done and duly certified, are fit expressions to us of the fact that He can do for us all that we want. Doubtless it is a great and difficult thing to regenerate a fallen nature; no person, really awake to his miserable and dreadful bondage, ever thought otherwise. But He that touched the blind eyes and commanded the leprosy away, He that trod the sea, and raised the dead, and burst the bars of death Himself, can tame the passions, sweeten the bitter affections, regenerate the inbred diseases, and roll back all the storms of the mind. Assured in this manner by His miracles, they become arguments of trust, a storehouse of powerful images, that invigorate courage and stimulate hope. Broken as we are by our sorrow, cast down as we are by our guiltiness, ashamed, and weak, and ready to despair, we can yet venture a hope that our great soul-miracle may be done; that if we can but touch the hem of Christ's garment, a virtue will go out of Him to heal us. In all dark days and darker struggles of the mind, in all outward disasters, and amid all storms upon the sea of life, we can yet descry Him treading the billows and hear Him saying, "It is I, be not afraid." And lest we should believe the miracles faintly, for there is a busy infidel lurking always in our hearts to cheat us of our faith when he cannot reason it away, the character of Jesus is ever shining with and through them, in clear self-evidence, leaving them never to stand as raw wonders only of might, but covering them with glory, as tokens of a heavenly love, and acts that only suit the proportions of His personal greatness and majesty.

There are many in our day, as we know, who, without mak ing any speculative point of the objection we are discussing, have so far yielded to the current misbelief as to profess, with a certain air of self-compliment, that they are quite content to accept the spirit of Jesus; and let the miracles go for what they are worth. Little figure will they make as Christians in that kind of gospel. They will not, in fact, receive the spirit of Jesus; for that unabridged is itself the Grand Miracle of Christianity, about which all the others play as scintillations only of the central fire. Still less will they believe that Jesus can do anything in them which their sin requires. They will only compliment His beauty, imitate or ape His ways in a feeble lifting of themselves, but that He can roll back the currents of nature, loosened by the disorders of sin, and raise them to a new birth in holiness, they will not believe. No such watery gospel of imitation, separated from grace, will have any living power in their life, or set them in any bond of unity with God. Nothing but to say—"Jesus of Nazareth, a man approved of God by miracles and signs which God did by him"—can draw the soul to faith and open it to the power of a supernatural and new-creative mercy.

We come back then, in closing, to the grand first principle of evidence, and there we rest. The character and doctrine of Jesus are the sun that holds all the minor orbs of revelation to their places, and pours a sovereign self-evidencing light into all religious knowledge. We have been debating much, and rang ing over a wide field, in chase of the many phantoms of doubt and false argument, still we have not far to go for light, if only we could cease debating and sit down to see. It is no ingenious fetches of argument that we want ; no external testi mony, gathered here and there from the records of past ages, suffices to end our doubts ; but it is the new sense opened in us by Jesus Himself—a sense deeper than words and more im mediate than inference—of the miraculous grandeur of His life ; a glorious agreement felt between His works and His person, such that His miracles themselves are proved to us in our feel ing, believed in by that inward testimony. On this inward testi mony we are willing to stake everything, even the life that now is, and that which is to come. If the miracles, if revelation itself, cannot stand upon the superhuman character of Jesus. then let it fall. If that character does not contain all truth and centralize all truth in itself, then let there be no truth. If there is anything worthy of belief not found in this, we may well con sent to live and die without it. Before this sovereign light. streaming out from God, the deep questions, and dark surmises, and doubts unresolved, which make a night so gloomy and terrible about us, hurry away to their native abyss. God, who com- manded the light to shine out of darkness, hath shined in our hearts to give the light of the knowledge of the glory of God in the face of Jesus Christ. This it is that has conquered the assaults of doubt and false learning in all past ages, and will in all ages to come. No argument against the sun will drive it from the sky. No mole-eyed scepticism, dazzled by its bright ness, can turn away the shining it refuses to look upon. And they who long after God, will be ever turning their eyes thither ward, and either with reason or without reason, or, if need be, against manifold impediments of reason, will see and believe.

CHAPTER XII.

WATER-MARKS IN THE CHRISTIAN DOCTRINE.

There is no kind of evidence that is so convincing, or is re
ceived with so great satisfaction, as that which, after long and
doubtful search, is suddenly discovered to have all the while
been on hand, incorporated, though unobserved, in the very sub
ject-matter of inquiry. Thus, for example, a suit upon a note
at hand had long been pending in one of the courts of our com
monwealth, payment of which was resisted on the ground that
it was and must be a forgery, no such note having ever been
given. But the difficulty was in the trial to make out any con
clusive evidence of what the defending party knew to be the
truth. His counsel was, in fact, despairing utterly of success ;
but it happened that, just as he was about closing his plea, hav
ing the note in his hand, and bringing it up, in the motion of
his hand, so that the light struck through, his eye caught the
glimpse of a mark in the paper. He stopped, held it up deli.
berately to the light, and behold the name, in water-mark,
of a company that had begun the manufacture of paper after
the date of the instrument! Here was evidence, without going
far to seek it—evidence enough to turn the plaintiff forthwith
into a felon, and consign him, as it did, to a felon's punish
ment.

Just so there is, we now propose to show, a certain divine
water-mark in the Christian doctrine, which, whether we see it
or not, is there waiting at all times to be seen, and to give to
all who will look for it indubitable proof of its supernatural and
divine origin.

And, first of all, we select for an example or principal in
stance, the grand comprehensive distinction of the Christian

system, viz., the assumption it everywhere makes of a neces sarily twofold economy in the training of souls. This assump tion or assumed necessity appears and reappears on almost every page of the New Testament. The two economies are "two covenants;" two ministrations—a "ministration of condemna tion," and a "ministration of righteousness;" "law and grace;" "bondage and liberty;" "the letter that killeth, and the spirit that giveth life;" "the law that makes nothing perfect;" and "charity which is the bond of perfectness."

We have spoken already[1] of this twofold process in the training of a soul, and shown the privative condition it is necessarily in till it has passed through the first stage or economy, and come forth in the second. Our object here, in recurring to the subject, is different, viz., to show the remark able advantage Christianity or the Christian gospel has in the positive and deliberate recognition of a truth so plainly funda mental, and one that, as soon as it is definitely stated, inevit ably verifies itself and becomes an immovable conviction in every thoughtful mind. Christianity is just here quite alone; alone, that is, in the deepest and most radical of all conceptions that pertain to the discipline of virtue; alone, that is, in per ceiving beforehand the necessary duality of the process, and conforming itself deliberately to what is required, in the pre paration of a grand dual economy. In this fact all the human philosophers are left behind. For, while the Christian Scrip tures are so forward, and full, and explicit in asserting the two testaments, and displaying their relative use and power, throw ing themselves out boldly on their doctrine, in the noble confi dence of truth, the philosophers do not appear as yet even to have had their attention attracted to the question. Such of them as were educated under Christianity, appear to have re garded its manifold representations of letter and spirit, law and grace, a ministration of condemnation and a ministration of righteousness, as the unmeaning jingle or pious cant only of revelation, entitled in that view, to no philosophic respect. Indeed, it is not a little remarkable that some of the heathen philosophers appear to have approached the Christian doctrine more closely than they.

Our Christian philosophers, so called—Christian, not because they teach anything that deserves the name, but because they

[1] Chapter iv. p. 76.

are born in Christian countries—commonly begin with man as being simply a conscious intelligence, conceiving him to be in his proper normal state, and to have, in that view, certain sus ceptibilities to virtue ; a conscience, a free will, a power of doing good and receiving injury.   Then, ignoring as a fact of no con sequence the abnormal and diseased state of sin, they go on to build up their schemes of ethical practice, showing what the foundations of virtue may be, and upon those foundations erect ing their codes of observance.   But as they never allow them selves to look on the fact of depravity, and the consequent state of psychological disorder, so they never trouble themselves about any such superlative notions of virtuous living, as respect the perfection and final beatitude of the soul.   Their concern is simply to determine the authority of what is called virtue, and show the matters of good behaviour that are binding on men, in the relations of domestic, social, and public life.   They in culcate nothing but legalities.   It is virtue enough to do the right things, no matter whether they are done grudgingly and by hard constraint, or willingly, cheerfully, and gladly, as the spontaneous tribute of a full and ready heart ; no matter, in deed, whether it be only the doing of some right things such as concern human society, leaving out the duties owed to God, or whether it include all duty and so the possibility of a principle ! Meagre, sad-looking impostures, these ethical schemes, that bear the name of philosophy !

But the heathen philosophers, as we have already intimated, often do better.   It is not any part of philosophy with them to steer wide of the truths of Christianity, and ignore all the great questions of revealed religion.   Their ignorance of Chris tianity delivers them of any such feeble and absurd jealousy. Accordingly they go directly into the great and solemn problems of human existence with a free mind and a universal aim. They take up the question of evil ; they recognize in the fullest manner, as we have shown already, the depravity of human nature, and the state of general distemper produced by sin ; they recognize also the sense of bondage encountered by every soul in its endeavours to resume self-government and re-establish the harmony of virtue.   They go farther, they conceive a new and higher state of possible assimilation to God, or the gods, which they celebrate as the liberty of virtue.   Thus Plato shows that " the more conformed the soul is to the Divine Will, so

much the more perfect and free it is."[1]   Even Aristotle recog
nizes the necessity of freedom in virtuous exercises, as being the
only sufficient ground of stability in them, "because blessed
souls live and dwell always in such exercises without tedious-
ness or staleness of mind."[2]   Epictetus, in like manner, shows
that "submitting the mind to the mind that governs all things,
as good citizens to the law, is perfect liberty."[3]   And Seneca
coincides with all such testimonies, in the declaration "that it
is a great and free mind that has given itself up to God."   It
could also be shown, by abundant citations, that they even dis
allowed the name of virtue to any merely legal or constrained
practice.   Having advanced so far in the right direction, we
almost look to see them taking up the impression of some ne
cessary twofold process in the grand economy of virtue.   But
they are in a limitation.   The assimilation to God, in which
they rest their hope of liberty, or the complete state of virtue,
is not prepared by a gospel and a new, supernatural, and
redemptive movement, but only, as they conceive, by an appli
cation of their minds to God.   "The philosopher," says Plato,
"conversing with what is divine and excellent, becomes, as far
as what is human may, divine and excellent."[4]   Again, "Assimi
lation to God, in righteousness and holiness, is the result of
wisdom or philosophy."[5]   They had no conception, therefore,
of two ministrations, and could not be expected, under a scheme
of truth so deficient, to take up the yet deeper conception of
a necessarily twofold process in the economy of virtue.   As
the Christian philosophers have never taken the hint of this
antecedent necessity from the manifold declarations of the Scripture, so these others have fallen short of it because they had
nothing to yield them such a hint.

And yet how easy it seems, having the hint of it once given,
to verify this necessity!   Though no one of the philosophers
was ever able to take up such a conception, it requires no phi
losopher, when it is once given, but only a thoughtful man, to
perceive the certain truth of it.   If (1.) there is to be a moral
regimen set up in souls, it must begin with law, or imposed
obligation; no matter whether it be only pronounced in the
conscience, or outwardly also in a revelation.   Again, (2.) it is
equally plain that mere law can bring nothing to perfection.
The experiment of disobedience will be tried.   The very motive

[1] *Leg.* 4.   [2] *Eth.* l. i. c. 10.   [3] In Arrian, i. 2.   [4] *Repub.*   [5] *Theatet.*

it supplies to virtue, viz., retribution, makes the virtue weari
some, and a burden certain to be cast off. It has no motivity
that generates liberty; on the contrary, the motivity it has,
appealing only to interest, detains from liberty. And yet, (3.)
the law, it is equally manifest, will be a necessary condition or
first stage in the process of holy training. It will impress
the sense of law as a condition of wellbeing. It will also develope the knowledge of sin—what it is, and does, and deserves.
And the bondage it creates, or which is created under it, the
hopelessness, the death, will prepare the want of a deliverer.
The regimen of abstract law, again, (4.) is, in this view, seen
to be inherently faulty, even though the precept be perfect;
hence that nothing but a personal homage, or faith in a Divine
person—whose character and life, embraced in love, suppose
the embrace of all law—can finally bring in its principle, and
establish it in the liberty of an eternal and celestial love.

See, then, how distinctly all this and more is said in the
Christian documents. Hold them up to the light, and let the
Divine water-mark, or inwrought signature of God, appear!
Whence comes it that these Gospels and Epistles, clothed in no
pomp of philosophy, and decked with no literary pretensions, so
far transcend all the philosophy of all ages, opening up deeper
truths regarding the great problem of human existence, than
have anywhere else been discovered to the thought of man?
They tell us in the utmost simplicity of manner, and with no air
of discovery, that God has two ministrations for us—letter and
spirit, law and grace. As regards the first, they tell us that it
is a fundamental and first fact in God's economy, no jot or tittle
of which can ever fail—a perfect law, and so the basis or formal
idea of all perfection. Yet, as an abstraction, commanded by
authority, and enforced by power, it makes nothing perfect. It
is only a schoolmaster that sets the training on foot, and brings
it on a single stage. It is more unfortunate, however, than
most schoolmasters, for the stage it prepares is one of loss and
defeat, and not of gain—ordained to be unto life, it is found to
be unto death. It is a ministration of condemnation. It is the
letter that killeth. It entered that the offence might abound.
Weak through the flesh, it accomplishes nothing but a state of
bondage, and the loosing of retributive causes that set the whole
creation groaning and travailing in pain together. And all this,
we perceive, was understood as well at the beginning as after-

ward. For, if there had been a law given that could have given life, then, verily, righteousness should have been by the law. But that was inherently impossible, and the impossibility is re cognized from the first. The legal state was instituted, not as a finality, but as a first stage in the process of training; to develope the sense of guilt and spiritual want, to beget a know ledge of sin, its exceeding sinfulness, and the insupportable bondage it creates. And then appears, in the person of the in carnate Redeemer, a new and higher ministration, designed from the foundation of the world to complement, or even in supersed ing to establish the other. Now He hath obtained a more excel lent ministry, by how much also He is the mediator of a better covenant, which was established upon better promises. For, if that first covenant had been faultless, then should no place have been sought for the second. Now, it is no more a question of works; there never could have been a rational expectation of human perfection on that basis; but it is a question of simple faith. The righteousness of God without, or apart from the law, is now manifested, even the righteousness of God which is by faith of Jesus Christ, unto all and upon all them that believe. What we call our virtue now is no more a will-work, or a some thing done according to law, but it is a continuous and living ingeneration of God, who has thus become a divine impulse or quickening in us, and so the life of our life. Therefore now we are free. Embracing the person of Christ, and yielding the homage of our hearts to Him, we do, in fact, resume the law, in our deliverance from its bondage. We keep His command ments because we adhere to His person, and we enter thus into a liberty that fulfils all law, the liberty of love. There is there-fore now no condemnation to them that are in Christ Jesus. For the law of the spirit of life in Christ Jesus hath made us free from the law of sin and death. For what the law could not do, in that it was weak through the flesh, God sending his own Son in the likeness of sinful flesh, and for sin condemned sin in the flesh, that the righteousness of the law [i.e., of the precept] might be fulfilled in us, who walk not after the flesh, but after the Spirit. The bondage now is gone. The stage of liberty is come. This is the Spirit that giveth life. This is the minis-tration of righteousness. And if the ministration of condemna-tion be glorious, much more doth the ministration of righteous-ness exceed in glory.

This exposition of the two ministrations we have given as
nearly as possible in the language of Scripture. Not to be
struck by the magnificence of the thought, would argue great
dulness. All known speculations of philosophy regarding the
moral economy of human life, sink into littleness and utter in-
competency by the side of it.

A very curious question, then, it is, whence came this doc
trine, and what should have set any writer, or any Christian
school of writers, on the conception of it ? Why does it ap
pear in the Scriptures of the New Testament, and nowhere
else ? It has, at first, a canting sound, it wears a strange,
peculiar air, and comes to us in strange, half-mystic words —
" letter " and " spirit," " law" and " grace," two "covenants,"
two " testaments," two " ministrations"—but it grows under
inspection, fills itself out in the sublimity of its reasons, and
finally stands confessed as the only adequate, the only true and
real philosophy. It is no crude suggestion, or new thought
half discovered. It is fully wrought out ; all the points are
stated. Everything is set in complete working order ; yet with
no parade of science or of definition, and, as it were, no consci
ousness of the transcendent superiority it reveals. Whence,
then, came it ? that is the question. And there is but one
answer. We could sooner believe that Plato's dialogues were
written by some wild herdsman of Scythia, than that this grand
distinctive doctrine of the Scripture is of human invention. It
bears the eternal water-mark of divinity, and that ends all
inquiry.

We pass on now to observe another most impressive distinction of Christianity, in what may be called the grouping of its
ideas ; and especially the fact that they group themselves in
such beautiful order and harmony about the grand, supernatu
ral fact of the incarnation. That it is a fact supernatural in
its form, will not be denied ; this indeed is one of the chief
grounds of impeachment against the gospels. It will also be
agreed, that if any such divine movement is really inaugurated
in the world, there needs to be also a whole system of ideas
and doctrines, springing forth and grouping themselves in
order round it. Otherwise we have no sufficient instrumenta
tion, for our human use or handling of so great a fact, and our
personal appropriation of it—no fit medium of thought re
specting it.

Here then we discover, again, upon a large scale, the secret evidence of a higher presence in the gospel. To frame such a fitting of ideas and doctrines, by human invention, out of the materials of natural sagacity and reason, we may fairly say is impossible. There have been as many as nine avatars or incarnations, the Brahmins tell us, of their god Vishnu; and multitudes of incarnations can be cited from the various pagan mythologies; but when has there been developed, round the pretended supernatural fact, any scheme of ideas or truths, internally agreeing with it and having their roots of life in it? It is a very easy thing, we may admit, to imagine a supernatural fact, an incarnation for example, but to fit it with a range of doctrines and holy ideas, such as will connect it with human experience and make it practical, is what no mortal wisdom was ever able to do. Thus, if there were given the fact of the incarnation of Jesus Christ, or His miraculous birth as the Son of Mary, there is no philosopher of mankind who could invent, around that central fact, a system of ideas and doctrines that would not, by their wild extravagance, and also by their manifest want of any vital agreement or coherence with it, turn it into mockery. Much less could he form a vehicle of doctrine, that would make that central fact a power, in the practical life, and dovetail it into the experience of mankind.

But all this we shall see accomplished, in the easiest and most natural manner possible in the Christian doctrine. And this is the line of our argument: that all the capital points or ideas of Christianity, frame into the supernatural, on one hand, in such beautiful order and facility, and without any strain of contrivance or logical adaptation; and into human experience, on the other, in a way so consonant to the dignity of reason, and the wants and disabilities of sin, that the signature of God is plainly legible in the documents. The examples to be cited are numerous, and we set them forth under numerical notations.

1. The new religion, or that of the divine advent, is called a *gospel*. Why a gospel more than a wisdom, or philosophy, or doctrine? These, and such like, are the names assumed by a the world's great teachers; but it occurs to none of them to call their utterance, whatever it be, good news or a gospel Whence the distinction? It grows out of the simple fact that they offer a doctrine drawn out of premises in nature, and the

contents of natural reason, a doctrine which, being in those premises, is already given, and only waits to be deduced. Whereas, Christ comes into the world from without, and above it, and brings in with Him new premises, not here before. He is therefore proclaimed as news, good news—"Behold, I bring you good tidings of great joy which shall be to all people." Christ also conceives Himself and His work in the same manner - " Go ye into all the world and preach the gospel to every crea· ture." His apostles all follow testifying the fact, as new tid· ings—" God was in Christ reconciling the world unto Himself." If it should be said that the work of Christ is called a gospel by mere natural suggestion, because it is a real communication from another world to this, we care not to object, because the term is thus accounted for in a way that supposes the fact of a supernatural mission; though, if the supposed mission were a fact given, it is doubtful whether any human skill, left to itself, would ever suit the fact with a name that so exactly corre sponds with its peculiarity, as a fact appearing in the world, but not of it. It would be called by any other name, probably, as soon as by the name gospel, and if some name in great repute with men were at hand, such as would mark it with a special honour, probably sooner. But suppose there were no super· natural fact at all in the case, and that all we find of that character in the work were reducible to myth, or quite ex plained away by a rationalistic interpretation. Whence, in that view, will the name gospel come ? If there is no supernatural fact at all, nor anything more than a pretence of it, who is going to handle even that fiction so nicely, as to fit it with the very peculiar name, *gospel ?*

2. We have another of the radical notions of this gospel pre· sented in the word *salvation.* The work is called a salvation. The incarnate Word is named Jesus by anticipation; because He will save the people from their sins. He declares finally, that He came to seek and to save ; and His work is published, after He is gone, as the grace of God that bringeth salvation. Meantime no human teacher has ever come to men with any- thing called by that name. The human teachers come with disquisitions, theories, philosophies, pedagogies, schemes of reformation, ideal republics, doctrines of association. But they, none of them speak of salvation. And that, for the simple reason, that they have not conceived the state of unnature under

sin as a really lost or undone state, requiring a supernatural and divine interposition to restore the ruin suffered This is the point distinctly conceived by Christianity, and therefore it is called a salvation. Plato saw distinctly enough the depravity of human nature, and his doctrine of virtue, we have seen, was that it can be formed in the soul, only by a divine communica tion. It is therefore only the more impressive, as a contrast that, having these two elements of Christianity on hand he no where conceives the virtue wrought to be a salvation. After all, the state of sin is not to him a practically lost state, but the transition to virtue, slurred by indistinctness, is virtually regarded as a growth or advance on the footing of nature · not a rescue from nature by a power above nature ; therefore, not a salvation.

3 The doctrine of this salvation makes it a salvation by *faith;* in which we have another ruling idea of the scheme that coincides with its supernatural facts and character. Chris tianity differs from all philosophies and ethical doctrines of men in the fact that it rests all virtue in faith ; exactly as it should, if it be a grace imported into nature from without, an advent in the world of one who is from above. Such a salva tion lies not within the premises of natural fact and reason · it is not therefore a matter of science or of logical deduction It makes its address, therefore, not to reason, but to faith reason may be allowed to have a tribunitial veto against it, provided the doctrine is certainly proved to be contrary to reason ; but it cannot be received by reason. It is only re ceived, when faith comes, laden with sin and fettered by its iron bondage, to rest herself, in holy trust, on the transcendent fact of such an appearing, and to find by experiment that it is, n sacred reality and power, what it assumes to be. It finds the new premise true, proves it to be true, intuits it, in and by the immediate experience of the mind. The new salvation is by faith, because it is a supernatural salvation ; for whatever virtue the plan ministers must be in and by the receiver's faith, practically trusting soul and spirit to the fact of such a Saviour and salvation.

There is much quarrelling with the New Testament on this ground. It becomes an offence because it requires faith. Where is the merit of mere believing, that it should be made the necessary condition of salvation ? In one view there is none, we answer, and it is not required because there is any. There is no merit in trusting a physician, but it may be a matter of some consequence that his medicines be taken; as they will not be, without some kind of faith in him. So it is a matter of consequence that the Christian grace be accepted, as it certainly will not be, unless the soul is practically trusted to it and the giver. If there is to be a healing, a new ingeneration of life and holy virtue, it can never be, save by the efficacy of a supernatural remedy. Believing in that remedy is the same thing as coming into its power; and, therefore, on this faith the gospel hangs salvation. It could not be otherwise. If Christianity, being supernatural, offered salvation on any other terms than faith, the offer would even be absurd, having no agreement with the grace offered. That it hangs salvation on this condition, indicates a thorough insight of its own nature, and the more ready the shallow wit of man is to find fault with such a condition, as humiliating or insulting to reason, the more evidently it is not from man, but from a superior and superhuman source.

Regarding faith, in this manner, as having its value, not in its own merit, but in what it receives, we would not be understood to represent it as an optional matter, without any positive obligation. It is a duty binding on every moral being, to believe and practically receive everything that is true; and this on the principle that mind, honestly used, will distinguish all important truth. Doubtless one may become so entangled by the ingenious sophistries of sin, or so darkened by its baleful shadow, that he cannot in a moment find, or finding, cannot embrace the truth. In such a case, the blame must rest upon his guilty past, and the mental distortion he has created, by his former abuse of truth, until such time as he can recover his sight. And this he may do rapidly, if only, trusting in God, he will take into practice, for medicine, every single truth he is able to find. All his unbeliefs and misbeliefs will be certainly cleared in this manner. And therefore Christ requires it of him, that they shall be; throwing his salvation even upon his belief of the truth.

4. Justification by faith is another distinctive point of the Christian gospel. And this includes two principal matters combined; that the transgressor, believing, has a righteousness generated in him, which is not built up under the law, by his own practice; and that something has been done to compensate

the law, violated by his past offences, and save it in honour, when his sin is forgiven.

As to the former, the righteousness ingenerated, the manner is sufficiently indicated, when it is called the righteousness that is of God by faith, unto and upon all them that believe. It is unto and upon such only as believe; because, as we just now said, speaking of salvation, it is only by faith that the soul is so trusted to, and deposited in, the supernatural grace of God, as to be invested with His righteousness, or assimilated to it. Be sides, it will be observed that this is called justification, partly because the natural laws of retributive justice, which are penally chastising the sinner, holding him fast in the meshes of inex tricable disorder and woe, can be controverted, or turned aside, only by a power supernatural and divine.

As to the latter point concerned, the implied compensation to law, in the supposed free justification, it is not that something is done to be a spectacle before unknown worlds, or something to square up a legal account of pains and penalties, according to some small scheme of book-keeping philosophy, but it is simply this: that, as there must be two stages of discipline to carry on the world—viz., letter and spirit, law and grace—the introduc tion of pardon, or the universal and free remission of sins, must be so prepared, as not to do away with the law stage that is precedent, but must let them both exist together, to act concur rently on the world. And this is done by the obedience of Christ, obedience unto death. Who can say or think that God yields up His law, in the forgiveness of sins, when the Word incarnate, having it on Him as a bond of love, the same that our human sin has broken, renders up His life to it, and bows to the awful passion of the cross, that He may fulfil its require ments. Magnified and made honourable by such a contribution of respect, no free remission or removal of penalties running against us can be felt to shake its authority.

It is hardly necessary to suggest the fact, that Christianity is radically distinguished, in this matter of justification, from the philosophies and the known religions. They see nothing in sin or its penal disorders that requires a distinctly supernatural remedy; or, when they are removed, any apparent infringement of law and justice. They only think to make men better by something done upon the natural footing; which, if they can do, they have no farther concern. They have no such conception

of a twofold economy of God as makes it a matter of consequence
to see that, when He forgives, the law is saved to the world and
kept on foot, as an element of training and discipline. If they
speak of pardon, it is no such pardon as partakes a judicial
character. Or if they speak of expiation, offering up their
children, it may be, to buy the release of their sin, it is the
passions of their God they seek to arrest, and not His desecrated
authority they will sanctify. They have no care for law, and no
suspicion that their God has any. They have no conception of
any such solemn relations between their sin and the eternal
government of the world, as creates a difficulty in the way of
releasing their punishment. No difficulty is apprehended, save
in the ill-nature of their God; and they expect to appease Him
by giving Him pains enough, and gory bodies enough of the
innocent, to satisfy Him. But the Christian truth is deeper in its
reasons, and has a more benign character. It comes into the world
as a divine advent, to fulfil a second stage in the moral eco
nomy of holiness. As the law begins with nature, so this finishes
with supernatural grace. As one binds, the other liberates; as
one kills, the other makes alive; and yet so tempered are they
both, that they are kept in perpetual action together. Let the
philosophers and human teachers show us that they have some
comprehension of the great problem of life, and of God's relation
to it, equally comprehensive in its breadth, and deep in its reasons.

5. It is another of the grand distinctions of Christianity that
it sets up a kingdom of God on earth. It is called " the king
dom of God" or " of heaven," because the organic force by
which so many wills and finally all mankind are to be gathered
into unity, is not in nature, but comes down out of heaven, in
the person of Christ the king. It is very natural that the
different political organizations of the world should be em
ployed figuratively, as terms of representation, in matters not
political. Thus we have theoretic commonwealths and ideal
republics. Truth is conceived as an empire. In the natural
sciences we have what are called three kingdoms, the animal,
and vegetable, and mineral. But here we have, what is not
elsewhere conceived, a supernatural kingdom in souls, the king
dom of God; a real, living polity, organized by a real king, and
swayed and propagated by the powers of truth and love, centred
in His divine person. Jesus coming into the world, as the
incarnate Word of God, brings a new force with Him, entering

into souls as the advent of a new divine power. In Him therefore begins, of course, a new organization, the kingdom of God in souls—righteousness, and peace, and joy in the Holy Ghost. This accordingly is the great thought of Christianity—the kingdom of God ; the implanting of a divine rule in lost men, and the gathering in, at last, of all people and kindreds of the earth, into a vast, universal order of peace and truth under Christ the anointed king.

The fact grows out of the incarnation, so that when Jesus is about to appear, the kingdom of heaven is at hand. No other religion, no priest or seer, no avatar of deity, has ever raised such a conception. It is the peculiar thought or fact of Chris tianity. And yet, daring as the proposition is, so extravagant that no mere man could make it without a charge of lunacy, Christ undertakes it—Christ, the Nazarene carpenter—and what is more, assumes the dominion and makes His kingdom good. And yet, if He could not make it good, His incarnation could not stand as an accepted fact. So closely interwoven are these two, the incarnate appearing, and the kingdom of God.

6. The Holy Spirit also is a Christian conception, standing in profound agreement with the supernatural fact of the gospel. As Christ, incarnate, is a supernatural embodiment, or manifes tation localized in space, so the Holy Spirit is a supernatural indwelling force, by which Christ is perpetuated in the world, universalized in all localities, and brought nigh to every being, in every place. And that there may be no mistake regarding the supernatural character of His agency, He is represented as being inaugurated by external signs, and by gifts of utterance and healing, that transcend all human power. He is not to be confounded, in this respect, with conceptions often taken up by the Eastern sages and philosophers, that are analogous in form, but really suppose, in their minds, no agency of God, save that which is implied in His omnipresent dominion over nature. " God, they conceived, permeates or passes through all things ;"[1] and they called Him in this view, " the divine spirit."[2] Thus Apuleius says, that " nothing is so excellent, or great in power, as to be content with its own nature alone, void of the divine aid or influence.". Philoponus, with our very point of need in his eye, calls what should be the Spirit, simply a providence. " Though the soul be lapsed into a

[1] *Cud.* ii. 498.   [2] *De Mundo,* 68.

preternatural or unnatural state, still it is yet not neglected by Providence, but has a constant care taken of it, in order to its recovery."[1]   Seneca distinctly conceives a divine spirit, active in us, and yet this spirit dwindles into a minister only of natural retribution.   " The sacred spirit dwells in us, observer of our evil things, guardian of our good, and He treats us as we treat Him."[2]   None of these conceptions really meet the case of a supernatural religion.   This demands a Spirit engaged to deliver, and competent to deliver from the lapse of nature, by acting on the fallen subject, and separating him from the retributive action of natural causes; dwelling in him thus, holding him up, guiding him on, extricating his liberty, and witnessing in him, as a divine revelation to his consciousness.

There is also a profound necessity for the Holy Spirit, thus conceived, in the miraculous advent of Christ itself.   Christ and the Spirit are complementary forces, and, both together, constitute a complete whole ; such a kind of whole as no man, or myth, or accident ever invented.   There was an inherent necessity that whatever supernatural movement, for the regene ration of man, might be undertaken, should include both a moral and an efficient agency ; one before the understanding, and the other back of it, in the secret springs of the disordered nature ; a divine object clothed in beauty, and love, and jus tice, to be a mould into which the soul may be formed, the type of a divine life in which it may consentingly be crystallized ; an efficient grace, working within the soul, pre paring it to will and to do, and rolling back the currents of retributive causes in it, opening it to the power of its glorious exemplar, and drawing it ever into that, and a life proceeding from it.   Without the former before the mind, whatever is done within, by efficiency, would be only a work of repair, a something executed, of whose way or method we should know as little as we do of health restored by hidden causes.   The change would be merely physical, not any change of character at all, more than when the secretions of the body are changed. Without the latter—the efficient working—the model set before us in the divine beauty of Christ and His death, would find us dulled in understanding, blurred in perception, and held fast in the penal bondage of our sins ; approving the good before us only faintly, desiring it coldly, endeavouring

1 Proem in Aristotle de Anima.   2 Ep. 41.

after it if at all, impotently, even as a bird might try to rise whose wings are cut.

Such is the profound agreement of Christ and the Holy Spirit. One is naught without the other. Given then the fact of the incarnation, and of Christ's human appearing, by whom was this remarkable counterpart or complement to His appearing invented? Who, in other words, contrived the day of Pentecost? Was it a man? was it several men of only common faith? or was it done by the loose gossip of a wondering and credulous age? The history says that Christ Himself gave the Spirit, by direct promise; declaring that it was expedient now for Him to retire from before the eyes, that the Spirit might come, and taking his exemplar into men's bosoms, in every place, all over the world, show it to them there. Who but Christ and He, the eternal Son of God, ever generated this conception?

7. The doctrine of spiritual regeneration, propounded in the gospel, is another point where it meets at once our human state and the fact of a supernatural economy. This truth of regeneration supposes a loss out of human nature, of the seed-principle of a good and holy life; such that the subject has really no good in his character, and never can by himself generate, or set himself in, the principle of good. He can do many good things, such as men call good, according to the standard of ethics or of human custom (which is the world's law of virtue), and may fitly enough be praised for the comely parts that make up the figure of his life. But these comelinesses are a virtue of items, mere will-works that proceed from no seed-principle of good. Sometimes even the worldly-minded teachers of Christianity take up with this kind of virtue, and form their estimates of character by inspecting the atoms collected in the life. Some things done, they say, are good, and some are bad—the good things ought to be increased, and the bad reduced. They see, of course, no radical defect back of the particulars noted, and therefore no need of a radical change in the life. It is the things done that make the character, and not the principle, or want of it, that gives character to the things. Their gospel is even more shallow than a pagan's philosophy. According to Seneca. who penetrates the real ground-work of human character—" All sins are in all men, but do not appear in each man. He that hath one sin hath all. We say that all men are intemperate, avari-

cious, luxurious, malign—not that these sins appear in all, but because they may be, yea, are, in all, though latent." [1] Nothing is more rational ; for, if nothing is done from any right principle, then nothing done is right, and there is no seed of right-doing in us.   The doings may be kept up by our will, without any seed-principle, so attentively and punctiliously as even to become tastes ; but tastes are not inspirations, and the only true virtue of man is that which he does from God, in the inspiration of a divine liberty.   Separated from God, he is a monster, and not a proper man, however plausible the show he makes.   And this is the effect of sin.   It alienates the subject from the life of God. Under sin, he is no more conscious of God, as in his normal state he was and must be.   He is therefore uncentralized by it, dead at the core.   The seed-principle of eternal life and beauty and order is gone.   He centres in himself, gravitates downward into, collapses in, himself; and he could as easily leap out of the malstrom, as set himself in the true liberty and seed-principle of holiness.

It is therefore declared, as the necessary condition of our salvation, that we must be born again, born not of blood, nor of the will of the flesh, nor of the will of man, but of God.   And this great change is the beginning and spring of all true heavenly virtue, because it is the revelation of God in the soul.   Now the soul is conscious of God again.   Now it moves in the line of the divine movement, which is moving in the Spirit ; which, again, is the inspiration of liberty.   All this, of course, not without consent in the subject, probably not without some deep and violent struggles on his part, to make way for the divine revelation.   He must offer up himself to the divine will, and to all the approaches of the divine love ; and this includes much—a removal of all obstructions, a renunciation of self, a free commit ment of all things to Christ, and a pliant, unequivocal, and humble faith in Him.   But none of these are, by themselves, regeneration.   That is of God, and is, in fact, the soul's assump tion, or resumption, by God.   To say that it is a change of the soul's love, is only another version of the same truth ; for the love is changed by the entering in of God and His love, into the soul's faith.   For love is of God, and every one that loveth is born of God, and knoweth God.   Old things are passed away, and all things are become new ; because God is revealed within,

1 *Ep.* 60.

changing, of course, the principle of all action, and the meaning of all experience. That this new revelation is supernatural coinciding, in everything said of it, with the grand central fact of the incarnation, need not be shown. Enough that it is the initiation of a sinner and alien into the kingdom of God Except a man be born again, he cannot see the kingdom of God.

8. The Christian doctrine of Providence coincides, also, with the fact of a supernatural work in the redemption of mankind. It assumes, without misgiving, the bold conception of a super natural Providence, under which the world itself is ruled in the interest of Christianity; a conception that will be verified in the next or following chapter, and therefore need not be dis cussed here. Nothing more is necessary to our present purpose, than just to call attention to the remarkable fact that this myth, this marvel of superstition, this gossip of miracle, that we call Christianity, dares to claim the government of the world (as in real consistency it should) in its interest, and, what is more, history, as we shall see, audits the claim, and makes it good.

9. We name, as another point of the Christian doctrine, strangely and surprisingly coincident with the supernatural idea of the plan, introduced by the incarnate appearing of Christ, the Trinity of God. I say, strangely and surprisingly coin cident, because the last thing that would occur to any human being, in the exercise of his natural wisdom, would be the introduction of a new or modified conception of God, to accom modate the new fact of a gospel. And yet, exactly this is what we discover in the matter of that gospel; and, what is more, having the fact before us, we can easily enough distin guish a practical reason for it, in the requisite instrumental use, or handling of that gospel; or, what is no wise different, in the practical adjustment of our relations to God, under the twofold conditions of nature and grace, in which He is now set before us.

We cannot here go into the learning of this great question. Suffice it to say, that the Old Testament Scriptures contain the rudiments of a trinity, and that the Platonic, Alexandrian, and Christian trinities are either suggested by, or developed from these rudiments. That the Old Testament Scriptures are prior in date, even by hundreds of years, to the writings of Plato, is not to be denied. The East was full of traditions from these Scriptures, and he himself, a traveller in those parts, professed that he derived many things from the traditions of the "Bar barians." It cannot therefore be charged that the Christian trinity, as given by Christ, in the baptismal formula, was origin ally a product of natural reason, and was transferred from Plato's theosophy. No trinity was ever suggested by mere thought, or generated by mere natural reason. Reason takes the road of unity, and the conception of a triad comes out, if at all, from the process of a supernatural revelation. Thus came the Christian trinity, as a fact historically developed; first in the Almighty Creator and Father, the Jehovah-angel or Word of the Lord, and the Holy Spirit, of the Old Testament; then in the Father, Son, and Holy Ghost, of the New. It is a conception gene rated by supernatural transactions, and is needed to accommodate the uses of a supernatural salvation.

Thus, if there were but one economy. or ministration of God, known to us, viz., that of nature, we should never need, and, in fact, should never have, any conception of the Divine Being, save that which is named by the terms God, the Almighty, the Creator, and others, conformed to the notion of the divine unity. But, having fallen into a state of retributive disorder, from which we can be delivered only by a supernatural salva tion, we are obliged to adjust ourselves toward God as filling two economies, and that requires a new machinery of thought. If now we have only the single term God, we must speak of God as dealing with God, or of the grace-force of God, as delivering from the nature-force of God. If the work includes an incarnation, as we suppose it must, then it must be God sending God into the world; and, if it includes a renovating, new-revealing agency within, then we can only go to God to give us God and ask of God to roll back the retributive causa tions of God, that are fastening their penal bondage on us. All which, we may see, is a method too clumsy and confused to serve at all the practical uses of the salvation provided. There is, in short, no intellectual machinery, in a close theoretic mono theism, for any such thing as a work of grace or supernatural redemption. In the Christian trinity, this want is supplied. First, we have the Father, setting God before us as the author and ground of all natural things and causes. Then we have the Son and the Spirit, which represent what God may do, acting on the lines of causes in nature; one as coming into nature from without, to be incarnate in it, the other as working internally in the power of the Son, to dispense to the soul what He addressed outwardly to human thought, and configure the soul to Him, as an exemplar embraced by its faith. Then, putting our trust in the Son, as coming down from God, offering Himself before God, going up to Him, interceding before Him, reigning with Him, by Him accepted, honoured, glorified; invoking also God and Christ to send down the Spirit, and let Him be the power of a new indwelling life, breathing health into our diseases. and rolling back the penal currents of justice to free us of our sin, we are able to act ourselves before the new salvation, so as to receive the full force of it. Having these instruments of thought and feeling and faith toward God, and suffering no foolish quibbles of speculative logic to plague us, asking never how many Gods there are! nor how it is possible for one to send another, act before another, reconcile us to another? but, assured that God is one eternally, however multiform our con ceptions of His working, how lively and full and blessed is the converse we get, through these living personations, so pliant to our use as finite men, so gloriously accommodated to the two fold economy of our salvation as sinners! Is this now a con ception gotten up by man, upon his natural level? Is there any philosophic, theosophic, or mythologic mark upon it?

We have thus brought into review as many as nine of the principal facts and prominent articles of Christianity, and find them crystallizing into a perfectly harmonious and orderly system, round the one central fact of a supernatural religion, initiated in the incarnate appearing of Christ. His work is called a gospel on this account, precisely as it should be, and yet by no human suggestion would be. It is also called a sal vation, differing from all theosophies and mythologies, in the fact that it is a supernatural restorative force, and, in that view, the only real salvation ever known. It brings the salvation also to faith and hangs it on faith, as by the conditions of the case it must, and as no other known scheme of virtue does. It jus tifies also by faith, communicating, in this manner, the righteous ness of God, and preparing acquittal in a way that keeps the law in full force, as the nature-side and necessary element of human training. A kingdom of God, or of heaven, is erected by it on earth; in which we see, by the name itself, that the reigning force of the new kingdom is not of nature, but from without and above the world. The Holy Spirit is inaugurated as a conception of the divine working, different from that which is included in the laws of nature, and delivering from the re tributive action of those laws. This deliverance, connected with a renovated principle of life in the soul, it calls regeneration, conceiving, in a way peculiar to itself, that without the change thus denominated, as a second birth, or newly regenerated life, there is and can be no seed-principle of heavenly virtue. Here too is proposed, for the first time in the world, a properly super natural providence ; that is, a providence which governs the world, in the interest of salvation, or regenerated holiness. Accordantly also with such a conception of God, as presiding over a double administration of law and grace, nature and the supernatural, the divine unity is reproduced as trinity ; in which, whatever may be the thought of other trinities, Christianity holds, at least, the honourable distinction of being the only doc trine that conceives a trinity, in and through, and practically operative with, a double economy of divine government.

Is there not something remarkable in this general consent of the Christian names, facts, ideas, and doctrines ? and the more remarkable that it appears in matters where we should least look for it, if left to ourselves and the natural processes of our thoughts ? And still the list might be indefinitely extended. Thus preaching is to be the means of propagation for this gospel, and what but a supernatural gift to the world could ever be heralded or preached ? Prophesying in the Spirit is a supernatural utterance. The ministry are conceived to be set apart by the Holy Spirit, which is true of no other class of teachers, on the footing of reason or of natural science. Spiri tual gifts belong to a plan transcending nature. The sacraments are consecrated vehicles of grace and power. Visions and re velations are from above. The resurrection of the dead is not of nature. The history of the original propagation of Chris tianity, taken as a whole, is, in fact, a miraculous process, and nothing less. In short, the whole fabric of the Christian insti tution—thought, name, office, fact, and doctrine—centres, we discover, in the one grand idea of a supernatural movement on the world. There is nothing eccentric that will not fall into the general aim of the plan and chime with it ; no fantastic matter that is unreducible, as we should expect, if human wis dom only had undertaken the devising and the adjustment of the parts. As Napoleon noticed, with an impression of wonder, " One thing follows another like the ranks of a celestial army." He knew what an army was, and the order of a well-set discipline, but he finds a higher, even celestial order, which his phalanx is a thing too loose to represent, in the gloriously compacted truths of a heaven-born, supernatural faith.

Even Mr Hennel admits a correspondent impression of the compact unity, and the admirable working order of the Christian plan ; admitting, strangely enough, that it excels all other fruits of human learning and philosophy in this respect, and yet con ceiving that, with all its high pretensions of a supernatural origin, and the undeniably supernatural guise in which it stands, it is itself a strictly human product ! He says, " Christianity has presented to the world a system of moral excellence. It has led forth the principles of humanity and benevolence from the recesses of the schools and groves, and compelled them to take an active part in the affairs of life. It has consolidated the moral and religious sentiments into a more definite, in fluential form than had before existed, and thereby constituted an engine that has worked powerfully towards humanizing and civilizing the world." [1] Moral and religious sentiments ! as if it were only a compact of these, and such like human qualities, when it is talking all the while of the incarnation, of faith, of justification, of the better covenant, of regeneration, of the re surrection of the dead, and commanding its apostles to preach the trinity of God ! Are these staple matters of Christianity our " moral and religious sentiments ?" " Consolidated " also they are " into a more definite and influential form !" Is it in such lofty and transcendent spiritualities as these which are named, that our mere human notions are wont to get consoli dated ? And why could not the philosophers, such men as Plato, Socrates, Aristotle, Cicero, and Seneca, consolidate such human notions as well, or to as good effect, as the rude fisher man of Galilee ? And yet what is there of solidity, in giving to these mere natural things or sentiments, a form so fantastical and flighty, and calling them by names to which no human thought can reach ? Doubtless Christianity is " more influen tial," but it is so, because it is so truly unsolid, so spiritual, and so visibly superior to the world, and to all those dull im becilities sometimes called religious sentiments. God is in

.   [1] *Inquiry*, p. 48.   '

Christ, reconciling the world unto Himself—that is influential , that is power!

And now the question is—Whence comes this supernatural, world-transcending institute, erected among us, in so many tokens of a perfect intelligence? Whence this more than logical, this organic unity in things so remote, and to mere human thought undiscoverable ; for if it be possible that human thought should stumble on a fiction so magnificent, it certainly could not frame it into order, and offer it as a truth of salvation.

In adjusting our answer to this question, it is important, first of all, to observe that the Christian truth has obviously nothing of the form of a scheme thought out by the natural understanding. It is not metaphysical or deductive. It proposes itself to faith, under laws of expression, and is plainly seen to be no product of mental analysis or constructive logic. t has the form not of something generated by, but of some thing offered to, the world. It comes down into history, as t represents, from a point above history ; standing out in symbols of fact and expression, that are to report and verify themselves. It is, in form, a something to be believed, not a something reasoned—incarnation, love, miracle, a calling of God after men, a communication of the divine nature. Admitting, as we safely enough may, for the present, that criticism dis covers tokens of human activity and frailty in the record, still the operative system stands forth in its own simple confidence, in its own heavenly form, as a gospel to the world, and as such it reveals the solid unity, the glorious depths of harmony and self-understanding, we have discovered in its doctrine. It speaks as if it never had a thought of system, and yet reveals a reach of system wider than all human philosophy.

But this will be denied, and still it will be maintained that this unconscious, inartificial fabric, is a work of art. That, if we know anything of what is in man, is impossible. If the scheme were down upon the footing of nature, as on the face it declares it is not, then it might not be difficult to admit that human skill, or even the silent process of human history, as in the case of the English common law, should shape it into a system of apparent order and scientific unity. But being a scheme supernatural, not even the first facts or premises were included in our knowledge, as derived from our natural experi-

ence, and required therefore to be invented by us; and to sup
pose that our human faculties, breaking over the confines in this
manner of all knowledge, could there build up, in the cloud-land
of unknown, merely imagined fact, a sober, thoroughly coherent
scheme of truth and renovating life, adjusting the infinite to the
finite, law to mercy, discord and death to liberty and salvation,
and setting all its grand array of facts, names, doctrines, and
powers, in a frame of solid and compact unity—such a supposi
tion is too extravagant to be rationally entertained. It is, sup
posing that we are able to build in the realm of fiction itself,
a vaster and more solid economy of intellectual and practical
truth, than has ever yet been built on the basis of experience.

Three suppositions may be raised in regard to the matter in
question; viz., that the work is all of man; that it is partly
of man; and that it is all of God. The first of these we have
discussed already; for, if such a work could not be invented,
much less could it be accomplished by the haphazard process
of myth and wild tradition. The second, which supposes some
central point of a supernatural plan being given—the fact, for
example, of the incarnation—that this fact was wrought up by
the human understanding, through a course of active develop
ment, into the complete scheme and perfect unity we have
described, need not be particularly discussed, because it allows
the fact of a supernatural root and beginning, which is the
principal matter in question.

The third supposition is the only one that is rationally
tenable; viz., that this grand out-birth of a new divine economy,
called the gospel, is, in fact, supernatural, and stands in the
compact order of a complete intellectual unity, because it was
given by a comprehending mind equal to the reach of the plan.
Not that everything written, or advanced in the canonical books
of the New Testament, is historic fact or infallible truth—our
present supposition does not reach so far as that, but leaves a
space to be filled up by other kinds of argument—it simply
supposes that all such prominent ideas, tokens, facts, and
doctrines as we have named—that is, everything which goes to
shape the new economy, as being integral to it—is brought
into knowledge and published to the world supernaturally.
And the proof is that already given; viz., that the consent of
so many parts and tokens in one central fact and design, can
not otherwise be accounted for, and is otherwise truly impos-

sible. The human understanding may frame a theory out of data or phenomena supplied by experience; it may scheme out a system or hypothesis, regarding matters known, that is coherent, and stands in the complete unity of reason ; but it is a very different thing to make up a supernatural kosmos of fact, doctrine, idea, relatively consistent, and converging all on the common point of a spiritual renovation of souls. That, we may affirm with entire confidence, is not within the compass of any human power.

Of this, too, we have abundant evidence, besides that which rests in any mere judgment of human capacity. The whole religious and mythologic history of the world is such evidence. In the first place, every pagan religion, every mythology, is in form a supernatural machinery ; a fact which Mr Parker and others who endeavour to reduce Christianity to a common foot ing with such mythologies, and so to a mere product of nature, have strangely overlooked. In the next place, what one of these pagan supernaturalisms has ever proposed the problem of salva tion, or the deliverance of man from sin and the restoration of his divine consciousness ?—the only real problem, manifestly, that requires to be supernaturally solved. Again, what one of these mythologies proposes to erect the kingdom of God among men, or has any consistent and concentrated action bearing on that one result, or indeed on any other ? What one of them, we may ask, even proposes a pure morality ? So plainly im possible is it for man or human history to develope any intelli gent and rationally harmonious scheme of supernaturalism.

And yet we have more convincing proofs even than these. See what figure is made by Mormonism, Mohammedanism, and the Romish Church, all of which begin with supernatural con ceptions or data furnished by Christianity. If we will ascer tain what it is in man to do, in the way of composing super natural verities, see what additions or amendments these have furnished. The new faith of Mormon pretends to be Christian still, only it is a more complete and finished form of the Chris tian truth. But the ungodly and profane mummeries it has added, in the new revelations of the book, the new priesthood, and the new sainthood, all of which are boasted and accepted as improvements, it is very plain are only mockeries of all the practical aims of the gospel, and of the virtues it came to restore. Mohammedanism, borrowing from the Christian Scriptures, proposes for its aim, to perfect in men a heavenly virtue. But the doctrine of fatalism it establishes, forbids, at the outset, every struggle after such heavenly virtue, and the sensual para dise it promises, generates, as far as it goes, a habit opposite to everything in the nature of that virtue.

But these, it will be said, are not, in any proper sense, developments of the Christian supernaturalism, at which they begin; but tricks of knavery, or ravings of fanaticism. Pass then to the Romish Church, and see what the venerable, slow-moving wisdom of ages can do. Here we meet the councils, age after age, in their high deliberations. All the learning of the world, for many hundreds of years, is here concentrated. Heretical additions are here carefully scented, and promptly burnt out by the fires of purification. All determinations pass by debate, and sometimes by the debates of ages. The history is a process slow and laborious, like that which generates the common or the civil law; and the result is even called a development of Christianity. What then do we find? Is the glorious order and regenerative unity of the gospel, as a power of salvation, preserved and augmented, or is it overlaid and stifled, by a mass of antichristian inventions and corrupt tradi tions, that have really no agreement with it? And yet they are all introduced to give it greater effect. The exorcisms were to expel devils; but the solemn trifling of the ceremony only turned the disciple away from faith, to look after powers of magic. The amulets were to be pledges, on the person, of God's keeping and defence, against devils and all disasters; but these were accepted as charms also of magic. The sacra ment itself of Christ's body and blood, ordained to be the vehicle and sign of a co-operative grace to the recipient, must needs be farther intensified in its power, and, to this end, was transmuted into the very substance of Christ, by a perpetual miracle; which miracle, again, was taken as another feat of priestly magic, and watched as a pious incantation by the receiver. Celibacy and monastic retirement were to beget a higher and more superlative virtue; turning out, instead, to be only the scandal and disgust of the world. Pictures were added to assist the mind in conceiving things high and remote; operating, instead, as a stricture upon it, and chaining it down to a new antichristian idolatry. Ascetic practices were added, to chasten the soul and refine its spiritual fires; only kindling, instead, the fires of a new fanaticism. The way to Christ would be more easy, it was conceived, if His mother could be invoked to present the cause of the suppliant; and lo! Christianity becomes no more a gospel of life, but a fantastic scheme of Mariolatry. A vicar of Christ was wanted, many thought, to represent Him on earth, and be a visible mark for their faith; but the vicar displaced the principal, becoming a mark, instead, of superstitious homage, and a receiver of deific honours.

And thus we have a proof irresistible of what man can do, in the way of thinking out or dressing up a scheme of supernatural truth. Four or five common persons, without learning or culture, assisted by one other distinguished by higher advantages, have presented, we have seen, such a scheme. All the parts they have set in harmony with each other, and made them crystallize into the perfect unity of the plan. But here we find all the great minds of the Church, the learned, the wise, the prudent, and even the good, slowly elaborating their additions, or, as some will say, their developments, of the doctrine handed down to them, and producing just that which has no agreement whatever with its genuine import and the real movement it proposes—joining, as the classic poet says, a "horse's neck to a man's head," and expanding the simple, life-giving truth, into such theatrical pomps and scholastic wisdoms, that a cap and bells would scarcely be a less appropriate honour.

What, then, have we to do, after such a reference as this, but to gather up all these prominent facts, ideas, names, and doctrines, which we have seen coalesce so perfectly in the central fact of a supernatural grace for the world, composing, when taken together, the total frame-work and complete virtuality of the gospel, and say that, in this secret and everywhere present water-mark, we read the signature of God. None but He could have organized this heavenly kosmos that we call the gospel.

CHAPTER XIII.

THE WORLD IS GOVERNED SUPERNATURALLY, IN THE INTEREST OF CHRISTIANITY.

CHRISTIANITY, as planted by Christ, is a divine institute in the world, the particular design of which is to act remedially, as against the mischiefs introduced by sin, and propagated by the retributive causes of nature. The Holy Spirit also is, by the supposition, a divine force or deific agency inaugurated in the world, to carry on, through all the coming ages, this same new-creating work. Now, as there is but one Divine Being or God, who is entered thus into so great a work, with tokens of feeling so impressively indicated, it follows by a very short inference, if indeed by any inference at all, that the one God of the world, governing it always accordantly with Himself, must govern it in the interest of Christianity. Christianity, plainly, is either nothing to Him, or else it is more than any secondary thing; the hinge of His counsel, the mission of His love, the grand, all-inclusive, and eternal aim of His purposes. And if this be true, He will not govern the world in a way that forgets or over looks Christianity, but will govern it rather for Christianity's sake; which, again, is the same as to say that He will govern it by a supernatural regimen, even as Christianity itself is a supernatural institution.

Exactly this, too, is the assumption of Christ Himself. He openly claims the government of the world, as being in His interest, or at the disposal of his cause and kingdom, saying, —" All power is given unto me in heaven and in earth." He is also declared by His apostle to have " ascended on high, leading captivity captive," that He might be a dispenser of divine gifts in this manner; " for God hath set him at his own right hand, in the heavenly places, far above all principality and power, and nath put all things under his feet, that he might be head over all things to the Church." He also publishes, Himself, a doctrine of prayer that supposes the same thing; or that, if any one will ask in His name, or as abiding in Him and doing His will, he shall have his petition—guidance, light, deliverance, healing of the sick, support against enemies, power to work, patience to suffer—everything that supposes the government to be enlisted, as a supernatural providence, in the furtherance of his Christian welfare.

Indeed, we shall not sufficiently understand the Christian ideas of providence, till we conceive it to be a twofold scheme of order and divine dispensation. Nature, in the first place, is a kind of providence, being so adjusted as to meet all the future uses it can, as nature, meet. But it requires little insight to perceive that it cannot meet those uses that suppose a need of deliverance from nature. Manifestly nature cannot rescue from the disorders produced by a retributive action of her own causes. And if all God's action were included in the operations of nature, nothing plainly could ever be done for man, as regards the wants of his sin, the cries of his repentance, or the struggles of his faith. Nature can throw him, and trample him, by her retributive causes, but she has no help to give him in rising or rolling back her causes.

On this subject of providence, there is much of unregulated thought and crude speculation. Thus it is a greatly debated question, whether there is a special or only a general providence? For it is conceived, by a certain class, that God has a special meaning or design, in some few things of their experience, and not in others. This plainly is a faith of credulity, and one that accommodates God to the measures of human ignorance. Another class, who assume to be more philosophic, holding a general, and denying a special providence, only substitute an absurdity for a superstition; for what is a general providence, that comprehends no special providence, but a generality made up of no particulars; that is, made out of nothing? The only intelligent conception is, that every event is special, one as truly as another; for nothing comes to pass in God's world without some particular meaning or design. And so the general providence is perfect, because the special is complete.

And yet even this is no sufficient conception of providence. There is yet, after all, a real truth associated with the specialty view just stated, and covered, in part, by the scanty garb in which it is dressed ; viz., that God is more warmly reciprocal with us and the struggles of our faith, in some things than in others—more reciprocal, that is, and closer to our want, and warmer to our feeling, in His supernatural providence, than He is in His natural.

The truth will be set in a more definite light, if we conceive, first of all, that nature is a kind of constant quantity and fixed term between us and God. It needed to be so for many reasons. We could not even keep our feet if the ground had no stable quality. We could do nothing in the way of industry, attain to no exercise of power; there would be no law, no science, nothing to meet our intelligence ; we could not act responsibly toward each other without some constant, calculable, or known medium between us. We could apprehend no retributive force in nature, waiting by the laws of obligation, to be their sanction. Even God Himself would be a vague and desultory phantom, if He were not represented to us by the fixed laws and the orderly, enduring processes of nature. Without these, even the light and shade of His supernatural manifestation would be insignifi cant—just as the living play of a countenance would signify nothing, if it had no lines of repose at which the play begins, and into which it returns.

But, while such is nature, it is yet, as we have seen, sub mitted, by its very laws, both to our supernatural action, and to that of God. As we act our liberty in it and upon it, never suspending or defrauding, even for a moment, any one of its laws, so it would be singular if He could not do the same, and that upon a scale correspondent with the magnificence of His attributes. So, in millions of ways, at every minute, the courses of things may be touched by His will, and turned about, as the holy Poet says of the cloud, " to do whatsoever he commandeth upon the face of the earth." By means of the con stant element between us and God—limbered, though constant, to our common action—we are set in terms of reciprocity as living persons or powers, and are found acting, as toward each other, in a perpetual dialogue of parts. Taken thus, in the whole comprehension of its import, our world is nothing but a vast, special, supernatural, reciprocal providence, in which our God

is reigning as an ever-present, ever-mindful counsellor and
guide and friend, a Redeemer of our sin, a hearer of our
prayers.   It is not that He, long time ago, put causes at work
to meet our wants, and answer our prayers, but that He
worketh hitherto.   He is no dead majesty, but a living ; and,
if we want a special providence, He is special enough to give
us His recognition.   He will even teach us how to pray,
correcting our petitions to make them meet His counsel, and
giving us desires, levelled to the exact aim of His purposes ;
even as the eagle teaches her young how to set their wings,
and rest them on the air in flight.   Not that He means, when
speaking of things " agreeable to His will," that we are merely
to come, guessing at things already fixed, and trying to suit
our petition to the motion of the wheel as it rolls, sliding it
carefully in at the right place, but that He will have us pray
as in power ; for it is agreeable to His will that we have
power with God, and prevail—power to come and lay our hand
on His, as His is laid on the world's causes, and, by the suit
of our want, emboldened by the acquaintanceship of our faith,
to move that hand.   And to just this end, as Christ Himself
teaches, all things in heaven and earth are submitted pliantly
to him, so that, without shock or miracle, He can, if He will,
turn them to His friendly and gracious purposes.   The world
and its affairs are so to become co-efficients only of His gospel.

Such is the conception Christianity holds of providence, or the
providential government of the world—it is supernatural, it is
Christly, and is to be relied upon ever, as a power operating for
Christianity in the earth.   Is the conception true, is it borne
out by sufficient proofs ?   This I shall now undertake to show.

Let us note, in passing, however, as a fact introductory, that
just such a government, as respects the mode, would be wanted
and really required, apart from any fall of sin, or work of
deliverance from it.   For, if there be only nature, with her
constant quantities and endlessly propagated causes, if there be
no divine supernatural agency in the world, then there is no
conceivable footing of society, or social relationship with God
left us.   Nature, in such a scheme, is only a machine, and that
machine is all that we have contact with.   And if we should
maintain our uprightness, holding on in ways of unfaltering
obedience, we shall none the less want to know God, and have
our society with Him.   But we get no terms of society in a

machine, we cannot seek unto a wall. Acting supernaturally ourselves, we need also to be supernaturally met and acted on. Without this, we have no terms of reciprocity with God more than with a volcano or a tide of the sea. Society between us there is none. Society is rigidly definable, as being a super-natural commerce between parties acting supernaturally. As between us and God, it is a doing and receiving; if we do not sin, a righteousness looking up to God in confidence, and a smile of approval looking down to commend and bless. But if there be no such thing as a Divine supernatural agency, then is no such footing of society conceivable. We exist as a solitary party. Nature is our cage, and the nearest approach we get to a recognition, is to find that we are shut up in it. Is it so? Do any of us think it is so? Did we really believe it, what could our existence be but a conscious defeat and mockery, a longing that is objectless, a breathing without air?

But our state is not a state of sinless obedience. We have set the retributive causes of nature against us, and Christianity undertakes to be our deliverer. And the claim now is, that the government of the world is supernaturally administered, so as to work with it. We allege, then, in evidence—

I. That facts do not take place here, in human society, government, and the Church, as they should, if events were left to the mere causalities of nature, and were no way con trollable by a supernatural ministration of divine government, or by some genuinely Christian providence, in the management of human affairs.

The fact of sin is palpable, and is shown by evidences not to be questioned. What shock of disorder it must have given, or has in fact given, to the mundane kosmos, in all its parts, we have also shown. Taking now the supposition that there is nothing else but nature, and nature a scheme of universal cause and effect, that is, a machine, propagating its activities by its own organic laws, we ought to see no improvement, no advance, but a regular running down rather from bad to worse, and a final disappearance of all vestiges of order. Society and human capacity ought to sink away universally toward barbarism, and nature itself to grow weaker, more sterile, deeper in deformity and confusion. So it ought to be—speculatively viewed, or according to conditions of scientific order and law, nothing else could be. And yet we are just now taken with such confidence of progress in our human history, as to imagine that progress is even a prime law of natural development itself.　In which we are doubtless right as regards the general fact of progress (it is no fact as regards the savage races), but are only the more strangely blind to the higher fact which that progress indicates ; viz., the regenerative action of supernatural forces, that, in spite of the downward tendency of mere nature under sin, are creating always a new heavens and earth out of the ruins of the former beauty, and making even the losing experiences of evil conditions of spiritual and social progress.　Plainly no such progress ever ought to be, or ever would be made, apart from the supernatural causes which are its spring.

But there is a more deliberate way of testing this point, and a method of inquest that reaches farther.　We turn ourselves to the courses and the grand events of human history, all that we include in the providential history of the world—the wars, diplomacies, emigrations, revolutions, persecutions, discoveries, and scientific developments of the world—and we are imme diately met by the appearance of some wonderful consent or understanding between Christianity and the providential courses of things.　Christianity is, in form, the supernatural kingdom and working of God in the earth.　It begins with a supernatural advent of divinity, and closes with a supernatural exit of divinity ; and the divine visitant, thus entered into the world and going out from it, is Himself a divine miracle in His own person ; His works are miracles, and His doctrine quite as truly, and the whole transaction, taken as a movement on the world, or in it, that is not of it, supposes, in fact, a new and superior kind of administration, instituted by God Himself.　Accordingly, if it be true that God is in such a work, having all the highest and last ends of existence rested in it, he ought to govern the world, as we have already said, for it, and so as to forward this as the main interest included in it.

Now, whatever may be true as respects the positive and direct evidence of such a fact, this, at least, is a matter that will strike any one as being truly remarkable, and, moreover, as being quite unaccountable, except on the ground of its truth, that Christianity has never been exterminated, but still lives, and even holds a reigning power at the head of all learning, art, commerce, society, polity, and political dominion in the earth. Pythagoras, Socrates, Plato, Zeno, Aristotle, Seneca, all these great founders and lawgivers in the world of philosophy are gone ; the Academy and the Porch, and all the schools that were gathered ·by the wisdom and the mighty and beautiful thought of these first minds of the world, are scattered ; but Jesus, the unlettered rustic, lives, and His simple words, distinguished by no literary pretensions, and recorded only in the simplest and most fragmentary way, by the unlettered men that caught them, live also.   Studied in deepest reverence, and expounded by all the richest, nicest learning of the world, and fed on by the pray ing souls of the faithful in all walks and conditions of life, they are continually gathering new followers, and composing a larger school, to which no inclosures of Academy or Porch, nothing but kingdoms and continents, can think to give their name.   Why now is it that time and the world's government conspire so powerfully with Jesus, and not with such a great and deeply cultured soul as Plato ?   Why with Christianity, and not with any proudest school of human opinion ?   All the mere human teachers are much closer to nature certainly than Jesus was ; and if the world's government is wholly natural, or in the interest of nature, it would seem to be a very plain inference that what belongs to nature will be most easily perpetuated.   Why should a government, in the interest of nature, concur to enthrone and crown what is really supernatural ?   •

Besides, nature, as we have seen, is a power acting retri· butively, in a process of self-chastisement and deterioration naturally endless, and upon this falling flood, or into it, Chris tianity settles, to grapple with its mad causations, and roll them back, and hush their elemental war, by its words of peace ; how then is it, that a new, supernatural dispensation, which arrays itself at all points against nature and its penal disorders, erects upon the unsteady waters of so fickle and wild a sea, the only institution that for the last eighteen hundred years has been able to challenge the honours of per manence ?   If there be no power but nature, no government superior to the interest of nature, it certainly ought not to be so. On the contrary, whatever pretends to be supernatural, ought to die soonest, and show the greatest frailty—even as the pouring waters of Niagara may well enough keep on over the rapids, down the fatal leap, and no cessation make, even for millions of years ; whereas the slender, light-trimmed vessel, that sets her sails for the ascent of those same rapids, ought not to stem them by one inch, and least of all, to become an institution in them, stiffly and steadily breasting the current for ages. And yet, if there were some Higher Providence governing those falls in the interest of the vessel, and not, as nature would, the vessel in the interest of the falls, then plainly it would no longer be absurd for that same frail craft to become an institution, even half way down the final leap itself.

If it be suggested that other religions, such, for example, as Buddhism and Mohammedanism, are also supernatural in their form, and have survived, one of them a third longer, and the other two-thirds as long as Christianity, it is enough to reply, as regards the latter, that all the forces of reality it had were stolen from Christianity, and that, in spite of these, it is now just upon the death ; and, as regards the former, that while its machineries are in form supernatural, it really undertakes to do nothing as against the lapse and disability of nature, but rather settles into .the same disorder with it, and takes a show of perpetuity, because it flows with the current, and wins a kind of permanence which is only another name for the disability it creates. This is true of all the false religions ; they belong to nature, and become constituent elements in that hell of disability which nature makes out of sin. Christianity rises, and raises its adherent races with it. These others fall, and finally die, when their adherent races die out of the world, assisting and hastening that event, each in its own way. When, therefore, we consider that Christianity goes directly into a conflict with nature, calling nature death, and engaging to combat the death by its regenerative power, and that still, after so many centuries, it holds on victorious, what shall we infer with greater certainty, than that the government of the world is with it, in its interest, engaged to give it success ? Without or apart from this fact, it plainly could not have held its ground, even for a single year. No ! Christianity stands, and will, because the God of Christianity is the God of the world. The kingdom is not moved, and cannot be, as it certainly should under a mere providence of natural causes, and that for the manifest reason that all power in heaven and in earth is given into the hands of the king. And this brings us to a

II. Argument which is more general and more positive, viz., this, that, if we could make a perfectly intelligent survey of the great world's history itself, and see how its principal events are turned, we should only discover the same thing on a larger scale; that the world itself is governed in the interest of Christianity or the supernatural grace and kingdom of Jesus Christ. We plainly cannot undertake any such review, for the reason that no human insight is equal to the task; but if we just glance along the inventory, so to speak, of the matters of this history, recalling chapters by their titles, and only having in mind the relation of so many things to the central figure, Christ and His kingdom, we shall find that, in His glorious person, we get the key by which their mystery and meaning are solved, their practical harmony expounded.

Thus we have the Jewish dispersion, before Christ, in all the principal cities of the world, and the establishment there of the synagogue worship; so that, when the apostles go abroad with their message, they have places in which to speak made ready, assemblies gathered, and what is more than all, minds prepared by Jewish symbols and associations, to receive the meaning of the new gospel, as related to a first dispensation of law; with out which, as we have seen, its true place in God's economy is undiscovered; without which, too, it is bolted into the world, separately from all historic connexions, and from all the evi dences to be shown for it, by its fulfilment of ideas hid in ancient rites and forms.

Next we observe that philosophy had just now culminated among the Greeks and Romans, and was giving way as a force that is spent. The Sophists had run it into the ground. Faith in it was gone, and with that, all faith too in the gods of their religion. In this manner a deep and painful hunger was pre. pared, and multitudes of the most thoughtful minds were actually groping after the very food which Christ was to bring.

At this time, too, the Greek tongue, which, for ages to come, was to be the general vehicle of thought and commerce between the peoples of the world, had become, to a great extent, the vernacular of the country, and a Gentile speech or medium was thus made ready to receive and convey the grace that is given to the Gentiles.

The Romans, too, are now masters of the country, and the Roman empire, of which it is become an integral part, is well nigh universal. When Christ therefore is crucified, it is, as it should be, the public act of the world, decreed by the Roman procurator in the name of the world. There is also now a more open state of society between the nations and races of mankind than was ever known before; because they are all, in fact, one empire. The apostles, therefore, may well enough go into all the world, as they are bidden, because the pass of a Roman citizen is good in all the world.

It has also been noted as a remarkable fact, that when the Incarnate Word appears it is a time of general peace; and it is remarkable, not only as a matter of poetic fitness or æsthetic propriety, but still more in the deeper and more cogent sense of a practical necessity; for if Christ had come, in the tumult of a time of war, His glorious but gentle appeal of truth and love would have been utterly drowned and lost. In the din of so great noise and passion, who could feel his want of a salva tion? who be attracted by the beauty of a character? who de scend to a cross to look for the Incarnate Word, and catch His mournful testimony?

Take now these familiar facts, and what are they all but a visible preparation of human history for Christ, showing on how vast a scale the world is managed in the interests of Christ and His supernatural advent? Why else, too, do they all con cur in time, when they might as well have happened centuries apart? Whence comes it that, when human history has been brewing in so great a ferment for so many ages, all these great preparations should just now be ready, calling for the king with their common voice and saying, "the fulness of time is come?"

As it was with the events that preceded and prepared the gospel, so it has been with those which followed its publication. They give us their true sense and gauge of power, in the fact that they inaugurate a new era, called the Christian era. And what are we to see in the simple *Anno Domini* of our dates and superscriptions but that, for some reason, the great world-history has been bending itself to the lowly person of Jesus, from the hour of His miraculous advent onward through so many centuries of time. The Christian era! a new forma tion, speaking geologically, in the domain of human life and society! Christ, who is called by many the impossible, the in credible person, the gospelled carpenter raised into a mythic divinity—to Him it is that the great world has so long bent itself, and dated its history from His year! So clearly is it

signified, that the government of the world is waiting on Chris
tianity, and working in its interest, and is thus, in highest
virtuality, a supernatural kingdom.

The events themselves of the new era indicate the same thing.
First, we hear Porphyry, and other assailants of the gospel,
complaining strangely that their gods are grown dumb, refusing
any more to heal or give oracles. The Jewish unbelievers are
smitten next with a token of discouragement even more appal
ling in the terrible siege and dreadful overthrow of their holy
city ; in which they are shown, as convincingly as possible, that
God has brought their ancient specialty of theocratic rule and
distinction to a full end—just that which even prophecy had
foretold as the inaugural of a universal religion. After long and
bitter persecutions, Constantine is finally enrolled as a convert,
and Christianity takes the ascendant above all the gods of the
empire. The northern hordes begin to pour down the Alps,
over-running the distracted and worn-out civilizations of the
empire, and conquering, in fact, a religion by which they are
themselves to be tamed and socially regenerated. The false
prophet appears, propagating his new dispensation by the fierce
apostleship of arms, and the world is to be shown what is the
value of a triune grace and gospel, by a grand collateral experi
ment, in which both trinity and grace are wanting. The cru
saders follow in successive repetitions of defeat and disaster ; as
if God's purpose were to stamp it on the Christian sense of the
nations that Christianity is forbidden by the eternal proprieties
of its mission to strengthen itself by any victories but those of
peace. The discovery of the mariner's compass leads off the
discoveries of Vasco de Gama and Columbus. Printing is in·
vented, and the age of learning revived. This prepares the
great Reformation of religion ; for it, Luther ; and for Luther,
God so musters forces, as to give him always civil protection,
keeping him in fortress, and compelling even the combined fury
of kings and kingdoms to pass by harmless. The Puritans are
driven out of England to plant their gospel of liberty and light
on the shores of a new world. Cromwell breaks down the mon
archy to inaugurate, in England, religious toleration ; so to
regenerate the laws and political liberties of the English nation.
The American Revolution, followed by the federal constitution,
fulfils the Christian aim of Puritanism, and lays all claims and
titles of legitimacy at the feet of human liberty and progress,

The wars of Napoleon follow, by which the oppressive dynasties of Europe are broken up or shattered, to let in the light of a new age of improvement.   The revelations of Christian science, meantime, are uncovering and transforming the world, tenfolding its forces and uses, and all that constitutes its value, in a single generation.   The grand commercial apostleship of steam and telegraph, hurrying the intercourse and shortening the dis tances of the ends of the world, fixes the superiority of the Christian nations, and prepares the speedy sovereignty of the Christian ideas.

What now do we distinguish in these facts, but an outstand ing, world-wide proof of the truth we just now stated, that the government of the world is in the interest of Christianity, and so far is itself a really continuous supernatural administration ! These events are a kind of providential procession that we see, marching on to accomplish the one given result, the universal and final ascendency of Jesus Christ.   They march, too, in the beat of time, preserving their right order, and appearing, each, just when it is wanted, not before or after.   When has it ever been seen that the government of the world was conspiring, in this large historic way, across the distance of remote ages, with any merely natural man, his teachings, or plans, or work ? Whatever else may be true, this at least is plain, that between Christianity as a fabric all-supernatural, concerned for nothing but to do a supernatural work, and the world as mere nature, suffering nothing above nature to be, there ought to be, and indeed never could be any such concurrence.   Besides, the progress indicated by these facts is plainly impossible on the footing of mere nature; for nature, under sin, becomes, we have seen, a grand destructive causality rather, such as, running by its own mechanical laws, can of course breed no result of self-restoration, but must run itself downward, instead, into a worse and more fatal deterioration.

But it will be imagined by some, that these are facts which we obtain by gleaning ; that, meantime, there is an abundance equally copious of adverse facts, such as have no concurrence with the gospel of Christ, but seem, instead, to offer only hindrance. What account, for example, can we make of the dark ages so called, and of the confessedly base corruptions that have been al lowed to over-run Christianity as a doctrine of faith and salvation ? To this I answer, that, by this question, rightly viewed, is opened one of the most fruitful and convincing chapters of Christian evidence; showing, as no other does, that Christianity is upheld by nothing but the fact, that the government of the world is with it. What could follow, but a corruption of Chris tianity, at the beginning, from our very belief in it ? for by our faith we bring ourselves to it as a contribution; contributing, of course, our misbegotten opinions, our confused passions, our habits, prejudices, weaknesses of every kind, and so infusing our poison, more or less hurtfully, into that which saves us ; even as the patient will communicate his plague to his physician, or the bad wine give its smell to the jar into which it is poured. The disciple will as certainly give his form to Christianity, when he preaches it, or commends it, as he will receive a regenerated life from it. The new gospel, accordingly—it could not be other wise—will go into a grand process of corruption, at first, such as will perchance be called improvement, and the problem of history will be, to settle and discriminate the truth, by winnow ing out the forms of human error and corruption from it. With out some process of this kind, it could never be seen what really belongs to the gospel, and what to the unwisdom and unbelief of those in whom it dwells. As the gospel was revealed to sin, so there was a different kind of necessity that the gospel should be revealed experimentally through sin. Man, the believer, must, in other words, be allowed to try his hand upon it, and make it his gospel—make it wiser by his philosophy, stronger by his regal patronage, more conspicuous and stately by the paraphernalia of forms and the robed officials he may dress up for its due embodiment.

This is that mystery of iniquity that an apostle saw, even in his time, beginning to work ; which he said must work, till it should be taken out of the way. This is that falling away first, that must come, the man of sin that must be revealed. It is not the papacy exactly, but that which made the papacy; viz., faith, not able, without a severe schooling, to mind the distinc tion between a subjection to and a supervision of the gospel ; for, in becoming responsible for it as a servant, what will the new believer more certainly do than take it in charge, patronize it, mend it, that is, disfigure and hide it ? And there will be no limit to this wrong. Unable to stay content with the humble guise and the simple doctrine of the cross, he will exalt himself unwittingly above what is called God in the work, and will go on

to be so grand a supervisor, that finally, as his sins are added
to the forwardness of his service, we shall begin to see that he
has contributed his whole self, and even taken God's seat, in his
preposterous ambition ; becoming first the minister, then the
vicar, and last of all, to give a true name, the usurper of God's
authority.   Christianity is now in his charge, and is not im
proved by his additions.   Disappointment follows ; this compels
a reconsideration, this a reformation, and so the true gospel is
finally restored, with its reasons only certified, by the human
abuse through which it has passed, and the lines of contrast
drawn by so many miserable corruptions.

Thus, at a very early period, we hear such men as Justin
and Clement of Alexandria, proposing to give the Christian
doctrine the dress of a philosophy, and find them earnestly at
work to accomplish a point of so great consequence, imagining
that so it will be more able to command the respect of the
learned, and will better satisfy the want of the world.   The
work goes on, till, at last, some centuries of dialectic industry
may be said to have completely finished all that could be done,
when lo ! the beautiful life-giving truths of Christ, offered by
Him to faith, are converted into a dry, scholastic jingle, ad
dressed to speculative reason, without value even to that, and
as easily rejected as embraced.   Monasticism and vows of
celibacy are added in the same way, to give Christianity, in
certain special examples, the advantage of a more superlative
virtue than God had planned for, in the practical relations of
life ; finally to result in corruptions too monstrous ever to have
been gendered in those relations.   Constantine, having become
a disciple, must needs contribute not his person only, but all
the power of his throne, to the gospel, expecting in that man
ner to make it partake of his imperial pre-eminence, and be
come strong by a strength thus contributed.   Uniting it, in
this manner, to the state, he not only stays the woes of perse
cution, but he lifts the Church into a rank of political ascen
dency ; which is the same as to say that he dooms it, for ages
to come, to be the mother of all unholy arts and oppressions,
and the source of unspeakable public miseries.   Gregory the
Great can find no rest to his prayers, till the Church is consoli
dated under the acknowledged primacy of St Peter ; and when
it is done, he may fitly rest in his prayers, having made the
Church such an organ of abuses, oppressions, and religious woes,

as the world had never seen before, and never will see again. Images and pictures are at length set up in the holy places, under the fair pretence that they are needed to represent the spiritual truths of religion to the eye, and so to accommodate the apprehension of weak and ignorant minds. And, then, finally, behold ! as the fruit of so great an improvement, whole nations of people worshipping the images, and before them, transformed into nations of idolaters !

So the mystery works, and so the true gospel is becoming distinguished from the false, the gospel of the Son of God from man's gospel of additions, improvements, and airy conceits. As Christ revealed His gospel by communication, so here it is revealed again, as it needs must be, by the light and shade of historical experiment; settled, or adjusted, or practically de-fined, by use and abuse. These facts appear to be entirely adverse to Christianity. They are so, and, in that, have their value. That the government of the world, therefore, has passed by on the other side, and let Christianity fall in these facts, we are not to suppose. Being a gift to human liberty, it could not otherwise be established. When the experiment is finished, then the Divine Word will burst up into a second com ing, through the human incrustations, consuming by His breath and destroying by His brightness the accumulated wisdoms and pomps of His mistaken followers. In all these losing agencies, there is yet no loss. The dark ages we speak of are yet in no backward motion. Still the march of Christian history is on ward. If these bad impediments were not already raised, why, then, they were yet to be raised. Just so far on its way to the state of universal dominion, is the gospel and supernatural kingdom of Jesus Christ.

Still there have been events, it must be admitted, in what is called Christian history, which are darker and more difficult of solution. They appear, at first view, to have no place under a scheme of providential government, such as we are now sup posing. And yet if we could hold a longer reach of times, and seize the connexions of history with a broader grasp of in telligence, they might fall into place and become as transparent, under such a scheme, as any other. As it is, we can only suggest possibilities, and start guesses, and rest till our facul ties grow to the dimensions of the subjects. What does it mean, for example, that the Jesuits and the Council of Trent

were able to stop, or set a limit to, the Reformation of the
Church? We cannot answer, and probably shall never know.
Like all evil, it may be referrible to the necessary scope of
human liberty. Or it may be that the Reformation itself was
a thing too incomplete and partial to be allowed a sweep of
universal triumph. It might have been a great disaster to the
religion of Christ, to be resolved into a mere reformationism,
and left confronted by no antagonistic force. Why, again, was
it, or how, that the Churches of Northern Africa were allowed
to be over-run by barbarians, and finally, in the loss of their
faith, to give way utterly, and fall into extinction, before a bar
barous religion? Was it that occasional examples of loss and
retrocession must be suffered, in order to the enforcement of a
just responsibility for the gospel in its adherents and followers,
otherwise ready to assume that, having God for its author, it
will take care of itself? This we cannot answer, but we can
without difficulty imagine it to be so. Why, again, were the
French Huguenots, the religious hope and glory of their time,
suffered to be butchered or expelled the kingdom? Was it
that so many great and noble men might endanger again the
simplicity of the truth, and could only give their most valuable
testimony for Christ by their death or exile? Or was it that
Calvinism itself, preparing, at this time, to establish a new
type of individualism under its doctrine of an electing and
special grace, and so to inaugurate a new state of ecclesiastical
and civil liberty, might have stiffened, having God's decrees all
with it, into a form of Christian absolutism too closely resem
bled to the faith of Mahommed, and must needs be tempered
therefore, in this manner, by the experience of a predestinating
counsel opposite, shaking even it to its fall? Or, if we ask
why it is that so great decay of faith is suffered in Germany
and in the Christian world generally, at the present time; why
it is that learning is turned against the gospel, to explain it
away, or reduce it to the terms of nature and speculative
reason? the question may be dark to many, and may seem to
admit no satisfactory answer. Still, to any one who has
thought deeply, it will be something to ask whether it was
possible for the principle of faith ever to be set in its true post
of honour, till the relations of nature and the supernatural are
settled by a thorough discussion, such as brings every truth of
Christianity into question?

On the whole, we discover nothing in any of these darkest and most adverse facts of history, to shake our conviction that the world is governed, as we said at the beginning, in the in terest of the incarnation or supernatural advent of Jesus Christ. Almost all the great staple events of history reveal this fact, in forms of palpable evidence, and if in some it seems to be less plain, there is yet nothing in them to dislodge our faith, even for a moment.   Besides, we have always before us the one majestic fact, that Christianity still lives.   The Church, being a supernatural institution, all history bends to it, and it proves its sublime peculiarity in the fact, that it is for ever indestruc tible by time and its changes.   The schools of Pythagoras, and all the great teachers after him, have flourished for a day, and vanished—tokens all of the necessary frailty of mere natural wisdom—but the Church of Jesus Christ, the Nazarene teacher, stands from age to age.   It began with a feeble knot of dis ciples, it has spread itself over a vast field or kingdom, includ ing in its ample scope all the foremost nations and peoples of the world.   Persecution has not crushed it, power has not beaten it back, time has not abated its force, and, what is most wonderful of all, the abuses and treasons of its own friends have never shaken its stability.   Mohammedanism, punctually served, and to the letter, by the bigoted fidelity of its adherents, grows old and dies in a much shorter time.   Christianity, be trayed, corrupted, made to be the instrument of unutterable woes, by its disciples, is yet forbidden to die.   God will not let the dissensions, the treasons, the unutterable and abominable profligacies, that are mortal to the life of other institutions, have any power of death upon it; upholding it visibly Himself, and showing by that sign, as He could by nothing else, that the settled purpose of His will is to establish it as the universal religion.

But the government of the world includes, in its largest view, the interior history of souls.   Before we arrive at Christianity, therefore, what we there call the domain of the Spirit, and of spiritual experience, is to be classed under providential history. We cite, therefore, in this connexion,

III.   As a distinct argument, the spiritual changes wrought in men, and the testimony given by the subjects of such changes. Nothing is better attested than the fact that men of our race, whether under Christianity or without any knowledge of its truths, do undergo changes of character and life, that can no way be accounted for without some reference to a supernatural power, such as Christianity affirms in the doctrine of the Spirit. The subjects themselves can nowise account for the change, except by the supposition of a Divine agency in them superior to the laws of natural development, and also to any force of will they could themselves exert on their own dispositions, and the moral habit of their previous life. ·

To change the type of a character, and above all to do it in such a manner that, from and after a given date, it shall be confessedly different, more widely different than if a thief were to become suddenly honest, a licentious man suddenly and deli cately pure, a violent gentle, a cowardly heroic—this, it will be agreed, is a thing most difficult to be accomplished. Many will even declare it to be impossible; nothing more is possible, they will say, than for the subjects to set their will to a refor mation, which doubtless they may do at any given moment, but, in doing it, how far off are they still from any change of character ; persisting against what struggles of perverse habit, heaving spasmodically under what loads of corruption, ready to fall again, how easily, back into what has all the while been and still is their character. But if they do, perchance, succeed in finally changing anything, how slowly must the change be wrought. Even as one habit gives way to another by a long and wearisome reiteration of practice. Exactly so it is, we ad mit, with all changes in mere natural character, all improve ments in the plane of the natural life. If there is no force but mere will, acting in this plane, to change us, there can be no sudden reverse of character ; no reverse at all, which is more radical than what the phrenologist give us to expect, when they set us on courses of practice, to increase or diminish, given lobes of brain under the bony casement of the skull. Whoever undertakes any such improvement of his character, in a bad point, doing it by his will, we expect to see relapse and fall back. We have a way, indeed, of saying, " It is in him," when a bad man is repressing his particular sin ; by which we mean to intimate our conviction that what is in him will assuredly come out and show itself, even more flagrantly than ever. Thus we reason, and we are right in it, if no account be made of faith and the influence of a supernatural power.

Thus it was that Celsus reasoned, utterly denying the credibility of any sudden change of character from bad to good, such as the Christians spoke of; for, not being in the faith of Christ, he had no conception of the supernatural efficacy embodied in His plan of salvation. He says, " Those who are disposed by nature to vice, and accustomed to it, cannot be transformed by punishment much less by mercy ; for to transform nature is a matter of extreme difficulty." He did not understand, alas ! what " mercy " is. But Origen does. Having it revealed in him, by his own holy experience, he replies, how beautifully, " When we see the doctrine Celsus calls foolish, operate as with magical power, when we see how it brings a multitude at once from a life of lawless excesses to a well regulated one, from un righteousness to goodness, from timidity to such strength of principle that, for the sake of religion, they despise even death, have we not good reason for admiring the power of this doctrine ?"[1]

The picture given by Justin Martyr corresponds ; at once proving itself by its own beauty, and revealing the hand of the Divine Spirit by whom it is wrought. " We, who once were slaves to lust, now delight in purity of morals ; we, who once prized riches and possessions above all things, now contribute what we have to the common use ; we, who once hated and murdered each other, and on account of our differences would not have a common hearth with those of the same tribe, now live in common with them, and pray for our enemies, and endeavour to persuade those who hate us unjustly, that, living according to the admirable counsels of Christ, they may enjoy a good hope of obtaining the same blessings with ourselves, from God the ruler of us all."[2]

That changes such as these are sometimes wrought in men and societies of men, under the gospel of Christ, we certainly know. There is almost no one who has not some time witnessed such examples. And yet, where communities are taken, the results will be so far mixed by cases of spurious faith, of hypocrisy, of backsliding, and apostasy, as to blur and sadly confuse the evidence displayed. Our best and least ambiguous examples of spiritual renovation, therefore, will be found in the case of individual persons.

The case of Paul is familiar, and it is remarkable that no other ancient human character comes to us attested, in its

[1] Neander's *Memorials of Christian Life*, p. 17. [2] *Ibid.* p. 61.

genuineness, by such evidence. Whatever the learned critics
say or assume to show, concerning the Gospels, there is cer .
tainly no myth in the Epistles. When they come to these,
their theory breaks down, their occupation is gone. That such
a man as Pliny lived, and such a man as Cicero, is not as well
attested, or shown by as good evidence, as that Paul the apostle
lived, wrote the epistles ascribed to him, and bore the double
character, first of a persecutor and fierce enemy of the cross,
then, by the grace of God revealed in him, that of a preacher of
the cross ; sacrificing all things, enduring all pains and severities,
ᴵᵒᵛ the name of Christ, his Master. This change, he tells us,
was a change supernaturally wrought, gives us the day and the
ꜟour on which his bad career was stopped, and shows him-
lt to us and all the world from that moment onward to be
another man. From a most bitter and relentless persecutor he
has become a believer in Christ—the most powerful and chief
aavocate of His gospel. A profound self-evidence verifies the
man and the change, and the divine life in him is not less
visible. His own account of the change, which he testifies
openly in every place, is that, " by the grace of God," he is
ꙡꜵꙇ ꙇꙇꙅ ꙇꙅ—" new-created in Christ Jesus unto good works."
    And of such examples the Church is full in all ages. By
some wondrous providence in souls, if we do not accept the
Christian mystery of the Spirit, a stream of new creative power
from God is entering into men's hearts, transforming their lives,
and with this one uniform result that, if Christianity is a fiction
or a myth, it makes them, as certainly its friends and disciples
as it makes them bitter and more akin to God.
    Augustine, for example, was, before his conversion, a less
violent and bloody man than Paul, had far less pretence of
virtue and a much feebler sense of principle, and was, in fact,
a really less hopeful person as regards the prospect of his be
coming a holy character. And yet, from a given moment, on
ward, which moment is exactly specified in his " Confessions "
he becomes another character. Neither can it be said that he
was turned about thus suddenly by some fit of superstition.
He was not a superstitious character, but a loose, free-thinking,
sensual person, whose habit was opposed to the spiritualities in
every form. His own account of his conversion is, that it was
the prayers of his saintly mother which took hold of him,
drawing down upon him from above that divine influence and

grace by which his life was so remarkably changed. We can see, too, for ourselves, in his whole subsequent life, his action, his temper, his great and massive thoughts, his burning con templations, that he is lifted above his natural force, to be a man above himself. The rhetorician is gone, and the apostle has taken his place.

The conversion of Raymond Lull, of Colonel Gardiner, of John Newton, of Dr Nelson, and of hundreds whom we know, as our living contemporaries in the Church, corresponds. The number is so great in fact, examples of the kind so familiar, that any attempt to specify names must be insignificant. A great many supposed changes of the kind turn out, as we admit, to have no sound reality, and are followed by no correspondent change of life. It would be so as a matter of course ; just as there will be spurious examples of honesty, honour, and courage. But the spurious no more disproves the true in one case than in the other. The question is simply this, whether, in given cases, we do not see men entered, more or less sud denly, by what is called their conversion, into another and dif ferent kind of life ; the violent becoming gentle, the deceitful true, the covetous unworldly and liberal, the selfish benevolent and self-denying, profanity changed to prayer, drunkenness to sobriety, revenge to long-suffering, blood-thirstiness to love and compassion ; the subject becoming thus, in truth, from that time onward, a confessedly new man, in all these his several habits and relations ? We are all familiar, certainly, with such examples. They are among the most prominent and impressive facts in the interior personal history of mankind. And they are so well attested, in myriads of cases, by the practical re sults of the life, as to make the unbelief which denies their verity, or classes them as examples of spiritual illusion, a pre judice that amounts to weakness, or supposes a real incapacity for evidence.

Now in these changes of spiritual experience, called conver sions, the Christian word, and the truths of the life of Jesus, are commonly supposed to have an important instrumentality. The subjects uniformly say it, in the confessions they witness. They suppose that God, revealed in Christ, is so, by a trans mission inward, revealed in their consciousness. But if Christ was only a simple, natural man, and if all which is reported of Him in the Gospels, transcending the supposition of His simple humanity, is wild excess or legendary exaggeration, the account which refers these inward changes or conversions to Christ, can hardly be true. That any mere illusion should be followed, age after age, by such wondrous and manifestly real changes, mak ing human souls visibly akin to God, is not to be supposed. That would be to account for the soundest and profoundest facts of human history, by referring them to causes most purely fanci ful, and doctrines wide of all true intelligence.

Here, then, we find ourselves, with these facts on our hands, without any Christian truth to account for them. For when we have dismissed the Gospels, or thrown them aside as unre liable or incredible, these facts are not annihilated. These con verts, these transformed men—the grandest truths, and most quickening powers, and most glorious characters, in human history—are still left, living and blooming and blessing their times, for all these eighteen centuries. They certainly are no fictions, or myths, or fables of tradition. They testify all that they are consciously transformed by some Divine power. A kind of gospel is in them. God has wrought in them, if Chris tianity has not. Only it is remarkable that when they are so transformed by His inner visitation, they immediately declare for Christ, and cleave to Him with ineradicable affection. We seem thus, in fact, to discover that, as we are casting Christi anity away, the government of the world is turning the inmost heart of the repenting and holy toward it, and giving, in that manner, indisputable evidence that it is itself willing, whether we are so or not, to serve in the interest of Christianity.

It does not appear to have been as carefully considered as it should be by the disciples of naturalism in what manner these converts, and the testimony they give, is to be disposed of. For, in our view, they are even a more intractable subject to handle than the Gospels themselves. To deny the reality of their change, and reduce their whole life and experience to a matter of illusion, requires a degree of effrontery and personal conceit that would repel any critic of only ordinary intelligence. For in these Christian myriads are grouped almost all the greatest scholars, philosophers, and lawgivers, the most revered and stateliest names, the most beautiful and holiest characters of Christendom.

It cannot be said that these conversions are in any sense natural, or produced by natural causes, in the feeling and con

dition of the subjects. Their affinities are all visibly transcendent, and their life itself is, in one view, a kind of protest
against nature and withdrawment from it.

They are not changed, in this manner, by their own mere
will. Whoever believes that a mortal man can take hold of the
moral jargon into which his thoughts and passions are cast by
sin, willing himself back, item by item, into peace and harmony
and the ennobled consciousness of good, ought to be able to
believe in Christianity much more easily. A bad man may
reduce or hold in check the evil instigations of his habit by his
mere will; he may even drag himself into positive acts of duty
and observance, and become a sturdy legalist in the practices of
virtue; but to bring himself out into a luminous, joyous, and
spontaneous virtue, and make himself free in good, as having
the principle installed in his heart, is a different thing. No
thing, in short, is wider of all rational belief than that the con
verted men or disciples of Christianity could make the beginning
act the part, fashion the character, kindle the fires, and conquer
the elevations, visibly displayed in their life, doing it by their
human will.

But there is a certain inspiration, it may be said, that flows
into men from the ideas they assume. Thus it may be con
ceived that the supposed convert, in these remarkable transfor
mations of life and character, received first a theological pre
conception that a change thus and thus described is necessary
to his salvation; and then, having his imagination powerfully
excited by the struggles of supposed guilt and danger he is in,
he conceives at last, that the change required is actually passed
upon him; whereupon he is set forward in high impulse into a
new style of life, correspondent with the auspicious hallucina
tion that has triumphed over his sin. And this is really the
most plausible account that can be made of these changes in
the interior history of souls, which does not suppose them to be
referrible to a supernatural divine agency or providence.

But what kind of mind is it that can be satisfied with one
of its wise inventions, when, to account for the highest and
divinest range of fact in man's spiritual history, it supposes
whole myriads of the strongest minds and noblest characters to
have been inspired with so much goodness all their lives long
by a hallucination?

In the next place, we are led to inquire why it is that men

pass no such crisis of inspiration in other matters ? Whence comes it that, having formed some preconception of honesty, truth, purity, wisdom, art, the auspicious hallucination that is to shape their transformation does not suddenly take them up as here, and carry them forward into the inspired liberty ? Why do not men become heroes, poets, lawgivers, in this man ner ? Have they not thoughts enough of being thus distin guished ? and are not such kind of thoughts in them commonly hallucinations ?

But it is not true, in a very great multitude of cases, that any such preconception has been taken up. What thought had Paul, on the way to Damascus, of being converted to Christ as the necessary condition of his salvation ? As little had Augustine, till his mind was opened from within to such a thought. Besides, we have multitudes of cases in our own time, where any such manner of accounting for the change of character actually wrought is plainly inadequate ; cases, for example, where there is too little of personal vigour to carry out any preconception, even if a beginning were made in that manner. Thus a ministerial acquaintance, whose name is before the nation and the world, as a public name, had living in the place where he was pastor, a short-witted person, gene rally taken for an idiot, who, in addition to his natural dis advantages, was deep in the vices of profanity and drunkenness. At a time of general attention to the things of religion, this forlorn being came to him to inquire the way of salvation. The first impulse of prudence was to put him off, as being incapable of religious experience, and as one who would only turn it into mockery by his absurdities. On farther consideration, it was found to be rather a duty to give him even the greater atten tion, according to the proportion of his want. In a few days, it became a subject of mirth, with all the light-minded class of the community, that this man was a convert. The Christian people looked on him with pity, and were silent ; they had no hope of him. But from that hour to this—and many years have now passed away—he has never faltered in his course, never yielded so much as an inch to his vicious habits. His constancy and consistency are even as much superior to that of other disciples, as his simplicity is greater than theirs. He is always in his place. He has worn out two or three Bibles, for he had before learned to read a little, and now put himself to the task in earnest. He gets a few dollars of earnings, which he does not want, and goes to his pastor, requesting him to apply it to some good use, which he does not know how to select. When asked by his friends—for that is the general wonder—how it is that his old habits of profanity and drunkenness have never once gotten advantage of him, his uniform reply is, " Why, I have seen Jesus !" The critic of naturalism can not, of course, admit any such mystic notion as that—Jesus was a man, and, if He is anything now, He is still a man. Will he account for such a character, initiated by a sudden change, by supposing a preconception that shapes it, and main tains it against infirmities so great, for such a course of years ? There is a much deeper and more adequate philosophy in the subject himself. Take his own account of it, and the fact is possible ; take this other, and it is not.

There are multitudes of cases also, in every age, where heathens who have never heard of Christ, or of any terms of salvation at all, and sometimes even the rudest of heathens. are passed into a manifestly new character, by a change corre spondent, in every respect, with what is called conversion under the gospel. And if God, as we maintain, is reigning super- naturally over the world and in it, to establish and complete the kingdom of His Son, what shall we look for but to find sporadic cases of conversion, or spiritual illumination, even among the heathen peoples, before the knowledge of Christ is received ?

Socrates is best conceived in this manner, and according to his own impressions, he was guided supernaturally, by a secret grace and ministry, in whose teaching he received all that most distinguished his personal history. Clement of Rome, as we have already observed, was a man mysteriously led, as by some divine impulse, and appears to have come into the spirit of a new-born life, before he had even heard of Christ. In Him. therefore, his heart instantly rested, finding there the grace that he wanted, and the divine beauty that he already longed for.

And what forbids that we include in the reckoning examples of a class more wild, where it is impossible to suspect any dis- temper of the experience, under preconceptions imposed, either by philosophy or by the gospel—such, for example, as the strange devotee discovered by Brainard, among the children of the forest, and called by him " the conjurer." " He said," so

Brainard represents, "that God had taught him his religion, and he wanted to find others who would join heartily with him in it. He believed God had some good people somewhere, who felt as he did. He had not always felt as now, but had formerly been like the rest of the Indians till about four years before that time. Then his heart, he said, was much distressed, so that he could not live among the Indians, but got away into the woods and lived alone there for months. At length, he said, God comforted his heart, and showed him what he should do, and since that time he had known God, and tried to serve Him, and loved all men, be they who they would, so as he never did before."

Brainard was also told by the Indians, "that he opposed their drinking strong liquor with all his power, and that if, at any time, he could not dissuade them from it, he would leave them, and go crying into the woods. He was looked upon and derided, among most of the Indians, as a precise zealot, who made a needless noise about religious matters. There was something in his temper and disposition which looked more like true religion, than any I have ever observed among other heathens."[1]

In the same manner, a forlorn woman, discovered by one of our missionaries, in the depths of Central Africa, is reported by him to have broken out, in the most affecting demonstrations of joy, when Christ was presented to her mind, saying, " O, that is He who has come to me so often in my prayers. I could not find who He was!" And if God holds any terms of society and reciprocal feeling with our race, what should we more naturally expect, than that He will always be revealed, in this manner, to such as earnestly seek the right, and give play to their inborn though distracted affinities, longing and searching, if haply they may find Him? But if God is revealed thus tenderly, even to minds in the darkness of heathenism, it is plain as it can be, that the great, internal changes of character we are discussing, are not to be accounted for by the preconceptions that are taken up and become operative in the subjects.

After all, this question is more naturally and satisfactorily handled, in the more ordinary form; viz., as a question of Christian experience; what it is, whether it supposes, neces-

1 *Memoir*, pp. 171, 175

sarily, a supernatural power, and what is the real significance
of the testimony given by so many witnesses for Christ ? For
the work of the Spirit, which is the Christian conception, is
but another name, as already intimated, for that supernatural
providence or government of the world in souls, which, we are
endeavouring to show, is dispensed in the interest of Chris
tianity.

Thus we have vast crowds of witnesses, rising up in every
age, who testify, out of their own consciousness, to the work of
the Spirit, and the new-creating power of Jesus, who, by the
Spirit, is revealed in their hearts.   In nothing do they consent
with a more hymn-like harmony than in the testimony that
their inward transformation is a divine work—a new revelation
of God, by the Spirit, in their human consciousness.   They are
such men too as the world are most wont to believe on all
other subjects.   Neither has any one a particle of evidence to
set against their testimony.   All which the stiffest unbeliever
can allege against them is, that he himself has no such con
sciousness, or has found no such discovery verified to his parti
cular experience.   They testify, on their part, with one voice,
to a truth positive, and the whole opposing world can offer
nothing, on its part, against their testimony, but the simple
negative fact of having in themselves no such experience.

Meantime, their very word itself conveys a look of verisimi
litude, and makes a show of God, so necessary to us, and so
honourable to Him, that it challenges the spontaneous faith of
every ingenuous and thoughtful soul.   We never hear any single
man of them speak of his better life as a development, or a
something merely unfolded in him, by natural laws.   No
preacher preaches, no martyr goes to the fires in that vein.
But they all talk of their faith, and of what God gives to their
faith ; the conscious impotence of all their struggles with them
selves, and the easy victory they find in God ; how they are
borne up as on eagle's wings, their wonderful light, their peace,
the love they could not have to their enemies, but now, by
Christ revealed within, are able to exercise, unstinted and free.
Consciously they are not living in the plane of nature, they do
and suffer things which nature can as little do, as she can raise
the dead.   They conquer their fears, God helping their faith.
Pride, passion, habit, they subdue in the same manner.   Religious prejudices also, animosities of race, the contempt of

learning, and the bigotry of schools melt away in them, leaving a character that is visibly a new creation. Even the sceptic who has come to such a state of intellectual disease, that he can no longer find how to believe anything, is filled and flooded with the light of God, in Christ and the Spirit, as soon as he can heartily ask it, with a will to be taught. And so we have a vast cloud of witnesses, testifying in all ages, to the reality of a supernatural grace, which is the root and power of all their works, and the hidden spring of their unspeakable joys. They know it to be so ; for they consciously get their impulse wholly from without any terms of power in themselves, or of causality in nature. They could as easily believe that they make the rain in their own cisterns, as that their holy experiences are not from God Himself. So do they all testify with one voice— Paul, Clement, Origen, St Bernard, Huss, Gerson, Luther, Fenelon, Baxter, Flavel, Doddridge, Wesley, Edwards, Brainard, Taylor, all the innumerable host of believers that have entered into rest, whether it be the persecuted saint of the first age, driven home in his chariot of blood, or the saint who died but yesterday in the arms of his family. They live in the common consciousness of a power supernatural. saying, " Yet not I, but Christ liveth in me." Nothing, in short, would violate, or in real truth obliterate, so much of the Christian history, as to qualify it down to the mere terms of natural development. In deed it would be the virtual expurgation from it of all the saints of God, whatever they have done, or been, or said.

Holding the subject in this form, our critics of the naturalistic school commonly turn their account of the matter in some such way as this. They say to Paul, Luther, Knox, Edwards, and, in fact, the whole Church of God : " We do you full credit, as being made just as much better men as you say you are, and as being exercised subjectively, in just the way you think you are. You are only mistaken, as we have now dis-covered, in respect to the manner and grounds of your ex perience. You have prayed and thought you were heard, you have believed and thought your success was a gift of faith, you have been strengthened against fears and pains of death— all you that have been martyrs—others have been strengthened in their times of temptation, and you all think it was God who bore you up by the immediate gift of Himself; but we are able now to tell you that you were, so far, mistaken.

There is a law of nature by which all these things come to pass, and it is so fixed that nature will help you always, or even inspire you, just according to what you do. All this which you think comes from God by a regenerative dispensation, is the development of nature by a generative."

There would seem to be a rather remarkable defect of modesty in this assumption, of which it cannot be supposed that its authors are themselves aware. It not only shows the whole Church of God, that their conceptions of Christian experience are mistaken, but it corrects them in precisely that which they testify, in the philosophic method itself. This, they say, we find by experiment. It is not our speculation, it is not any theoretic interpretation put on our experience, but it is our experience itself. When they say that God consciously strengthens them in their day of trial, gives them what to say, hears their prayers, keeps them in peace by the testimony that they please Him, fills them day and night with His fulness, and our modern critic runs to them to mend their phraseology, and shows them how to come at the same things in a more rational way, even by letting the divinity that is in them already have a free development according to natural laws, it would not be strange if they should answer with a sigh, "Ah! dear child, we cannot get on thus; for all that bread on which we feed is manna that we gather, and not a loaf that is hid in our nature. Turn us down thus upon nature for a gospel, and our wings are cut. All that we know of God and divine things, we know by stretching upward and away from nature, and believing in God as in Christ revealed. Every success we get, every joy we reach, comes of rejecting just that method by which thou proposest to regulate our experience. May it not be that what thou hast discovered by reason has kept thee from faith, and that still thou needest some one to teach thee what be the first principles of the doctrine of Christ ?"

What we find, then, as the result of our inquiry is, that the government of the world shows the same hand which appears in the character and work of Jesus. In the first place, we discover that nothing takes place in the world that ought to take place, and even must take place, if the government and supreme law of things were confined to mere nature and her processes. Next, we find that the issues of wars and dis-

:overies, the migrations, diplomacies, and great historic eras of races and nations, the extinctions and revivals of learning, and the persecutions and corruptions, not less than the refor mations of churches, are all so modulated by the superintend ing government of the world, as to perpetuate the gospel of Christ, and, as far as we can see, to insure its ultimate triumph. Then passing into the interior history of souls, which, after all, is the chief field of God's government in the earth, we meet vast myriads of witnesses in all the walks of life, and in all the past ages, who profess to know God in the witness of their eternal life and show, by tokens manifold and clear, that they are raised above themselves in all that makes the character of their life. To sum up all in one brief expression, we have found a New Testament in the government of the world. It penetrates all depths of matter, heave: in the roll of the sea, administers back of the thrones, tempers the courses of history, restraining remainders and excesses of wrath, overturning, conserving, restoring, healing, and reaffirm ing thus, in all the grand affairs of human life, without and within, just what Christ the Word declares, when ascending to reign—All power is given unto me in heaven and in earth. What, in fact, do we see with our eyes, but that the scheme of the four Gospels is the scheme of universal government itself?

CHAPTER XIV.

MIRACLES AND SPIRITUAL GIFTS NOT DISCONTINUED.

IF the world is managed supernaturally, or as being in the interest of Christianity, which is the doctrine maintained in the last chapter, a subordinate and vastly inferior, though to many, much more pressing question, remains to be settled; viz., what has become of the miracles and supernatural gifts of the gospel era? These were associated historically with the planting of Christianity. By such tokens Christ authenticated His mission, giving the like signs to His apostles, to be the authentication of theirs. What, then, it is peremptorily required of us to answer, has become of these miracles, these tongues, gifts of healing, prophecies? what, also, of the dreams, presentiments, visits of angels? what of judgments falling visibly on the head of daring and sacrilegious crimes? what of possessions, magic, sorcery, necromancy? If these once were facts, why should they not be now? If they are incredible now, when were they less so? Does a fact become rational and possible by being carried back into other centuries of time? Is it given us to see that Christianity throws itself out boldly on its facts, in these matters, or does it come in the shy and cautious manner some appear to suppose, asserting a few miracles and half-mythologic marvels that occurred in the romantic ages of history, where no investigation can reach them; adding, to escape all demand of such now in terms of present evidence, that they are discontinued, because the canon is closed, and there is no longer any use for them?

Such a disposal of the question, it must be seen, wears a suspicious look. If miracles are inherently incredible, which is the impression at the root of our modern unbelief, evidently nothing is gained by thrusting them back into remote ages of time. If, on the other hand, they are inherently credible, why treat them as if they were not ? raising ingenious and forced hypotheses to account for their non-occurrence ? Christianity, it is true, is in some sense a complete organization, a work done that wants nothing added to finish it ; but it does not follow that the canon of Scripture is closed—that is a naked and violent assumption, supported by no word of Scripture, and justified by no inference from the complete organization of the Gospel. For still, even according to Christ's own thought, it was a complete mustard seed only ; which, though it is com plete as a seed, so that no additions can be made to it, has yet, nevertheless, much to do in the way of growth, and no one can be sure that other books of Scripture may not some time be necessary for that. We do not even know that a new dis pensation, or many such, may not be required to unfold this seed, and make it the full grown tree. It may not be so. ⹁ have no present suspicion that any such new contributions, or varieties of ministration are needed. But it is better not to assume that of which we have and can have no possible evi dence ; least of all are we called to do it, when the assumption itself is evidently made for a purpose, and wears a look of sus picion that weakens the respect of really important truths.

As little does it follow that, if the canon of Scripture is closed up, there is no longer any use or place for miracles and spiritual gifts. That is a conclusion taken by a mere act of judgment, when plainly no judgment of man is able to penetrate the secrets and grasp the economic reasons of God's empire, with sufficient insight to affirm anything on a subject so deep and difficult. There may certainly be reasons for such miracles and gifts of the Spirit, apart from any authentication of new books of Scripture. Indeed, they might possibly be wanted even the more, to break up the monotony likely to follow, when reve lations have ceased and the word of Scripture is for ever closed up ; wanted also possibly to lift the Church out of the abysses of a mere second-hand religion, keeping it alive and open to the realities of God's immediate visitation.

And yet, for these and such like reasons, it is very commonly assumed, and has been since the days of Chrysostom, that miracles and all similar externalities of divine power have been

NOT FOLLOW THAT THE GIFTS ARE DISCONTINUED. 315

discontinued. It is not observed that the date itself is contra dicted by the reasons ; for no book of Scripture had then been written for at least two hundred and fifty years ; though the miracles had never come, as a matter of fact, to any supposed vanishing point till that time. But that miracles continued for two hundred and fifty years, after there was no reason for them, is no great obstruction to a theory of the fact and the reasons, after it has once gained acceptance. Hence there is almost nothing, known to be derived from the Scripture itself, which is affirmed more positively, or with a more settled air of authority, than this discontinuance of miracles and spiritual gifts. Possibly some may even take it as a heresy and a great scandal to the cause of truth, to suggest a possibility of mistake in the assumption. Nay, there are probably many Christian teachers who would even think it a disorder in God's realm itself, if now, in these modern times, these days of science, the well-graduated uniformity of things were to be disturbed by an irruption of miraculous demonstrations. It would upset many whole chap ters of theory.

At the same time, there are classes of teachers and disciples, now and then, who spring up raising the question whether miracles are not restored, or some time to be restored ? Even Archbishop Tillotson was of opinion that they probably enough might be, in the case of an attempt to publish the Gospel among heathen nations.[1] But in all these cases, the point is virtually conceded that miracles have been discontinued ; whereas the truer and more rational question is, whether they have not always remained as in the apostolic age ? Of course there have been cessations, here and there, just as there have been cessations of faith and decays of holy living ; just as there are cessations of spiritual influence for the same reason ; though no one supposes, on that account, that the work of the Holy Spirit has been discontinued, and requires to be reinsti- tuted in order to be an existing fact. There is no likelihood that a miraculous dispensation would be restored after being quite passed by and lost. But there may be casual suspensions and reappearances, sometimes in one place and sometimes in another, that are quite consistent with the conviction that the dispensation is perpetual, never withdrawn, and never to be withdrawn.

1 *Works*, vol. x. p. 230.

And this, on very deliberate and careful search, appears to be the true opinion. We are able too, it will be seen, to verify this opinion by abundant facts. Of course it is not implied, if we assert the continuance of these supernatural demonstrations in all ages, that they will, in our time, be mere repetitions, or formal continuations, of those which distinguished the apostolic age; it must be enough that such works appear in forms adapted to our particular time and stage of advancement. Many persons demand that Christianity shall do precisely the same things which it did, or claims to have done, in the first times; not observing that the doing of a given thing is commonly a good reason why it should not be done again, and that the great law of adaptation, which is a first law of reason, will always require that there should be a change of administration, correspondent with our changes of stage or condition. No one ever charges it as a defect of evidence for the supernatural gift of the decalogue, that God has not continued, since that day, to give decalogues from every hill. On the contrary, when Christ appears, taking away, in some sense, the first covenant, that he may establish the second, we recognize a degree of evidence for both in the fact itself that there is a show of progress in the transition. This progress of manner and kind we want in things supernatural, as well as in things natural; else, if God were for ever to repeat his old works in their old forms, we should have a dull time of existence. What, then, if it should appear that our prophesyings, interpretations, healings, and other such gifts, have so far disguised their form as to be sometimes recognized only with difficulty? Instead of discovering an objection to Christianity in the fact, what have we in it, possibly, but a confirmation of its rational evidence? And yet it is chiefly remarkable, that the forms of the gifts are continued with so little apparent variation.

It is very obvious, or ought to be, beforehand, that these prodigies are not Christianity; the substance is not in them; they are only signs and tokens of the substance. Their propagation, therefore, is no principal interest of Christianity, and the living power of Christianity is never to be tested by their frequency, or the impressiveness of their operations. There may evidently be too many of them, as well as too few. As soon as they begin to be taken for things principal, or for the real substance, they become idols and hindrances to faith.

When the world that ought to be repenting is taken up with staring, the sobriety of faith is lost in the gospel of credulity. And then, instead of a solid, ever-during reign of Providence, that is governing the world in the interest of Christianity, we should have a glittering firework around us, that really governs nothing, has no power to regenerate souls, or strengthen the kingdom of Christ in the earth. Indeed, we actually see this olly beginning, in a very short time, to get possession of men's minds, and find the apostles, on that account, contending most deliberately against it.[1] It was a great evil that so many were more ready to figure in the gifts, or go after and admire the gifts, than to live by faith, and walk with Christ, and bear fruits meet for repentance.

It is our impression, to speak frankly, that the party of dis continuance, and the party of restoration, and the party also of denial, who make so much of the fact that these prodigies are gone by, and are even conceded to be now incredible, do all concur in a partial misconception of their place in God's eco nomy, and of their relative importance to it. To distinguish truly their office, we need to consider the two opposite extremes of character to which they are related. We are never to look at God's means, as being perfect or not in themselves ; they are good only as medicine for a fevered and disordered nature in man, requiring also to be increased or withdrawn, according to the oscillations of that imperfect and disjointed nature, as it swings to this or that opposite of excess.

To see how these gifts operate, or what place they fill, let us suppose it to be an accepted fact that God is reigning in a grand supernatural scheme of order, and governing the world, externally and in souls, for Christianity's sake ; let it be under stood and asserted that, even in things supernatural, God rules by eternal and fixed laws ; and it will not be long before the sottish habit of remaining sin will begin to settle even Christian souls into a stupor of intellectual fatality. Does not everything continue as it was from the beginning ? Prayer becomes a kind of dumb-bell exercise, good as exercise, but never to be answered. The word is good to be exegetically handled, but there is no light of interpretation in souls, more immediate ; all truth is to be second-hand truth, never a vital beam of God's own light. To subside into sacraments, that are only priestly

1 Cor. xii.-xv.

manipulations, is now easy. The drill of repetitions it is more readily hoped will wear into the rock, than that grace will dissolve it. A church-worship is easily taken for piety. Or, if there be no external change of the modes of religion, it is itself lowered and disempowered, as much as if a lower and more earthly form were chosen. All the possibilities are narrowed and shrunk away. Expectation is gone—God is too far off, too much imprisoned by laws, to allow expectation from Him. The Christian world has been gravitating, visibly, more and more, toward this vanishing point of faith, for whole centuries, and especially since the modern era of science began to shape the thoughts of men by only scientific methods. Religion has fallen into the domain of the mere understanding, and so it has become a kind of wisdom not to believe much, therefore to expect as little.

Now it is this descent to mere rationality that makes an occasion for the signs and wonders of the Spirit. The unbelieving and false spirit in half-sanctified minds, converts order into immobility, laws into lethargy, and the piety that ought to be strong because God is great, grows turbid and weak under His greatness. Let Him now break forth in miracle and holy gifts, let it be seen that He is still the living God, in the midst of His dead people, and they will be quickened to a resurrection by the sight. Now they see that God can do something still, and has His liberty. He can hear prayers, He can help them triumph in dark hours, their bosom-sins He can help them master, all His promises in the Scripture He can fulfil, and they go to Him with great expectations. They see, in these gifts, that the Scripture stands, that the graces, and works, and holy fruits of the apostolic age, are also for them. It is as if they had now a proof experimental of the resources embodied in the Christian plan. The living God, immediately revealed, and not historically only, begets a feeling of present life and power, and religion is no more a tradition, a second-hand light, but a grace of God unto salvation, operative now.

But it will shortly begin to be decerned, now that the sin-spirit is weak on the opposite side, and runs to the opposite excess. Before, it went back to the understanding, to nature, and to general unbelief. Now it rushes on to fanaticism, and has even a pride in believing things really incredible. It does not follow, because one heals the sick, or speaks with tongues, that he is therefore clear of his moral infirmities as a fallen man. He is taken with the stare of multitudes, gives way to a subtle ambition, magnifies overmuch his particular gift, runs into shows of conceit, grows impatient of contradiction, and loosens the rage of passion—by that, driving himself into even wild excesses both of opinion and practice—and finally coming to a full end, as one burnt up in the fierceness of his own heat. As before, without the miracles and the gifts, religion went down to extinction, under the wear of mere routine, so now the miracles and the gifts have issued in a wild Corinthianism, which whole chapters of apostolic lecture can hardly reduce to sobriety. And the result is, that now all the supernatural de monstrations are brought into disrespect, and a process begins of oscillation backward, to the ordinary and regular; then toward rationalism again, unbelief, and spiritual impotence.

Now, between these two kinds of excess, the Church is always swinging, and by a kind of moral necessity must be. It is not that God's administration is irregular and desultory, but that such is the unsteadiness and unreliableness of our poor disjointed humanity. The oscillation back toward order and reason is commonly longer and more gradual; that toward miracles and gifts shorter and sharper, because there is more heat and celerity in it, and less time is requisite to bring it to its limit.

It need hardly be observed that every outbreak of supposed miracle and supernatural demonstration has run its career in just this manner. It has begun with a most fervent seeking unto God, and a remarkable singleness of devotion to Christ. The mighty works appeared as revelations of divine power, scarcely expected by the subjects themselves, and there was no excess, except as the ideas and maxims of a non-expectant piety in the Church were scandalized by such displays of God. But there was no sufficient balance in the moral infirmities of a state of sin to keep down the passions, and hold in check the wildness of conceit, and the consequence was, that the subjects, unable to distinguish what was from God, and what from them selves, took their thoughts for oracles, and their fancies for visions, and very shortly ran the true work of God in them, into the ground. So it has been hitherto, and so it probably will be, till some age or state is reached, where men are suffi ciently modulated and sobered by truth, to have the heavenly gifts in terms of heavenly order, and be fired with all highest mountings of love, without setting on fire also the course of nature, in their corrupted hearts and bodies. Then the oscilla tions of which we have spoken will cease, the ordinary and regular life will be raised up to meet the extraordinary, and become a state of immediate divine knowledge and experience. Then the extraordinary, the miracles and gifts, will lose out their explosive violence, and become the steady, calculable quantities of a really godly life. That is the true kingdom of God, fulfilled in its idea—His tabernacle pitched with men. Life is now an open state of first-hand experience, full of God, where the young men see visions, and the old men dream dreams, without becoming either visionary or dreamy in their excesses; where feeling and reason coalesce, and the dear humility of love chastens all the flaming victories of faith and prayer.

It has been a very common thing with Christian teachers, and even with the writers of deliberate history, to discredit all appearances of supernatural wonders, such as miracles and spiritual gifts, because they make so bad a figure in the end. Whereas the true, and only true test of them is their beginning. We may as well test the opposite oscillation in this manner, and because it ends in the state of unbelief and all impotence— a religion without life and sanctifying power—have it as our conclusion that the convictions of order and holy regularity, which it set up at the beginning, are a dismal and cold illusion, dishonoured by its fruits. It is, doubtless, true that, as men judge, the excesses of fanaticism are less respectable than the excesses of deadness and immobility. It is so, because the common vote of the world is on that side, making it always a most creditable thing to live in such deadness to God and all holy things, as answers no one of the intelligent uses of life. But whoever ponders thoughtfully the question, will find ample room to doubt, which is really widest of a just respect, the excesses of fanaticism and false fire, or the comatose and dull impotence of a religion that worships God without expectation.

It may occur to some, to raise the question, why it is, that the lying wonders of necromancy, and magic, and demoniacal possessions are wont to be grouped contemporaneously with the true wonders of prophecy and divine gifts. The answer is readily supplied by the general solution of the subject here offered. The two kinds, probably, are not strictly contempo raneous, and it is very likely that the bad wonders will precede the others; even as they seem to do just at this particular crisis. For, after all the facts and functions of religion are reduced to a second-hand character—a reported history, a contrived and reasoned dogma, a drill of observances, where no fire burns, and no glimpses into eternity are opened by visions and revelations of the Lord, or where no God appears to be found, who is nigh enough to support expectation in His wor shippers—then, at length, even the outer people of unbelief begin to ache in the sense of vacuity, and there, not unlikely, the pain is first felt. Their religious and supernatural instincts have been so long defrauded, that it would be a kind of satisfac tion to get the silence broken, if only by some vision of a ghost — anything to show or set open the world unknown. They would even go hunting, with Clement, for some one to raise them a spirit. Hence the strange zeal observable in the new sorcery of our day. Why, it shows the other world as a living fact! proves immortality! does more than any gospel ever did to certify us of these things! But the secret of this greedy, undistinguishing haste of delusion is the sharpness of the previous appetite; and that was caused by the abstinence of long privation. We had so far come into the kingdom of nullities—calling it the kingdom of God—we had become so rational, and gotten even God's own liberty into such close terms of natural order, that the immediate, living realities of religion, or religious experience, were under a doom of suppres sion. It was as if there were no atmosphere to breathe, and the minds most remote from the impressions and associations of piety naturally enough felt the hunger first. Which hunger, alas! they are thinking to feed, by a superstitious trust, in the badly written, silly oracles of our new-discovered, scientific necromancy. But the Church also, or Christian discipleship, begins of course to ache with the same kind of pain, feeling after some way out of the dulness of a second-hand faith, and the dryness of a merely reasoned gospel, and many of the most longing, most expectant souls, are seen waiting for some livelier, more apostolic demonstrations. They are tired, beyond bearing, of the mere school forms and defined notions; they want some kind of faith that shows God in living commerce with men, such as He vouchsafed them in the former times. And if we

can trust their report, they are not wholly disappointed. Probably enough, therefore, there may just now be coming forth
a more distinct and widely-attested dispensation of gifts and
miracles, than has been witnessed for centuries. If so, it will
raise great expectations of the speedy and last triumph of holi
ness in the earth. But these expectations may be delayed.
By and by the subjects of the gifts, or those who think to go
beyond them, may begin to approach the bad extreme on this
side. Ambition may stimulate pretence, and the false heat of
passion. Then come wild excesses ; then a general collapse,
in which the wonders cease. And perhaps only this may be
gained ; that the sense of something more immediate than a
religion of second causes has been burned into Christian souls,
which it will take a century or two to exhaust. However, as
the sense of laws becomes more pervasively fixed in human
thought, it is allowed us to believe that, as the gifts are them
selves dispensed by fixed laws, the Church will gradually come
to be in them in that manner, and hold them in the even way
of intelligence.

Holding this general view of miracles and supernatural gifts,
it should not surprise us to find sporadic cases reported here and
there, in this or that age of the world ; as little, to fall on
periods in the Church history, where large bodies of disciples,
driven out into exile, or persecuted and hunted in their own
country, are brought so close to God, and opened so completely
to His Spirit, as to become prophets and doers of mighty works.
It may not be true in any age of the world, and probably is
not, that such gifts are absolutely discontinued ; so that no
supernatural wonder of any kind takes place. Such wonders
will vary their form ; but in some form, scriptural or provi
dential, ancient or new, social or only personal, they could be
distinguished probably by any one having a sufficient knowledge
of facts.

What is wanted, therefore, on this subject, in order to any
sufficient impression, is a full, consecutive inventory of the su
pernatural events or phenomena of the world. There is reason
to suspect that many would, in that case, be greatly surprised
by the commonness of the instances. Could they be collected
and chronicled, in their real multitude, what is now felt to be
their strangeness would quite vanish away, and possibly they
would even seem to recur, much as in the more ancient times

of the world. But no such revision of history is possible. The material is accessible only in the most partial manner, and if it were all at hand, could not be managed, or even be summed up in such a recapitulation as our present limits will permit

The first thing arrived at, by any one who prosecutes this kind of inquiry, apart from all prepossessions and saws of tradition, will certainly be, that the clumsy assumption commonly held, of a cessation of the original apostolic gifts, at about some given date, is for ever exploded ; for, as in fact they never consented to be stayed or concluded by any given time, so in history they persist in running by all time, till finally the investigator, unable to set down any date after which they were not comes into the discovery that the stream is a river, flowing continuously through all ages, and always to flow. He could not give us the wonders of Ignatius, Polycarp, Justin Martyr, Athenagoras, Irenæus, Tertullian, Origen, and there declare the point of cessation to be reached. He would not come down to Cyprian or Augustine, and settle it there, or down to Paul the Hermit, and settle it there. The dreams of Huss, the prophesyings of Luther, and Fox, and Archbishop Usher, the ecstasies t Xavier, with innumerable other wonders, and visitations of God, in the saints of the Church, during all the intervening ages bridge the gulf between us and the ancient times, and bring us to a question of miracles and gifts, as a question of our own day and time. Such demonstrations became more nearly frivolous, when everything was frivolous, and more visibly infected with superstition when the Church itself fell under the shadow of this baleful power ; but, though the evidences of supernatural facts were correspondently diminished, there was never any sufficient reason for the conclusion that they were quite gone by and finally discontinued.

It has been a subject of wonder that Mr Newman, with all his remarkable powers as a writer and a man of genius, should venture on the deliberate attempt to vindicate the authenticity of the Church miracles. And, probably enough, it is a fair subject of wonder, considering that his purpose required him to vindicate as well those which are trivial and ridiculous as those which wear the dignity of truth and reason. His argument must, of course, break down under such a load of absurdities ; but it does not follow that a more discriminative argument, unencumbered by Church restrictions, would not fare differently.

Descending now to the times we call modern, the times, for example, subsequent to the Reformation, nothing is easier, exactly contrary to the very common impression, than to show that the same kind of prodigies are current here, in the last three, as in the first three centuries of the Church.   Whoever has read that Christian classic, *The Scots Worthies*, has followed a stream of prophecies, and healings, and visible judgments, and specific answers to prayer, and discernments of spirits, corre sponding, at all points, with the gifts and wonders of the apos tolic age.   And the men that figure in these gifts and powers, are the great names of the heroic age of religion in their coun try—Wishart, Knox, Erskine, Craig, Davidson, Simpson, Welch, Guthrie, Blair, Welwood, Cameron, Cargill, and Peden.   And it is a curious fact, in regard to this great subject, that, while we believe so little and deny so much, and hold so many oppo site assumptions, this same book of Howie, that chronicles in beautiful simplicity more gifts and wonders than all of Irving's, is published by one of the largest and most conservative bodies of Christians in our country, and is read by thousands, young and old, with eager delight.   Is it that we like miracles and supernatural wonders, so far off that we need not, or that we can, believe them ?

At a later period, on the repeal of the edict of Nantz, and in the persecutions that followed, a large body of the Protestant or Reformed disciples, called Huguenots, hunted by their pur suers, fled to the mountains of Cevennes.   Some of them also escaped to England and other Protestant countries.   Among these unhappy people the miraculous gifts were developed, and by them were more or less widely disseminated abroad.   They had tongues and interpretations of tongues.   They had healings and the discerning of spirits.   They prophesied in the Spirit. Intelligent persons went out from Paris, to hear, observe, and make inquiry, and these people were much discussed as " Les Trembleurs des Cevennes."   In England they were also dis cussed as the " French Prophets," and the fire they kindled in England caught among some of the English disciples, and burned for many years.[1]

About forty years after this appearing of the gifts among the Huguenots, a very similar development appeared among the Catholic or Jansenist population of Paris.   Cures began to be

[1] *Morning Watch*, vol. iv. p. 383.

wrought at the tomb of St Medard, and particularly of persons afflicted with convulsions. And as the Jansenists were, at this time, under persecution at the hands of the Jesuits, and bearing witness, as they believed, for the truth of Christ, it is not won derful that they began to be exercised, much as the Huguenots of the Cevennes had been. They had the gift of tongues, the discerning of spirits, and the gift of prophesying. These were called "Convulsionnaires de Saint Medard," because of the ecstatic state into which they seemed to be raised.[1]

The sect of Friends, from George Fox downward, have had it as a principle to expect gifts, revelations, discernings of spirits, and indeed a complete divine movement. Thus Fox, over and above his many revelations, wrought, as multitudes believed, works of healing in the sick. Take the following references from the Index of his "Journal," as affording, in the briefest form, a conception of the wonders he was supposed, and sup posed himself to have wrought:—"Miracles wrought by the power of God—the lame made whole—the diseased restored— A distracted woman healed—A great man given over by physi cians restored—Speaks to a sick man in Maryland, who was raised up by the Lord's power—Prays the Lord to rebuke J. C.'s infirmity, and the Lord by His power soon gave him ease."

Led on thus by Fox, the Friends have always claimed the continuance of the original gifts of the Spirit in the apostolic age, and have looked for them, we may almost say, in the ordi nary course of their Christian demonstrations. We are not surprised, therefore, to find such a man of policy and incompar able shrewdness as Isaac T. Hooper, believing as firmly in the prophetic gifts of his friend, Arthur Howell, as in those of Isaiah or Paul. This Howell was a preacher and leather-currier in Philadelphia, a man of perfect integrity in all the business of his life, and also a most gentle and benignant soul, in all his intercourse and society with men. One Sunday morning, on his way to Germantown, he met a funeral proces sion, when, knowing nothing of the deceased, "it was suddenly revealed to him," so says the history, "that the occupant of the coffin before him was a woman, whose life had been saddened by the suspicion of a crime which she never committed. The impression became strong on his mind, that she wished him to make certain statements at her funeral. When the customary

1 *Morning Watch*, vol. iv. p. 385.

services were finished, Arthur Howell rose and asked permis
sion to speak. " I did not know the deceased even by name,"
said he, " but it is given me to say that she suffered much, and
unjustly. Her neighbours generally suspected her of a crime
that she did not commit; and, in a few weeks from this time,
it will be clearly made manifest that she was innocent. A few
hours before her death, she talked on this subject with the
clergyman who attended upon her, and who is now present;
and it is now given me to declare the communication she made
to him on that occasion."

He then proceeded to relate the particulars of the interview;
to which the clergyman listened with evident astonishment.
When the communication was finished, he said, " I do not know
who this man is, or how he has obtained information on this sub
ject; but certain it is, that he has repeated, word for word, a
conversation which I supposed was known only to myself and
the deceased." [1] The explanation came, it is added, in exact
accordance with Howell's promise.

We are brought down, thus, to our own age and time—is it
credible that the apostolic gifts and all the original wonders of
the Church are extant, or in real bestowment, even now? My
argument does not imperatively require it of me to go this
length, and say that they are. It is only a little better sus
tained on the supposition that they are. I am well aware, at
the same time, that a sober recapitulation of what appear to be
the facts of the question, will appear to many to be even a
kind of weakness. Enough that, consciously to myself, it re
quires a much stronger balance of equilibrium, and a much
firmer intellectual justice, saying nothing of the necessary
courage, to report these facts, without any protestations of
dissent or discredit, than it would to toss them by, with
derision, in compliance with the mere conventional notions, and
current judgments of the times. I shall therefore dare to re
port as true, facts which neither I nor anybody else has even
so much as a tolerable show of reason for denying or treating
with lightness.

How many cases of definite answers to prayers, such as are
reported in the cases of Stilling, Franke, and others, are brought
to our knowledge every week in the year. Cases of definite
premonition are reported so familiarly and circumstantially, as

[1] *Life of Isaac T. Hooper*, pp. 258-260.

to make a considerable item in the newspaper literature of our time. Prophecies of good men, or sometimes of poets and other literary men, are so often and particularly fulfilled, as to be the common wonder of the merely curious, who profess no faith in their verity, as communications from God. Dreams are reported, how often, foreshadowing facts, in a manner so peculiar, as to forbid any supposition of accident under condi tions of chance. The state of trance is exemplified in Flavel and Tennent, and indeed hundreds of others, as remarkably as in Paul in his vision of the third heaven. Cases are reported in every community, where the defiant wrath of blasphemy has been suddenly struck down, as by some bolt of invisible judg ment ; others, where a slowly coming retribution has so exactly retaliated the shape of a sin, as to raise the impression, that nothing but some directing will of God can account for the correspondence. A great sensation was made in the Christian world, only a few years ago, by the recurrence of tongues, heal ings, prophecies, and other gifts, both in London, as connected with the preaching of Mr Irving, and at Port-Glasgow in Scot land, in the more humble but not less respectable demonstra tions of the two MacDonalds. The question has been very summarily disposed of, and the conclusion has been generally taken, that these reported cases of spiritual gifts were un worthy of credit—mere hallucinations of the parties concerned. On a deliberate revision of the question, I am induced to admit, and, since I have it, to express a very different impression. These MacDonalds, for example, are men of unimpeachable character, one of them, as will be seen, from the cogent articles he wrote, remonstrating against the new Churchism taken up at length by Mr Irving, a man of great calmness, and remarkably well poised in the balance of his understanding. And yet this man is not only gifted with a power of healing the sick, but he is overtaken unexpectedly with the strange gift of tongues; viz., an ecstatic utterance, in words and sounds, which neither he, nor any that hear him, understand. Now there is nothing in this apparent gibberish, that could anyhow become a tempta tion to the enthusiast or the pretender. It seems, at first view, to be an exercise so wide of intelligence, as to create no impres sion of respect. And for just that reason it has the stronger evidence when it occurs ; for, notwithstanding all that is said by the commentators about tongues imparted for the preaching of the gospel, I have found no one of all the reported cases of tongues, in which the tongue was intelligible, either to the speaker or the hearers, except as it was made so by a supernatural interpretation—which accords exactly, also, with what is said of tongues in the New Testament. And yet, on second thought, they have all the greater dignity and propriety, for just the reason that they require another gift to make them intelligible. For this gift of tongues, representing the Divine Spirit as play ing the vocal organs of a man, which are the delivering powers of intelligence in his organization, is designed to be a symbol to the world of the possibility and fact of a divine access to the soul, and a divine operation in it—a symbol more expressive, in fact, than any other could be. And then it is the more exactly appropriate in its adaptation, that it wants another gift in the hearer, exactly correspondent, to understand it or give the interpretation. For so it is with all revelations of the Spirit, they are not only uttered or penned by inspiration, but they want a light of the Spirit in the receiver, to really appre hend their power. Not even the prophets understood their visions. Besides, there is, I know not what, sublimity in this gift of tongues, as related to the great mystery of language ; suggesting, possibly, that all our tongues are from the Eternal Word, in souls ; there being, in his intelligent nature as Word, millions doubtless of possible tongues, that are as real to him as the spoken tongues of the world.

Tongues were also spoken every week in London, and there was much discussion there of the case, in particular, of Miss Fancourt as a case of healing. She was a cripple, reduced to a bed-ridden state, by a curve of the spine, and the painful dis order of almost all the joints of her body. She had been lying for two years on a couch, padded and curved, to suit her dis torted form. Her family belonged to the Established Church, and she was herself a deeply Christian person. A Christian friend, who had been greatly interested in her behalf, called one evening, when the subject of miraculous healing was discussed. The friend, Mr Graves. was a believer in such gifts, but Mr Fancourt, the father, a genuinely Christian person, was not. After a time he disappeared, and during his absence from the room, Mr G. arose, as Miss F. supposed, to take his leave. But instead of the " good-night " she expected, he commanded her to stand on her feet and walk. Forthwith she rose up, stood, walked, was clear of her pains, took on all the characters of a well person, and so continued. A great discussion was raised immediately in the public journals, and particularly between the *Morning Watch* and the *Christian Observer ;* in which the *Observer* took precisely the ground of Mr Hume, as respects the credibility of miracles performed now ; insisting that henceforth, since the Scripture time, " we must admit any solution rather than a miracle." Little wonder is it that we have difficulty in sustaining the historic facts of Christianity, when the most Christian, most evangelic teachers, assume so readily the utter incredibility of any such gifts and wonders as the gospels report, and as they themselves have it for a righte ousness to believe.

But the doubt will be thrust upon us here, at the outset, as we come down to our own times—and it might as well be dis cussed here, before we proceed to other cases in hand—whether such things are really credible now, or entitled to even so much as the respectful consideration of thinking men. And I make no question that the class called thinking men in our age will be ready, with few exceptions, to reject, in the gross, and with out hesitation, all such pretended facts. They are the illusions, it will be said, of ignorant minds, weakened by superstition, heated by religious enthusiasm ; stories that are published, it may be, with honest intentions, but which any philosopher will dismiss without a moment's consideration.

But whoever is ready, in this manner, I reply, to erect the thinking men of an age into a tribunal of authoritative judg ment on such questions, has studied history to little purpose. There certainly is such a thing as religious delusion, or a faith of ignorance, in the world, and the humbler class of people are somewhat more exposed to this kind of infirmity. But their demonstrations have never been as eccentric, or their mistakes as contagious, or as difficult to rectify, as those of the thinking class. In matters of thought and opinion, there is no end either to the new crudities generated, or the newer criticisms by which they are extirpated. New types of thought sway the successive ages. One school or system expels another. No. thing rests, nothing gets a final form, in which it either can or ought to stand. The thinking and educated class of minds, too, are less capable of many truths, because they are so generally preoccupied, wittingly or unwittingly, by a contrary fashion, and have such an explicit faith in what the learned world pretends just then to have settled. On which account our Saviour Himself was obliged to seek His adherents, and raise up His apostles, among the ingenuous and humble poor, saying—I thank Thee, O Father, Lord of heaven and earth, that thou hast hid these things from the wise and prudent, and hast revealed them unto babes. The wise and prudent knew so much, as even to be incapable of faith in Him ; and if there had been no other class but these learned gentlemen, these thinking men of their time, He would scarcely have left a follower. But the fishermen, the babes of poverty, were less preoccupied, and capable of better things. And for just this reason, abating their greater exposure to fantastic and extrava gant delusions, it will be found, as a matter of fact, that the gospel of Christ has been more genuinely and evenly held, among this class, than it has among the professors and learned disciples. They testify one faith, and live one common life of grace, in all ages.

In view of considerations like these, how much does it signify, that the thinking men of our time are so ready to pro nounce on the incredibility, or even inadmissibility, of the supernatural facts just referred to ? Nothing, it may be, but simply this ; that the human mind, as educated mind, is just now at the point of religious apogee ; where it is occupied, or preoccupied by nature, and cannot think it rational to suppose that God does anything longer, which exceeds the causalities of nature. Is there, in this, any proper ground of assurance, that, within fifty years from this time, it will not be set in a position to regard the faith of supernatural facts, as being even necessary to the rationality, and the complete system of the universe ? If, as I have shown, by the argument here constructed, we act supernaturally ourselves, and if the fact of sin supposes a higher ground of unity in God's plan than is comprehended in mere nature, what less ought we to expect, than that, when the thinking mind of the world has finally worn a way through nature, ceasing to be hampered and shut in by it as now, it will strike into a broader field, and be as ready to believe these supernatural facts, as it is at present to reject them ? Indeed, there is a kind of law in scepticism itself that must finally bring it back from its denial of a supernatural revelation to a hearty and hungry embrace of it ; for, no longer staggered by the supposition, as thousands now are, that the Scriptures re present a dispensation gone by, which is henceforth incredible, it will finally discover that they may be rationally believed, for just the reason that God is doing similar wonders now. And as certainly as no human soul can rest in mere negation, or, what is no better, in nature as the only medium and symbol of religion, this discovery will be made. There are, in fact, two roads into this faith; the direct road, and the indirect or round about road of doubt and denial. One is taken by the humble, godly souls, whose only want it is to find their Lord, and walk with Him; these go straight into His seat, know Him in His private testimony, and the glorious induement of His power. The others, wanting only to find Him scientifically, begin at nature, jealous of all but nature. They go round and round their idol, looking to find a Creator, and Christianity, and a present living God in it, and, after they have torn their feet long enough, in beating through the briars of scientific reason, they will finally come in, as laggards, weary and sore, and join themselves to the little ones of faith, saying truly, "This, after all, is reason; to believe the Scriptures, just because the God of the Scriptures is the God of to-day; as conversible now as ever, working as mightily, redeeming as gloriously; to believe in the supernatural, too, because we believe in nature; which, without and apart from this necessary complement, were only a worthless abortion, a fraction whose integer is lost."

It is also a matter worthy of particular note, when we are falling into the impression, that a verdict of the thinking men of our time is entitled to authority on such a question as this, that we have so many characters in history which they can no way interpret, and which are, in fact, impossible to exist under their theory. How awkwardly do they handle such characters, and how poorly do they get on in their attempts to solve, or even to conceive them. Joan of Arc, for instance—who has not observed the strange figure of imbecility made by the mo dern school of literary unbelief, in the attempt to find a place for any such character? They can do nothing with her. In their view, she is impossible. And yet she has a place in his tory, and enters into the public life of the French nation, as a determining cause of great events, in the same manner as Charle magne or any celebrated commander. She is a phenomenon, for which naturalism has no account, and which, under that kind of philosophy, had no right to happen. It can say that she was a prodigy of straw got up by the leaders, who sought in that manner to retrieve the desperate state of their cause; or, that she was insane, or that she was romantic, or that she was a nervous and flighty girl, doing she scarce knew what, or, finally, that she is a myth, and no real personage. And yet the history laughs at all such wisdom, showing us a character real and true, that refuses to be explained by any such feeble inven tions in the plane of nature, and can be nowise comprehended in that manner. She begins to be intelligible only when she is classed with Deborah, as a chieftain called out from the retirment of her sex, by the election of God, and prepared, supernaturally, in the place of secret vision.

The same thing, in general, may be said of the interpreters of Cromwell. Nothing can be made of him as a mere natural man. Hume and Clarendon call him a religious hypocrite, as if a hypo crite could be a hero? Lamartine, simply because he believes in a light which is not church light, calls him a fanatic. Carlyle is wiser, and, as far as possible, contrives to let him report himself; but as soon as he chances to loosen his own self-reten tion, for a moment, and let us see the man through his panthe istic glasses, a strange letting down will be observed, however slight or casual the glimpse taken—it is Cromwell by moon light, and not the real hero. He ceases to be inspired, and begins to phosphoresce. He is no more a battle-axe, swung by the Lord Almighty, but one that lays on automatically, with force enough to make us think that he is. He is great in his faith, only it turns out that his faith, meeting no real object, is, though he thinks it not, a merely subjective impulse. Known to be a stout predestinarian, he is fitly shown to be a thunder-shock in battle, as by the momentum of God's eternal will in his person; only it is recollected that predestination, by God, is more philosophically phrased by the single word destiny; a force without will, or counsel, or end. He is great in power, therefore invincible, irresistible, as being set on by the universal Nobody. Is this Cromwell? No genuine Cromwell is found, till he is shown by the side of Moses, a man who takes power as a burden set upon him by God, and wields it only the more sternly and faithfully as power; a man "not eloquent," but "slow of speech," coming down out of the mount, where God has taught him, to be the leader, liberator, and lawgiver of his people. This is the view of Cromwell toward which historic criticism runs more and more distinctly, and when, at some future day, our literature has gotten over the shallows of natural ism, and dares to speak of faith, this will be the Cromwell shown. He may not be counted a man equal to Moses, but all that is most distinctive and greatest in his life will as certainly be referred to a supernatural and divine movement in him.

And how many characters are there in the history of our modern world who can as little be conceived on the footing of mere nature as these ! Savonarola, " the fanatic" of history, will emerge, not unlikely, clad in the honours of a prophet. So of Columbus, Fenelon, Fox, Franke, and a thousand others, who walked, consciously or unconsciously, by a supernatural in stigation—they were nothing, it will be seen, save by the secret inspiration that bore them on. And how many of God's little ones, living and dying in obscurity, have yet done as great won- ders in His name as if they had been teachers and heroes !

But why is it, some will ask, that we have only to hear of these things, and do not see them ? Why must we know them only through a degree of distance that takes away knowledge ? But the truth is not exactly so. We come a great deal closer to them than we think. Having had this great question of super natural fact upon my hands now for a number of years, in a determination also to be concluded by no mere conventionalities, to observe, inquire, listen, and judge, I have been surprised to find how many things were coming to my knowledge and ac quaintance that most persons take it for granted are utterly incredible, except in what they call the age of miracles and apostolic gifts ; that is, in the first three centuries of the Church. Indeed, they are become so familiar, after only a few years of attention thus directed, and without inquiring after them, that their unfamiliar and strange look is gone ; they even appear to belong, more or less commonly, to the Church and the general economy of the Spirit.

I will instance, first of all, a case not so clearly religious, but explicable in no way, by the mere causalities of nature. As I sat by the fire, one stormy November night, in a hotel parlour, in the Napa Valley of California, there came in a most vener able and benignant looking person, with his wife, taking their seats in the circle. The stranger, as I afterwards learned, was Captain Yonnt, a man who came over into California, as a

trapper, more than forty years ago.   Here he has lived, apart
from the great world and its questions, acquiring an immense
landed estate, and becoming a kind of acknowledged patriarch
in the country.   His tall, manly person, and his gracious.
paternal look, as totally unsophisticated in the expression, as if
he had never heard of a philosophic doubt or question in his
life, marked him as the true patriarch.   The conversation turned,
I know not how, on spiritism and the modern necromancy, and
he discovered a degree of inclination to believe in the reported
mysteries.   His wife, a much younger and apparently Christian
person, intimated that probably he was predisposed to this
kind of faith, by a very peculiar experience of his own, and
evidently desired that he might be drawn out by some intelli
gent discussion of his queries.

At my request he gave me his story.   About six or seven
years previous, in a mid-winter's night, he had a dream, in
which he saw what appeared to be a company of emigrants,
arrested by the snows of the mountains, and perishing rapidly
by cold and hunger.   He noted the very cast of the scenery,
marked by a huge perpendicular front of white rock cliff; he
saw the men cutting off what appeared to be tree tops, rising
out of deep gulfs of snow ; he distinguished the very features
of the persons, and the look of their particular distress.   He
woke, profoundly impressed with the distinctness and apparent
reality of his dream.   At length he fell asleep, and dreamed
exactly the same dream again.   In the morning he could not
expel it from his mind.   Falling in shortly with an old hunter
comrade, he told him the story, and was only the more deeply
impressed, by his recognizing, without hesitation, the scenery
of the dream.   This comrade came over the Sierra, by the Car
son Valley Pass, and declared that a spot in the pass answered
exactly to his description.   By this, the unsophisticated patri
arch was decided.   He immediately collected a company of
men, with mules and blankets, and all necessary provisions.
The neighbours were laughing in the meantime at his credulity.
" No matter," said he, " I am able to do this, and I will, for
I verily believe that the fact is according to my dream."   The
men were sent into the mountains, one hundred and fifty miles
distant, directly to the Carson Valley Pass.   And there they
found the company in exactly the condition of the dream, and
brought in the remnant alive.

A gentleman present said, " You need have no doubt of this; for we Californians all know the facts, and the names of the families brought in, who now look upon our venerable friend as a kind of saviour." These names he gave, and the places where they reside, and I found afterwards that the California people were ready everywhere to second his testimony.

Nothing could be more natural than for the good-hearted patriarch himself to add, that the brightest thing in his life, and that which gave him greatest joy, was his simple faith in that dream. I thought also I could see in that joy, the glimmer of a true Christian love and life, into which, unawares to himself, he had really been entered by that faith. Let any one attempt now to account for the coincidences of that dream, by mere natural causalities, and he will be glad enough to ease his labour by the acknowledgment of a supernatural providence.

I fell in also, in that new world, with a different and more directly Christian example, in the case of an acquaintance, whom I had known for the last twenty years; an educated man, in successful practice as a physician; a man who makes no affectations of piety, and puts on no airs of sanctimony; living always in a kind of jovial element, and serving everybody but himself. He laughs at the current incredulity of men respecting prayer, and relates many instances, out of his own experience, to show—for that is his doctrine—that God will certainly hear every man's prayer, if only he is honest in it. Among others, he gave the following:—He had hired his little house, of one room, in a new trading town that was planted last year, agreeing to give a rent for it of ten dollars per month. At length, on the day preceding the rent day, he found that he had nothing in hand to meet the payment, and could not see at all whence the money was to come. Consulting with his wife, they agreed that prayer, so often tried, was their only hope. They went, accordingly, to prayer, and found assurance that their want should be supplied. That was the end of their trouble, and there they rested, dismissing farther concern. But the morning came, and the money did not. The rent owner made his appearance earlier than usual. As he entered the door, their hearts began to sink, whispering that now, for once, they must give it up, and allow that prayer had failed. But before the demand was made, a neighbour coming in, called out the untimely visitor, engaging him in conversation, a few minutes, at the door. Meantime a stranger came in, saying, "Dr ——, I owe you ten dollars, for attending me in a fever, at such a time, and here is the money." He could muster no recollection, either of the man or of the service, but was willing to be convinced, and so had the money in hand, after all, when the demand was made. When Stilling and Franke recite their multitudes of specific answers to prayer, their reports are very hastily discredited by many, because of their strangeness. But I have heard so many examples, personally, of the kind just cited, that I begin to think they are even common.

Nothing is farther off from the Christian expectation of our New England communities than the gift of tongues. So distant is their practical habit from any belief in the possible occurrence, that not even the question occurs to their thought. And yet a very near Christian friend, intelligent in the highest degree, and perfectly reliable to me as my right hand, who was present at a rather private, social gathering of Christian disciples, assembled to converse and pray together, as in reference to some of the higher possibilities of Christian sanctification, relates that, after one of the brethren had been speaking, in a strain of discouraging self-accusation, another present shortly rose, with a strangely beaming look, and, fixing his eye on the confessing brother, broke out in a discourse of sounds, wholly unintelligible, though apparently a true language, accompanying the utterances with a very strange and peculiarly impressive gesture, such as he never made at any other time; coming finally to a kind of pause, and commencing again, as if at the same point, to go over in English, with exactly the same gestures, what had just been said. It appeared to be an interpretation, and the matter of it was, a beautifully emphatic utterance of the great principle of self-renunciation, by which the desired victory over self is to be obtained. There had been no conversation respecting gifts of any kind, and no reference to their possibility. The circle were astounded by the demonstration, not knowing what to make of it. The instinct of prudence threw them on observing a general silence, and it is a curious fact that the public in H —— have never, to this hour, been startled by so much as a rumour of the gift of tongues, neither has the name of the speaker been associated with so much as a surmise of the real or supposed fact, by which he would be, perhaps, unenviably distinguished. It has been a great trial to him, it is said, to submit himself to this demonstration; which has recurred several times.

I have heard also of as many as three distinct cases of heal ing near at hand ; one where a father whose nearly grown-up daughter, supposed to be near to death, under the ravages of a brain fever, was permitted, in answer to his prayers, to see her rise up almost immediately, and the next day walking forth completely well ; one where a bad and dangerous swelling was immediately cured ; another where a sick man was restored, when life was despaired of by his family.

In addition to these more domestic examples, I became acquainted, about two years ago, in a distant part of the world, with an English gentleman, whose faith in the gift of healing had been established by his own personal exercise of it. He was a man whose connexions and culture, whose well-formed, tall, and robust-looking person, whose beautifully simple and humble manners, and whose blameless, universally respected life among strangers not of the same faith, and knowing him only by his virtues and the sacrifices he was making for his opinions, were so many conspiring tokens winning him a char acter of confidence that excluded any rational distrust of his representations. He gave me a full account, in manuscript, of some of the cases in which the healing power appeared to be given him, with liberty to use them, as may best serve the con venience of my present subject.

It became a question with him, soon after his conversion, whether, as he had been healed spiritually, he ought not also to expect and receive the healing of his body by the same faith ; for he had then been an invalid for a long time, with only a slender hope of recovery. After a hard struggle of mind, he was able, dismissing all his prescribed remedies, to throw him self on God, and was immediately and permanently made whole.

At length one of his children, whom he had with him away from home, was taken ill with a scarlet fever. And " now the question was," I give his own words, " what was to be done ? The Lord had indeed healed my own sicknesses, but would he heal my son ? I conferred with a brother in the Lord, who, having no faith in Christ's healing power, urged me to send instantly for the doctor, and despatched his groom on horseback to fetch him. Before the doctor arrived, my mind was filled with revelation on the subject. I saw that I had fallen into a

snare, by turning away from the Lord's healing hand. to lean
on medical skill.   I felt grievously condemned in my con
science.   A fear also fell on me, that if I persevered in this
unbelieving course, my son would die, as his eldest brother had.
The symptoms in both were precisely similar.   The doctor
arrived.   My son, he said, was suffering from a scarlet fever,
and medicine should be sent immediately.   While he stood pre
scribing, I resolved to withdraw the child, and cast him on the
Lord.   And when he was gone, I called the nurse and told her
to take the child into the nursery and lay him on the bed.   I
then fell on my knees confessing the sin I had committed against
the Lord's healing power.   I also prayed most earnestly that it
would please my Heavenly Father to forgive my sin. and to
show that He forgave it, by causing the fever to be rebuked.
I received a mighty conviction that my prayer was heard, and
I arose and went to the nursery, at the end of a long passage,
to see what the Lord had done, and on opening the door, to
my astonishment, the boy was sitting up in his bed, and on see
ing me cried out, ' I am quite well and want to have my dinner.'
In an hour he was dressed, and well, and eating his dinner ;
and when the physic arrived it was cast out of the window.
Next morning the doctor returned, and on meeting me at the
garden gate, he said, ' I hope your son is no worse ?'   ' He is
very well, I thank you,' said I, in reply.   ' What can you
mean ?' rejoined the doctor.   ' I will tell you, come in and sit
down.'   I then told him all that had occurred, at which he
fairly gasped with surprise.   ' May I see your son ?' he asked.
' Certainly, doctor, but I see that you do not believe.'   We
proceeded up stairs, and my son was playing with his brother
on the floor.   The doctor felt his pulse and said, ' Yes, the
fever is gone.'   Finding also a fine, healthy surface on his
tongue, he added, ' Yes, he is quite well, I suppose it was the
crisis of his disease !' "

Another of the cases which he reports shows more fully the
working of his own mind, on the instant of healing.   It was
the case of a poor man's child, who had heard him advocate the
faith of healing, and now that the physician, after attending
him for many months of illness, had given the little patient up,
saying that he could do no more, the parents sent for him, in
their extremity, to come and heal their son.   He replied to the
father, " My dear friend, I cannot heal your son, I can do

nothing to help him. All that I can do is to ask you to kneel down and pray with me, to Christ, that we may know what is His will in this matter." "He immediately knelt down with me," and, the written account continues, "my prayer was a reminding of the Lord Jesus Christ of His mercy to the sick, when He was on the earth, and that He never sent any sick away unhealed. I then presented the petition of the father and mother, that their son might be healed, and besought the Lord to show what His will was in the case. Whilst I was making the supplication, it was revealed to me through the Holy Spirit, that I was to lay hands on the boy, and receiving at the time great faith to do so, I rose and, not wishing to be observed by the father, I laid my hand on the lad's head, and said in a low tone of voice, 'I lay my hand on thee in the name of Jesus Christ.' In an instant I saw colour rush into his pale cheeks, and it seemed as if a glow of health was given, in somuch that I said involuntarily, 'I think your son will recover.' I then hastily left the room. In less than an hour, the mother came to my house and insisted on seeing me, to tell me the wonderful things that had happened to her son. The result was that the boy was about the next day."

The other cases narrated by him are scarcely less remarkable. At the same time, he admits, with characteristic ingenuousness, that no such gift has been vouchsafed him now, for a number of years, and that most of the expectations he had in connexion with the apostolic wonder, thus restored, have been disappointed. What God's design was, in the gift thus temporarily bestowed, is a profound mystery to him, and he submits himself calmly in it to the better, though inscrutable wisdom of God. Probably enough, the reason of his gift was exhausted in affording, to these truths of faith, that evidence which is necessary to their just equilibrium.

I have hesitated much whether to speak of a case that, in all its varied stages, has been under my own personal inspection, and I am decided by the consideration that, while it shows no healing, by a gift, it does show, only the more convincingly, a supernatural grace of healing entered into the faith of the subject herself. She is an intelligent, well-educated young woman, of a more than commonly strong and somewhat restive natural temperament, the daughter of a Christian man, living in rather depressed circumstances, but profoundly respected for his character. Eleven years ago this daughter, who before had begun to show symptoms of disease, in a considerable distortion of the spine, became a great sufferer in the still worse complica tions of a hip disease. I have never looked on such scenes of distress in any other case, and hope I may never witness such again. Several times she was given up by her physicians, and her death was expected daily; I should hardly tell the whole truth, if I did not say, longed for, even more constantly. After about two years, however, her disease took a more quiet shape, and the suffering was greatly diminished. Thus she lay for nine long years of helplessness, with both feet drawn up under her, and one of them so close that it was difficult to get in a thickness of cloth under the knee to prevent inflammation. The physicians agreed that there was nothing more to be done, and that she must wait her time; which, after a while she had learned to do, with the sweetest patience and equa nimity. Every impulse in her restive nature was now tamed to God's will, and she blessed the hand which was pressing her so close to the divine friendship. If inquired of, at any time, whether she would like to get well, she uniformly answered, "No;" adding that she was afraid she might not stand fast, but might turn away from her fidelity, in which she was now so profoundly peaceful and happy.

But it occurred to her finally that, if God could restore her, He might also keep her, and the question rose whether she ought not to trust Him. At last, she was beginning to think it might be her duty to believe in God's healing as well as keep ing, and in that manner to pray. Having some attack of acute disease, a physician was called in, and, after the attack was quelled, he began to give some hopeful answers to her queries about the possibility of a restoration of her limbs. Shortly before this, too, her father, who was visited with a great accu mulation of trials, went through an awful struggle with God's justice rising up against Him in agonies of accusation. But he was quelled and comforted, and filled, as the result, with all divinest peace. And shortly after that he had a dream, which presented his daughter as well, completely healed, before him. But it raised no expectation, either then, or afterwards, and he does not refer to it now as having had any connexion at all with the subsequent facts—he does not much confide in dreams. But his daughter was beginning now to believe that she might be made well, and really set herself to it as her settled faith ; and he himself was allowing often the thought that possibly it might somehow be otherwise with her. Remedies were not discarded, but applied faithfully and perseveringly. The pro blem was, how to use natural causes with a faith in super natural helps. In a short time the limbs were brought down, one of them to touch the floor, then both, then she stood, and next she walked. I knew the change that was going on, but, not having seen her for some weeks, I was none the less sur prised, when walking in a neighbouring street, to see her skip- ing down a high flight of steps, with scarcely a perceptible token of lameness. Ask her family now what this means, and by what power it has come to pass, and they answer promptly, " By the power of God." She herself says the same, answering out of her own consciousness. She believes that her physician has done well, and that God sent him to be a minister to her faith, but she declares that she has all the while felt the vigour coming into her by and through her faith, and that, when she first stood, she consciously stood by a divine power, and could no more have stood without the sense of it, or the day before it came, than she could have supported the world. This protes tation of hers I feel bound to honour ; though very well aware that the case may be turned, by saying that the second causes appealed to wrought the cure. But is it not more philosophical, a great deal, to take the inward testimony of the subject, and see the higher consciousness of her faith struggling *with* the re medies, and contributing a force superior, in fact, to all remedies ? Indeed, I have a peculiar satisfaction in the facts of this case, just because the natural and supernatural are so rationally and soundly combined. The problem of their possible concur- ence is evenly held, and there is time enough occupied, in the cure, to show a process. " Go to the pool of Siloam, and wash "—even Christ himself used nature as a means, to pro voke the necessary faith, when nature had, in fact, no virtue in itself.

I cite only one more witness ; a man who carries the manner and supports the office of a prophet, though without claiming the repute of it himself. He is a fugitive from slavery, whose name I had barely heard, but whose character and life have been known to many in our community, for the last twenty years. He called at my door, about the time I was sketching the outline of this chapter, requesting an interview. As I entered the room, it was quite evident that he was struggling with a good deal of mental agitation, though his manner was firm, and even dignified. He said immediately, that he had come to me " with a message from de Lord." I replied, that I was glad if he had any so good thing as that for me, and hoped he would deliver it faithfully. He told me, in terms of great delicacy, and with a seriousness that excluded all appear ance of a design to win his way by flattery, that he had con ceived the greatest personal interest in me, because, in hearing me once or twice, he had discovered that God was teaching me, and discovering Himself to me in a way that was specially hope ful ; and that, for this very reason, he had been suffering the greatest personal burdens of feeling on my account. For more than a year he had been praying for me, and sometimes in the night, because of his apprehension that I had made a false step, and been disobedient to the heavenly vision. During all this time he had been struggling also with the question, whether he might come and see me, and testify his concern for me ? One must be a very poor Christian, not to be deeply touched by such a discovery—one of the humblest of God's children, a stranger, trembling and watching for Him, in his place of obscurity, and daring, only with the greatest difficulty, to come and disburden his heart.

I asked him to explain, and not to suffer any feeling of con straint. In a manner of the greatest deference possible, and with a most singularly beautiful skill, he went on, gathering round his point, and keeping it all the while concealed as he was nearing it, straightening up his tall manly form, dropping out his Africanisms, rising in the port of his language, beaming with a look of intelligence and spiritual beauty, all in a manner to second his prophetic formulas—" The Lord said to me" thus and thus ; " The Lord has sent me to say ;" till I also, as I gazed upon him, was obliged internally to confess, " Verily, Nathan the prophet has come again ! " It was really a scene such as any painter might look a long time to find—such dignity in one so humble ; expression so lofty and yet so gentle and respectful ; the air of a prophet so commanding and posi tive, and yet in such divine authority as to allow no sense of forwardness or presumption.

It came out finally, as the burden of the message, that on a certain occasion, and in reference to a certain public matter, I had undertaken that which could not but withdraw me from God's teaching, and was certain to obscure the revelations otherwise ready and waiting to be made. " Yes," I replied, " but there was nothing wrong in what I undertook to set forward. It brought no scandal on religion. It concerned, you will admit, the real benefit of the public in all future times." " Ah, yes," he answered, " it was well enough to be done, but it was not for you. God had other and better things for you. He was calling you to Himself, and it was yours to go with Him, not to be labouring in things more properly belonging to other men." I had given him the plea by which, drawing on my natural judgment, I had justified myself in going into the en gagement in question. Indeed, to have had any scruple on this account, I have no doubt would be commonly considered by intelligent persons to be even a weakness. And yet, I am obliged to confess to a strong and even prevalent impression that my humble brother was right. For the real stress of his message lay, not so much in the particular instance referred to, as in that more general infirmity or mistake, which the instance might be used to represent ; viz., the tendency of every most earnest soul to be diverted from its aims by things external. His spiritual perceptions were deep enough to lay hold of a general infirmity, which was only the more impressively cor rected by a particular example, and in this manner his piercing words of love were answered by the settled assent of my Chris tian consciousness.

I thanked him for his message, and even looked upon him with a kind of reverence as we parted. I found, on inquiry, that he was a man without blame, industrious, pure, a husband and father, faithful to his office, and always in the same high key of Christian living. But the people of his colour, know ing him well, and having nothing to say against him, could yet offer no opinion at all concerning him. He was plainly enough a strange being to them ; they could make nothing of him. The most they could say was, that he is always the same.

I have since visited him in his little shop, and drawn out of him the story of his life. He became a Christian about the time of his arrival at manhood, and gives a very clear and beautiful account of his conversion. And the Lord, he says,

told him at that time that he should be free, soul and body
To which he answered, " Yea, Lord, I know it." A promise
that was afterwards fulfilled in a very strange and wonderful
deliverance   I observed that in the account he gave me,
he was continually saying, in the manner of the prophet ,
" The Lord said," and " the Lord commanded," and " the
Lord promised," and I called his attention to the fact, asking.
.... ?   Do you hear words audibly
spoken ?   " Oh no."   " What then ?   Do you *think* what appears to be said to you, and call that the saying of the Lord ? "
"Yes, I think it, but that is not all."   " How then do you
know that it is anything more than ———'s thought ? "   " Well,
I know it, I feel it to be not from me, and I can tell you things
that show it to be so;" reciting facts which, if they are true,
prove beyond a question the certainty of some illumination not
of himself.   " Why, then," I asked, " does God teach you in
his manner and not me ?   I feel a strong conviction, some
times, that I am in the will, I know not how, and the d recting
counsel of God but I could never say as you do, ' The Lord
said thus to me.' "   " Ah," said he, " but you have the means,
you can read as I cannot, you have great learning   But I
am a poor ignorant child, and God does with me just as He
an.   Whatever may be thought of his revelations, none, I
think, ill deny im in his reply the credit of a true philosophy.   What can be worthier of God than to be the guide
of this faithful and otherwise dejected man, making up for
                    of ignorance by the fuller and more open vision
.. .. ;

        y   s ould leave a wrong impression were I not to say
that this Christian fugitive, this unlettered body servant, now of
Christ, a once of his   rthly master, 's deep n the wisd
Scriptures, quotes them continually with a remarkable elo
quence and propriety, and with a degree of insight which many
            e uc   preachers might envy.   He also believes
tha God   a..... l d th sick, in many instances, in   ate
connexion with 1   prayers, giving the names and particulars
without scruple.
   Such now are the kinds of religion s exercises and demonstrations that are still extant, even in our own time, in certain
walks of society.   In that humbler stratum of life where the
conventionalities and carnal judgments of the world have le

power, there are characters blooming in the holiest type of Christian love and beauty, who talk and pray, and, as they think, operate apostolically, as if God were all to them that He ever was to the Church in the days of her primitive grace. And it is much to know that, while the higher tiers of the wise and prudent are assuming so confidently the absolute discon tinuance of all apostolic gifts, there are yet, in every age, great numbers of godly souls, and especially in the lower ranges of life, to whom the conventionalities of opinion are nothing, and the walk with God everything, who dare to claim an open state with Him ; to pray with the same expectation, and to speak of faith in the same manner, as if they had lived in the apostolic times. And they are not the noisy, violent class who delight in the bodily exercises that profit little, mistaking the fumes of passion for the revelations of God, but they are, for the most part, such as walk in silence and dwell in the shades of obscurity. And that man has lived to little purpose, who has not learned that what the great world pities, and its teachers disallow, even though mixed with tokens of weakness, is many times deepest in truth, and closest to the real sublimities of life and religion.

That I may not leave a wrong impression, or an impression that is not according to truth, I feel obliged to add, in con cluding this chapter, that I do not seem to be as positive and full in my faith on this subject as I ought to be, and as my arguments themselves may seem to indicate. As regards the general truth that supernatural facts, such as healings, tongues, and other gifts, may as well be manifested now as at any former time, and that there has never been a formal discontinuance, I am perfectly satisfied. I know no proof to the contrary that appears to me to have a straw's weight. And yet, when I come to the question of being in such gifts, or of receiving into easy credit those who appear to be, I acknowledge that, for some reason, either because of some latent subjection to the conventionalities of philosophy, or to the worse conventionalities of sin, belief does not follow, save in a somewhat faltering and equivocal way. Arguments for the possibility are good, but evidences for the fact do not correspond. But there is nothing peculiar in this ; it is even so with many great questions of God and immortality. The arguments are good and clear, but, for some reason, they do not make faith, and we are still surprised to find, in our practice, that we only doubtfully believe. To believe these supernatural things, in the form of particular facts, is certainly difficult; and how conscious are we, as we set ourselves to the questions, of the weakness of our vacilla tions! Pardon us, Lord, that when we make so much of mere credibilities and rationalities of opinion, we are yet so slow to believe that what we have shown to be credible and rational is actually coming to pass.

CHAPTER XV.

CONCLUSION STATED.   USES AND RESULTS.

THE course of argument proposed in this treatise is now completed. It only remains to state, as definitely as may be, how far it goes, or in what way and degree it establishes the main point in issue ; and also to gather up some of the remote and subordinate results that appear to be involved in it.

It was undertaken mainly to establish the credibility and historic fact of what is supernatural in the Christian gospels. The problem was, in fact, to frame an argument that, on one hand, will virtually settle the question of a mythical origin of the gospels, without going into a direct controversy on that footing, where the points made are too many and loose to allow any very decisive result ; also to frame an argument that, avoiding, on the other, the issue of infallible inspiration, which involves insuperable difficulties in the statement, will yet virtually gain all that is sought for the Christian revelation under that issue ; viz., a genuine, comprehensive faith in its supernatural origin as a gift of God to man.

The argument presented turns principally on two facts ; viz., the fact that we act supernaturally ourselves, which God and other created spirits may as well do as we ; and the fact of sin, which is both a fact of universal observation and of univer sal consciousness. On the ground of these two facts, it has been shown, first, that nature is not the proper system of God, but only an inferior, subordinate, and merely instrumental part, and, in that sense, a part complemental to the grand super natural empire, in which the real system of God is centred ; secondly, that what is commonly called nature is no such integer of order and harmony as is commonly assumed, but is, in fact, a condition of unnature, being a scheme of causalities disordered by sin, and set on courses of retributive action that imply perpetual misdirection ; so that, apart from a co-eternal factor of supernatural redemption, what the naturalists regard as the real totality, or system of nature, is not only become a whole that groaneth and travaileth in pain together, but must inevit ably continue to groan, till relief and deliverance are brought, by some force supernatural that is equal to the occasion.

A supernatural work of redemption becomes, in this view, a kind of intellectual necessity; because otherwise the integrity and real unity of counsel, in a proper frame of order, appear to be wanting.   The strongest possible presumption is raised, in this manner, for just such a work as Christianity undertakes and declares to be undertaken—as it should be—from before the foundation of the world ; a work that is no afterthought, but enters into the original unity of the great scheme of exist ence itself.   When Christ appears, therefore, we take up the record of His life, and show that He is not only a supernatural person, as all men are, but a supernatural person in the still higher degree of being also superhuman ; that He has come into our world as not being of it, that His character can be nowise classed with human characters ; in short, that He is a living, self-evidencing miracle in His person.   Then, that He should perform miracles is scarcely less than a necessary con sequence.   We also show that Christianity, as a plan of super-natural grace, contains hidden marks of verity, which only appear when it is held up in a light to show them, and which, as being latent in this manner, could not be of man.   We have also shown that the world itself is governed in the interest of Christianity, and that supernatural facts are occurring now, or have never been finally discontinued.   It may be too much to claim that we have unanswerably established the fact of miracles performed in our time—it is more exact to say, that we have shown the assumption of their non-performance, of which so much is made by many critics, to be groundless, and that their continuance, which may be asserted with sufficient reason, they can no way disprove.

What now is the precise bearing of all this on the historic verity and the supernatural origin of the gospels, or of the Christian revelation generally ?   As regards the matter of an

exact verbal inspiration, nothing directly; that is a question
waived, or kept out of sight; and yet the mind is brought to
a landing-place, where, without being perplexed by impossible
definitions and strained arguments in their behalf, it will
acquiesce, as it were, naturally, in the fact of a general, un
defined inspiration, having no longer any quarrel to maintain,
because the conditions of quarrel are taken away. The question
of inspired verity is not left, by our argument, in any such
position, as when it is held that the moral ideas and spiritual
truths only of the Scriptures are infallibly given, and their
historic matter left to be disposed of as it may; for the great,
commanding, principal facts are shown to be historically true.
If any debate is to be had, it must be regarding certain sub
ordinate and particular facts that are questioned, because of
some specially suspicious indications that stumble belief. And
little stress is likely to be laid on these, because the working
plan of Christianity, as a regenerative, supernatural grace, is
now on foot as a verity already established; so that the mind
is set on a higher plane of thought than when it only admits
a Christianity qualified, or about to be qualified, down to a
mere doctrine of nature and natural development, and is pre
pared, in that manner, to be stumbled by the smallest difficulties.

The mythical origin of the gospels is, in this manner, refuted,
without any particular notice of its proofs, by a process farther
back and more summary. To untwist, one by one, its perverse
ingenuities, and wade through its mires of false learning, will
be necessary to no one who has found a Christ among men,
impossible to be classed with men; doing His miracles, and
erecting, on the earth, His supernatural kingdom. Not even
Dr Strauss would ever have undertaken this kind of argument, if
he had not first assumed the incredibility of anything super
natural; in which assumption, after all, the main plausibility
of his argument consists.

It is very true that we have not proved the historic verity
of all the miracles. We have only shown that Christ was a
miracle Himself, in His own person, and performed miracles.
Whether he performed this or that miracle, exactly as related,
may yet be questioned. Some of the facts reported as miracles,
looking only at the form of the language, may be otherwise
explained; as, for example, the disturbing of the water by the
angel in the pool of Bethesda; where it may have been the

writer's intention only to give the current faith or impression of the time. If any one chooses to deny the cursing of the fig-tree because it was an act of ill-nature, he can take that low view of the transaction ; only he is likely, when confronted with the suggestion that it was done as an eloquent exhibition of the great moral truth, that God will blast every tree that bears no fruit— a truth which could not be as impressively taught in words—to feel the lowness and perversity of his construction too sensibly to find much comfort in it. The miraculous nativity of Jesus may be questioned, by any one who can see nothing in it but an extravagance shocking to reason, or a myth, in the sem blance of narrative, that displaces any supposition of historic verity in the fact. But given the fact that an incarnation is wanted, that Christ is declared to be the Word incarnate, and shown, by His character, to have come into the world as not being of it, what more can be needed than to put the objector on the question, in what other manner a real incarnation of the divine in the human could be accomplished, that should be as close to human feeling, and as strictly historic in its introduc tion, as this of the miraculous nativity ? And if the objector will but let his imagination rise to the real pitch of the subject, it will be strange if he does not even begin to feel himself kindled with Mary in her song of triumph, and accept the whole history as one transcendently beautiful and sublime. In the same man ner, any one is at liberty still, as far as our argument is con cerned, to speak of discrepancies between the Gospels, or between the Acts of the Apostles and the Epistles, but now that Christ. and His miracles, and His supernatural kingdom, are seen stand ing forth as facts already established, facts which cannot be shaken by any mere discrepancies in the narrative, he is much more likely to accept these apparent disagreements, in matters trivial, as confirmations of the Christian truth, and use them as commendations of it to our confidence.

But it may be objected, contrary to this, by some over-strenuous or over-punctual believer, that our argument, which stops short of proving everything, leaves a gate open to every sort of looseness ; that, as the issue is here qualified, a war begun on each particular fact will finally cut off, in detail, all that seemed to be established in the general ; so that nothing will, in fact, be left. I think otherwise. The difficulty never has been to establish this or that miracle, but to establish any miracle at all, or the credibility of any. One miracle proved, or the credibility of one, is virtually an end of all debate, for the back of scepticism is there broken. Besides, the argument we institute puts the doubter in a new and advanced position. He has verified Christ, the grand, central wonder, the disorder and fall of nature, the need of a supernatural grace and power, even to complete the intelligent unity of God's plan, and what is more, the fact that he himself exists in a heavenly, super natural kingdom, where he meets, on every side, the manifested love and reconciling grace of God. The atmosphere of doubt and debate is already cleared. To break loose now, on some particular miracle, or question of fact, is impossible. Even if he gain his point, he is the loser; for he only mars the glory of a faith that is already established, and spots with blemish the religion that already has a right to his faith. He does not break Christianity down, he only makes it a faith less welcome and clear. In such a position, he will naturally prefer to have the gospel of his faith strong as it may be; holding always a presumption against the suggestions of doubt, and allowing to all the minor points of difficulty, that favourable construction by which they will be cleared.

On the whole, we seem to make out by our argument a vin dication of the supernatural truth of the Gospels, that it is not only sufficient, but practically complete, and, besides, one that has many advantages. We go into no debate about the canon, which is likely to issue in a manner that is not really convinc ing; we start no claim of verbal inspiration, such as takes away the confidence and establishes the rational disrespect of the sceptic before the argument is begun; we sharpen no point of infallibility down so as to prick and fasten each particular iota of the book, afterwards to concede variations of copy, de facts of style, mistakes in numerals, and as many other little discrepancies as we must. But we try to establish by a pro cess that is intelligent and worthy of respect, the historic out posts, Christ and his miracles, and with these, also, the grand working-plan of a supernatural grace and salvation. After this, the mind will gravitate, as of course, toward a general, inclusive, comprehensive faith, and we shall find no language that so fitly expresses our conviction, as to say, " All scripture is given by inspiration of God, and is profitable for doctrine, for reproof, for correction, for instruction in righteousness."

Superficially viewed, there is a certain parallelism between this argument for the supernatural in religion, and that of Mr Parker and the naturalistic school generally against it, and it is possible that some will be perverse enough to accuse me of a similar treatment of revelation. I will never condescend to widen purposely, or for reasons politic and prudential, the dis tance between me and another who has offended the Christian public. But it may show the method of my argument more exactly if I sketch a brief comparison—just as I have been referring heretofore to Mr Parker, to get light and shade for my subject, without raising any special controversy with him.

Mr Parker undertakes to frame a rational view of religion that sets it on the footing of nature. I have undertaken to frame a rational view of religion that comprehends nature and the supernatural as co-eternal factors in the universal system of God.

He maintains the complete universality of natural laws, and refuses to believe in a miracle, because it is a suspension of the laws of nature. I believe as firmly in the universality of laws, but not of natural laws; maintaining that the human will itself is regulated by no laws of natural causality, and has power even to act upon the lines of cause and effect in nature. God, of course, may do the same; which, if he do it, is a miracle. Not a miracle because the laws of nature are suspended; for they are not, but are only varied in their action by the intervention of a power external, as when we vary their results ourselves. Yet still there is a law for the intervention of God, viz., the law of His end; which, though it be no term of nature, but a rule of intelligence and rational sovereignty, would require Him to perform the same miracle again a thousand times over in exactly the same conditions. To define a miracle, therefore, to be a suspension of the laws of nature, is irrational and wholly below the subject. With Mr Parker, I believe in no such miracle. And yet, in the result of this argument, I am brought to accept all the miracles of Christ, while he rejects them all.

Mr Parker takes up the admission, so frequently and gra tuitously made, that miracles and all supernatural gifts have been discontinued, and are now no longer credible, and presses the inference that, being now incredible, they never were any less so ; that pushing them back, in time. is only a trick to get their incredibility so far off that we shall not feel it, and that the only ingenuous conclusion is that, not occurring now, they never did occur. It is certainly a very remarkable turn, as I think any one must admit, that supernatural facts, being credible down to some certain year of the world's almanac, then begin to be incredible ; incredible in their very nature, so that any one who pretends to believe in them is, of course, to be set down as an enthusiast or a charlatan. Mr Parker takes the assumption tendered, and reasons from it. I reject the assumption, and his inferences with it.

Mr Parker has much to say of inspiration. He believes that every man will be inspired under fixed laws of nature, just according to his goodness. In maintaining that all God's supernatural works, which include inspirations, of course, are ordered by fixed laws, I may seem to coincide. But the fixed laws of intelligence or counsel, the laws of reason as related to his end, are a very different matter from the fixed laws of causality in nature. Besides, if we look at the question with Christian eyes, there appears to be a little inversion of method in the doctrine that, if men will be good, they shall be rewarded by a consequent inspiration. It would be as much more ra tional, as it is more Christian, to put the inspiration in advance of the goodness, and say that men will be good accordingly as God inspires them. Not even this will hold, however, for God no doubt exerts an inspiring force in men to make them good, which they may even fatally obstruct by their perversity. The true doctrine of inspiration cannot be stated in any such sum mary manner. All inspirations are acts of divine sovereignty, under laws of reason which regulate that sovereignty. And then there are two modes of inspiration, one that is concerned to re establish the normal state of being, or the state of divine consciousness, in which the soul as a free spirit comes to abide and live in the divine movement, and is kept, strengthened, guided, exalted, by the inward revelation of God ; where it may be truly said that the soul is inspired accordingly as it yields itself conformably to God's will, and trustfully to the inspiring grace. The other mode of inspiration may be called the inspi· ration of use ; where the doctrine is, that God inspires men according to the use He will make of them. And here the kinds or qualities are as many as the uses. He inspires the

shepherd Amos, not to write Isaiah's prophecy, but the pro
phecy of Amos.   He inspires Bezaleel to devise cunning works,
to work in gold, and in silver, and in brass, and in cutting of
stones, and Moses to be the leader and lawgiver of His people.
He will give the same man a variable inspiration, setting Paul,
for example, in one mood of power when he lays his scorching
rebuke on the head of the Corinthians, and in a very different,
when he chants in the fifteenth chapter his sublime lyric on the
resurrection.   It is doubtless true, also, that as God has a place
and a use for every man, so He has an inspiration for him ;
adding honour thus, and comfort and capacity to every employ
ment.   The degree also of this inspiration may be supposed to
have some fixed relation to the faith and faithfulness of the sub
ject, though it is difficult to say what we mean by degrees where
the kinds are and must be different.   The doctrine of Mr Parker
wholly ignores or disallows this inspiration of use, and recognizes
nothing but the inspiration of character.   If a prophet, there
fore, writes a book of scripture with a higher inspiration than
another man has, who writes nothing, it is because he is a better
man.   Let all men be good then, and all will be able to write
as good books as he.   A very convenient and short way of let
ting down the honours of Scripture ; but it may be that God
wants only a few men for this particular use, or to write books
of scripture, as He wanted only one to be a Moses and one to
be a Bezaleel.   And if this be so, it is very certain that He will
inspire as many as He wants for the uses wanted, and no more.
It may be that, as He never wants another Moses, so He never
wants another book of scripture written, and it may be that He
does.   Should He ever want another, He will be able to qualify
His man ; if not, no other will be qualified.   Meantime, it must
be enough that He will have His own counsel, and will aid and
qualify all men for the uses He appoints.   On this ground it is
no such offence to reason to suppose that God has inspired par
ticular men to have a part in the written revelation of His will,
as Mr Parker thinks it to be, and the air of confidence he as
sumes when setting forth the conditions under which all men
may have as good or the same inspiration as the writers of Scrip
tures, indicates rather a want of due consideration than a philo
sophic superiority.   God conducts things to their uses by laws
of causality ; spirits to their uses by inspirations ; and, as the
different kinds of things ponderable and imponderable, solid and

fluid, elastic and inelastic, organic and inorganic, are kept to their uses by different kinds of laws, so it is but rational to believe that God will prepare men to their different places and uses by different kinds of inspiration.

I make no apology, then, for any look of parallelism that may be observed between the shaping of my argument and that of Mr Parker. On the contrary, I prefer to recognize the fact, thus far indicated, that he is pressed by the real difficulties of the question, and conceives intelligently many of the points that must appear, in any genuinely intellectual solution. It has sometimes seemed to me that, with all his aversion to supernaturalism, he might as well be satisfied with the general solution I have given, upon the footing of supernaturalism, as with his own upon the footing of nature. Had he sufficiently weighed certain questions that are fundamental, but which he virtually ignores ; had he determined what is the exact definition of the supernatural, as related to nature, and, in that manner, come upon the fact that we are supernaturally ourselves ; had he also brought his mind closely enough to the great question of sin, to expel all ambiguity concerning it—holding the fact of sin as positively, in the field of criticism, as he does when he attacks slavery as a reformer, and tracing that fact to its legitimate results—I see not how he could have escaped a different con clusion. Instead of making nature the kingdom of God, he would have made it the instrument only, or mere field of the kingdom ; a theatre in which the powers of the kingdom have their parts. Instead of looking for inspiration by the laws of nature, which, if the word has any meaning deeper than sem blance, is even absurd, he would have seen it to be a fact super natural. He would have found a place for prayer, better than a dumb-bell exercise before the terms of natural causality and consequence. His remorseless fidelity to a mistaken argument would not have compelled him to rob the Christian Scriptures of their glorious distinction, as a revelation of God. He would not have been obliged to spot the divine beauty of Christ, to reduce Him to his own human level, or to shock his own better sense and that of the world, by giving out the expectation that other and better Christs will yet be developed, by the progress of his sinful race. Faith he would have discovered, as the sister of reason ; grace, as the medicine of nature. In a word, he would have been a Christian in his doctrine, which now he is not; for, if there be any sufficient, infallible, and always applicable distinction, that separates a Christian from one who is not, it is the faith, practically held, of a supernatural grace or religion. There is no vestige of Christian life in the working-plan of nature. Christianity exists only to have a remedial action upon the contents and conditions of nature. That is development; this is regeneration. No one fatally departs from Christianity, who rests the struggles of holy character on help supernatural from God. No one really is in it, however plausible the semblance of his approach to it, who rests in the terms of morality, or self-culture, or self-magnetizing practice.

If the argument we have traced should be found to have established a solid conviction of truth in the supernatural facts and powers of Christianity, it will go far to invert the relative opinion of nature and faith in all Christian believers, and must therefore work important changes in many things pertaining to the interests of the Christian truth. It must vary the estimate, for example, that is currently held of natural theology. It is even a principal distinction of our modern Christianity, that it has submitted itself, so implicitly, to the dominating ideas and fashions of the new religion, science, or supposed science, that passes by this name. It is a kind of revised Christianity, a gospel that is preached in the method, set up in the plane, saturated with the spirit, and even where it is not suspected, compounded of the matter, of the science. The Christian schools begin with natural theology, because it is conceived to be fundamental, and the young men are long in disabusing themselves of their mistake; for any thing which can be proved for religion out of nature, and in the field of natural reason, is conceived to be specially solid, and impossible to be doubted longer. All which I call a mistake, however, not because of any positive mischief in deductions of this kind. The evil suffered is due, not so much to what our natural theology does, as to what it requires to be left undone; or, to be more explicit, to the fact that it requires all super natural evidences to give way to it, as being themselves a more questionable kind of verity; even as the ill-favoured and lean kine of Pharaoh's dream devoured those which were better. The opposite pole is represented here by Dr Henry More, who builds his argument for the existence of God to a considerable degree, on the basis of supernatural facts; such as dreams, prophecies, premonitions, visions, revelations. and the like—a curious and striking evidence, when viewed in contrast with our present conceptions, of the change of mental position that may be wrought in the thinking world, in a comparatively brief space of time. The modern advances in science compelled the change, and it could not be resisted. Neither was it desirable that it should be; for, when the new theology of nature is once qualified, by restoring the other pole of the subject, which belongs more distinctly to Christianity, it will be found to have expelled multitudes of superstitious and unilluminated vagaries, necessary to be expelled, before it was possible to hold the supernatural evidences, in the manner of true intelligence necessary to their genuine effect. Then the two worlds of evidences are seen to be complementary to each other, and the argument for God, the Christian God, is complete as never before.

The evil in our present stage of thought is, that natural theology has the whole ground to itself, and the God established is not a being who meets the conditions of Christianity at all. We get, of course, no proofs out of nature that go farther than to prove a God of nature, least of all do we get any that show Him to be acting supernaturally to restore the disorders of nature. What we discover is a God who institutes, is revealed by, and, as many will suspect, *is* the causes of nature. A latent pantheism lurks in the argument. Calling the God we prove a personal being, and meaning it in good faith, we yet find ourselves living before causes, and looking for consequences. We only half believe in prayer. We expect to be delivered of sin by a long course of duty and self-reformation, that will finally pacify the offended laws of nature and bring them on our side again. That God will do anything for us Himself, or hold any terms of real society with us we but faintly believe. That used to be the opinion of ancient times, but the world, we imagine, is now growing more philosophical. The result is that, professing Christianity in the most orthodox manner, we live in natural theology, half way on the road to pantheism. Even the incarnation and the miracles of Jesus drop into a virtually dead faith, becoming forms in place of living and life-giving realities.

And the reason is, that our God, derived from nature, is a monosyllable only, or at best a mechanical first cause, and no such

being as the soul wants, or as Christianity supposes in its doctrines
of regenerated life, and in all its supernatural machineries. Rest
ing here, therefore, or allowing ourselves, to be retained by what
we call our natural theology, Christianity dies out on our
hands for the want of a Christian God. And, accordingly it
is a remarkable fact, even in history, that we have lost faith in
God just in proportion to the industry we have spent in proving
His existence by the natural evidences. First, because, the
God we prove does not meet our living wants, being only a
name for causes, or a God of causes; secondly, because, in
turning to Christianity for help, we have rather to turn away
from the God we have proved than toward Him. We may
seem to have established the fact of God's existence, but if God
is gained, Christianity is lost!

There is no relief to this mischief, but to conceive, at the be
ginning, that nature is but a fraction of the complete system of
God, and no integer; that the true, living God, beautifully ex
pressed in a small way in nature, is a vastly superior being
still, who holds the worlds of nature in His hands, and acts
upon them as the Rectifier, Redeemer, Regenerator, and is even
more visibly, convincingly, and gloriously expressed in Christi
anity that He is in the worlds. Show Him at the head of the
great kingdom of minds, compassionate to sin, conversant with
sinners, a hearer of prayer, an illuminator of experience, a de
liverer from the retributions of nature, the glorious new-creator
of all the most glorious characters in the world. Display the
self-evidencing tokens of His feeling and work as the God
supernatural—God in Christ, reconciling the world unto Him
self. There is more convincing evidence for God in the life and
passion of Jesus than in all the mechanical adaptations of the
worlds. The God of the Bible and the Church, the God that
rules the world in the interest of Christ and salvation, mani
fested in the divine beauty, and the mighty works and heroic
sufferings of His saints—this is the God that speaks to our true
wants. Provoke such wants, and let Him speak. This kind
of evidence restores the equilibrium of the mere natural evi
dences, makes the God established a person, the true living God,
and the supernatural facts of Christianity are sustained and not
discredited by our belief in Him.

It does not appear to be suspected that our modern ten
dencies to pantheism are at all related to our overdoing in the

matter of natural theology, but it will by and by be discovered that we are greatly imposed upon by our zeal, and took our ingenuity in this kind of proof-building for a good deal more than it was worth. Never is God conceived to be really personal till He is shown outside of nature, acting upon nature even as we do ourselves. The proofs we seek are genuine only when they correspond and show us what wants to be shown.

It is also a matter of consequence in our argument, as related to the wants of the age, that it provides a place for the positive institutions of religion, and prepares a rational basis for their authority. It is frequently remarked that, for some reason, these positive institutions are falling rapidly into disrespect, as if destined finally to be quite lost or sunk in oblivion. Various reasons are assigned for this fact, which amount to nothing more definite than that such is the spirit of the times. The true reason is the growth and pervading influence of naturalism, which not only does not want, but excludes such institutions. This doctrine assumed, they are theoretically im possible. As the word *institution* itself indicates, they are supernatural creations; that is, something *set up on* the world of nature, not developments out of nature. Besides, it is the manner and temper of naturalism to be impatient of anything not established in terms of natural reason, and spurn it as having no sufficient authority. Accordingly it will be seen, that as we grow more naturalistic, just in the same proportion do these institutions lose their hold of us. What have we to do with the Church—can we not be as good Christians out of the Church as in it? What signify the sacraments, even if they were distinctly appointed by Christ? they cannot save us, and we can well enough be saved without them. And what is a holy day but a needless restriction, when one time ought to be as holy as another? So too of the Bible; that, as related to nature, is a positive institution. And so again of Christianity itself, which began to be instituted in the ancient ritual, and was finished, or fully completed when the higher sense of that ritual was displayed in the terms of the Christian salvation. It was set up on the world by a God who is not imprisoned in it but is acting on it from without, to rescue it from the action of its disordered causalities. What are all these pretended institutions of God but incumbrances and encroachments on our liberty ? And what necessary use do they serve ? They are, I answer, what body is to soul. All vital or vitalizing powers are organific, and live by means of their embodiment. These institutions are the body of religious organization, the conditions in that manner of religious power and perpetuity. Cast away this body, and religion is a disembodied ghost only, flitting across the world, but never resting in it. Truth becomes a vagrant. Worship has no time or seat. Preachers have no calling or commission. And the no-church, no-observance people come into the world to merely wear out and die, without faith, without holy virtue, without great sentiments to conserve society, or illuminate the night of their virtual atheism. If we talk of an " Absolute Religion," that is going to abide and reign without institutions, it will reign as Absolute Vacuity. However eloquently preached for the time, and however promising the show it makes by works of reform and social philanthropy, it will be seen to organize nothing, and when once its aim is accom plished in the extinction of all that Christianity organizes, it will simply cease to work, as all poison does when the subject is dead.

That Christianity will utterly die, however, for this or any other cause, we are not to believe. But the tendency of our time is one that must be finally arrested, by one or the other of these two methods ; by restoring a distinct and properly intelli gent faith in the supernatural reign of Christ, such as I have here undertaken to set forth, or else by a blind recoil, such as mere vacuity and the pains of vagrancy will instigate. In the first and true method, we shall have the positive institutions, holding them in respect, and observing them in practice, be cause we conceive a God who is not waiting for the development of nature, but working to regenerate nature, by what he can erect upon it and do in it. But if religion gets no body and no organized state by this rational and true method, then it will have them by a worse ; for, when we have gone loose for a long time, in this kind of dissipation, and scattered the body of reli gion as fine dust on the winds, there will finally come a reaction, a painful want of forms, observances, and organizations, and a greedy, irrational hurrying back to the Church that offers such a bountiful supply. The Absolute Religion that excludes a Church will conduct us back to the Absolute Church, and there, as disappointed victims of one, we shall go in, to be busied and fooled by observances and sacraments of the other, losing out our intelligence, and even God's light itself, under an immense overgrowth of institutions which he did not appoint, and which have really no agreement with His truth.

The conception we have raised of Christianity, as a regenera tive work and institution of God, separates it, by a wide chasm, from any mere scheme of philanthropy or social reform. As to reforms that begin at the outside, and stop at the rectification of the outward conduct, they may be beneficial or they may not. There is a degree of vice, and consequent misery, that, for the time, incapacitates the subject for the reception of truth and the Christian influences. There are also external wrongs and disorders of sin, that only represent to men the inward state of their hearts; holding up the glass in which they may see themselves; and it is no genuine interest of Christianity to get these smoothed away. It is even a great part of God's wisdom, in casting the plan of our life, that He has set us in conditions to bring out the evil that is in us. For it is by this medley that we make of wrongs, fears, pains of the mind, and pains of the body, all the woes of all shapes and sizes that fol low at the heels of our sin—by these it is that He dislodges our perversity, and draws us to Himself. If, therefore, by a grand comprehensive sweep of reform, we could get all the mis doings, that we call sins, out of sight, and the sin of the spirit, as a state separated from the consciousness of God, shut in, so as nowhere to appear, it would be the greatest imaginable mis fortune. We should have a race acting paradisiacally in their behaviour, when they have no principle of good in their life. It is very true that no mere reform is likely to reach this point; for it is very certain that men will do sins enough or have vices enough to represent and shame their sin. And yet the merely naturalistic reformers go to just this task; the task, that is, of an external purgation of the world. This is their religion, and they take on often such airs, in what they imagine to be the superior philanthropy, or the superior fidelity and boldness of their course, that they seem even to be holding out a challenge to Christianity to come and try, if it can do as much as they! Are they not going to take care of the progress of society? Are they not also going finally to get all the evils of life away ?   Christianity undertakes no such thing—unless by undertaking more.   It goes only a certain way in the matter of reforms ; viz., far enough to show its true interest in every thing human, and especially far enough to get those vices and sins in hospital, which, as they continue to rage, take away self-possession, abate the force of reason, and disqualify the subject for the gospel.   But it has a quiet perception of the folly and absurdity of any plan, which expects to smooth up the world in its sin, or its alienation from God.   Back of sins it recognizes sin ; back of the acts, a state which they ex press and represent.   This it regenerates ; and so, working outward from the inmost centre, it proposes to reform every thing.

Great reforms are certainly wanted.   No Christian, there fore, will dishonour the faith of a supernatural remedy in Christ, by taking refuge behind it, and avoiding, in that manner, his responsibilities—how is he going to regenerate all the sin of the world, when he dare not speak of the sins ?   On the other hand, he will not be intimidated by the outcry of the reformers, that upbraid his Christian slowness, or beguiled by their pretentious airs, when they make it a religion, or even a more superlative religion, to be doing such prodigious things for society.   Their appeal is to public opinion, not to God. They make their own gospel as they go, and have undertaken themselves to do such things for the world, that men will say, " Behold Christianity was a failure ! "   The force too by which they operate is in their will, and this strikes fire into the nitrous element of their passion the moment they encounter resistance.   They grow hot and violent.   Denunciation be. comes their element, and, as numbers are added, they run to a genuine fanaticism.   No Christian has any place on this level. As far as he undertakes to co-operate in reforms, he must do it as one who stays above with Christ, and works with him ; re taining his passions, by not losing his will ; mixing his reproofs with his prayers, and moderating his ambition by resting his cause, in the mighty power of God.

To admit, in its full force, the reality of our Christian or supernatural relations to God, would also very certainly result in a more apostolic manner of preaching.   For preaching deals appropriately in the supernatural, publishing to guilty

souls what has come into the world from above the world—
Christ and His salvation. We ask, how often, with real sadness, whence the remarkable impotence of preaching in our
time? It is because we concoct our gospels too much in the
laboratories of our understanding; because we preach too many
disquisitions, and look for effects correspondent only with the
natural forces exerted. True preaching is a testimony; it
offers not things reasoned in any principal degree, but things
given, supernatural things, testifying them as being in their
power, by an utterance which they fill and inspire. It brings
new premises, which, of course, no argument can create, and
therefore speaks to faith. And, what is most of all peculiar,
it assumes the fact in men of a religious nature, higher than a
merely thinking nature, which, if it can be duly awakened,
cleaves to Christ and His salvation with an almost irresistible
affinity. This religious nature is a capacity for the super
natural; that is, for the divinely supernatural; in other words,
it is that quality by which we become inspirable creatures,
permeable by God's life, as a crystal by the light, permeable in
a sense that no other creature is. Indeed, the great problem
of the gospel is in one view, to inspire us again, at a point
where we are uninspired; to permeate us again by the divine
nature, and make us conscious again of God. In this view, it
assumes to speak as to a want, and what a want it is, that a
capacity even for God, in the soul, stands empty! And hence
it is that so many infidels have been converted under preaching,
that went directly by their doubts, only bringing up the mighty
themes of God and salvation, and throwing them in as torches
into the dark, blank cavern of their empty heart. They are
not put upon their reason, but the burning glow of their inborn
affinities for the Divine are kindled, and the blaze of these
overtops their speculations, and scorches them down by its
glare. Doubtless there are times and occasions, where something may be gained by raising a trial before the understanding.
But there may also be something lost, even in cases where that
kind of issue is fairly gained. Many a time nothing is wanting
but to speak as to a soul already hungry and thirsty; or, if
not consciously so, ready to hunger and thirst, as soon as the
bread and water of life are presented. If the problem is to get
souls under sin inspired again, which it certainly is, then it is
required that the preacher shall drop lecturing on religion and

preach it ; testify it, prophesy it, speak to faith as being in faith, bring inspiration as being inspired, and so become the vehicle, in his own person, of the power he will communicate, that he may truly beget in the gospel such as will be saved by it.　No man is a preacher, because he has something like, or about a gospel, in his head.　He really preaches only when his person is the living embodiment, the inspired organ of the gospel ; in that manner no mere human power, but the demonstration of a Christly and Divine power.　It is in this manner that preaching has had, in former times, effects so remarkable.　At present we are almost all under the power, more or less, of the age in which we live.　Infected with naturalism ourselves and having hearers that are so, we can hardly find what account to make of our barrenness.

It is also a matter of consequence to be anticipated in a just and full establishment of supernatural verities, that intellectual and moral philosophy are destined, in this way, to be finally Christianized ; and so, that all science will, at last, be melted into unity with the religion of Christ.　Our professors of philosophy leave it to the theologians to settle the question whether man is a sinner or not, and go on to assume that he is in the normal state of his being, acting precisely according to his nature ; when, if the theologians chance to doubt any of their conclusions, the reply is, that they do not understand philosophy.

Now it is either true that man is a sinner, or it is not.　If he is not a sinner, then he exists normally, and what he is in his action, he is in his nature, and a great many questions will be settled accordingly.　On the other hand, if he is a sinner, acting against God, acting as he was not made to act, then he is, by the supposition, a disordered nature, a being in the state of unnature.　Any philosophy therefore which does not recog- nize the fact, but deduces his nature from his present demon- strations, must be wholly at fault.

And how different any philosophy of man must be, which ignores the fact of sin, from one that does not, may be easily seen.　Let the subject be the relation of our powers and capacities to our ideals.　One who makes no account of sin, will say, develope the capacities and you have the ideals—he will even infer the capacities from the ideals.　But to one who duly recognizes sin, there is nothing so sad, as the fact that the mind flowers into ideals that it cannot reach, conceiving a beauty, a perfectly crystalline order, when it can as little drag itself into this beauty, this crystalline order, as it could a shattered firmament.

Or, let the subject be, what is the nature of virtue, or, more particularly, whether self-love is the determining motive in all virtue ? Taking it for granted that, what men do they are made to do, and finding that the common world of men are actuated by self-love in their virtue, the inference is that such is the manner of all virtue ; it is what men do for fear, for gain, or for some matter of mere self-interest ; in which virtue and vice are exactly alike. But one who recognizes the fact of sin immediately suspects that the self-love power enters into men's virtue thus largely because they are sinners. In the highest, the truly Divine virtue, he looks for a spontaneous or inspired movement, where the good is followed because it is good, the right because it is right, God because He is God. And the conclusion is, that what the other calls virtue is only a form of sin.

Or again, the question may be, what is the perfect state of man ? Ignoring the fact of sin, the conclusion will be that he is perfected, in squaring himself by the rules of virtue ; he is consummated, that is, in the matter of ethics. But where sin is taken into account, it will be recollected that men, as commonly observed, are out of place and out of the true line of experience ; that they have departed from God; and that their properly religious nature is detained by sin, or closed up. To be completely filled with God, and perfected in the eternal movement of God ; in a word, to be conscious of God, and dwell in the Divine impulse or inspiration—that is the perfect state. He has found, in other words, that man is just what he most entirely omitted to be, or perhaps never once thought of in his fallen life, an inspirable creature, having, in that fact, the real summit, the grandeur, and glory of his being. He culminates in God, not in any rules of ethics. His goodness is not the perfect drill he submits to, and tries to observe, but it is the freedom of a spontaneous, inspired, and truly divine beauty.

How different a thing must it be, to philosophize about a substance that acts according to its nature, and about one that acts in contradiction both of its nature and its God ! Doubtless the latter is a much higher form of being than the other ; for it can not be a thing, it can be nothing less than a power, glorious and transcendent ; and therefore it is that man, contemplated at just this point of sin, rises to a pitch of tragic sublimity and grandeur, as nowhere else. Why then should our philosophy refuse to look at him, just where his real stature is revealed ? When this fact of sin is referred back to theologians, and de clared, either with or without a sneer, to be in their province, a much greater compliment is paid them than is commonly thought. It is giving them up all that belongs to man's real greatness, and claiming the husk that is left.

This separation of intellectual and moral philosophy from the great religious problem of our existence, the fact of sin, and the want of salvation, is the more remarkable, that it is a descent from the more dignified and nobler conceptions of the ancient heathen masters. It is unnatural, and even unintelligent. How can philosophy, dealing with a supernatural subject, stand off from the facts of his supernatural history ? Endeavouring to stay by nature, and magnify the natural history, it only takes a brick for Babylon, and gives a science of the brick. There is to be a speedy revision of this false method. No real philoso pher can long ignore the supernatural. Religion then takes hold of philosophy, and sets it to the study of her problems. All natural science will follow, setting itself in affinity with things supernatural. The philosophies are then baptized, in being simply inducted into a just conception of the one system of God. Now the young minds trained in such studies are not led away, but led directly up to Christ and the glorious truth of His mission. That mission is become the pole star of learning, and how great the change that must follow !

Once more it appears to be an important consequence of the argument we have instituted, that, in assigning the supernatural a definite place, and a firm, intellectual ground, it contributes a valuable aid to Christian experience. There is a feeling widely prevalent, that when we talk of faith we are covering up the want of intelligence ; that when we speak of the supernatural, we mean something ghostly, supplied by the imagination, and verified only by our superstitions ; that when we name the mat ter of religious experience, we suppose a drivelling, and, as it were, forced admission of the soul, to what a rational philosophy must of course reject. All such impressions will, I trust, be removed, as unworthy and really unjust by the argument I have now presented.

It finds a place for the supernatural in the scheme of exist ence itself; showing that we ourselves are supernatural agents as really, only not in the same degree of power, as Christ in His miracles. It gets a footing, in this manner, for super natural facts and agencies, among the known realities. More than this, it shows that nature is not, by itself, any complete whole or real universe, but is, in fact, only a scaffolding, the smallest, humblest part of the intellectual whole, or system of God's empire; while, on the other hand, the supernatural side of His plan, concerned with free intelligences, their government and redemption, and the building of them into a temple of eter nal Love and Beauty round Himself, comprises all the real and last ends of His throne.

Everything is thus made ready for best advances in religious experience. For there is a close relation, scarcely different from identity, between faith and what is called experience; and both are terms that have a fixed reference to the fact, that Christ and Christianity are supernatural bestowments. If they could be reasoned out of premises already in the mind, they would not require faith. But Christ comes into the world from without, to bestow himself by a presentation. He is a new premise, that could not be reasoned, but must first be, and then can be re ceived only by faith. When He is so received or appropriated, He is, of course, experienced or known by experiment; in that manner verified—he that believeth hath the witness in himself. The manner, therefore, of this divine experience, called faith, is strictly Baconian. And the result is an experimental know ledge of God, or an experimental acquaintance with God, in the reception of his supernatural communications. Which know- ledge, again, or acquaintance, is, in fact, a revelation within, a divine manifestation, a restored consciousness of God, or we may call it peace, joy, strength, a growth into the divine purity —it is any and all these together. And it should not be strange that, in such a participation of God, we are lifted, empowered, assimilated, or finally glorified.

It will be admitted that what is properly called religious experience runs low in our time. Even the phrase itself is care fully eschewed by many as a term of cant, that lacks, or is suspected of lacking, any basis of intelligence. We learn to be familiar with the phrase " philosophic consciousness," and speak with satisfaction of " cultivating the philosophic consciousness," but religious experience belongs to a lower class of people, who cannot ascend to so high a matter. One pertains to a rational culture, the other is a relic of pietism, now gone by, with all but the feebler minds. No fact presents the intellectual habit of our time in a more pitiable light. To get experience of our selves, or a practical consciousness of our own little subjectivity, we account to be something of importance ; but to recover, un fold, grow into, and become ennobled by the consciousness of God, united to Him as the all-sufficient object and fulness of our life—this, we think, is something related to weakness ! And to this folly we are shrunk by the wretched conceit of our na turalism. What if it should happen to be true, that we are all inherently related to God, having our summits of thought, power, quality, greatness in Him, made to be conscious of Him as of ourselves, and in that nobler consciousness to live ! What if this too should happen to be the truth waiting our embrace, at the point of littleness and mere self-consciousness sharpened by our sin ! How sorry the picture we make, when we figure it in this manner, as the superlative wisdom. to have a cultivated power of self-reflection, and only another name for weakness to speak of religious experience ! If I am right in the matter of my argument, a very different impression is justified. Mere naturalism it shows, in fact, to be a fraud against nature. It soundly authenticates the grand supernatural verities of the gospel and of Christian experience, showing that without them there is no rational unity even in what we call the universe.

The utmost confidence may now be felt in all the expecta tions and exploits of faith ; in prayer, in divine guidance, in the cares of a supernatural providence, in all the heavenly gifts. Clear of all reserve the disciple may go to his calling, as one detained by no misgivings or lurking suspicions. And his success will be according to his confidence. Weakened by no foolish suspicion of being at fault intellectually, he will go on manfully and boldly, instructed always by his experience, and advancing always upon it ; removing greater mountains as he gets more faith ; and giving all men to see. who chance to observe him, what power and lustre there is in a life thus hid with Christ in God. Verily, such it is that we want as the

preachers and pastors and saints of our time; men whose
strength is the joy of the Lord; men who dwell in the secret
place of the Most High; men who walk in glorious liberty,
living no more to themselves, but to Christ who bought them:
preaching Christ by their example, their prayers, their prophesyings, and witnessing, by the blessed fruits of their faith, to
its ennobling verity and greatness.

The argument we have traced prepares also a yet further
contribution to Christian experience, in bringing more distinctly
forward the question of a possible discovery and statement of
the laws of the supernatural. How great a change has been
wrought in the creative and productive processes of human
industry by a scientific discovery of the laws of nature. The
address we make to nature, and the forces of nature, is now
intelligent, and our productive powers are as much greater, as
the forces we harness are stronger and more obedient. The
world itself is quite another world, displaying new and vastly
higher possibilities. What now is wanted in the domain of
Christian experience, is a similar development of the laws of
the supernatural; when a correspondent change will be observed
in the productive forces and the progressive conquests of the
spiritual life. When these laws are once developed, the men
of the kingdom will see it, as never before, to be a kingdom,
and will know exactly by what process to be advanced and
established in it. It will be as when alchemy gave way to
chemistry, astrology to astronomic computations, the divining-
rod and other saws and superstitions of mining to the intelli
gent prospecting of geologic science, agriculture in the times of
the moon to agriculture in the terms of experimental and
scientific guidance. Not that any science of supernatural
things, or things of religious experience, is possible to be
created, that shall prove itself in the same manner to the mere
natural judgment or intellect. It must be a science if we use
that term, that pertains to the higher realm of the Spirit. It
must, therefore, stand in terms of analogy and figure, which can
fully unfold their meaning only to minds enlightened in a degree
by holy experience. It must be a contribution to faith, of the
laws by which it may address itself to the supernatural forces of
grace, and the manifestations of God. In the initial points of
faith it must approve itself to the mere intelligence; in points
further on it must approve itself more and more to spiritual

insight in its advanced stages.   Hitherto there has been a large
mixture of superstition in religious experience.   Proposing to
get on by application, it has yet trusted more to heat than to
light.   It has looked for visions and revelations without law.
It has been a kind of spiritual alchemy, taken by wonderful
surprises, and blown up as often by fanatical explosions.   The
progress it has made has been fantastic, and it has finally
reached the abiding place of order and sobriety only by a long
course of eccentricities and blindfold experiments.   There has
even been a kind of impression that God Himself is irregular,
and, in some good sense, capricious in His supernatural gifts,
therefore to be reached by no certain method, but only by a
sort of adventure that will some time chance to find Him.
How different the fortunes of religious experience, when it is
regarded—which in some future time it will be—as a coming
unto God by the laws that regulate His bestowments; when
the world of His supernatural kingdom is conceived to be as
truly under laws as the world of nature, and these laws,
accurately distinguished, enable the disciple to address himself
accurately to the powers of grace, as now to the forces of
nature.

Our argument favours such an expectation.   It brings the
supernatural into the grand, fore-ordinated circle of existence,
and makes it even a central part of that stupendous whole or
integer which we call the universe.   It also conceives that
God works by laws in the supernatural, in the incarnation and
the miracles of Jesus, in His sacrifice and death, in the mission
of the Spirit and all spiritual gifts.   Indeed, there is no being
but a bad one, a sinner, that is not punctually and exactly de
termined by some law.   Not even the atoms of a crystal are
more exactly set by law, than the thoughts and choices of a
perfect mind.   And though it be not any law of physical
necessity, such as we discover in the causalities of nature, it is
none the less a law of unalterable and undeviating control.   In
God Himself, it is the law by which, as presiding over the
thoughts, the ends, and the determinations of His perfect mind,
the laws of nature were themselves conceived and appointed—the
higher law of His goodness and His moral reason.   Neither let
it be imagined that this higher tier of law, which governs God
in His supernatural dispensations, is to us inaccessible or undis-
cernible.   As the fall of an apple showed to Newton's eye the

law that presides over the remotest worlds of the physical universe, so we shall find, not seldom, in the most familiar principles of duty and sentiments of religion, things in ourselves that infallibly interpret Him. A large inference may be also derived from the admitted fact of His perfection; for, while nothing definite or certain can be predicated of imperfection in a subject unknown as regards its law, the exact ideal imperfection of God, like that of the astronomic order, suffers a large and free deduction respecting all His tempers, ends, and methods. Much also may be gathered from the general economy of the supernatural, as displayed in the work and counsel of human redemption. Much is given by express revelation; for though it is not common to regard, as definite and fixed laws of divine action or bestowment, the familiar rules by which our approach to God is regulated in the Scripture, they do yet suppose that He is regulated Himself by terms correspondent. The rule —to him that hath shall be given—first be reconciled to thy brother—if two of you shall agree as touching anything— if our heart condemn us not—if a man hate his brother—as we forgive them that trespass against us—if ye keep my command ment—if ye search for me with all the heart—all these con ditions of prayer and terms of approach to God are in a yet higher view laws of the Spirit, supposing that God's gifts themselves are dispensable only in terms that correspond. And besides all these, a large discovery also can be made of things supernatural and their laws by our own experience; for as he that loveth knoweth God, so the whole life of faith is an ex perience and spiritual discovery of God. And no discovery of natural science is more valid. Nor is there anything in which a ripe Christian can do more for experimental religion, than in giving to the help of such as will seek after God, a treatise drawn from all these sources on the laws of God's supernatural kingdom—the kingdom of grace and salvation. No other con tribution to the truth of Christ is so much needed, or promises results of so great moment. First, that which is natural, after ward that which is spiritual. It was necessary to this higher kind of progress that the discoveries of natural science should precede and raise the expectation of laws here also to be veri fied. And when it is done, as it will not be in any brief space of time, the world may begin to think of a general consumma tion at hand. Faith will now grow solid, and overtop the temples of reason with its grandeur. Religious experience, conceived and proved to be the revelation of God, will become a general embodiment of the divine in human history, fulfilling the idea of the incarnation, never till then completely intelligible. There will be order without constraint, and liberty without fanaticism. The desultory will give place to the regular, and a kind of holy skill will distinguish all the approaches of men to God, and all the works they do in His name. The power of Christian piety will be as much greater than now, as it knows how to connect more certainly and more in the manner of science with the resources of God.

Until then the highest and even truest principles of Christian experience are likely to involve some danger of fanaticism. I cannot be sure that persons will not appear who, professing to lay hold of points advanced in this treatise, use them fanatically, as the fuel of their strange fire. Fanaticism can certainly find a shelter under it, and gather out of it many pretexts for extravagance and delusion, even as it has done in all ages out of Christianity itself; but I cherish a degree of confidence, that what I have advanced will be a contribution rather to the intelligence than to the delusions of the Christian world. It has been my endeavour to put honour on faith—to restore, if possible, the genuine apostolic faith. I have even wished, shall I dare to say hoped, that I might do something to inaugurate that faith in the field of modern science, and claim for it t re that respect to which, in the sublimity of its reasons it is entitled. And great will be the day when faith, laying hold of science and rising into intellectual majesty with it, is acknowledged in the glorious sisterhood of a common purpose, and both lead in the realms they occupy, reconciled to God, cleared of the disorders and woes of sin, to set them in that final unity which represents the eternal Headship of Christ.

PRINTED BY VIRTUE AND CO., CITY ROAD, LONDON.

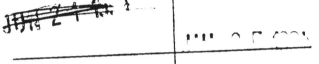